MEXICO

*To the political prisoners,
the disappeared,
and the politically persecuted*

James D. Cockcroft

MEXICO

Class Formation, Capital Accumulation, and the State

Monthly Review Press
New York

Library of Congress Cataloging in Publication Data
Cockcroft, James D.
Mexico: class formation, capital accumulation,
and the state.
Bibliography: p.
Includes index.
1. Mexico—Economic conditions. 2. Mexico—
Politics and government. 3. Mexico—Social conditions.
4. Social classes—Mexico—History. I. Title.
HC133.C6   1983   330.972   81-84748
ISBN 0-85345-560-0
ISBN 0-85345-561-9 (pbk.)

Monthly Review Press
155 West 23rd Street
New York, N.Y. 10011

Manufactured in the United States of America

10 9 8 7 6 5 4 3 2 1

Contents

Tables

Acknowledgments

This book represents many years of research, during which so many workers, peasants, students, and scholars of Mexico have assisted me that it would be impossible to list them all. Many colleagues in the United States and Europe have also been generous with their critical suggestions. In the notes I acknowledge individuals or works whose suggestions proved specifically useful in the corresponding section of the book.

Grants or released time from the following institutions facilitated the research: Foreign Area Fellowship Program research grant on transnational corporations (the fellowship is awarded by the Joint Committee of the Social Science Research Council and the American Council of Learned Societies), 1974–1975; Rutgers University sabbatical year, 1979–1980; Visiting Professorship, Sociology Department, Universität Bielefeld (West Germany), 1980; Fulbright-Hays Research Grant on migration and border problems, 1980–1981; and Visiting Professorship, Departamento de Sociología, Universidad Autónoma Metropolitana (UAM)—Azcapotzalco, Mexico City, 1980–1981.

None of these institutions or individuals is responsible for the content of this book. Some of the seminal ideas, prior to their final elaboration here, appeared in the following: *Intellectual Precursors of the Mexican Revolution, 1900–1913* (Austin: The University of Texas Press, 1968; paperback ed. with "Note to Chicano Readers," 1976); chapter on Mexico in Ronald Chilcote and Joel Edelstein, eds., *Latin America: The Struggle with Dependency and Beyond* (Cambridge, Mass.: Schenkman, 1974); *El imperialismo, la lucha de clases y el estado en México* (Mexico: Nuestro Tiempo, 1979); and "Subordinated Technological Development: The Case of Mexico," in *Research in Social Movements, Conflicts and Change*, vol. 4, ed. Louis Kriesberg, (Greenwich, Conn.: JAI Press, Inc., 1981).

Special thanks go to graphic artist Rini Templeton; to indexer Hedda Garza; to typist Blanca E. Rincón Castro of the Departamento de Sociología, UAM—Azcapotzalco; to cartographer Kevin Beede; and to editor Susan Lowes and the entire staff of Monthly Review Press.

Finally, a word or two about the dedication. It has both a universal and a specific meaning. In 1968, I dedicated my first book on Mexico "to the political prisoners." In 1979, I dedicated my second book "a los desaparecidos" but through editorial oversight the dedication did not appear in the first edition. Now I sadly add to this list "the politically persecuted." Illustrative of the sweep of repression affecting Mexico is the shooting of various progressive individuals from all walks of life, including my colleague of the Departamento de Economía, UAM—Azcapotzalco, Edur Velasco, wounded in 1982. I gratefully acknowledge Edur's help in confirming the statistics provided in the tables of this book, and I wish him a complete recovery.

—James D. Cockcroft

Friends Lake, Chestertown, N.Y.
May 1, 1983

Introduction
to Modern Mexico

In 1982 Mexico became the world's fourth largest oil producer, inflation approached 100 percent, the government was unable to meet payments on the huge foreign debt, nearly a million workers were dismissed from their jobs, and the nation's leaders acknowledged that the "crisis" of the 1970s had given way to the "national emergency" of the 1980s. This book is intended to present a comprehensive analysis of the Mexican political economy and its crisis, tracing their historical roots in the process of class struggle, capital accumulation, and the development of the modern technocratic-authoritarian state.

While for more than a generation most Latin American nations have experienced severe political instability and one or another form of military dictatorship, two exceptions stand out: for almost a quarter century the Communist Party has steered Cuba through stormy times, and for more than half a century a single party (known today as the Institutional Revolutionary Party—PRI) has overseen the industrialization of Mexico. If we search Cuban and Mexican history for the secret of these parties' staying power, we find that both countries share a similar and singular experience: in the twentieth century they passed through the most influential revolutions of the Western hemisphere. In Cuba, a socialist revolution brought stability, with a government committed to addressing people's need for food, clothes, housing, schools, medicine, and jobs; in Mexico, the 1910–1920 Revolution and the changes it made possible in the 1930s ushered in the post-1940 era of industrial transformation, which has produced today's system of dependent state monopoly-capitalism—some forty years of "stability." In Mexico, unlike most of the rest of Latin America, by 1940 the power of the Catholic Church had been checked, the sails of coup-minded generals had been trimmed, a serious agrarian reform had been introduced, and key natural resources had been nationalized. In subsequent years, foreign capital was often obliged to go "half-and-half" with domestic capital in new industrial ventures and, in spite of U.S. opposition, a foreign policy that recognized new revolutions in the region held relatively firm.

1

Yet Mexico's much-vaunted "stability" has come to resemble that of a well-guarded zoo, with lions in cages and zebras on a grassless pasture. At night the caged animals roar to get a bone; the starving herds in the dusty compound try to swim the river around it. For the other side of the coin is that Mexico's revolution has brought forth a sophisticated centralized state that Mussolini would envy. Workers in factories, railways, mines, schools, clinics, and offices are trapped in their "cages": government-controlled unions with institutional "rights" that keep wages low and strikes at a minimum. And who is outside in the dusty compound? At least half of Mexico's 72 million people: all those superexploited peasants and ex-peasants on whose backs the country's post-World War II capitalist economic growth was built.

Today these 36 million are the landless peasants, the migrant workers, the urban jobless, the sierra Indians, the shivering prostitutes, the homeless, wandering beggars and bandits, and the nameless semiliterates who are, according to the voices of big business, "unemployed and unemployable." Many of these immiserated have no identity papers; they are undocumented aliens in their own country. In search of survival they trek from harvest to harvest and from city to city. Three million are street vendors in the capital. Some make it across the U.S. border; about half of these have previously worked in Mexico's cities but at starvation wages. Less than 40 percent of Mexico's labor force earns the legal minimum wage, which in 1982 was not half of what a working-class family of five needed to maintain itself. Not even half of the labor force is regularly employed. "Today is like yesterday," wails the popular song, "in a world without tomorrow."

> How sad the rain beats
> On the tin roofs
> Of the cardboard houses.

Economists examining Mexico's income pie agree on the following: in 1958 the top 5 percent of income recipients had 22 times the income of the bottom 10 percent; by 1977 the share of the top layer had jumped to 47 times that of the bottom. Thirteen million Mexicans live in extreme poverty, and have incomes below those in Latin America's poorest country, Haiti. Over half the population suffers from malnutrition, including 90 percent of preschool children, who constitute one-third of the population. The fodder consumed by the cattle contains more protein than does the diet of the peasants who tend them. There is a housing shortage of 6 million units, and 40 percent of existing "homes" consist of only one room with primitive roofing. A million families are homeless, and about half the population lacks sewage services, toilets, potable drinking water, electricity, running water, floors other than dirt, social security, adequate footwear, or an income of more than $.25 (U.S.) per person per day.

And who are the keepers of the zoo? They are the agribusiness owners, real-estate speculators, captains of industry and commerce, bankers and department store owners, corporation managers, very successful professionals, army brass, top politicians, and high-level bureaucrats—10 percent of the population, earning over 50 percent of the income. Another 20 percent of the income goes to the 20 percent just below the elite: shopowners, wholesalers, army lieutenants, state doctors, union bureaucrats, federal schoolteachers, civil servants, and skilled industrial operatives. About 17 percent goes to 20 percent who are regularly employed wage earners, and what is left (13 percent) is divided among the remaining 50 percent of the population—the under- and unemployed.

Mexico's capitalist economy is rife with paradoxes. An agrarian nation imports its tortillas: one-fifth of the corn eaten in corn-growing Mexico comes from the United States. Half the nation's deaths occur without medical attention, yet there are 80,000 medical students, 20 percent more than in the United States. Some 16,000 doctors are unemployed in greater Mexico City, yet almost half the urban and rural municipalities have no doctors at all. Mexico's stores brim with goods made by the transnational corporations. For example, the Aurora Supermarket regularly displays twenty shelves of toilet paper in different brands, textures, colors, and prices, but few Mexicans can afford it: the majority use newspaper or, in the countryside, a smooth stone. The dozens of models of automobiles that choke Mexico City's streets, exhaling a veil of smog that envelops the central plateau, are for 13 percent of the residents; the rest spend four hours a day going to and from work on overloaded buses and subways.

The tenth largest nation in the world, Mexico has a home market that potentially could build on economies of scale based on such abundant resources as a hard-working populace, and iron, coke, coal, silver, copper, manganese, lead, zinc, mercury, fluorspar, graphite, sulphur, rubber, sugar, tobacco, hemp—and oil. Its industry provides all sorts of consumer goods, but for the most part it does so as an assembly operation—importing 82 percent of the necessary machines, tools, materials, and spare parts, mainly from the United States. Mexico is the United States' third largest trading partner, after Canada and Japan. Were Washington to impose an economic boycott of the kind it laid down against China for twenty years and still maintains against Cuba, Mexico would lose its economic viability almost overnight.

This is something Mexican capitalists and politicians take seriously. In 1982 the Mexican government owed more than $50 billion to foreign banks and U.S.-dominated lending agencies, or fourteen times what it owed them in 1970—almost one-fourth of the nation's GNP. That is $1,000 for every adult Mexican—more than many make in a year. The United States has an even larger debt, but North Americans owe it to themselves and Mexicans owe it to foreigners. What if foreigners tighten the credit screws, as they did briefly in 1976 in response to nationalist rumblings from the president's office—or as they did against the democratically elected Allende government in Chile and the nationalistic military junta in Peru in the 1970s?

Over the past generation, wave after wave of popular resistance to the state and the domestic and foreign bourgeoisies it services has swelled into a veritable tide. The state has made various adjustments to this challenge, growing more sophisticated in its mixture of repression, concessions, revolutionary rhetoric, and acknowledgment of its failures. When class war reached a critical phase in the late 1960s and mid-1970s, the government unveiled a long well-kept secret: Mexico was sitting on a sea of oil. The people were assured that the economy would not be "petrolized," as had happened in Venezuela, and were told that the chaos that swept Iran after the Shah suddenly increased oil production would never erupt in Mexico. Rather, poverty would be gradually reduced and more jobs offered through skillful management of oil revenues for the country's next stage of industrial development. Yet this did not happen.

Why doesn't the oil benefit the poor? Why can't the money pay for medical care, housing, and education? It has that potential. But how can it go for the people's needs if the bureaucrats and capitalists spend it on wine, women, and song? How can capital investment increase or profits be maintained without a low wage scale, and how can this be guaranteed unless under- and unemployment in turn guarantee a reserve army of unemployed? This is the dilemma of the capitalist state.

U.S. labor unions and jobless white Americans complain about "millions" of Mexicans crossing into their territory. These migrants, whose numbers are actually lower than the press makes out, find temporary work and carry home to Mexico what is left of their wages—after they pay their living expenses and pay off the traffickers and loansharks who "help" in their migration. The annual migratory flow provides cheap nonunion labor to U.S. ag-

ribusinesses, hotels, restaurants, automotive plants, electronics
factories, and garment producers who depend on such labor at set
periods of time. But it also helps Mexico, and businesses in Mexico,
reproduce a labor force—future generations of workers—at no
cost to the Mexican government. The U.S. government allows the
"illegals" to go on cleaning toilets in Houston, packing meat in
Chicago, picking crops in California's Imperial Valley, and as-
sembling parts in Los Angeles in exchange for easier and cheaper
U.S. access to Mexican gas and oil, and because capitalists like to
blame the migrants for high U.S. unemployment rates while bol-
stering sagging rates of profit through their exploitation. How long
will the majority of Mexicans put up with being exploited on both
sides of the border?

Throughout this book, I examine the interweaving of interests of
domestic elites with those of stronger foreign powers, and the periodic conflicts between such interests. It is out of a long, uneven
historical process of state formation, changes in the organization of
economic production, accumulation by ruling groups of the wealth
produced by the toiling masses, and internal and international conflict that Mexico's contemporary capitalist system has emerged.

The book is divided into two parts. Part I traces the process of
capital accumulation and state and class formation from the time of
the earliest Mexican states, through the colonial period of Spanish
rule, to the birth of the independent nation. It is written in the
belief that to understand modern Mexico we must delve into the
history of its peoples—each with unique customs and heritage—
their struggles to define and control the state, and their repeated
uprisings against domestic and foreign oppressors. It concludes
with the 1910–1920 Revolution and the consolidation of the roots
of today's state during the social upheavals of the 1930s. Part II
then examines the development of monopoly capitalism after 1940
and the class structure of contemporary Mexico, with particular
emphasis on how both have been affected by state policies and the
impact of immense U.S. investments and cultural influences.[1]

I

From the First Peoples
to the Modern State

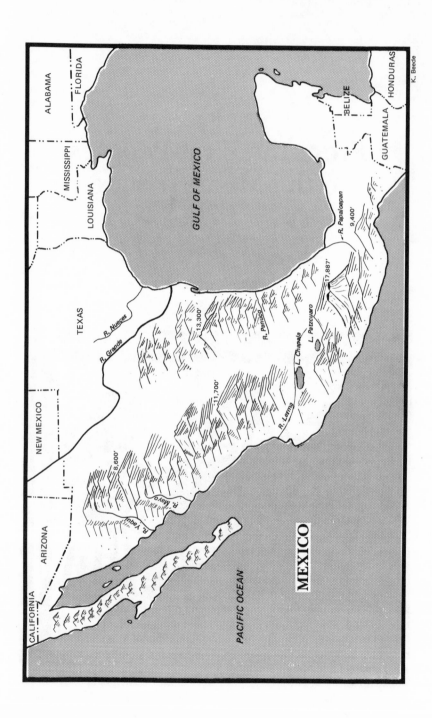

K. Beede

1
Conquest and Colonization

I come for gold, not to till the land like a peasant.
—Hernando Cortés

The sixteenth-century conquest and colonization of Mexico's peoples was a violent affair. The colony of "New Spain," as Mexico was called, produced gold, silver, and a number of other primary products (not the least of which were cochineal dye and medicinal plants, important in the development of European textile manufacture and medicine) for the benefit not only of Spain but also of nascent European capitalism. New World resources and labor fueled the accumulation of wealth in Europe, based on mercantilist trade, a growing division of labor, and global plunder. Marx characterized this period of "original accumulation" as the time when there grew in northern Europe an economic surplus sufficient to initiate the reproduction of a surplus on an ongoing basis—"the rosy dawn for the era of capitalist production."[1]

Although elements of division of labor and original accumulation in Mexico no doubt predated the assertion of Spanish colonial domination, events since then laid the groundwork for what was to become an unevenly developed capitalism heavily affected by external forces. The particular character of Mexico's postcolonial process of capital accumulation became defined in colonial times by the preference of the country's elites to rely on intensely exploited cheap labor much more than on modernizing the forces of production. Mexico's subsequent unequal exchange of products with foreign powers derived from this early colonial shaping of the character of accumulation and its corresponding low level of productivity.

Mexico's colonial class structure consisted of a mass base of peasants and workers highly exploited by privileged commercial, mining, agrarian, and—later—manufacturing interests. Some of these elites, whether Spaniards or criollos (whites born in Mexico), eventually evolved into an early productive bourgeoisie. At first, especially in mining and agriculture, Indians supplied the labor, generated some of the capital, and provided much of the necessary

9

technology and social organization for the production of goods. Eventually, Indians, Africans, the *castas* (people of racially mixed parentage), and the majority of whites (losing the description "criollos") became subjugated as, in main part, "free" wage labor—that is, separated from the means of production, one of the fundamental preconditions for the emergence of the capitalist mode of production. Throughout the colonial period, revolts by the lower classes were common but ruthlessly crushed. Meanwhile, the fruits of their long days and nights of labor were largely appropriated by the elites or their state allies, the royal bureaucrats.

Mexico's increased economic growth and the continued development of a home market in the eighteenth century—an embryonic capitalism stimulated by merchant capital in control of much of the appropriated mineral wealth—contributed to rapid social change. Together with events in Europe triggered by the transition there from mercantile capitalism to early industrial capitalism, such internal economic growth helped to disarticulate older forms of production (communal, slave, petty-commodity, etc.) and to create the conditions for a renewed and more explosive outbreak of class war. This chapter examines the precolonial and colonial conditions that lay behind state and class formation in the evolution of Mexican society up to 1770, when the process of internal economic growth and social change entered this new phase of dynamism, which ultimately generated the mass upheavals behind the nation's winning its independence.

First Peoples

Who the original peoples of Mexico were remains a subject of inquiry, but the radiocarbon (C-14) method of dating used by archaeologists, the use of computers in hieroglyphic deciphering, and other new developments in geography, geology, botany, ethnology, and physical anthropology have given rise to some hypotheses on which there is general agreement. The evidence suggests that humans have existed in America for between 35,000 and 50,000 years.[2] The common view is that the first peoples originated in Asia, using the Bering Strait between Siberia and Alaska as a crossing place. Archaeological excavation in Mesoamerica (a region comprising considerable parts of present-day Mexico and the Central American states) has unearthed small wheeled objects, considered to be toys or cult objects. The early inhabitants of Mexico, then, were familiar with the principle of the wheel—although neither the wheel nor the plough were used, since there were no draught animals. Agriculture developed in Mesoamerica as it did in Mesopotamia but, in contrast with the latter, apparently preceded permanent settlement. Maize (corn) was the prevalent crop; beans, sapots, squash, pumpkins, chile peppers, avocado pears, and tuber plants were also harvested. Productive technology consisted of highly finished implements of stone, obsidian, and jade, as well as the wooden digging stick, or *coa*, still in use today. Robert S. MacNeish believes animal husbandry in the region of Tehuacán (south-central Mexico) began as far back as 7,000 years ago, as did pumpkin cultivation in Tamaulipas (northeast Mexico). Excavations in central Mexico have revealed agrarian villages 3,500 years old. In the fields, houses, and burial grounds, thousands of clay female heads and figures have been found, implying that women had either temporal power or religious significance or both (the figures might be fertility gods).[3] Compact agricultural villages were commonplace in much of Mexico by 1500 B.C. Many of these village communities were small and relatively undifferentiated in terms of livelihood; much of the farming was done communally. How and under what pressures they evolved into larger, more complex units is not clear.

The rise and fall of class-stratified civilizations such as those of the Olmecs,[4] Monte Albán,[5] the Maya, or Teotihuacán continues to be the focus of research and controversy, some emphasizing environmental factors and some the social and economic aspects of power. There is general agreement that the scientific, artistic, architectural, and state-building achievements of these pre-Columbian societies could not have occurred without the production of an economic surplus (freeing portions of the population from direct food production), a significant division of labor, a degree of political centralization in the form of a state representing the interests of a ruling elite, a high level of organization and discipline of labor, a growth in long-distance trade, and in many cases the concentration of people into cities often more densely populated than any in Europe. The sheer size and the fine art of the monumental architecture, wall paintings, pottery, and sculpture suggest something less simple and egalitarian than either "primitive communism" or scattered "democratic city-states." The Pyramid of the Sun, 689 square feet at the base and 210 feet high, constructed during the Teotihuacán civilization (ca. A.D. 100–600) near today's Mexico City, must have taken the labor of thousands and many years. The use of irrigation and intensive agriculture, the importation of raw materials from the lowlands, the exportation of finished products (particularly carved obsidian and pottery—there were specialists *within* obsidian carving), and the concentration of up to 100,000 people in the urban center of Teotihuacán by ca. A.D. 500—all these testified to an economic surplus and dynamism that carried Teotihuacán influence as far south as Kaminaljuyu (modern Guatemala City).

Perhaps most difficult to explain is the origin, growth, and decline of Maya civilization. Its most prominent intellectual and religious centers were located in the least inhabitable tropical, forested lowlands of southern Mexico and northeastern Guatemala, where few people have lived in the last thousand years. Noted for the highest intellectual achievements of pre-Columbian America, the Maya (Classic Period, A.D. 325–925) extended from the highlands of today's Guatemala and El Salvador to the semi-arid frontier zones of the Yucatán in Mexico. Early signs of their civilization appear ca. 300 B.C. in Guatemala's highlands, where the first religious buildings of any size were constructed. Archaeologists estimate a labor force of up to 15,000 for their construction, suggesting a high degree of political centralization.

There are conflicting theories as to how a predominantly egalitarian society, most of whose members engaged in slash-and-burn agriculture in the tropical lowlands, developed the degree of class stratification that characterized Maya civilization. The lack of pressure to irrigate and so centralize production did not deter a process of social differentiation that led to outstanding accomplishments in astronomy, the calendar, mathematics, architectural sculpture, graphology, mural art, and painting. In astronomy, the Maya could accurately chart the course of such planets as Venus without a telescope; they could calculate the exact dates of solar eclipses. They had a chronology and calendar that defined the 365-day solar year more accurately than was done a thousand years later under Pope Gregory in 1582. In mathematics, they mastered the positional notation system unknown to the Greeks and Romans. Using a vigesimal system and the figure zero, they devoted their mathematic precision largely to astrological-religious purposes, including the construction of their monumental religious centers (Europeans did not become acquainted with the figure zero until A.D. 1202, when the Arabs introduced it from India). Maya hieroglyphic writing, much of it still undeciphered, shows elaborate developments in graphology, including pictographic, ideographic, and phonetic elements.

The Maya social organization revolved around small agricultural villages of twenty to forty households. Land was owned in common by lineage groups whose members were not permitted to marry within their own group; each household farmed a plot of communal land. It is estimated that the Maya agricultural household could produce twice the food it needed in four months, leaving ample time to labor on public works, temples, and other services for the benefit of the upper classes. Gordon Willey's excavations in small Maya villages suggest a relatively comfortable standard of living for the non-elites, as evidenced by the survival of platform foundations in all the houses. As for the Maya "urban" centers, it is believed that these were largely ceremonial—inhabited by fewer than 5,000 people, mainly the elites, their servants, and a few others. Defining the elites and their system of power is not easy. Egon Z. Vogt has hypothesized that the Maya had a democratic social organization, with religious and administrative functions distributed and rotated according to a complex system of time periods, services rendered, wealth, and social prestige—in other words, there was not a single professional group as such, and the nobility was not hereditary.[6] The absence of signs of large war fortifications has led many to view the Maya cities as peaceful theocracies: independent city-states governed by a priesthood.

Various hypotheses have been put forth to explain the disappearance of these city-states (whether democratic or authoritarian) and of other civilizations before the emergence of the more secular and complexly class-divided societies encountered by the Spaniards. Among these are population growth exceeding food supplies and a relative deterioration in agriculture; natural catastrophes, famines, or epidemics; and warfare. The details and social character of these transformations and/or battles are vague. For all practical purposes, a hiatus of knowledge exists for the period between the end of the Classic pre-Columbian civilizations, ca. A.D. 1,000, and the rise of the Aztec Empire (A.D. 1327–1519). The general conclusion of scholars is that expanding groups from Mexico's north swept down over the central plateau and on south, destroying the earlier civilizations; rival states from other directions (e.g., that of the Mixtecans in the southeast) expanded as well. From A.D. 900 to 1300 the Toltecs moved southward and gradually incorporated other peoples of central Mexico into a tribute system, extending their influence at least as far as Oaxaca and the Guatemalan highlands, either through conquest or alliance building. Andean cultures apparently were contacted in this period, explaining perhaps the appearance of metallurgy and related Peruvian techniques. But famines, catastrophes, drought, and maybe even climatic changes or failures in irrigation systems in the late Toltec period led to a decline in population and the Toltecs' vulnerability to invasion by other peoples from the north, known as the Chichimeca, whose area of influence soon extended over the vast network of lakes that then constituted the Valley of Mexico, site of today's Mexico City. But these peoples engaged in warfare among themselves, with the result that many of them sought to consolidate their societies into small tight-knit city-states. Then, in the fifteenth century, the Aztecs began to assert their power. By the time of the Aztecs, new inventions in metallurgy, greatly expanded irrigation works, more centralized social organization, greater contact between peoples, a higher degree of state centralization, and the supremacy of a military elite and secular nobility rather than a priesthood were all in evidence. Knowledge about the Aztecs, like that about all the ancient peoples of Mexico, is still far from complete. Much of the ethnohistorical material is based on early accounts by Spanish conquerors, missionaries, and administrators—thus reflecting the biases and motivations of an alien culture. Indian accounts are often filtered through those who received a Christian education from the Franciscan friars and thus reflect some bias as well (Indians learned Latin and theology quickly enough to become the tutors of the sons of the *conquistadores,* and the friars used them to convert Nahuatl to a written language). Nonetheless, these sources, as well as those brought to light by Lord Kinsborough—for example, the Aztec MSS., Ixtlilxochitl, the Mendoza Codex—show beyond any doubt that social stratification, class conflict, and state systems of complex social organization had developed and flourished long before the arrival of the Europeans.[7]

Little is known of the historical roots of the Aztecs, although they themselves believed their ancestors came from a far-off place called "Aztlan." For years they lived as conquered subjects in the Valley of Mexico, doing military service for their overlords. They were driven repeatedly to the poorest lands by each conquering city-state or band, until in 1327 they were allotted a marshy, dismal island in the lake district of the Valley of Mexico. Their mythology describes them as welcoming this outpost because it fulfilled the prophecy and order of their god of the sun (and later, war), Huitzilopochtli, or Hummingbird on the Left: "Go thither where the cactus Tenochtli grows, on which an eagle sits . . . there we shall meet a number of tribes and with our arrow or with our shield we shall conquer them." Within a century, Tenochtitlán (today's Mexico City), as they called their city-state, was the dominant city in the region—the capital of an emergent empire (the eagle atop the cactus is the symbol on the national flag today).

Economically, the Aztecs accumulated surplus through conquest and tribute exacted from other states and peoples. The Aztecs appropriated not only much of the production but also some of the producers from these other societies, forcing them to work on the construction of Tenochtitlán's irrigation and drainage system, to build the houses of the nobility, or to fight in further Aztec wars of expansion. A vastly expanded and improved system of irrigation, including the *chinampa* system (later misnamed "floating gardens"),[8] together with increased division of labor, artisan production, and trade (which characterized other states as well, such as those of the Mixtecs and Zapotecs), generated a sizable economic surplus distributed among the Aztec elite of military officers, state bureaucrats, priests, and nobles.[9]

Socially, the expanded material base of production enabled increased class differentiation. Even within segments of the laboring classes—for example, the freemen of the *calpulli* (literally, large house, an institution that antedated the Aztecs and was a community endowed with inalienable land that each member was obliged to work)—there occurred a division of labor, specialization, social ranking, and the buying and selling of slaves (who in turn often purchased their freedom with war booty acquired in military service). Based on quantity and quality of land, degree of access to water, influence with the state, priesthood, or nobility, and proof of prowess in military combat there was opportunity to improve one's station in life.

Politically, a complex use of the state or state-regulated apparatuses (e.g., trade networks, religion, warfare) characterized Aztec domination of outlying regions and helped enforce labor discipline inside the Valley of Mexico. A ruling army maintained order, a state bureaucracy collected and channeled tribute in goods and labor on a supracommunal basis, and the priesthood oversaw religious practices and education.[10]

At the heart of the Aztec state were the *calpulli*: economic, religious, military, and (by the middle of the fifteenth century) administrative units. The *calpullec*, or head of the *calpulli*, was elected by community members. He was always from the same family, so that there developed a hereditary nobility. A council of elders supported the *calpullec*. In 1376 the Aztecs initiated the rank of "Chief Speaker," who, with his descendants, enjoyed the highest authority and exceptional rights, including polygamy. These descendants *(pipiltin)* added numbers to the nobility. In addition there existed a meritorious nobility, consisting largely of warriors who distinguished themselves in battle. Organized into military orders, they were awarded shares of tribute monies and conquered lands, as well as high state offices. This military aristocracy became the authority that decided on the succession to the Chief Speaker, thereby removing this power from representatives of the *calpulli*. All nobles had the right to private land ownership (their estates were farmed by slaves and bondsmen).

Beneath the ruling elites were the merchants, artisans, and laboring classes. The merchants, some of whom shared the privileges of the nobility, helped the Aztecs in their expansion of wealth and power, often bringing back from their travels messages and useful military-political information. Wielding significant power, they had their own judiciary; but they always remained under the ultimate control of the ruling class. In Tenochtitlán's neighboring city Tlatelolco, the main marketplace, they enjoyed an economic autonomy that was rapidly moving an otherwise state-dominated system toward a free-market economy in commodities (though not in land and labor).[11] The *conquistador* Hernando Cortés reported 60,000 people gathering every day at Tlatelolco "to buy and sell every imaginable kind of merchandise." His aide, Captain Bernal Díaz del Castillo, marveling at the quantities of gold and silver products, wrote: "It was like the enchantments they tell of in the legend of Amadis . . . gazing on such wonderful sights we did not know what to say or whether what appeared before us was real." But Cortés knew it was real and what to say, telling the Aztecs: "We Spaniards are troubled by a disease of the heart for which the specific remedy is gold."[12] The merchants brought from the tropical lowlands raw materials for the artisans and took back the plateau's textile, pottery, and metal products. Yet they encountered limits to their ability to accumulate great wealth—because of the *calpulli* system they had little chance to accumulate land, and they were not permitted to break into the tight guild structure of the artisans.

The position of the artisans was quite inferior to that of the merchants but above the rest of the working population. They were permitted a voice in the city councils, and the more successful ones had sizable labor crews at their beck and call.

The working masses in Aztec society consisted of three groups: the freemen (i.e., members of the *calpulli* who held most of the land in the Valley of Mexico); the bondsmen, or *mayeques*, who composed a third of the Valley of Mexico's population; and the so-called slaves, or *tlacotin*, who constituted about 5 percent of the population (this does not include the numerous conquered peoples).[13] In addition to these major groups in Aztec society there plied their trades various thieves, murderers, prostitutes, and so on. These miscellaneous elements grew in number as more traditional disciplines and loyalties began to disintegrate before the inexorable march of Aztec conquest and state centralization.[14]

The Aztec state was extremely powerful, as almost all of the powers formerly allotted to the *calpulli* became concentrated in it. Toward the end of the fifteenth century, it ruled over a population of diverse peoples across Mesoamerica estimated at from 5 to 35 million.[15] Since the Aztecs were also known as the "Mexica," their rulers called their empire "Mexica" (in Spanish, Mexico). Yet they did not conquer, integrate, or administer all of Mesoamerica—trade and, when necessary, military forays served to assert Aztec hegemony. Rather than incorporate conquered peoples into their society (a job made difficult by geography, language, and customs), the Aztecs preferred to exact tribute from them, both in wealth and labor. In this regard, Aztec colonization was far less complete than the Spanish version that replaced it.

In the early phases of their empire-building, the Aztecs sacrificed their prisoners to the gods—a likely reason for the remarkable "stability" of their rule (earlier ruling groups had also used human sacrifice as an instrument of statecraft).[16] Their religion asserted that sacrifice was necessary to keep the sun in movement,[17] first through the sacrificial deaths of the gods and later of human beings. "Periods" of the sun ended in catastrophe, and the fifth period, coming to a close at the time of the Spanish Conquest, had benefited the faithful with a new material basis for life: maize.[18] In the last years of Aztec rule, human sacrifices notably increased—as did internal dissension within the Aztecs' domains, especially from other Indian societies, which revolted in various parts of Mexica. Additional factors undermining the stability of Aztec rule and economic growth were population increase, which strained the capacity of the irrigation system; natural disasters (floods, drought, famine, disease); the labor-intensive character of the productive and trade system; a waste of resources in religious activities; and the arbitrary character of the class system. In spite of an elaborate system of social regulation, the Aztec system contained within it the seeds of its own internal unraveling: a diversified network of forced labor, tied labor, tribute, specialized producers and distributors, and an increasingly free exchange of commodities. It is thus not surprising that subject peoples resisted Aztec dominance or that groups more directly embedded in Aztec society also strained against the constraints placed on their daily lives. Struggle and revolt came mainly from the toiling masses but, after a devastating famine in 1505, better-off elements also rebelled. Thus, increased human sacrifices paralleled the state's need to maintain fear, and thereby stability.

The Tlaxcala and Tarascan Indians, fiercely independent peoples who survive today, proved particularly unyielding when the Aztecs tried to conquer them in the late fifteenth century. Then, after the 1505 famine, the emperor Moctezuma (Montezuma) faced rising tensions within the Valley of Mexico, from allied cities and even from groups inside Tenochtitlán. His response was to massacre opponents, dismiss all high state officials who were not nobles, crack down on aspiring merchants, and deify himself so that all loyalty had to go not to the ruler and the state—as in the past—but to the god-emperor, Moctezuma.

Conquest and Colonization

When the Spaniards arrived in 1519, warfare broke out between Cortés's soldiers and the Indians. Once subdued, however, the Otomí and Tlaxcala, resentful of Aztec domination, opened negotiations with the Spaniards, and were recruited by Cortés to march on Tenochtitlán. En route, Cortés sought to strengthen his hand by massacring the unarmed residents of the Aztec-controlled city of Chololan (Cholula). Duly intimidated, Moctezuma sought to prevent a similar fate for Tenochtitlán by plying Cortés with gifts of gold, silver, and headfeathers. Cortés accepted the gifts and made Moctezuma his prisoner. Then, while Cortés was making a return trip to the port city of Veracruz to meet with a new landing of Spaniards sent by his superior, the Governor of Cuba, who earlier had ordered him *not* to advance to Tenochtitlán, his second-in-command, Pedro de Alvarado, led a gruesome massacre of the capital's residents, who were armed only with wooden staves.

Thus, after winning over the newly arrived Spanish soldiers in Veracruz, Cortés returned to an agitated Tenochtitlán, where he met an aroused and angry people. United under the leadership of Moctezuma's brother Cuitlahuac, the Aztecs used their superior numbers and familiarity with the system of bridges and canals linking the neighborhoods of the lake regions to isolate and almost decimate Cortés's army. Cortés sought to retrieve the situation by presenting Moctezuma to the people as a peace gesture, but the disgraced emperor was promptly stoned to death by his former subjects. In what Western history books call the "Noche Triste" (Sad Night), Cortés and the remnants of his army slipped out of Tenochtitlán under cover of darkness.

The Aztec's victory was short-lived, however. Cortés regrouped his remaining forces, buttressing them with soldiers from Tlaxcala anxious to end Aztec tyranny. With this immense army of Indians and the superior Spanish technology of firearms, swords, plated armor, and horses, he then re-invaded Tenochtitlán in 1521. An epidemic of smallpox, a disease unknown in Mesoamerica, debilitated the Aztec forces and took the life of Cuitlahuac; his nephew Cuauhtémoc assumed leadership. In a prolonged siege, during which the canals ran red with blood and the stench of the dead made Cortés ill, the Spaniards had to destroy Tenochtitlán in order to capture it. They wrecked the intricate irrigation system and slaughtered most of the citizens. They took Cuauhtémoc prisoner, and some time later executed him. On August 13, 1521, the Aztecs capitulated, bringing to an end their already unstable reign.

Aided by the Catholic clergy, the *conquistadores* set about their immediate business: to harness the wealth, land, and labor of the Indians the better to enrich themselves and the Crown. In the words of Cortés, "I come for gold, not to till the land like a peasant"; to which Bishop Alonso de la Mota y Escobar added, "Where there is no silver, the gospel does not enter . . . where there are no Indians, there is no silver."[19] The Spanish Conquest destroyed the economic and political autonomy of the conquered Indian states, restructuring those parts that the Crown, Church, and colonists could use for their own aggrandizement; thus, the heterogeneous Indian societies gradually became reduced to a more homogeneous, tribute-paying population—and eventually a disciplined labor force.

Cortés estimated that 100,000 were killed at Tenochtitlán, and subsequent overwork, malnutrition, poor hygiene, starvation, floggings, killings, and disease caused more than 90 percent of Mexico's Indian population to be wiped out by 1650. Many perished from diseases imported by the Spaniards or on slave ships, especially smallpox, but also typhoid, measles, malaria, yellow fever, diphtheria, and mumps.[20] The Indians' agrarian communities—though permitted to continue because of their stabilizing influence and provision of labor power—were reduced or damaged by Spanish importation of sheep and plows and production of wheat for the whites. (Sheep destroyed lands with their root-killing grazing, while plows required more cultivable land per unit of food produced.) The Spaniards drained the lake that supported *chinampa* agriculture and monopolized sources of water, thereby furthering malnutrition and starvation. Table 1, based on the conservative demographic estimates of Charles Gibson, shows the marked decimation and partial recovery of the Indian population in the Valley of Mexico between 1520 and 1800, as well as the years of extreme epidemics.[21]

This population decline heightened Indian suffering as the whites competed for increasingly scarce labor power. The whip, gibbet, and stock, imprisonment, torture, rape, and occasional killing became standard weapons for enforcing labor discipline. Though exempted from taxes and tithes, Indians had to pay a

Table 1
Indian Population and Extreme Epidemics, Valley of Mexico

Est. population	Year	Extreme epidemics
1.5 million	1520	1521
300,000	1570	1545–1548, 1576–1579
70,000	1650	1629–1634
120,000	1742	1736–1739, 1761–1762
275,000	1800	1784–1787

Source: Charles Gibson, *The Aztecs under Spanish Rule* (Stanford: Stanford University Press, 1964).

yearly head-tax, called tribute. Men, women, and children were herded into mines and *obrajes* (textile workshops), sacrificed "to the production of objects intended to serve no end beyond the maximization of profit and glory for the individual conqueror."[22] Describing the laborers as "pitilessly exploited," one writer notes that some "*obraje* owners locked their Indians up at night in guarded dormitories."[23]

The *conquistadores* were aiming for wealth and power. Cortés was representative of the new "free-enterprise" spirit. He started gold placer-mining in southern Mexico, opened the first silver mines at Taxco, and established himself in a wide range of business activities besides agriculture. His 25,000-square-mile estate (hacienda) in Oaxaca was netting his son 80,000 gold pesos a year in tribute by 1569. The Cortés hacienda included a nascent silk industry based on the mulberry tree, two sugar mills, wheat, fruit, horses, cattle, sheep, pigs, and corrals for the mules bred in Tehuántepec to service the mines to the north. In Mexico, the successful *conquistador* or colonist became a mining entrepreneur, a rancher, a merchant, and a producer of commercial crops on haciendas and textiles in *obrajes*.

The Spaniards at first sought to maintain remnants of the old ruling classes to assist them in exacting tribute and organizing and disciplining the labor force. Most of the former nobles and high bureaucrats cooperated (after initial resistance), retaining their domineering ways under the new conditions. They became known as *caciques* (bosses),[24] and some of them in turn became "governors," elected by the Indian communities they administered. Each community had its own *cabildo* (town council), to which it elected five to ten councillors from the old ruling class. The governor and councillors were responsible for managing the village's internal affairs. They oversaw the maintenance of order, the supervision of communal lands, food, water, and the local market, the collection of tribute on behalf of the *corregidores* (local Spanish officials in charge of districts and tribute collection), church attendance, and organization of labor for the colonists. In exchange, they were allowed to own land and pass it on to their children (entail), engage in trade, own slaves, and pretend to Spanish ways. Some became landowners and traders on a significant scale (with slaves and mulatto servants) and lorded it over the commoners. In performing their tasks, the *caciques* delegated authority to an intermediate class of lesser officers, who were also exempted from labor for the colonists.

Initially, the *conquistadores* divided up the Indians for their own use—as concubines, slaves, and sources of new generations of desperately needed labor power. Cortés assigned Indians to himself and his officers, using them as unpaid labor and as soldiers. Crown approval was taken for granted, since earlier practices in the Spanish Caribbean had included such labor-recruitment devices as *repartimiento* and *encomienda*. The *encomienda* derived from a Crown decree giving Christopher Columbus access to Indians and their labor—but *not* their land—"in trust" *(en encomienda)*. In return the *conquistadores* were to Christianize the indigenous peoples. By 1542, some 30 *encomiendas* incorporated an estimated 180,000 Indian laborers, whose production went to the *encomenderos*. Under the *repartimiento* system, colonists had to hire Indian labor at a royal labor exchange at predetermined wages for set periods of time.

The zeal of the Catholic clergy in helping to subdue and discipline the Indians was enormous. A Franciscan father, Juan de Zumárraga, boasted in 1531 of the destruction of over 20,000 idols. Missionaries frowned on Indian practices of polygamy and homosexuality, which they suppressed. They forced the occasionally bare-breasted women to cover themselves with the typical Indian blouse, the *huipil*. They had men in loincloths cover their legs with white trousers, standard peasant dress for centuries to come. Shortly after the Conquest, the papacy conferred on the Castillian monarchy complete supervision of the ecclesiastical establishment in the New World, in return for the conversion of Indians and economic maintenance of the Church. In 1536 this church-state alliance introduced the Inquisition, by means of which heresy and treason became synonymous—and the clergy meted out harsh punishments.[25] Supported by tithes, religious fees, and income from food produced by Indian labor on immense tracts of Church land, the curates also financed and administered schools, hospitals, and charity, while indoctrinating the populace in the new faith.

Benefiting from state privileges, the Church emerged as a dynamizing, productive economic force, calculating its varied enterprises along rational, profit-oriented lines. Its 10 percent tithe on gross output, charged mainly on the whites' large estates (haciendas), while cutting into the private agrarian sector's profits, had the effect of stimulating private investment in other sectors. The Church itself became a significant agricultural producer (along with the Indian villages). By 1700, income from Church funds in the New World was maintaining the ecclesiastical establishment not only in Spain and Portugal but also in Italy. Moreover, by investing much of its revenues in mortgage loans and other credits to private enterprises in mining, trade, and agriculture at interest rates lower than the market rate, the Church became the major credit institution in Mexico. Its rural "banks," for instance, greased the entire agrarian economy. Active in various productive ventures, the Church was simultaneously landlord, banker, and capitalist.

Despite biological holocaust, cultural disruption, and unprecedented economic exploitation, many Indians managed to adjust to their new situation. The Catholic Church's lavish, exotic rituals and orderly hierarchy contained forms already familiar to them, and they transferred much of their old religious identity to the new doctrine imposed in place of their smashed (and obviously unsuccessful) idols. In 1531 a humble Indian named Juan Diego claimed to have seen an image of the "Virgin of Guadalupe" (mother of the gods) miraculously coming to bless and heal her suffering people. Although the friars of the evangelical orders initially resisted accepting Juan's vision, the more pragmatic secular clergy encouraged its popularization. Then, after publication of a widely distributed book on the subject in 1648, the myth of the Indian Virgin received official blessing, and statues, carvings, and paintings of the Virgin of Guadalupe began to appear in churches and public places. This amalgam of Catholic and Indian superstition continues uninterrupted to this day. So, however, do the ambivalent feelings of Indians and mestizos (persons of mixed Indian/white descent who today constitute the vast majority of the population) about the clergy, who are viewed as oppressors as often as saviors.

More important than the Indians' religious incorporation, however, was the integration of many of their social practices into the Spanish system of exploitation. For example, the Maya had practiced a system of *compadrazgo* (literally, co-fatherhood), which readily became amalgamated with the European "godfather" system. Maya *compadrazgo* contained certain pre-Spanish roots of *machismo* (the ideology of male supremacy with its corresponding emphasis on bravery, virility, woman's "frailty," etc.), as did the Aztecs' male-dominated military and religious traditions of strict obedience and hierarchy.[26] Under the Spaniards, *compadrazgo* served as a patriarchical form of harnessing Indian labor and fortifying class hierarchy. It provided a patron-client form of exchange that remains common today, through which the better-off *compadre* is expected to assist the family of the peasant or worker godson in its economic survival.

Crown Policies and Early Intercolonial Rivalries

In the course of the Catholic Crusades, the expulsion of the Muslims (the so-called Reconquest of 1031–1492), and the reunification of the kingdoms of Castile and Aragon (1479), Spain had established a centralized state, administered by a bureaucracy of *letrados* (university-trained lawyers) and dependent on the export of primary products (more than manufactures) to other parts of Europe. Since the Spanish textile industry could not compete with cheaper woolens and silks from France, Holland, or England, the privately controlled livestock monopoly *(mesta)* found it more profitable to export raw wool than Castilian cloth. Spain's lifeline was based on a thriving mercantile system of production guilds, private monopolies, shipping companies, and state-protected merchant monopolies. Consequently, with the recent advances in long-distance shipping possibilities, Spain naturally feasted its eyes on new riches abroad. State-backed merchants helped finance overseas exploration to discover maritime trade routes to the Indies and the precious embroidered fabrics, exotic spices, and other wealth reputed to be there. The militaristic tradition provided many a willing explorer, accustomed to acting boldly and greedily. To the surprise and delight of the merchants, explorers, and conquerors, a midway point was encountered—America (a better helmsman than geographer, Columbus thought he had discovered the Indies and so named America's inhabitants "Indians")—pregnant with wealth not even anticipated: gold, silver, and a local labor force accustomed to paying tribute, whether in products or work.

In the course of the Reconquest much of the military and political power of Spain's feudal nobility had been broken, and new values and institutions had emerged: strong authority vested in a monarchical state; a militant Catholicism; rewards for military

prowess and individual enterprise; use of family ties and connections to the court *(personalismo)* for garnering wealth or prestige; a
focus on trade, guild production, or direct seizure of land or wealth
rather than on new manufacturing production techniques; and a
corresponding emphasis on individual exploits for obtaining gran-
deur. Given these new values and the immense distances and risks
involved in overseas trade, the Crown found it practical to let state-
sponsored free enterprise conduct the Conquest. Private individuals or groups paid their own way. Wealth garnered in earlier
conquests (e.g., by Cortés in Cuba) financed further ones (Mexico,
and then Peru). To a significant degree, Mexican and Peruvian
Indians—through their gifts, labor, and forced tribute—paid for
their own conquest.[27]

But although it encouraged free enterprise, the Crown made
sure it retained the upper hand. It signed a *capitulación*, or contract,
with the head of every overseas expedition, assigning him an area
for conquest and granting him certain titles should the venture
succeed, as well as obliging him to pay the Crown tribute on the
wealth he obtained abroad. Those adventurers who conquered territory without first having signed such a contract usually signed
later, to protect themselves against competitors in the marketplace
of conquest. Bitter feuds among the colonists became legend, with
rivals even killing one another. Such strife made it easier for the
Crown to maintain its authority, although the *conquistadores* by no
means welcomed the Crown's restrictions.

No sooner had the conquest of Mexico been completed than the
Crown began to undermine the authority of the *conquistadores*, reducing their status to that of ordinary royal governors and in some
cases repealing earlier *capitulaciònes* and replacing them with royal
appointees. In 1523 the monarchy prohibited *encomiendas*, declaring all Spanish colonists, their descendants, and Indians vassals of
the king. Viceroys and other officials were sent to enforce royal
discipline on the unruly settlers. In 1542 the New Laws were
promulgated, forbidding further allocation of Indian lands to the
colonists. Local officials had to collaborate to survive—the common
expression "Obedezco pero no cumplo" (I obey but do not comply)
reflected the problem. They also worked with Franciscan and
Dominican friars to persuade Crown officials that strict enforcement of the New Laws was impossible, and in 1545 the monarchy
revoked the New Laws. Yet in 1550 it ordered further expeditions
of conquest to cease until the government could decide if they were
"just." The colonists chafed at the bit, and in 1566 a conspiracy by
Alonso de Avila (son of a prominent conqueror) to make Cortés's

son Don Martín Cortés king of Mexico was nipped in the bud; Avila and his brother were decapitated and their heads publicly displayed on pikes as grim warnings against future conspiracies against the Crown. Then, in 1573, the Standard Law resolved much of the Crown-colonist tension by replacing the word "conquest" with "pacification" and merely urging the colonists to moderate their use of force.[28]

Since Spain gained its relative prosperity through international trade, vastly enriched by the Crown's "royal fifth" *(quinto real)* of the New World's precious metals and of colonial trade revenues, the monarchy and Spanish merchants jealously guarded their monopolistic powers, epitomized by the authority vested in the Casa de Contratación (Board of Trade) and the Consulado (merchant guild) of Seville (and after 1717, Cádiz). State regulation and the power of wealthy import merchants prevented manufacturing in New Spain (Mexico) from reaching a point where it might challenge or supersede the import of luxury and manufactured goods from Europe. Economic conflicts between the Mexican merchants' Consulado in Mexico City and the merchant oligarchy of Seville were common. For example, from 1620 to 1670 the Mexican merchants were waxing rich on the Manila-Mexico-Peru trade. They handled the trade on Chinese silk processed by Puebla's textile manufacturers into finished garments and shipped to Peru and the rest of South America. They also exported to Peru textiles, clothing, books, leather goods, and jewelry. Mexican manufacturing production grew enormously in the first third of the seventeenth century, and Spain's oligarchy resented these threats to Spanish commerce and the draining of Peruvian silver into the Pacific trade. In 1631, and again in 1634, the king tried to prohibit trade between Mexico and Peru and to limit the Pacific trade to the Far East, but through collusion with local bureaucrats Mexico City's merchants continued the trade virtually unabated.

The Crown also periodically outlawed the production of olive oil, wine, certain textiles, and other goods that might compete with Spain's major items of trade. Consequently, most *obrajes* and successful artisan workshops clustered around mines, haciendas, and urban centers, although a few sold to national and international markets. Not even producers of agricultural commodities were permitted to develop too large-scale a production if the Crown became convinced by Spanish merchants in Veracruz that a competitive colonial elite might emerge. For example, cacao was a major export crop in early colonial Mexico, but by the mid-seventeenth century Spain had shifted its trade quotas and investment opportunities to Venezuela, thereby contributing to the demise of cacao as a money-earner for Mexican merchants and producers and its ascent to the position of leading export of Venezuela (in fact, Venezuela exported most of its cacao to Mexico, where it was a basic component of the daily diet).

In the meantime, the Crown sought new ways to structure the employment of labor. It first placed most of the largest *encomiendas* under royal jurisdiction (incorporated by the Crown), prohibited settlers from access to free labor, and permitted them instead tribute regulated by Crown-appointed *corregidores*. Although Cortés's own estates were exempted, by about 1575 the other large *encomiendas*, producing 75 percent of New Spain's tribute, had been incorporated by the Crown—assuring it or Spanish merchant monopolies of most of the corresponding revenues from such leading exports as sugar and hides, or cochineal (a red dye from insects) and indigo (a blue dye from a shrub-like plant) essential to Europe's expanding textile industry. By 1602 there remained only 140 Indian communities in privately held *encomiendas*, compared with 480 in 1560. Second, the Crown introduced to New Spain the *repartimiento*, also regulated by *corregidores*. This pitted the colonists in fierce competition with one another for the same precious surplus-producing commodity, labor power. The fabulous silver discoveries of 1546 and the corresponding high wages and *partidos* (minority shares of ore mined) offered to laborers attracted large numbers of Indians to the northern mines.

After the 1576–1579 epidemic, labor shortages grew even more severe, and the Crown permitted the *repartimiento* system to give way to one of "free" labor on an open market. By the start of the seventeenth century, free (wage) labor prevailed at most mines and on a majority of haciendas. In New Spain's largest silver-producing area, Zacatecas, by 1598 there were no *repartimiento* Indians at all and only 130 African slaves, compared with 1,014 free laborers. Free labor also became common in the textile *obrajes,* in other workshops, in transport, and in trade, as well as among artisans, servants, haulers, sweepers, and the work crews engaged in Mexico City's public drainage operations *(desague).* Few of the colonists—least of all merchants, miners, *hacendados* (owners of haciendas), and manufacturers—complained when the Crown decreed an official end to *repartimiento* in 1632.[29]

Thus, by the early seventeenth century, free labor (and different forms of debt-labor) had become a common practice. There continued regional variations, of course—instances of slavery in some coastal areas and parts of the northeast, and a late-colonial shift toward debt-peonage on haciendas.[30] And free labor often amounted to paid forced labor, debt-labor, or payment in kind, only rarely alleviating the intense exploitation suffered by Indians. Many Indians ostensibly hired for a wage became entrapped in a web of debts for their purchases of basic necessities—the first steps in the long process that led to the nineteenth-century institutionalization of "company stores" *(tiendas de raya)*. In addition, they had to pay Church and brotherhood fees and (relatively low) royal taxes. Also, they had tasks to perform in their communities, under the surveillance of the *caciques* and lesser officers.

Given the low wage structure and the large amounts of unpaid household labor and subsistence production engaged in by women and children, the reproduction costs of Indian labor power were borne largely by the Indians themselves. Peasant producers had their surplus appropriated by others, forcing them to resort to unpaid family labor in subsistence farming and household handicraft production simply to stay alive. This, of course, by helping to maintain wages below the minimum, reinforced the dominant system of labor exploitation. The best-off of colonists in turn—given their reliance on cheap labor and use of means of production less capitalized than those of foreign competitors—were rarely able to develop New Spain's home market more than regionally. To grow wealthy, most of them transferred to the international market their mining and agricultural surpluses, which they obtained on the basis of "superexploitation" (i.e., payment of labor power below its value, or what it takes for a laborer to sustain his or her family). Thus, for the toiling masses, noncapitalist forms of economic activity like petty trade, domestic handicraft, and small-parcel subsistence farming became absolutely necessary and, in a contradictory fashion, functional for the elites' original accumulation of capital.

Early in the colonial period, then, the Crown's decrees to make most of the American territories royal provinces instead of proprietary domains served its interests well (and those of Spain's merchant oligarchy and, as we shall see, of nascent-capitalist groups in northern Europe), while still allowing some of the colonists enough opportunity to accumulate handsome surpluses. All political and economic rights were circumscribed by the Crown, which legally owned all the land and controlled the main source of wealth, the labor of Indians. The Crown had thus taken sufficient steps—for the moment, at least—to prohibit the formation of a rival group of miners, merchants, manufacturers, or landowners able to seriously threaten its hegemony.

After the defeat of the Spanish Armada (1583–1588), Spanish

mercantilist strength was increasingly challenged by rival colonial powers. Consolidation of Dutch commercial supremacy and British naval supremacy during the next half century was accompanied by the penetration of Spanish America. During the peak years of Mexico's early mining production at the outset of the seventeenth century, the first significant north-European incursions into the Caribbean and South America occurred. Piracy, smuggling, slave-running, and pillage were the hallmarks of the next two centuries. "The treasures captured outside Europe by undisguised looting, enslavement, and murder floated back" to Holland, England, and other European powers to be "turned into capital."[31] Mexican silver and gold flowed through Spain to pay for north-European manufactured goods or the costs of war and empire, ending more often than not in the hands of Genoese, Dutch, and German bankers or England's nascent industrialists. In effect, the Spanish merchant guild (Consulado) became a front or funnel for the capital of north-European merchants and early manufacturers.

Spanish merchants settling in Mexico established commercial monopolies, conducting their trade through the ports of Veracruz and Acapulco. They and their descendants resided for the most part in Mexico City, itself a growing commercial center. At times, more than half of Spain's shipping to the New World was bound for Mexico. From Acapulco ships carried Mexican and Peruvian silver to the East Indies in exchange for the silks and spices coveted by Europeans. In the words of Adam Smith:

> In China and Indostan, the value of the precious metals, when the Europeans first began to trade to those countries, was much higher than in Europe and it still continues to be so. . . . The silver of the new continent seems in this manner to be one of the principal commodities by which the commerce between the two extremities of the old one [Europe and Asia] is carried on, and it is by means of it, in great measure, that these distant parts of the world are connected to one another.[32]

Spanish merchants thrived in this expanded trade, but at the same time they found themselves transferring their profits to banking and insurance operations on which they depended. As Tomás de Mercado, a Dominican theologian in New Spain writing about Seville's merchants, observed: "To all the Indies they ship great cargoes of every kind of merchandise, and return with gold, silver, pearls, cochineal, and hides in vast quantities. . . . to insure their cargoes (which are worth millions) they have to take out insurances in Lisbon, Burgos, Lyons, and Flanders, because so vast are their shipments that neither the merchants of Seville nor of twenty cities like Seville are capable of insuring them."[33] Meanwhile, manufacturing development in Spain was further inhibited by the inflationary impact of silver from the colonies.

The monopoly structure of this expanded worldwide trade facilitated draining enormous surpluses from Mexico, since prices on colonial exports were quite unfavorable compared with those of European manufactured imports. The most conservative estimate available for the start of the eighteenth century puts the value of Mexican exports at 2 million pesos for every million pesos imported. Other estimates put the ratio at five to one. Adding direct tribute collection, we can appreciate Mexico's loss to the "mother" country. A typical annual report of Royal Treasury income in New Spain in the late eighteenth century shows over 11 million pesos collected, 72 percent of which went to Spain and most of the remainder to the colonial bureaucracy in Mexico.

The Rise of Commercial Agriculture

As mining flourished and more people moved to the mining areas, the demand for agricultural goods increased, as did the need for labor. Both led to a reduction of Indian lands. Landowners sought to enlarge the pool of landless labor by dispossessing the Indians, which also served to eliminate the competition of Indian producers in what were becoming ever larger internal and external markets. To service the booming mining centers, agriculture was put on a more commercial basis: breeding mules and horses to transfer the wealth; cultivation of sugar and maize to feed the labor force that produced it; and establishment of immense wheat fields, grinding mills, and sugar mills (or *ingenios*—literally, engines) on haciendas that spread throughout much of New Spain. In the words of German geographer and man of letters Alexander von Humboldt:

> Trips through the mountainous part of Mexico offer the most obvious examples of the beneficent influence of the mines on agriculture. Without the establishments formed for the working of the mines, how many places would have remained unpopulated, how much land uncultivated, in the four districts of Guanajuato, Zacatecas, San Luis Potosí, and Durango. . . . The foundation of a city follows immediately after the discovery of a large mine. . . . Haciendas are established nearby; the scarcity of foodstuffs and the high prices caused by consumer competition favors agricultural products, compensates the grower for the deprivations of life in the mountains. In this way, arising only out of the desire for profit . . . a mine . . . is very quickly linked up with lands long under cultivation.[34]

Or, as Lucas Alamán, a prominent nineteenth-century entrepreneur and historian, observed: "The great sums poured into the mining *reales* [firms] were diffused for many leagues, fomenting agriculture and industry by providing consumers for the products of the one and by the installation of equipment, draining machinery, and refineries for the other."[35]

Hacendados employing cheap labor that worked from dawn to sunset and Spanish colonist merchants in whose businesses they sometimes participated made fabulous fortunes in the course of agriculture's commercialization. New Spain's agricultural goods—cochineal, indigo, silk, cotton, hides, tallow, leather products, sugar—were increasingly traded for European manufactures, including Spanish arms, paper, fine cloth, books, wine, olive oil, and soap. Even regions removed from the main locations of mineral or agricultural production for export developed farming for profit. For example, to service the provincial center of Guadalajara, cattle and other livestock production (sheep, horses, mules, etc.), and maize and wheat cultivation were developed according to carefully calculated profit considerations. Indeed, during declines in mining production, as in the mid-seventeenth century or between 1805 and 1810, agricultural production for the internal market tended to overtake mining in total value. (One observer estimated the value of agrarian production at almost four times that of mining in 1810.)[36]

Hacendados expanded not only at the expense of Indians. In some areas—for instance, in parts of the Bajío (greater Guanajuato area)—they also purchased mid-size farms. Shifting their investments according to market opportunities (in hard times parceling out their lands for cash), many *hacendados* also participated in mining or commerce. As social historian Doris M. Ladd has observed, rich *hacendados* were

> very active in the processing industries in New Spain. Miners invested great sums of money in refining haciendas to process the ores from their mines. Most harvest haciendas contained factories, installations for making bricks, for fermenting and distilling alcoholic beverages, for grinding grain, for curing hides, for drying and salting foodstuffs. . . . In Mexico, when great wealth was involved, "the merchant," "the miner," "the financier," "the *hacendado*" turned out to be, more often than not, the same person.[37]

Smallholders *(rancheros),* tenant farmers, and sharecroppers also existed, with the largest number of prosperous *rancheros* establishing themselves in the Bajío region. While most small producers experienced miserable conditions, those producing goods that required close supervision or highly motivated workers (garden products, cochineal, small animals, eggs, and even sometimes cotton, tobacco, or wine) were able to compete with the *hacendados*.

Agricultural activity was far from static. Production fluctuated with the ups and downs of mining and trade, and different geographical regions gave rise to variations in land-tenure patterns and agrarian practices. In the southeast there were few haciendas and many Indian villages. In Yucatán, technologically primitive haciendas exploited subsistence Indian communities. In central Mexico, there were more haciendas, though they were still outnumbered by Indian villages. In the north, haciendas barely outnumbered Indian villages, and there were even more *ranchos* (small estates or homestead farms, owned or rented). The commercial haciendas became increasingly concentrated near the mines and some of the provincial centers.

As the eighteenth century progressed, agricultural production received added impetus from new silver discoveries, population growth, and, in central Mexico at least, the demands of the internal market. Increasing numbers of Indians joined the ranks of the free labor force to work in the new mines and on the expanding commercial haciendas or the few successful small and medium-size agrarian parcels. (The fact that free laborers could get the support of colonial authorities if they were not permitted to leave the haciendas put a legal brake on debt-peonage.) Once more, Indian lands were reduced by aggressive *hacendados*, on whom many peasants became dependent during epidemics or economic hard times. In the middle of the century it became legal for landowners to transmit their workers with their land in cases of property sales; also, because of the *hacendados'* sheer power supremacy, debt-peonage did increase—although not in the extreme manner it was to assume after Mexico's gaining independence (1821) when, with the collapse in strong central government, the *hacendados* would be able to enforce it with private armies.

The expansion of the haciendas reflected their owners' need to separate the peasantry from its means of production (i.e., land) in order to obtain its labor power for increased production for the home market or export. The *hacendados* followed the Spanish tradition of organizing their estates to function as self-contained units, incorporating agrarian activities, artisanry, commerce, and even occasional *obrajes* within their far-flung borders. Besides wage laborers, they used tenants, sharecroppers, and peasants from neighboring Indian communities—all of whom they treated with patriarchical condescension. Yet historians have not uncovered one example of a completely autarchic hacienda.

Despite their expansion, and in part because of it, the haciendas ran into economic difficulties toward the end of the colonial period. Their owners owed immense sums to the Church and the merchants for loans, had to pay wages in cash, and needed further credit to expand. Competition in regional markets drove many *hacendados* to increase their scale of production, forcing new cash outlays and further indebtedness.

Constituting an emergent but unevenly developed agrarian bourgeoisie, the better-off *hacendados* overlapped with the most prosperous mining, commercial, and manufacturing families. The richest *hacendados* were often absentee landlords. The middle ranks of the emergent agrarian bourgeoisie consisted of *mayordomos* (administrators who received a minority share of profits), *arrendatarios capitalistas* (who paid the *hacendados* rent and retained the profits from production), and prosperous *rancheros*. Some of these elements also developed their own business enterprises on the side (e.g., *ingenios*, urban real estate, sugar trade, etc.).[38]

Indian, African, and *Casta* Resistance

Whether Indian, African, *casta* (of mixed race), or poor white, New Spain's lower classes (and later, some emergent intermediate-class elements as well) did not accept their subjugation or abuse passively. Many authors on Mexico's colonial period, using the language and perspective that permeates the primary source, equate "lower classes" with "nonwhite" or "Indian" groups, thereby blurring the important role that class position played in defining how a person acted or was stereotyped. Accepting many of their sources' stereotypes, some portray the Indians as having behaved "passively" and "obediently," while declining into "alcoholism" or "laziness"; or, alternatively, as having found in Christianity a solace preferable to their pre-Conquest exploitation.[39]

That in fact Indians actively engaged in rebellion after the Spanish Conquest has been well documented, and Indian revolts probably occurred more frequently than the written evidence indicates. In the face of the Conquest's spread, many Indians who did not actively rebel abandoned their communities or took refuge in the mountains instead. Some committed collective suicide rather than be enslaved, and some women refused to continue procreating. In addition, as under any system of exploitation, Indians resisted covertly and on a daily basis—slowing up their labor, doing less careful work, and so on.

Overt resistance was widespread and recurrent. For example, the Huasteca Indians along the Pánuco River (Veracruz, Hidalgo, San Luis Potosí) bitterly fought the Spaniards. Thousands were burned alive; others were captured and sent to the Caribbean as slaves; still others held out and conducted guerrilla actions for over two centuries. In fact, as late as the mid-nineteenth century some of the Huasteca were secure in their own communities, practicing a self-declared anarchism. Serious Indian revolts occurred in the Huasteca region during the last two decades of the dictatorship of Porfirio Díaz (1876–1911), and these Indians helped launch the Mexican Revolution of 1910.[40]

Maya communities in the Yucatán also held off the Spaniards for many years. Francisco de Montejo, and later his son and nephew (both also named Francisco), finally subdued them only after burning chieftains alive, cutting off the arms and legs of male prisoners, and hanging or drowning the women. Over 500 Spaniards perished in these early battles. Then, in 1761, the Maya rose up under the leadership of Jacinto Cano, protesting excessive tribute; and in 1846–1848 they launched a bloody revolution against the predominantly white upper classes (for which reason it has been called by many historians the "Caste War of Yucatán").

The Yopes in coastal Guerrero joined with some of their former enemies in 1531 to combat the greater threat of Spanish rule. The massive and sanguine Mixton Rebellion of 1541 in the Zacatecas-Jalisco area of western Mexico resulted in the death of the *conquistador* Alvarado and led to a prolonged period of guerrilla warfare. Churches and monasteries were prime targets. (This, like a few other *early* Indian revolts, involved the participation of *caciques* seeking autonomy from the Spaniards in order to establish independent control over Indian labor.) Also in the west, Tepic miners revolted in 1598 and again under Mariano in 1801. As late as the Díaz dictatorship, the Indians of this region took refuge in the Sierra de Nayarit, from where they launched forays against large-scale landowners.

The Chichimeca, as the northern groups of hunters and food-gatherers were called (Otomí, Zacatecos, etc.), fought the advancing Spaniards and their Indian auxiliaries with extreme ferocity in the triangle between Guadalajara, Saltillo, and Querétero, where the big silver finds were. With their raids along the Zacatecas-Mexico City road and elsewhere, they inflicted more losses in lives and property than in any previous Spanish-Indian conflict. By 1570 the entire frontier was aflame with rebellion, and the Chichimeca advanced on Guadalajara and to within twenty leagues of Mexico City. The Spaniards responded by organizing the first regular Spanish army in New Spain (made up mostly of criollos) and a network of armed garrisons *(presidios)* to carry out a war policy of "fire and death," combined with the enslavement of frontier Indians. Final Spanish and criollo victory (1600) occurred only by means of superior firepower combined with a pacification program that included recruitment of captured Chichimeca into the army; awarding them special privileges (including titles of nobility), money, food, and clothing; and assimilating them into a new religion (Catholicism). Indians as far north as New Mexico continued the by-then vain resistance into the seventeenth century. In the northwest, the Yaquis of Sonora held off much of the whites' advance until the twentieth century. Their revolts threatened the Díaz regime and were brutally repressed, the captured warriors being sent as slaves to harvest tobacco crops in Oaxaca.

In the south, Oaxaca's Indians jealously guarded their nearly autonomous communities throughout the colonial period, rising up repeatedly against abuses by *corregidores* or priests. For example, in 1660 over twenty Oaxacan towns revolted, protesting the *repartimiento;* peasants killed royal officials and looted royal coffers. In 1680 the Indians of Tehuántepec revolted and took control of much of the Isthmus for eight years. To this day, these Indians are known for their independence and dignity, which they had maintained during the reigns of the Zapotecs and Aztecs as well. Indians in Chiapas periodically mounted insurrections against outside domination, and in 1712 the Tzetzal revolt created a confederation based on a mythical avenging virgin.

Almost all of the Indian resistance focused on retaining or repossessing land, or opposing forced labor. Issues were defined regionally rather than nationally, and the fight to retain communal roots or identity was an important part of the struggle. Often colonial officials, in an effort to avoid military defeat or the spread of insurrection, as well as to maintain a steady source of out-migrating labor, negotiated truces and compromises with the rebellious communities—and then executed or imprisoned local leaders. Where negotiations failed, the state response was always one of brute force.[41]

Thus, Indian resistance to exploitation was not merely passive or cultural. It took an active form, although varying in intensity and success from region to region, and even from village to village. Few historians deny that throughout the colonial period the Indians retained a strong sense of identity and many of their traditional practices. By 1810 they still constituted a majority of the population—about 60 percent of an estimated 6 million. *(Caciques* and lesser officers made up about 7 percent of the Indian population in the early seventeenth century, but they increasingly migrated to the cities where, with occasional skilled peasant migrants, they emerged as a new type of Mexican: the Spanish-speaking Indian who imitated the manners of the whites and mestizos—the so-called *ladino*.)

Africans, first brought to New Spain on a regular basis in the late sixteenth century to help fill the void left by the precipitous demographic decline among Indians, also resisted subjugation. The first slaves arrived in Mexico in small numbers with Cortés, one of whose faithful lieutenants was a black Catholic named Juan Garrido who became a *conquistador* in his own right.[42] More slaves arrived in the following two decades, and the first black "scare" in Mexico dates from 1537, when a slave uprising was brutally crushed. The peak of slave importation (never conducted on a massive scale) was during the mining boom of 1580–1635—a time in which larger numbers of Spanish immigrants arrived as well. In general, the Crown discouraged slavery as a means of labor exploitation, particularly after the end of the mining boom. The *tlacotin* and *mayeques* of Aztec times were initially resettled in Indian communities, where they had the rights of commoners and joined them in laboring for or paying tribute to the whites. Thus only blacks were slaves in the colonial period.

By the mid-seventeenth century, mulattoes (persons of mixed black and white descent) outnumbered blacks almost four to one, the combined total being estimated at 165,000. Many blacks were free, having been able to purchase their freedom; others had run away and formed "maroon" bands. While some worked the mines, by 1650 those still enslaved were limited largely to the sugar-growing areas of Oaxaca or the coast of New Spain. The Spaniards (known as *peninsulares*) and the criollos often used slaves in specialized capacities—as servants, as overseers of Indian labor, and as mistresses and concubines for merchants and officials.

Resistance came from maroons and slaves alike. The maroon bands fought off *peninsular* and criollo attempts to reconquer them along both coasts and in the interior of New Spain from 1607 to 1611. They raided major transportation routes, like the one linking Puebla to Veracruz. One leader, an ex-African chieftain named Yanga, finally agreed to compromise with colonial authorities, and his followers were granted their own autonomous town in exchange for a promise to return future runaway slaves. There followed more maroon uprisings, in 1617–1618, which were put down by force and compromise. More rebels were permitted to establish a community in the sierra near Córdoba, Veracruz, which received the name of San Lorenzo de los Negros. And in 1646 fighting between mulatto and white soldiers broke out at the Veracruz garrison; the mulattoes were subdued, and the trouble did not spread.

In 1611, some 1,500 blacks rioted in Mexico City at the burial of a black woman said to have been flogged to death by her master. A plot was alleged, and in 1612 the authorities tortured or killed the leaders of the black brotherhoods, lynched about thirty-five other men and women in the central plaza, and displayed their severed heads on pikes. All restrictions on blacks, previously ignored or lifted, were reimposed and new ones added. In 1665 there were various outbreaks by blacks and mulattoes in Mexico City, all of which were suppressed with the aid of the Inquisition. Blacks and mulattoes in general opposed the royal bureaucracy and sought out the freer, less-regulated urban atmosphere of the criollos and mestizos, among whom they had a better chance of creating their own opportunities. By 1810, there remained fewer than 10,000 black slaves—and their rebellious spirit infused the Wars of Independence (1810–1821).

A small number of other minorities entered Mexico during the colonial period, including Jews, Italians, and Portuguese. Some Asians, mainly Filipinos and a smattering of Chinese, arrived on the Manila galleons. The Asians engaged in petty trading, usually as peddlers, and like other minorities tended to assume Spanish names.

The mixing of all the different races created what were known as the *castas:* mestizos, mulattoes, *zambos* (Afro-Indians), Afro-mestizos, and so on. In all their various combinations, members of the *castas* were generally poor; only a few gained positions that exploited Indians or blacks. Mulattoes, *zambos,* and Afro-mestizos suffered racist degradation more than did mestizos, who, to a degree, shared white racists' disdain for Indians and blacks. This was in part because of the sliding color scale of racism and the social emphasis placed by the ruling elites on light skin, something to which some members of the *castas* could reasonably lay claim. The *castas* numbered about 6 percent of the population in 1700 and 19 percent in 1810, roughly equal to the number of whites—although in fact most demographic estimates supposedly based on phenotype actually take class positions into account. For example, immigrant whites who sank into the lower classes were described and known as *castas*, "vagabonds," or any category other than white. Especially in the north, but also in the center and to a lesser degree in the southeast of the country, the vast majority of *castas*, as well as poor whites, worked alongside Indians, acting as direct competitors for land and for wages. It was these people who, after the Indians and blacks, suffered from racism the most. In the words of the Consulado of Mexico merchants writing to the Spanish Cortes (parliament) in 1811:

> The *castas*, whose lazy hands are employed in peonage, domestic service, trades, artifacts and the army, are of the same condition, the same character, the same temperament and the same negligence as the Indian . . . drunken, incontinent, lazy, without honor, gratitude, or fidelity. . . . The whites who call themselves American Spaniards [criollos] show their superiority over the . . . Indians and *castas* . . . by their inherited wealth, their career, their love of luxury, their manners and the refinement of their vices.[43]

Because of their oppression, the *castas* were quick to join the numerous underdog revolts in New Spain's cities known as *tumultos*, or, in the eyes of the white elites, "rioting of the rabble." Even criollos, however, though terrorized by these wild uprisings, would occasionally join, use, or attempt to lead the *tumultos* in order to threaten the *gachupines* (a derogatory term for Spaniards, or *peninsulares*), their rivals for power in control of commerce and the bureaucracy. In almost every *tumulto* the Indians, Africans, *castas*, and poor whites moved against the symbols of wealth and state power by looting stores and destroying government offices, the gibbet, and the stock. *Tumultos*, then, constituted the gravest and most recurrent threat to Spanish colonial power and to the hegemony of the white elites. They were a profoundly class phenomenon, with undertones of anticolonial nationalism.

After the particularly violent *tumulto* of 1624, provoked by Archbishop Juan Pérez de la Serna, a criollo, and Viceroy Marqués de Gelves, his rival, during which Mexico City was ravaged, the *visitador* (Crown-appointed inspector) Martín de Carrillo y Alderete sent the king a description of the conditions that provoked it:

> The *tumulto* shows three facts of great importance to the Spanish Government: first, the conspiracy was organized, directed, and led by the clergy, that is to say, by the class believed at court to be the principal and most firm support of the government of the mother country; second, if the matter were followed through, it would be found that all, or almost all, the populace were accomplices; third, the hatred of the mother country's domination is deeply rooted in all classes of society, especially among the Spaniards who come to establish themselves in Mexico City (criollos), and was one of the principal means used to excite the populace to action.[44]

Although the principal class division in colonial society was that separating a small bureaucratic-religious, mining, landed, and urban commercial set of elites from an immense peasantry and working class that produced the marketable wealth, the elites were not always united. They often found themselves in competition for

scarce labor, quarreling over the spoils of colonial power, dis-
agreeing about Crown policies, and feuding over the question of
status and power associated with "pure" Spanish blood (*peninsulares,* or *gachupines,* versus criollos). Within the clergy, the friars
tended to ally with the Crown, its bureaucracy, and the Indian
caciques, while the secular bishops and priests (who increasingly
were criollo) lined up with the colonist landholders, miners, and
merchants (also increasingly criollo). Consequently, when Viceroy
Gelves arrived in New Spain in 1621 to crack down on smuggling
and the general unruliness of the colonists, he also sought to discipline the secular priests, who responded by closing the churches. A
minor incident touched off the 1624 *tumulto,* joined in by almost all
groups. As wealthy whites locked their gates or boarded up their
windows, the *castas,* blacks, Indians, and poor whites left their
squalid quarters, took to the streets, and rioted in a crowd 30,000-
strong. Open warfare ensued. Angry mobs ransacked the palace,
hauled down royal banners, and forced the viceroy to flee for his
life. Only after militia opened fire on the crowd did the *tumulto*
subside.

The political struggle, however, dragged on, as secular clergy in
the churches (the only arena of relatively free speech) became the
chief spokesmen against the colonial bureaucracy and Crown authority. Some Inquisition officials and *peninsular* bishops went
along with the secular clergy. In 1642 Viceroy Juan de Palafox y
Mendoza conceded to the criollos some posts in the militia and
bureaucracy and granted *hacendados* some of their claims to Indian
labor and positions in the new trade fleet; over the next few years
he attempted to reduce the wealth and power of the Jesuit order.
But these concessions to the criollos were offset by the Crown's
increased taxes to finance the fleet and a general crackdown on
those economic activities of the colonists that posed a threat to the
royal monopolies, as well as by its appointing a majority of high
Church officials from among the Spanish-born. Tensions between
the viceroys and secular clergy simmered off and on right up to the
Wars of Independence.

In 1692 food shortages and skyrocketing food prices provoked
another *tumulto* in Mexico City. Indians, blacks, *castas,* and poor
whites went on a rampage of violence and looting, burning down
the viceregal palace, city hall, and offices of the Audiencia (royal
court), and ransacking 280 shops and stalls. As in 1624, there were
cries of "Death to the *gachupines!*" Church property went untouched. Order was restored when the viceroy's soldiers opened
fire on the people.[45]

Food riots, caused by poor harvests and price speculation, sometimes leading to full-scale *tumultos,* became a leading form of revolt

in the eighteenth century, much of which was marked by crop failures and poor economic conditions for the masses. Population recovery and periodic economic downturns led to a labor surplus, to Indian migrations in quest of employment, and to a significant amount of vagabondage and banditry. The "Bourbon reforms" in administrative institutions and economic policies in the 1760s and afterward (analyzed in Chapter 2)—particularly in their development of an army and a militia—weighed heavily on the lower classes, who suffered the forced troop levies.[46] This grievance, added to their other sufferings, triggered a series of revolts in major population centers like Puebla, San Luis Potosí, Guanajuato, Morelia, and Pátzcuaro.

The Crown's expulsion of over 400 Jesuits in 1766–1767, in an attempt to free the monarchy from excessive clerical influence by choosing the most vulnerable group to attack, served to enrich the elites, who grew fat off Jesuit lands and properties. But it also provided a further reason for political protest against the arbitrariness of Spanish colonialism. Many towns were seized by rioting workers, peasants, and unemployed, who stormed the jails, insulted public officials, and threatened local authorities.

The *visitador* José de Gálvez, often described by historians as a mild ruler, finally crushed this tide of rebellion by hanging 85 persons, lashing 73 into bloody ribbons, jailing 674 others, and banishing 117 in 1767. All the victims of this stern "justice" were Indians and *castas*. Unrest seethed in subsequent decades. The army, originally created to defend those of Spain's colonies under threat from rival European powers, rapidly developed into a police force for Mexico's masses, especially the Indians. In 1786 Mexico City's lower classes sacked and burned the granaries of some *hacendados,* and the following year *tumultos* erupted in Acayucan and Papantla near the Gulf Coast—both towns passed into Indian hands until troops could be dispatched from Veracruz. In 1808 Veracruz itself experienced a *tumulto.* All the *tumultos* were but forerunners of what was to come in 1810, when peasants and workers would take matters into their own hands, raid the granaries and arms depots, and commence the Wars of Independence—the inevitable result of the historical development of class hatred so acutely perceived by *visitador* de Carrillo y Alderete almost 200 years earlier.

Mining, Commerce, and Manufacturing

The discovery of fabulous new silver mines in 1546 and the introduction of the patio process in 1557 (by means of which silver is extracted from ore through its amalgamation with mercury, permitting profitable exploitation of low-grade ores) led to a rapid expansion of economic activity to the north of the Valley of Mexico in such mining centers as Guanajuato, San Luis Potosí, Pachuca, and, above all, Zacatecas. By 1609 some 65 percent of New Spain's exports were silver, and this expansion had generated vastly augmented internal and external trade, related productive activities, and the conquest and development of Santa Fe (in today's New Mexico) and Nuevo León (today's Monterrey).

Yet, while great fortunes were made in mining, it was a risky business, as the decline in the mid-seventeenth century showed. It depended heavily on the scarce resource of labor, much of which died in the mineshafts or revolted against working conditions; on credit; on mercury supplies; on royal bureaucratic decrees; and on machinery, transport, and marketing channels. There were small mining ventures as well as large ones, and competition was intense. Moreover, financial control over mining profits was in significant part exerted by intermediaries: miners had to accept the prices offered by the *aviadores*, the agents of the big silver dealers in Mexico City. The silver dealers in turn made their fortunes by selling for the internal and external markets.

In 1634 Spain decided to ship its mercury to Peru instead of New Spain and to collect the debt owed on the mercury and salt sent to New Spain. The development of New Spain's home market in food production, textiles, leather goods, and so on was one reason for this change; another was the Crown's momentarily reduced need for bullion remissions since it wished to let the silver remain in the New World to finance its defense systems in the Caribbean and the Philippines. The subsequent deline in mining production was not as serious as often supposed, since Mexico City's criollo merchants infused new credits into the mining sector, new discoveries were made, and local smelting of silver increased. Then, with the renewed availability of mercury from Spain in the late 1660s and the aid of local capital, mining recovered, exceeding in the 1675–1690 period Zacatecas's peak production of the 1620s.[47]

After 1700, the total annual value of minted silver and gold (mostly silver) rose gradually—from 3 million pesos to 13 million in 1775. From 1770 to 1820, the mining industry was organized as a guild, the Cuerpo de Minería, which was headed by a Tribunal General and led mainly by criollos. The tribunal stimulated a late eighteenth-century boom by cutting mercury prices, creating credit "banks" involving local capital, permitting foreigners to invest in mining, and encouraging engineering innovations to combat problems of underground flooding and to raise labor productivity.

Mine workers continued to strike and rebel, however, and new silver discoveries accomplished more than all the tribunal's reforms combined. The minted value of silver and gold jumped to over 27 million pesos a year by 1805, when more than 3,000 mines were employing an estimated 35,000 laborers. An additional large number of workers, refiners, artisans, carriers, street peddlers, shopkeepers, speculators, prostitutes, and so on, gravitated around the mines, a few making their fortunes, most not. In brief, throughout the colonial period mining was a center of economic life and the "motor" of internal economic growth.

Yet the fact that legal regulations and mercantile-capitalist monopolies were, for the most part, based in Spain made it difficult for Mexicans to retain control of the whole process: no Mexican miner, for example, was able to finance the importation of special pumping machines from Europe, even when in 1803 the Crown issued a decree permitting such importation. Digging deeper shafts in the frantic scramble for wealth had led to flooding the mines, and little was being done to remedy the situation. Spain did not respond to British attempts to sell it machinery for building drainage canals and similar tools for "mine modernization." The technical problems, combined with growing labor unrest, led to a severe slump at the end of the colonial period (mintage value dropping to under 4 million pesos in 1810).[48]

New Spain's rich merchants not only financed the mines but also exerted influence in agriculture, manufacturing, and a medley of speculative activities. And, as was typical during the mercantilist-capitalist era, they accumulated great wealth in high finance and trade. Seventeenth-century merchants in Mexico City, though mostly of European origin, included a number of criollos who augmented their capital by cultivating good relations with high state and Church officials and entering into creditor and partnership arrangements with lower-level bureaucrats (whose taking of bribes, loans, or promised shares of profits made them in effect the merchants' "employees"). Corruption was so widespread that every criollo entrepreneur was likely to have a contact in the state bureaucracy. The merchants colluded with the bureaucrats to outwit the Crown on taxes, trade and manufacturing prohibitions, and so on. This colonial tradition is the source of modern Mexico's famous "*mordida*" (literally, "little bite," a bribe accepted in everyday activities). Alliances, partnerships, and intermarriage cemented the common economic and social interests of wealthy criollos and *peninsulares* involved in commerce, mining, agriculture, or manufacturing.[49]

Merchant capital in New Spain, as in Europe, was a key agent in the development of capitalist institutions: if mining was the economic motor, merchant capital was the grease. By 1604 it had helped establish some 25 textile mills *(obrajes)* in Mexico City alone, plus many others in Cuernavaca, Puebla, Texcoco, Tlaxcala, and Querétero. One of the largest employed 120 workers, while others employed from 50 to 100—sizable figures for any manufacturing enterprise at the time. Producing mainly cotton and wool textiles (silk manufacture prospered for a century but gave way to competition from the Orient), the *obrajes* concentrated laborers in sweatshop conditions. Some *obrajes* used the "putting out" system, permitting nearby Indian villagers to do the initial spinning. *Trapiches* (one or two loom producers) were common and, though partly competitive with *obrajes,* were generally subordinated to them in the network of marketing, credits, and supplies. Some weavers and spinners were able to continue to work at home, but the tendency in most places was toward the concentration of production under one roof (manufacture) and toward centralized control by *obraje* owners or the merchant bourgeoisie, often one and the same. The technology of spinning wheel, reel, horizontal loom, and water-driven machinery, however, often remained primitive. The typical owner of an *obraje* was a Spanish settler (or his descendants) who had other economic interests, usually as a merchant *(mercader)* but increasingly in diversified areas. *Obraje* ownership was a means of upward mobility, opening doors to the principal elite groups of New Spain—and a few of the tens of thousands of new Spanish settlers who poured into Mexico in the sixteenth century actually did quite well in select parts of manufacturing industry, as well as in the less-developed cottage industries relating to leather goods, spurs, pottery, and textiles. The Spanish guild system was introduced early (iron guild, 1524; hatmakers, 1561; silk production, 1584; wool products, 1592; gold-thread sewing, 1599; etc.), and many immigrants worked as artisans, while others engaged in petty commerce as shopkeepers, served as overseers of laborers, or joined the ranks of the commoners.[50]

The merchants, though never gaining complete control over the textile productive process, dominated it from start to finish. In cotton textiles, for instance, they provided the raw materials (cotton from the lowlands, sometimes from merchant-owned farms), transportation, credit, productive instruments, and final distribution networks and sales outlets. Merchant *obraje* owners increasingly hired artisans on a wage basis. In woolen textiles, Spanish and criollo merchants dominated the productive and distribution process to an even greater extent, at first enslaving Indians and eventually relying on a form of wage labor that sometimes bound the workers through a system of debts. Thus artisans and others underwent a process of gradual, though incomplete, proletarianization, losing control of much of both their means of production and the sale of their final products. The colonial legal system caught up with these realities in 1790 and 1810, when the regulations assuring guild input into textile production were largely lifted in order to extend to the merchant bourgeoisie further control over textiles. Indians and impoverished urban female weavers were no longer required to have guild approval; in addition, any reference to production techniques was eliminated.

Nationally, the *obrajes* came to employ thousands, forming in some instances the economic hub of major population centers—for example, Puebla, with its 20,000 cotton-textile workers and population of 70,000 in 1810. Moreover, regions dominated by such manufacturing centers thrived on commerce—in Puebla's case, thirty *obrajes* at the start of the seventeenth century stimulating a lively trade linking the city to Veracruz, Havana, Caracas, and Lima, as well as to its own regional market in agriculture and manufactured and artisan-produced goods. This partial but vigorous growth in the home market is the reason recent scholarship has viewed the seventeenth century not as one of depression but as one of transition toward capitalism, economic diversification, and the development of strong regional economies.[51] Nevertheless, with the ups and downs of the market and of the supply of capital (credits from merchants or the Church, provision of raw materials, etc.), there was frequent turnover in *obraje* ownership, which discouraged the development of a cohesive manufacturing class; and periodic economic hard times led to massive layoffs of workers and a recurring problem of urban unemployment that grew worse during the last fifty years of the colonial period.

Moreover, generations of colonialism generated what sociologist Peter Singelmann has called a "disarticulation" of markets for the production and circulation of commodities.[52] One market, usually the more profitable one, was international, involving the trade of primary commodities for European luxury and capital goods imported by the upper classes. The other market was national or regional, including the distribution of food, clothing, and some instruments of production among the general population for its reproduction. Although both counted heavily on cheap labor, the export sector and the home market were not well synchronized, and the realization of surpluses in the former remained independent of the size of the latter. The elites continuously reinforced the ties to Europe by sending their money back to Spain, or reinvesting it in producing more for export, or importing capital goods for the same end, or purchasing imported items for their own consumption.

Wages in most sectors of the economy remained fairly stable from 1650 to the end of colonial times, and the level of exploitation of those incorporated into the work force did not noticeably change.[53] Whether in state monopolies like tobacco production or in the private sector, workers continued to labor from twelve to fifteen hours a day at miserable wages. On such a basis, for example, the Royal Tobacco Factory of Querétero employed 3,000 workers, 60 percent of them women, and made a regular profit of well over 100 percent a year. There was thus little incentive for either the state or New Spain's elites to increase production through mechanization—at least at the pace European manufacturers were setting. The corresponding greater productivity of European capital furthered a process of unequal exchange between New Spain and Europe. As economic historian Jeffrey Bortz has pointed out:

> European exports derived from a special productivity greater than that of the colonies, allowing the sending [to the colonies] of manufactured goods and the tools of production. Mexican exports derived from the fruits of nature and the low costs of labor power, allowing the sending abroad of goods complementary to European accumulation [and making Mexico dependent] in the sense that its economic reproduction was based upon the development of productivity in the metropolitan countries.[54]

Thus, the colonial period dialectically established in Mexico the conditions for an embryonic dependent capitalism and the impoverishment and blocked opportunities that were to generate the repeated mass uprisings that ultimately broke Mexico's ties to the "mother" country and went on to challenge the power of its traditional elites and emergent bourgeoisie.

2

Independence and Civil War, 1770–1880

We say one thing only to you and the venerable saintly priests. Why didn't you remember or take notice when the Governor began killing us?

—Reply of Indian captains
to the Bishop of Yucatán, 1848

Laboring citizens are condemned to be mere passive instruments of production for the exclusive profit of the capitalist.

—Ponciano Arriaga to the 1856–1857
constitutional convention

The late-colonial period witnessed a heightening of intercolonial rivalries, a transition from earlier mercantile forms of accumulation to emergent capitalist ones asserting ascendance, and a corresponding intensification of class struggle affecting all social classes. These developments led to Mexico's aborted social revolution and yet to its winning national independence in 1821. Because the class conflicts behind the independence movement continued to shape the embryonic national state and patterns of capital accumulation for decades to come, the 1770–1880 period can be viewed as a continuous economic process having two disruptive political moments: 1810–1821, known as the Independence Wars, and 1854–1867, starting as a liberal-conservative civil war and ending with a war of national liberation against French military occupation. The economy underwent a gradual dissolution of the mercantilist-capitalist mode of accumulation and its replacement by more capitalist ones. The first political moment established national sovereignty, while the second created a stable nation-state for the purpose of capitalist economic development.[1]

European Competition, Bourbon Reforms, and Class Struggle at Independence

In the late eighteenth century, Spain's European competitors flooded colonial markets and threatened the prosperity of the mo-

45

nopolistic Cádiz/America trade network. In 1762 the British seized
Havana and Manila and threatened to occupy Veracruz. In eleven
months of British occupation, Havana received fifty times the number of merchant vessels it was accustomed to handling, most of the
ships containing English manufactured goods or slaves. English,
French, Dutch, and (after 1776) U.S. contrabanders increasingly
penetrated Spain's colonial trade network and raked off growing
portions of New Spain's economic surplus.

In an effort to cope with these economic realities, Spain implemented a series of policy changes known as "the Bourbon reforms," after the Bourbon dynasty, which had replaced the
Hapsburgs in 1701. Most of the reforms occurred during the reign
of Charles III (1759–1788). Foremost among his reforms was the
series of Free-Trade Acts that, starting in 1765, gradually
liberalized trade over the next few decades. The acts reduced and
equalized duties for Veracruz, Buenos Aires, and other major
ports. The aim was to reduce contraband by opening limited channels through which foreign traders could legitimately operate and
by means of which Mexican traders could, for the first time, trade
with other parts of Latin America and—in the case of grains—with
the Spanish islands of the Caribbean. Since the intent was to augment the export of Spanish manufactures to the colonies, the acts
permitted no re-export of European imports. Nonetheless, the
steady expansion of the Free-Trade Acts in the last third of the
century helped create a golden age for European commerce.

In 1795, the Crown issued decrees creating new Consulados in
Veracruz and Guadalajara. By then, Crown revenues had become
dependent on the activities of Spanish and criollo merchants
operating in Mexico. The new Consulados represented one more
instance of legal and administrative changes catching up with material reality. In effect, they recognized the end of the monopoly of
the Mexico City Consulado. Veracruz merchants took over control
of the Oaxaca cochineal and other regional trade networks from
those of Mexico City. Native-born merchants gaining their wealth
from the growth in Mexico's home market found their ambitions
and expectations furthered. Almost all the Bourbon economic reforms had these effects.

Stimulated by the Free-Trade Acts and northern Europe's transition from mercantile capitalism to early industrial capitalism,
Mexico's economic activity expanded rapidly. By the late 1700s
manufacturing production was valued at 72 million pesos a year,
with 25 percent being the preparation of foodstuffs for shipment,
15 percent textiles, and 20 percent candles and soap. From 1779 to
1803, mining production almost doubled. Agricultural production

also rose sharply. The role of small and medium-size merchants and middle-level transport workers increased, although their distribution system remained cumbersome, utilizing as it did Indian carriers *(tamemes),* other "beasts of burden" (mules, etc.), and difficult mountain trails and roads. Adding the better paid mineworkers, successful artisans, small-scale miners, and comfortable *ladinos* to these elements, a start toward formation of a less-white middle social grouping with rising expectations was underway by 1800.

For their part, New Spain's elites increased investments in productive enterprises for both the internal and external markets. That profit ultimately ruled over prestige as a motivating factor among Mexico's elites was symbolized toward the end of the colonial period when the nobility (criollos were permitted to become nobles) readily agreed to give up the institution of entail. Prohibited by Spain earlier, entail had become so encumbered by liens as to be no longer economical.

The value of Mexican exports jumped over 50 percent in the 1780s as compared with the 1770s—in spite of a severe drought, an epidemic, and a consequent reduction in production from 1784 to 1787. An approximate doubling of grain, food, and livestock prices between 1779 and 1803 benefited hacienda agriculture, which vastly increased production. A rise in *diezmos* (one-tenth of produce delivered to the Church by peasants, artisans, and other small producers) similar to that in food prices drove most rural Mexicans to the edges of survival and furthered land concentration in the hands of a few. By 1800, the number of haciendas (large and medium-size) in the Valley of Mexico was 150. Some 50 of these, located in the valley's Chalco region, provided all the maize consumed in Mexico City, whose population had grown to 137,000. Less than half was sold through the state warehouse *(alhóndiga);* most was sold by speculators, hoarders, and landowners— particularly when the price was driven up by shortages and the growing demands of thousands of desperately hungry people. Maize prices more than doubled between 1778 and 1814.

Table 2 reveals the vitality of agricultural and industrial production—largely for New Spain's home market—during the last two decades of the colonial era.

Such growth in economic production, together with the Cádiz monopoly's preference for sustaining its old ties with European manufacturers, contributed to the Bourbon administration's recognition that more efficient management techniques and economic reforms in the colonies might sustain the empire better than the most dedicated efforts at fulfilling unrealistic dreams of a sudden

Table 2
Estimates of Mexico's Economic Product
ca. 1791–1809
(expressed as annual market in pesos)

Percent	Sector	Domestic market	Export market	Total
62	Agriculture	133,782,625	4,844,685	138,627,310
25	Industry	54,744,047	257,264	55,001,311
13	Mining	924,259	27,026,741	27,951,000
100		189,450,931	32,128,690	221,579,621
		86%	14%	100%

Source: These estimates are based on the consumer market estimates made by José María Quirós, *Memoria de estatuto* (Veracruz, 1817), as elaborated by Doris M. Ladd, *The Mexican Nobility at Independence, 1780–1826* (Austin: University of Texas Press, 1976), p. 26, and David A. Brading, *Miners and Merchants in Bourbon Mexico, 1763–1810* (Cambridge: Cambridge University Press, 1971), p. 18. They are ostensibly, but not always actually, speculations as to average annual consumption. In a long note Ladd explains the details of these compilations, drawing critical support from the calculations of economist Fernando Rosenzweig Hernández, "La economía novohispana al comenzar el siglo XIX," *Ciencias Políticas y Sociales* 9, no. 33 (July–September 1963): 455–94.

capitalist transformation of Spain capable of making Spanish merchants or manufacturers competitive with those of northern Europe. While maintaining or increasing the centralization of political power through the *intendencia* system, modeled after the French mode of administration, the Bourbon reforms included economic and occasional political concessions to Mexico's criollo elite. To finance its wars with France and England, Spain sought to increase revenues from the colonies from public funds remitted to Spain and from taxes on American trade. The Crown's income from Mexico's economic activities quadrupled from 1763 to 1792.[2]

Nevertheless, recurrent outbreaks of drought or frost, normally followed by bad harvests and epidemics, plagued Mexico. Economic historian Enrique Florescano has summarized the consequences of this: dying off of livestock; layoff of hacienda workers; ruin of small and medium farmers; ravenous hunger; strikes in mines and *obrajes;* decline in commerce; massive emigration of hundreds of unemployed toward zones less hit by scarcity and hunger; stagnation in rural salaries and those of urban day-workers; progressive rise in prices; more and more landless peasants and discontent in the countryside; and rising social tension in the cities.[3] The economic elites shrewdly utilized the periodic bad harvests to increase their own wealth and power through price speculation and land monopolization. Everywhere there began to appear tiny cultivated parcels, as people sought to cope with food shortages and inflation. Famine, epidemic, death, migration, and family disintegration accompanied the concentration of land and wealth, particularly after 1795.

Florescano attributes the sharp rise in population in the last third of the century in part to the earlier good harvests of the mid-1750s and of 1762–1770. But it seems just as likely that peasants and workers, suffering the extreme hardships of hunger, land reduction, and unemployment, resorted to having more children for the purposes of subsistence production and economic survival. Moreover, the demographic increase in labor power was more cause than effect of the bumper harvests and economic expansion of the late eighteenth century.

Those institutions that might have regulated the shady dealings of the *hacendados* and market speculators, the *pósito* and the *alhóndiga* (the state markets and warehouses founded in the 1580s and overseen by municipal authorities), declined in their influence after 1793. Some became irrelevant, as the free marketplace took over—often in stalls established in their very shadows. Others had already become economic pawns of *hacendados* or merchants.

Frightened by the French Revolution, the Crown severed its ties with republican France in 1793 and temporarily joined forces with England against the French revolutionary upsurge. England's aim, however, was to weaken Spain and gain control of the lucrative colonial trade with the American colonies. This led to a renewal of war between England and Spain in 1796. Needing its fleet for the war, Spain authorized the right of criollos to ship their goods in their own vessels to Spain and back. In practice, neutral nations were also allowed to engage in this shipping, so that by the first half of 1799, of thirty foreign ships landing at Veracruz, twenty-five were of U.S. registry. Thirteen years earlier, Thomas Jefferson had expressed the expansionist goals of the emergent republic to the north: "Our confederacy must be viewed as the nest, from which all America, North and South, is to be peopled."[4] U.S. merchants appointed agents at Veracruz, and leading Mexican trading houses did likewise in U.S. cities. Foreign agents also engaged in military adventures and conspiracies to try to "free" Mexico from Spanish domination (e.g., Wilkinson's "Mexican Association," 1805, with U.S. government support; the British agent Williams, sent in 1808; the increase in Bonapartist agents, 1809; U.S. armed expeditions into Texas, etc.).

Spain's turn-of-the-century wars curtailed its trade and contributed to a decline in royal incomes. From 1793 to 1807, remissions from the Indies' trade dropped from 20 percent of royal income to 9 percent. Efforts to keep the commerce alive by allowing neutral trade (1797–1799), assigning warships to carry merchandise and silver, and permitting the colonies to trade with nonbelligerents all failed.

European and U.S. suppliers, traders, and contrabanders—especially the British—easily broke through the old Spanish merchant monopoly. Mexican-based merchant guilds, which had controlled Havana, La Guaira, Maracaibo, and Campeche (important intercolonial ports of trade), also lost their dominance to European traders, as many European commodities circumvented Veracruz. On the other hand, some Veracruz merchants became commercial agents for the foreign traders. The final result was to place more imperial and intercolonial trade in the hands of multinational commercial interests, which accounted for almost half of Mexico's imports by the end of the colonial period. Spain's efforts at political and economic renewal, thus undermined, were brought to a humiliating end in 1808 by the military invasion and takeover of Spain by French forces advocating bourgeois-republican ideals.

During the first decade of the nineteenth century, some criollo merchants greedily eyed the expanding marketplace offered by Britain and looked with favor on selling their goods to the British. Parts of the Caribbean were already effectively under economic domination by the British. By 1810, British traders were solidifying commercial relations with all of "Spanish" America, while criollo advocates of independence like Francisco de Miranda and Simón Bolívar were counting on British and U.S. funds and guns. The "liberal" tie that began uniting British and criollo-elite commercial and political interests was not the liberalism of Jacobin ideologues and dark-skinned slave or proletarian insurgents (who smashed the British and French armies in Santo Domingo and Haiti), but economic liberalism—the liberalism of free trade—the key doctrine in the transition from mercantilism to capitalism worldwide.

On December 26, 1804, in a desperate move to make up for the decline in royal revenues and in response to the renewed outbreak of war with England, the Crown issued for New Spain the "Act of Consolidation of Royal Revenues." This act decreed the redemption of mortgages belonging to chantries and pious foundations. These mortgages had been willed to the Church's convents and the diocesan Juzgados de Capellanías y Obras Pías by New Spain's wealthy elites. The Act of Consolidation was implemented on September 6, 1805. In the next three years, some 12 million pesos, or one-quarter of the total debt to chantries and pious works, was collected by the Crown. This served to estrange segments of Mexico's merchant, mining, manufacturing, and landowning elite—although the very rich withstood the crisis and some merchants and moneylenders gained an advantage through the relative weakening of the Church credit system. But small and medium-size producers in all sectors were severely affected by the credit pinch and the higher commercial interest rates. The upper clergy, which lived off tithes, was unaffected, but the lower clergy, which depended heavily on the chantries, was affected. Even a relatively well-off parish priest like Miguel Hidalgo y Costilla (reputed "father" of Mexican Independence), criollo son of a hacienda manager, had one of his three farms embargoed when he could not redeem his debt.

The Spanish and criollo nobility depended heavily on the credit system to finance their economic affairs and the frills of "noble life," to pay royal taxes, to gain royal permissions for entails, and to maintain the primogeniture system allowing them to pass their wealth on to the oldest son in perpetuity. There soon occurred audible murmurs about "bad government," around which Mexicans of any class or race could rally. As one well-off landholder said, "This continuous extraction is why our colonies have been maintained in a state of infancy; agriculture kept behind. . . . Well, if in such a state we are to suffer the extraction of the pious funds, who will be able to doubt our total ruin?"[5]

Within Mexico's nascent commercial and productive bourgeoisie an ascendant group of criollo (and mestizo, considered "criollo") landowners, manufacturers, miners, and merchants who considered themselves "Spanish" in prestige but "criollo" in deprivation were growing anxious to solidify and extend their newly gained wealth—and, if the opportunity presented itself, to seize corresponding political power. Large and middle-size landlords, especially those expanding their wealth rapidly, were particularly aggressive in asserting their class interests. The main tension among elites was between the mainly Spanish bureaucratic-commercial colonial oligarchy (including high clergy and military), many of whom were connected to the Mexico City Consulado, and the emergent Mexican bourgeoisie, including the merchants of the Veracruz and Guadalajara Consulados, who advocated free trade.

The nascent Mexican bourgeoisie's capitalist ethos of profit maximization, however, was tempered by its historical formation in the context of Spanish traditionalism. All of New Spain's elites—including, technically, the Indian nobles—called themselves Spaniards and pretended to the values of European nobility. Titles were easily purchased. Both the clergy and the military enjoyed special privileges, known as *fueros*, including juridical immunity. Colonial bureaucrats also enjoyed special prestige—a lawyer in the bureaucracy often had as many rights as a wealthy merchant. The elites championed the values of progress and piety, innovative entrepreneurship and traditional prestige, class unity and kinship loyalty. Their favorite reading ranged from works on the newest technological innovations to religious stories of miracles. As Ladd has observed, "Great wealth was so organized as to maximize family relations and minimize Creole and Peninsular distinctions. It was focused on Mexican resources, and it was produced by Mexican labor, Mexican technology, and Mexican capital . . . wealthy entrepreneurs were capitalist in the Hispanic tradition."[6]

However draped in the rhetoric of the Enlightenment or the French and American revolutions, the most progressive demands of the Mexican elites were limited to modest reformism. The native-born wealthy resented the monopoly of political power held by the Spaniards, the *gachupines*. They advocated elimination of colonial restrictions on trade and sought ways to get around the plethora of regional marketing taxes *(acabalas)* and royal and Church taxes that were slowing their economic advance. They objected to having to pay for Spain's defenses in its endless wars with rival European powers. As Fray Servando Teresa de Mier complained: "Since Spain is unable to protect her commerce and unwilling to allow others to export our products and us to import theirs, and has deprived us of factories and industries, the European war is more cruel for us than for her, and is ultimately waged with our money."[7]

Future insurgent Carlos María de Bustamante opened the pages of his newspaper *Diario de México* in 1806 to structural criticisms of the system, addressing himself to the viceroy in a virulent attack against "a reduced number of cruel monopolists who in years of scarcity augment their fortune at the cost of the blood of the destitute."[8] Landowners had long objected to the protection the Crown had offered Indians and Indian lands, wanting instead to extend their haciendas. Many *hacendados* and expanding middle-size landlords began thinking of political autonomy for New Spain and an end to Church and royal taxes. Some clergy talked of reducing the large estates, and even an occasional viceroy denounced biglandlord greed. Michoacán's bishop bemoaned the "wretched, vile" conditions of the poor.

Yet, for all its fascination with the new bourgeois ideals emanating from abroad and its resentment of colonial despotism, Mexico's nascent bourgeoisie was still constrained by the contours of its colonial past. Rarely was it economically autonomous, and its political and cultural domination by an exterior state further limited its ability to think and act independently. It was far from "underdeveloped" in the skills or traits of early capitalist bourgeoisies— indeed, its greed and satisfaction in the exploitation of those beneath, judging from its own historical records (deeds, accounting books, proclamations, etc.), were equal to, if not in excess of, those of its European counterparts. It was, however, still relatively weak in the larger social context in which it operated and therefore incompletely developed as a class fully conscious of itself or capable of asserting control over its own destiny.

The confused character and relative debility of the early Mexican bourgeoisie, rooted in the colonial soil from which it had sprung, help explain its propensity to seek foreign allies among stronger bourgeoisies and its terror at being overthrown from below by a massive rebellion of those on whose exploitation it depended. The problem of protecting its class interests and assessing blame for the growing gap between rich and poor created conflict and tension within its own ranks. This helps explain why it welcomed expansion of the colonial army—developed in part to protect its own class interests—to some 40,000 by 1810. Half of the army was non-Spanish and some of its officers were criollo.[9]

And Mexico's elites needed the army. More and more peasants were being forced to surrender their lands to the expanding hacienda system; more and more unemployed or day laborers (*jornaleros*) were crowding into the already socially tense cities. In the early 1800s, the German scientist Alexander von Humboldt toured New Spain, in part to send reports back to British and other north-European industrialists and traders. He was struck by the depth of the colony's social problems and predicted an "explosion of social conflict."[10]

The poverty, desperation, and restlessness engulfing the general population were not undifferentiated. The separation of growing numbers of peasant producers from their means of production (land and other agricultural tools) and their increased incorporation into a "free" wage-labor force (even if later leading to debt-peonage) were stimulating processes of proletarianization and differentiation within the rural masses. Many became pauperized and survived by begging, engaging in day labor, farming on a tenant or sharecropping basis, or tilling subsistence parcels granted them by *hacendados*, whom they served as debt-peons. Those attaching themselves to the haciendas were sometimes better off than their job-seeking counterparts.

A few peasants managed to succeed as *rancheros*. Middle-size landlords, *arrendatarios capitalistas*, and *rancheros* found in the reduction of the peasantry an opportunity to enlarge their holdings and profits. Obtaining more field hands by advancing into the Indian *ejidos*, they also achieved, as Marx would observe in describing early capitalist transformation of rural areas in general, "more efficient cultivation [by making] use of the hired services of their poor neighbors."[11] In northern Mexico, the *vaquero* (cowboy) was becoming a colorful, independent-minded fixture—owner of his own horse and arms, free to transmit the patriarchal authority of the *hacendado* down to those "beneath" him or even to challenge the *hacendado* should occasion merit it.

A crisis in agricultural production from 1808 to 1810 crippled the economy and generated widespread unemployment. With the spread of epidemics and hunger, an immense floating population of restless, desperate workers stalked the land, the mines, the dismal *obrajes,* the teeming provincial centers of production and trade.

Adding to the social and political conditions in New Spain that led von Humboldt to foresee an "explosion of social conflict" were the intermediate classes—small in number but, like the masses, experiencing rapid social change and racial or social discrimination. Theoretical confusion abounds about the concept "intermediate classes." Some historians equate mestizos with "middle class," thereby mixing race and class. But class determined race much more than the other way around. Many people calling themselves Spanish were mestizo; many so-called mestizos and *castas* in general were working-class or peasant criollos or *ladino* Indians; and even many Indians, above all *caciques,* were considered mestizo. Other authors lump clergy, lawyers, and intellectuals together with small producers in the intermediate classes, thereby overlooking the fact that the petty bourgeoisie owns, or at least possesses, its own means of production and employs others. Intellectuals and professionals, with some exceptions of course, rarely own more than their labor power and personal possessions and are either self-employed or employed by others.

"Intermediate classes" is a more accurate concept than "middle class" because various groups compose the category and are intermediate not because of middle levels of income, property, or power but because they are situated in an intermediate position between major social classes that either own the means of production or apply their labor power to activate them. In other words, intermediate classes do not constitute a major pole of a bipolar class contradiction—such as landlord-serf, bougeoisie-proletariat, and so forth.

In late-colonial Mexico, the numerically insignificant intermediate classes included mainly owners of their own means of production, whether traditional peasant smallholders *(rancheros)* and artisans engaged in simple commodity production, or occasional incipient capitalists. Guild masters, scattered *rancheros,* owners of workshops *(talleres),* artisans employing others—these elements constituted the petty bourgeoisie. Their simple-commodity form of production was under great pressure at this point in time. Merchant capital had penetrated it on a significant scale, generating a growing separation of craft producers from their means of production. Merchant capital in this way was also weakening the control of guild organizations over guild members and over the employed labor force relating to artisan masters. It was well on its way to introducing early-capitalist manufactories, distribution of whose products it controlled through a system of regional, national, and international monopolies. While an occasional small producer was able to accumulate capital, expand sales or trade, and begin to organize production on a capitalistic basis, more often it was a section of the existing merchant class that began to take possession directly of production.[12]

Usually more powerful and influential than traditional petty commodity producers within Mexico's intermediate classes were petty-bourgeois elements active in agriculture and commerce. The rural petty bourgeoisie, whose most successful members rose into the ranks of the agrarian bourgeoisie, included prosperous *rancheros,* renters of small haciendas or Church estates, and some *mayordomos* who established cattle, sugarmill, or other enterprises of their own. The rural petty bourgeoisie employed others but generally had a difficult time competing within the agrarian bourgeoisie and merchant monopolies.

The commercial petty bourgeoisie included street peddlers, small and medium-size traders and merchants, smugglers, muleteers and middle-level transport operators, small shopkeepers, and so on. Some of its members—particularly successful smugglers and muleteers—accumulated tidy piles of capital, but most, like the majority of intermediate-class people at the time, lived hard-working, austere lives. Those able to sustain their capital accumulation were admitted into the ranks of the upper classes, and some even bought titles. Recent regional case studies by Mexican and foreign scholars have revealed a remarkable flexibility in access to upper-class status, something that probably provided a safety valve for putting off revolution in the colonial period for many years.

Various groups within the intermediate classes did not own any means of production or form part of the petty bourgeoisie, nor were they peasants, workers, landlords, or capitalists. They were professionals, *letrados* in the bureaucracy, intellectuals, priests, or military officers. During the eighteenth century, lawyers, journalists, teachers, parish priests, minor officials, and other professionals emerged as intermediate groups spawned by the flourishing universities and schools. The rapidly expanding economy at the end of the century increased some of their expectations, even as it did those of occasional better-paid mine workers or successful artisans, *rancheros*, or small-scale merchants and miners.

The race factor played a role in the intermediate classes' struggle for social definition. For most literate members of the *castas*, government patronage or enlistment in the army were the only means of achieving some degree of wealth. Many aspired not only to this but to the upper-class values associated with it and with white skin in colonial Mexico. Thus their "class" ideology was strongly marked by the values of the nascent bourgeoisie and the titular nobility. They looked down on manual labor—not from the heights of a class fully superior to it, but from the sides of the workbenches or cultivated furrows among which they might find themselves forced any day. Mexico's intermediate classes, then, lacked cohesiveness and a class ideology. Neither the petty bourgeoisie nor the intelligentsia and professional groups were socially or psychologically united around a common class or ideological program. Usually adhering to upper-class values, most of their members were blocked from even a middle level of income or prestige. Constantly being pressured down into the ranks of the working class, peasantry, or lowest echelons of the state, religious, or merchant establishments, the intermediate classes—especially the intelligentsia and professionals—were experiencing rising, yet blocked, economic and political expectations. And so, many of them became the voices of an anticolonial movement for independence. Readily would they cry out "Death to the *gachupines!*" Feeling themselves victimized by class and race, they easily gave expression to what in fact were mass demands for an end to slavery, tribute collection, and racism in all its forms—regardless of their own hypocrisy, given their tendency to exclude "Indians" from their circles. Economically pinched, the intermediate classes welcomed an end to royal and Church taxes, and agrarian reform could only benefit them.

Behind the embrace of bourgeois revolutionary ideas reaching Mexico from Europe and the United States were definite and clear economic interests with which the intermediate classes identified but of which they were as yet unable to partake. Insufficiently numerous or strong to assert power on their own, they shared one particular "class interest" with the nascent bourgeoisie, both emotionally and materially: fear of the toiling masses. While from their ranks might emerge an occasional revolutionary leader able to identify with the poor, for the most part they could assert leadership in an anticolonial struggle only by pooling their efforts with those bourgeois elements that shared their resentment of Spain.

Together, the intermediate classes and bourgeoisie might achieve what neither could accomplish alone.

Most Mexicans were peasants, field hands, miners, carriers, *obraje* employees, apprentices, workers of various kinds (including occasional slaves)—proletarians in the broad sense, yet not a modern industrial proletariat (even by nineteenth-century standards). Exploited for centuries by the forces of European mercantile capitalism and colonalism, these laboring masses had repeatedly fought, usually at the local or regional level, long and hard to overthrow the forces holding them down. The one common enemy that existed, making possible Mexican independence and some degree of cross-class and cross-race unity among Mexicans, was the colonial state itself and the *peninsulares* who constituted its voices of political command and loci of economic power. It was against this colonialism and these *gachupines* that many Mexicans, though by no means all, could agree, finally, to fight.

The driving force of New Spain's late-colonial economy was an embryonic capitalism, stimulated by merchant capital in control of most of the appropriated mineral wealth and much manufacturing production. But the forms this capitalism was taking in Mexico were varied and complex, reflecting the socioeconomic materials out of which it had grown—from Indian communal traditions to those of the Spanish nobility; from conquest, pillage, and "original accumulation" to the separation of laborers and artisans from the means of production and their development into free wage labor; from production for an external market and a growing home market to labor recruitment through starvation and the "tying" of labor through debt obligations. Yet assert themselves the forces of early capitalism did, both from within and from without—and it was these forces that ultimately lay behind the rapid social changes at the end of the colonial period and the birth of the Mexican nation.

Class Wars for Independence and Interelite Struggles for Hegemony

Mexico's Wars of Independence were profoundly anticolonial and interclass struggles that succeeded in establishing national sovereignty but failed to achieve a social revolution. No single class or class fraction was able to assert or maintain hegemony over the tide of mass rebellion that swept the land from 1810 to 1821. Politically, the foremost precondition for the movement of independence was the steady erosion of Spain's traditional system of control over the American colonies, which climaxed in 1808 when Napoleon's army occupied Spain and seized Charles IV. At that time, even New Spain's viceroy, José de Iturrigaray, sided with dissatisfied criollos against the old colonial system. This provoked a *gachupín* "loyalist" revolt against him led by sugar *hacendado* Gabriel Yermo. Meanwhile, secret societies like the Literary and Social Club of Querétaro and the Masons plotted to throw out the colonial bureaucrats.

Then, in 1810, the explosion occurred—not coincidentally, in that part of New Spain with the most capitalist-oriented economic activity and the most intense social differentiation: the north-central region known as the Bajío, rich in mining, manufacturing, and agriculture. A parish priest, Father Hidalgo, after receiving a message that the plot to revolt had been discovered by Spanish officials, called people to mass in Dolores, Guanajuato, where he issued his historic "Grito de Dolores" (Cry of Dolores) on September 16, 1810: "My children, will you make the effort to recover the lands stolen 300 years ago from your forefathers by the hated Spaniards? . . . Long live religion! Long live our most Holy Mother of Guadalupe! Long live America! Death to bad government! Death to the *gachupines!*"[13]

Thousands of desperately poor people took up Hidalgo's call. They grabbed machetes, clubs, and a few guns and stormed the *alhóndiga* granary in Guanajuato, a fortress filled with royal treasure guarding the entrance to the city. Members of the Spanish garrison were massacred, and then the inflamed masses murdered thousands of better-off civilians and plundered the commercial and mining hub of the Bajío. They moved on to storm, slay, and seize granaries, proprietors, officials, and lands representing the hated oppression of colonialism and class-race exploitation. Here, in the greater Bajío region, were bred the mixed traditions of armed class struggle and religious idolatry, symbolized by the Indians' carrying the banner of the Virgin of Guadalupe into the front lines of battle. For the Indians, the Virgin represented an avenging spiritual force to be marshaled against the pro-Crown banner of the Spanish Mary, Our Lady of Soledad.

Tens of thousands of peasants and workers massed behind Father Hidalgo, self-appointed "Captain-General of America." Together with the peasant army of Father José María Morelos to the south, they forced the wealthy criollos to ask Spain for help in putting down the uprisings.

It was this explosive class threat from below that ultimately, in 1821, persuaded the wealthy elites to opt for independence. As the criollo "Libertador" of South America, Simón Bolívar, put it in his

famous "Letter from Jamaica" of 1815, the criollos' grievance was
not so much Spain's intolerance of democracy as its refusal to permit criollos enough authority to preserve some "respect" among
the Indians and *castas* (and nonelite criollos, who outnumbered the
elite). These lower elements, Bolívar argued, threatened to disrupt
all America with revolution: "We have been deprived of an active
tyranny, since we have not been permitted to exercise its functions." In other words, ascendant economic groups had been kept
from the highest offices of government in Spanish America and
thereby deprived from exercising the class dictatorship so necessary to avoid the disruption and chaos of revolution from below.
On September 15, 1821, the Guatemalan Act of Independence
openly proclaimed independence "in order to prevent the consequences that would be fearful in the event that the people should
proclaim it."[14]

Thus threatened, most of Mexico's elites and some of the intermediate classes pragmatically hedged their bets by spreading their
financial backing and ideological support among all political
groups, from the most royalist through those seeking autonomy or
even independence. As the anti-Crown insurgent Carlos María de
Bustamante would later recall, "If we were to punish all those who
failed at their duties in this revolution, now making war on us
unashamedly, now doing a balancing act so as to land on their feet,
now staying home like hearth cats while their brothers knifed each
other in battle, it would be necessary to execute two-thirds of our
population." To which liberal ideologue José María Luis Mora,
who lost a brother in the insurgent cause, was to add:

> Many people would have powerfully supported the revolution with
> their influence and wealth were it not for the fact that they were
> profoundly afraid of losing everything in the general disorder; this is
> how . . . men who truly loved and were committed to their native land
> not only abandoned Hidalgo's cause but actually took arms against
> it.[15]

Hidalgo's ragtag but raging army swelled to 80,000 as it plundered city after city, finally arriving at the outskirts of Mexico City.
For reasons unknown, Hidalgo chose not to attack the metropolis
but instead led his troops westward and seized Guadalajara. Then,
in January 1811, royalist soldiers won a victory that demoralized
and scattered thousands of Hidalgo's troops. In July, Hidalgo himself was captured, tried by the Inquisition, defrocked, and executed.

The mestizo priest José María Morelos soon picked up where
Hidalgo left off, however, organizing a disciplined army of

thousands that closed in on Mexico City in the spring of 1813. Peasants and the impoverished rallied to Morelos's condemnation of "all the rich, criollos, and *gachupines,*" his advocacy of the distribution of idle hacienda lands for the benefit of small agriculturalists, and his plan to distribute half of all seized wealth to the poor. Profoundly antiracist, Morelos also forbade the use of racial terms like "mestizo" among his troops.

In 1813, Morelos called a meeting of all his forces at Chilpancingo in order to draft a revolutionary program and coordinate future actions. The congress resolved to end slavery and caste distinctions; initiate an income tax; abolish state monopolies, sales taxes, and tributes; and introduce higher wages for the poor—all of which would benefit the oppressed. These proposals constituted a frontal assault on the institutions blocking the advance of early capitalism and so were not welcomed by traditional criollo landowners or the top layers of the Church hierarchy—despite the fact that the congress guaranteed the virtues and rights of private property.

General Félix Calleja, a Spaniard, and his largely criollo army[16] attacked and eventually overwhelmed Morelos's guerrillas, and in 1815 Morelos too was defrocked and executed. Rebel actions continued for the next five years, but mainly along regional and guerrilla lines, with victories won in the mountains and forested regions south of Mexico City. One of the main leaders was Juan Alvarez, an Afro-Indian peasant.

In 1820, a military coup d'état in Spain overthrew Ferdinand VII and led to the reintroduction of the liberal Cadiz Constitution of 1812, whose provisions included laws protecting Indians and Indian lands and thereby threatened the criollos' shaky rural hegemony. The Spanish parliament (Cortes) also re-evoked the Acts of Consolidation, which again threatened the elites' source of internal credit, and vowed to limit the right of the Church to acquire property and to abolish ecclesiastical and military *fueros*—a direct challenge to the privileges of the military and clerics. Criollos now began to see loyalty to Spain as imprudent, and looked for a leader other than Calleja, one from among their own ranks.

They found their man in *hacendado* Augustín de Iturbide, son of a wealthy Spanish (Basque) merchant and a criolla mother, who earlier had fought on the side of Spain against Hidalgo, Morelos, and Alvarez, and who was strategically well placed to unite the elites and forge an alternative to the masses' war against them. This popular war represented a climax to the earlier series of revolts and *tumultos* by peasants and workers that had periodically interrupted the stability of colonial rule. Yet, as earlier, this war suffered from regional limitations and lack of a common program on class goals. Such limitations made it that much easier for Mexico's elites to control the anticolonial rebellion's ultimate outcome— although not the elites' contest for power among themselves. Iturbide succeeded in persuading the viceroy to name him commander of the Spanish army in the south. He then met with Vicente Guerrero, the south's Indian guerrilla leader, and convinced him to form an alliance to free Mexico from Spanish rule.

Pro-Iturbide officers agreed to give up the *fuero militar*, while those liberals joining Iturbide in turn forced him to agree to the abolition of slavery and the provision of full citizenship for blacks, orientals, and Europeans residing in Mexico. Iturbide also curried favor among royalists, gradually winning them over to his "Army of the Three Guarantees." These guarantees were: "Unity," among criollos and Spaniards; "Religion," to reassure the Church; and "Independence," meaning only autonomy from Spain. On September 27, 1821, Iturbide's army seized Mexico City, and he received communion at the Cathedral and installed a coalition parliament— in effect establishing home rule. The new nation's tricolor flag was unfurled: white for religion, green for independence, and red for the blood of union. A year later, in September 1822, Iturbide abolished racial definitions on citizenship documents and censuses—his only progressive sócial achievement.

In spite of Iturbide's having agreed to honor the Cádiz Constitution and the Cortes laws of 1820–1821, in February 1822 the Cortes rejected home rule for Mexico. This hardened the political position of the criollo elites and their new-found *gachupín* allies, who had already begun to experience some economic benefits from their having proclaimed home rule, particularly after the new government further opened Mexican ports to world trade. Duties were reduced from 16 to 6 percent, muleteers were allowed free trade overland to the northern frontiers, war taxes on pulque marketing and mining were reduced, and import duties were lifted on mercury and on machinery for use in mining, crafts, and farming. Mexican farm produce and manufactured goods could now be exported duty free. The tobacco and cotton-textile industries, which had entered a wartime boom in production for the sizable popular armies, received from the new home government protection via import restrictions.

Criollos in the merchant, mining, and agrarian sectors, in order to protect their commerce, had named their sons commanders of regional armies. While these military "protectors of commerce" occasionally became radical anticolonial caudillos, most formed themselves into regional networks of *caciques* and became influential in the series of coups and countercoups that were to follow independence.

Iturbide was unsympathetic to liberal republican ideas, however, and in May 1822 he proclaimed himself Emperor Augustín I of "independent" Mexico. Five months later he dissolved parliament. In the eyes of his republic-minded critics—many of them from the intermediate classes whom he had thrown in jail—the "emperor" had no clothes. Iturbide trusted no one, including his commander in the port of Veracruz, Antonio López de Santa Anna, a *hacendado* and former royalist officer whom Iturbide tried to recall to Mexico City. Sensing a rising republican tide of revolt against Iturbide, on December 1, 1822, Santa Anna seized control of Veracruz, proclaimed a republic, and called for the restoration of the 1821 parliament. Groups in other regions joined the revolt in the name of republican federalism and began to march on Mexico City. Rather than face a humiliating military defeat, in February 1823 Iturbide abdicated and went into exile. (He returned in July 1824, in an attempt to reassume political power, only to be captured and executed as a traitor.)

Thus Iturbide's experiment with autonomy from Spain under a constitutional monarch failed, in large part because of Spain's refusal to recognize home rule and Iturbide's own heavy-handed treatment of his opponents. It was the forces of republican liberalism (which Santa Anna opportunely claimed to represent) that consummated in 1823—through their overthrow of the "emperor"—the independence that Iturbide had earlier proclaimed.

From 1821 to 1857, the young nation experienced over fifty separate governments, ranging from monarchy or dictatorship to constitutional republicanism, as Mexico's elites scrambled for power while simultaneously seeking to hold back the demands of the masses. Powerful centrifugal forces, including intense differences of opinion on questions of religion and the form the new state should take, prevented the criollo bourgeoisie from settling their differences calmly. Interelite rivalries were heightened by the multiplication and fragmentation of markets, competing regional power blocs, and the economic leverage of foreign capitalists and states, whose financial support the elites welcomed but whose military intervention many feared.

Rancheros, blacksmiths, lawyers, artisan manufacturers, and other intermediate-class elements that had proven influential in the radical wing of the anticolonial insurgent forces now sought new opportunities for economic well-being, and the post-1821 expansion of international trade led to an intense upsurge in petty bourgeois commerce, production, and paperwork. Although some leaders of the anticolonial revolution from the intermediate classes achieved government positions after independence, this fact represented neither their assumption of economic (class) power nor that of political (state) hegemony. They were far too weak, fragmented, and confused to accomplish that.

There instead began an era in which local oligarchs and regional caudillos, many with their own armies, gained control over peasants, workers, and the unemployed. The control was institutionalized through a complex chain of command extending from caudillo to local *cacique,* priest, mayor, hacienda owner or *mayordomo,* factory or workshop owner or foreman, and block "captain." People were tied into the system through a dependence on personalized patronage, involving elaborate networks of payoffs and favors.

It is often assumed that the Wars of Independence shattered Mexico's economy, but there is considerable evidence that this was true only in selected areas, particularly Guanajuato and Michoacán. Most mines were unaffected by war damage, and the slowness of mining's recovery from the flooding problems of 1805–1821 had more to do with the loss of assured supplies of lower priced Spanish mercury than with actual war-caused destruction. Mining did not recover its 1805 level of production until 1850. Textile and tobacco production boomed from provisioning soldiers, and in the first decade after the independence war Mexican exports doubled. Wily officers carved out part of the cochineal trade for themselves or took to contraband, as a new class of speculators emerged—what one author has called the "merchant military" and another the "armies of commerce."[17]

Internal economic development was now by region, and was based on regional markets dominated by local oligarchs. There are many examples: silver exporter and cotton importer Isidro de la Torre in the northwest, and later his sons in the Morelos sugar industry; the Béistegui family in the Bajío; import-export merchants and early industrialists like Milmo in Monterrey; or the Martínez del Río brothers, big in textile manufacturing in Veracruz, Puebla, and Mexico City, as well as owners of one-tenth the land area of Chihuahua by 1860. Most successful merchants and capitalists had strong links to foreign capital, and at least one (Béistegui) had the majority of his investments in Europe. Many relied on land rent (rural and urban), state favors, commerce, moneylending, and speculative financial ventures for their initial accumulation of capital.

Despite regional growth and individual successes, the postindependence economic recovery of Mexico as a whole was slow and

uneven for many decades. There were a number of obstacles besides political instability. During the Wars of Independence more
than half a million people had been killed, mostly raw labor power
in whose absence capital accumulation had to proceed more slowly
than among the expanding U.S. and European populations. Additional deaths resulting from Mexico's internal and international
wars, high infant mortality, and shortened life spans caused by
malnutrition, disease, or overwork further limited the labor supply. The population grew slowly, from about 6 million in 1810 to
only 8.7 million in 1874. In addition, the rugged mountainous
geography and the primitive transportation system; the new nation's lack of economic surplus, earlier drained by the forces of
colonialism and subsequently held back by the withdrawal (or expulsion) of Spanish capital variously estimated at from 100 to 300
million pesos; the foreign debt; unequal exchange patterns in trade
with Europe and the United States; loss of over half the nation's
territory to the United States after 1848 (including the lucrative
gold veins of California); and inefficient economic organization—
exemplified by parts of hacienda agriculture or the Church's
diezmo, as well as by the maze of official permits and fiscal or customs regulations inherited from colonial times and maintained for
many decades—all held back progress.[18]

Here desperate people reverted to production of handicrafts or
subsistence farming, strengthening "domestic economies" of petty-
commodity production, while there a new textile factory, paper
mill, or export crop was introduced for production by wage or
piecework labor on a mass scale. Everywhere simmered revolt and
military conflict, while foreign powers hovered along the coasts
with gunships and troops, ever ready to recolonize a vulnerable
land rich in natural resources. From the viewpoint of the indus-
trializing and colonizing British bourgeoisie, for example, the
words spoken in 1824 by Foreign Minister George Canning promised an auspicious future: "The nail is driven, Spanish America is
free, and if we do not mismanage our affairs badly, she is English."[19]

British manufactured goods flooded the Mexican market. As
early as 1824 cotton textiles constituted 30 percent of imported
manufactures through Veracruz, thereby undermining Mexico's
textile industry, which accounted for about a quarter of Mexican
manufacturing enterprises. For the foreign bourgeoisies, particularly the British merchant houses, bankers, and industrialists, consolidation and extension of their power on a global basis depended
on preventing autonomous Latin American industrial development while opening up the world's markets through free

trade. Foreign capitalists thus sided with Mexico's *hacendados*, miners, and exporters against emergent Mexican industrial interests.

Yet in the first two postindependence decades Mexico did not fall under the control of another nation. Discouraged by the chaotic internal situation, foreign capitalists preferred to operate in the spheres of public debt, credits, and trade more than in new direct investments. Until 1850, only the Spaniards held large investments in Mexican manufacturing; French, German, British, and U.S. citizens held lesser amounts. The one area in which foreign capitalists maintained an active interest was mining. They continued to invest in rehabilitating the mines and received the greatest part of the profits from the increased production that followed. Mexico depended more than ever on silver and gold for its export earnings (86 percent in 1872), while hides, sisal, and ixtle (a cactus fiber used in making binding twine) led the way in agricultural exports, followed by coffee. By 1870, England and the United States accounted for about 70 percent of Mexico's trade. Until 1884, when dictator Porfirio Díaz renegotiated the foreign debt and invited foreign capital in, early industrialization attempts were largely a domestic matter. Nevertheless, even a nationally based industrial development was discouraged by free-trade practices (and the smuggling to evade state protectionist measures introduced in the 1820s) and by foreign bondholders' pressures on the government to repay them.

Given Mexico's foreign debts and budgetary and balance-of-payments deficits (which got worse the more "free" trade became), it was an easy matter for foreigners to continue the process of financing Mexican "economic development" begun much earlier; and there was very little protest against the continued transfer of economic surplus abroad. Foreign loans were followed by the collection of debts and the acquisition of property as payment, thereby augmenting the flow of capital out of Mexico. Mariano Otero was among a handful of Mexicans who bothered to complain, observing in 1842 that "trade is no more than the passive instrument of foreign industry and commerce . . . and today those cabinets, in everything submissive to the mercantile spirit, are profoundly interested in keeping us in a state of misery or backwardness from which foreign commerce draws all the advantages."[20] By 1867, the state's foreign debt had soared to 375 million pesos and its domestic debt to 79 million pesos—while public income had still not reached 20 million pesos. Currency devaluations and inflation, then as today, benefited merchants and large-scale property owners at the expense of those whose labor produced the wealth—

robbing artisans, workers, and peasants not only of their real income but also of much of their property.

Mexico was a nation founded on debt and desperately shy of liquid capital and credit. José María Quiros, writing in 1817, estimated that the previous seven years of warfare had cost the country 887 million pesos, 787 million of which were in circulating currency (much of it in capital's flight abroad to avoid the internal chaos). Successive governments exempted Spanish investors from expulsion orders if they made loans to the state. In this way, many Spaniards retained their status as leading members of the bourgeoisie. The newly independent government owed European citizens and governments—Great Britain in particular—over 76 million pesos, including monies advanced for the purchase of arms for the insurgents. Private British banking firms loaned an additional 16 million pesos in 1824. (Mexico defaulted on these in 1827, but granted the British a favorable trade treaty as part of the settlement.) British interests also invested 12 million pesos in mining, starting foreign capital on its way to eventual dominance in that sector of the economy.

Other than foreign loans, where could the new state get much-needed capital? The army, the Church, and the *hacendados* were one possibility. But if scarce capital were to be saved, it would mean cutting back the payroll of the 18,000 officers and 5,000 soldiers, who drained over half the federal budget, or confiscating Church property, or taxing the criollo bourgeoisie. They would hardly tolerate this, and the government would fall. So it turned to another source: the *agiotistas,* moneylenders who emerged as a powerful fraction of Mexico's commercial bourgeoisie.

Foreign capital was augmented by capital generated internally by the *agiotistas.* Far from acting like old-fashioned usurers, the *agiotistas* constituted a nascent banking community interested in gaining monopolistic control over diverse productive activities. Their influence over the state, desperate for funds, aided them in investing in manufacturing, commerce, mining, and agriculture. They bought up haciendas ruined by the 1808–1810 crisis or unable to meet debt payments, and organized them on a sound economic basis. They grew fat off Mexico's internal wars—each new triumphant general had first to settle up with the *agiotistas.* For the first decade after independence, *agiotista*-merchant-landlords were hegemonic within the bourgeoisie. Together with the Church credit system, *agiotista* capital tended to merge with landed capital in a stepped-up process of dispossessing the peasantry. The number of haciendas doubled between 1810 and 1854, with one-fifth belonging to the Church.

The brothers Manuel and Antonio Escandón were typical. The Escandóns made deals with British merchant houses and bankers, funded the nation's first railroads in the 1840s, backed General Santa Anna and the liberals in 1842 in spite of their conservative ideology, made millions from state public works and services, merged with other capitalists, like the Béistegui family in mining, and held lucrative portfolios in tobacco, salt, sugar machinery, textiles, haciendas, urban real estate, communications and transport, foreign trade, and public finance.

The profits the *agiotistas* made from lending to the government—the state paid them the cream off the customs duties collected at the ports—were plowed back into productive enterprises. The series of financial agreements made with the government by national and foreign entrepreneurs gave all capitalists not only government support but a steady stream of payments with which to increase their economic interests. Britain, France, and Spain settled both public and private debts by diplomatic convention—and no Mexican diplomat was free of the fear of foreign military intervention should the state not pay up or grant alternative economic concessions. As economic historian Barbara Tenenbaum has shown, the *agiotistas,* through their many deals with foreign capitalists, sometimes made use of the diplomatic conventions in order to improve their own chances at recovering their investments.[21] Other members of the commercial bourgeoisie, like the Martínez del Río brothers, also increased their capital in this way, transforming themselves later into an industrial bourgeoisie. In brief, the state's economic maneuvers typically contributed to an "original accumulation" of capital by both national and foreign capitalists.

For most of Mexico's richest families, independence meant the elimination of rival commercial intermediaries and Spanish monopolists and a strengthening of trade relations with Britain, in which Mexico produced and exported mineral and agricultural products in exchange for English manufactures. Interelite struggles for political power were more between families than between class fractions based on distinct capitals, since family monopolies usually extended into every major economic activity. In their rush to build up or consolidate monopolies in competition with one another, Mexico's wealthy families only occasionally advocated alternative emphases for national economic development. These emphases sometimes overlapped with political-ideological conflicts between the philosophies of "liberalism" and "conservatism" (which eventually became the banners of diverse contending class forces in the civil war of 1854–1867).

After independence, in the absence of political parties, the social network of freemasonry (a secret fraternal social organization influential in the European and U.S. bourgeois social ferment of the eighteenth and nineteenth centuries) became a convenient arena for political combat. Liberals, stronger in the provinces than in Mexico City and most involved in agriculture and mining, advocated a U.S.-style federation. Aided by the first U.S. ambassador to Mexico, Joel Robert Poinsett, a notorious meddler in Mexico's internal affairs who viewed Mexicans as "ignorant and debauched,"[22] the liberals organized freemason lodges of the York Rite. When they achieved state power, however momentarily, liberals attacked the Church, often for economic reasons. For instance, the Church-owned Juzgado was at the time Mexico's principal banking institution, and since it normally had its loans secured by real estate, the Church exercised considerable control over land. In addition, special privileges, or *fueros,* excused clergymen from normal civil procedures, which made it difficult for a liberal government to curtail Church power. To favor their own landed interests, the liberals repeatedly sought to eliminate the Church's tax on agricultural production. Tied to the export of minerals and agricultural products in exchange for imported manufactured and luxury goods, liberal oligarchs sought to maintain the free-trade-based export economy. Measures like tariffs to protect nascent industries held little attraction for them.

The conservatives, on the other hand, had close ties to the Church and advocated a strong central government. Many belonged to the Scottish Rite of freemasonry and had been sympathetic to Spain. They saw tariffs as a way to protect the local textile industry, fortify manufacturing, and move toward industrialization via control over the customs houses, which might prohibit free entry of European imports. Since there were frequent changes in government, each one in need of revenue, tariffs were used by the state to raise revenues although they also served from time to time to finance an industrialization program. Conservative leaders included large-scale landholders less interested in capitalist agriculture than the liberal *hacendados,* as well as some fabulously wealthy merchants and early industrialists. Like the liberals, the conservatives wished to reactivate the mines—but usually for the purpose of developing the home market. They sometimes found support among middle-level merchants in the interior who were integrated with the home market and wished to invest their surplus in manufacturing production, mining, or commercial agriculture.

In practice, liberal-conservative differences among the elites on issues of economic development were minor, so much did their economic interests overlap. Both liberals and conservatives among the bourgeoisie grew rich off the state, switched sides at moments of political change at the state level, and used the state to control or repress peasant revolts, strikes, or other forms of labor protest. In terms of industrial development, the liberal Estevan de Antuñano and the conservative Lucas Alamán each tried to launch a modern textile manufacturing industry. To help finance new industry, Alamán, a devout Catholic criollo from a mining and banking family with strong ties to British capital, founded the Banco de Avío in 1830, state-funded with a million pesos. But this development bank never really got off the ground.

Much of the liberal-conservative struggle for state power reflected competing interests within classes or groups other than the bourgeoisie. For example, some of the urban intermediate classes (professionals, bureaucrats, and liberal intellectuals) opposed the military and clergy. The military officer corps was split between liberals and conservatives, but united in its determination to maintain its *fueros*. The military retained the power of arms, as well as its new commercial interests. It, along with the *agiotistas*, was a potent arbiter in the nation's internal affairs. Landlords who survived the credit crunch often built alliances with the army and the Church in order to control peasant unrest and assure sources of credit. Much Mexican mining capital went into landed property, as did some merchant capital. Still other landlords sided with the liberals in their anticlericalism, foreseeing the day when Church properties would be confiscated and (presumably) added to their own.

While the most successful *agiotistas* diversified their investments into textiles and other home industries, internal production of many items was not sufficient to supply a fully developed home market. For example, not enough cotton was produced for the home clothing industry, and so Mexico imported raw cotton from the United States, processing it in Mexico. Protective tariffs, strong in much of the 1820s and 1830s, existed only on finished goods by the 1840s. Manuel Escandón and the *agiotistas* put in Alamán as head of the state's General Directorate of Industry in 1842, in part to oversee development of the home market. State decrees provided a basis for the formation of regional and national industrial committees and the creation of government departments to favor industry, along with educational and technological advances in agriculture. Industrialists organized themselves into manufacturing assemblies, which were given a veto power in the 1843 constitution on tariff questions.

British diplomatic correspondence of this period reveals that foreign bondholders frowned on these industrialization plans and pressured for continuing the pattern of export of agricultural and mineral products and import of manufactured goods. Alamán's job in the end was primarily not to introduce new industries but to compile statistics and screen for markets in order to expand Mexico's internal and external trade. The state, rather than industrialize Mexico, continued to help the *agiotistas* and related interest groups find the best markets, keep abreast of financial and related matters, and garner additional federal contracts for railway or other public construction projects.

But it remained an unstable state, whose problems were only compounded by the liberal-conservative quarreling among contending politicians. Only the U.S. invasion of 1846–1848 momentarily stopped the interelite feuding, provoking half-hearted attempts at defending the country against outside aggression and at forming class alliances not unlike those that had unleashed the Wars of Independence. Regional outbreaks of class war, pitting poor against rich, once again tempered the elites' new-found "nationalist" fervor.

Foreign Invasions

The United States was not the only foreign power to invade Mexico during this period. Between 1823 and 1861, Mexico suffered an average of one invasion every six years. In 1829, the Spanish briefly occupied Tampico. In 1838, during the so-called Pastry War, the French invaded Veracruz, leaving only when Mexico guaranteed payment of a 600,000-peso debt. Nevertheless, the United States was the most successful aggressor. Having gained its independence almost half a century earlier than Mexico, the northern republic had long coveted Latin American lands. In 1823, President James Monroe had enunciated the Monroe Doctrine, ineffectually warning European powers to stay out of the Americas. Ambassador Poinsett was then instructed to explore the possibility of incorporating northeastern Mexico (today's Texas), and to warn Mexico not to consider acquiring Cuba, which, if taken from Spain, also should be "attached" to the United States.[23] Starting in 1823, U.S. citizens began to colonize northeastern Mexico. Then in 1835–1836, U.S. citizens (and a few Mexicans) led a bloody but successful fight for secession from Mexico; in 1845 the United States annexed the Republic of Texas.

When U.S. and Mexican patrols clashed in April 1846, President

James K. Polk claimed American blood had been shed on U.S. soil. Congressman Abraham Lincoln asked Polk to indicate precisely where this had occurred, but to no avail. The battle had in fact taken place well inside Mexican territory, near the Río Grande, about 150 miles south of the Texas-Mexico border (the Nueces River), but nonetheless the United States used the incident as a pretext for declaring war. The United States invaded Mexico, ostensibly to force it to pay off a multimillion-dollar debt owed U.S. citizens who had lost properties during the Wars of Independence and subsequent internal strife, but in actuality to seize almost half of Mexico's territory. The doctrine of Manifest Destiny proclaimed that it was the "destiny" of the United States to occupy the entire North American continent.

Mexico City was captured on September 14, 1847. General Santa Anna fled, but young military cadets *(los niños héroes)* vainly defended Chapultepec Castle, some reportedly wrapping themselves in Mexican flags and leaping from the cliffs while shouting "Viva México!" A group of recent Irish Catholic immigrants, who had fled the potato famine and British colonialism only to be drafted into the U.S. army, deserted the Protestant General Winfield Scott to form the "Saint Patrick's Batallion" and fight on the side of their Mexican Catholic "brothers," similar victims of a big power. Most were killed or captured and put before a firing squad.

In the face of the "Yankee" onslaught, Mexico's elites were little more courageous than Santa Anna had been. They and their political representatives took care to prevent popular resistance from getting out of hand by delegating all military authority to the regular army, which they could control. The U.S. invasion happened at an inopportune time for them. They had their hands full attempting to crush the peasant revolt of 300,000 Maya in Yucatán and a series of uprisings against their class rule by peasants, workers, and squatters in central Mexico. A massive peasant uprising in Oaxaca, Guerrero, and Michoacán between 1842 and 1844, followed by one led by Luciano Velázquez in the Huasteca region of Veracruz from 1845 to 1849, had generated among Mexico's masses new calls for breaking up haciendas and giving back "land to the tiller." Agrarian movements were spreading to many areas of the country. They ranged from social banditry to Catholic millenarianism, from land takeovers to the establishment of free peasant communities.

The peasants directed their anger not only at landlords, merchants, and industrialists, but also at the Church hierarchy. For example, replying to the Bishop of Yucatán, who had asked them to lay down their arms, a group of Indian captains leading the Maya revolt wrote (through a scribe) in 1848:

We say one thing only to you and the venerable saintly priests. Why didn't you remember or take notice when the Governor began killing us? Why didn't you stand up or take interest in us when the whites were slaughtering us so much? Why didn't you do it when a certain Father Herrera did whatever he liked with impoverished Indians? This priest tossed his saddle on a poor Indian, mounted him, and began to whip him, lacerating his belly with lashes. Why didn't you have any concern when that happened? And now you remember, now you know there is a true God? . . . If the whites' houses and haciendas are burning, it's because earlier they had burned the town of Tepich and all the hamlets where poor Indians dwelled, and the whites ate all their cattle.[24]

Hoping to stem such peasant rebellions, many prominent families collaborated with the U.S. invaders, thereby hastening the defeat of a Mexican officer corps reluctant to fight and thousands of aroused peasants and workers who genuinely defended the nation's honor. The taking of Mexico City set the stage for arrangement of the terms for the war's settlement, enshrined in the 1848 Treaty of Guadalupe Hidalgo, through which the United States obtained most of northern Mexico. Mexico's elites welcomed the $15 million war indemnities allotted Mexico under the treaty's terms, hoping it would fill up the state's drained treasury and help reestablish a semblance of social order. They used the money to crush the Maya revolt, although fleeing Indians put up resistance in the jungles of eastern Yucatán until the army finally subdued them at the end of the century.

Agrarian revolts then erupted elsewhere. In 1849 Eleuterio Quirós led a thousand peasants in the takeover of Río Verde, San Luis Potosí, a revolt that quickly spread to Guanajuato and Querétaro and engulfed the Sierra Gorda. Liberal spokesman José María Luis Mora called for total suppression of all Indian revolts shaking the nation. In 1854, a U.S. payment of 10 million pesos known as the Gadsden Purchase, which ceded additional territory (now part of southern Arizona) to the United States, was again used to repress peasant revolts—as well as to finance the pageantry of the president, none other than that unprincipled ideological chameleon Santa Anna, by then an absolute monarch except in name.

From its conquest of Mexico, the United States obtained wealthy territory soon to be the scene of the fabulous Gold Rush. Mexico, on the other hand, lost an estimated 50,000 lives, mostly from among the urban unemployed, workers, and peasant soldiers who put up the only significant resistance. In addition, some 100,000 Mexicans in the conquered territories became labor power for U.S.

capital. U.S. railmen, miners, industrialists, ranchers, farmers, and land tycoons immediately began violating provisions of the Treaty of Guadalupe Hidalgo guaranteeing the property and civil rights of those Mexicans remaining at their homesites in today's southwestern United States. In the following few decades, U.S. citizens of Mexican descent lost some 20 million acres. Respect for the Mexicans' culture and language, guaranteed by the treaty (an often overlooked legal basis for twentieth-century experiments in bilingual education), was systematically violated. Poor whites were similarly pillaged or abused, although not subjected to the widespread lynchings suffered by Mexicans. Thus the U.S. doctrine of Manifest Destiny, a racist doctrine born from the genocidal wars against the peoples who first inhabited the lands occupied by the Pilgrims, was also a classist doctrine born from conquest and domination by the forces of expansive U.S. capitalism.

Most popular resistance against repeated foreign invasions was conducted with guerrilla tactics on the part of regional armies. Many radicals and liberals from the intermediate classes reasserted their voice in national affairs, and in some cases lent leadership to the uprisings of peasants and workers. Many of these same leaders went into exile when conservatives wielded dictatorial powers in the late 1840s and early 1850s. When they returned they brought with them the ideas of Fourier, Proudhon, Owen, Saint-Simon, and Marx, and infused the mass struggle with such new terms as "socialism," "anarchism," and "brotherhood." European exiles from the defeated revolutions of 1848 also brought these ideas to Mexican soil.

Until the late 1840s, the elites' interfamilial squabbles had rarely cost the life of one of their own. Each attempt to establish hegemony in the disputes over free trade and protectionism, federalism and centralism, limited Church activities and expanded ones, had called on the armies of the poor, while elite leaders had negotiated compromises or even switched sides according to the balance of forces and the availability of new opportunities for their own financial aggrandizement.

After the U.S. invasion, however, political and social issues became much more sharply defined. The lower classes escalated their demands for economic justice as their revolts spread and they experienced the power of guerrilla warfare. Many petty-bourgeois leadership types and commercial *hacendados* increased their demands for confiscating Church wealth. The bourgeoisie recognized the need to consolidate a constitutional republic, with a strong enough executive to further their economic interests and divert or contain the surging regional peasant and worker revolts. Then it

was that a charismatic leader, a self-made lawyer of Zapotec Indian
stock named Benito Juárez, emerged to lead the so-called Liberal
Reform movement of 1855–1867, which fought the diehard conservatives, the Church, and—in the longest and hardest-fought war
yet—a French army of occupation.

Civil War, Liberal Reform, and Consolidating a Capitalist State

By 1854, Santa Anna and his clerical and military allies had
established a repressive regime that jailed, executed, or exiled its
opponents on a massive scale. This had the effect of unifying warring factions among the liberals, known as the "purists" *(puros)* and
"moderates" *(moderados).* The purists drew their main support
from the urban petty bourgeoisie, *rancheros,* and an occasional
hacendado like firebrand anticlerical ideologue Melchor Ocampo.
Together with vocal urban or town-based liberal artisans, intellectuals, and lawyers, they advocated small and middle-size farms as
an alternative to the "inefficient" system of huge rural estates enslaving peasants in debt-peonage. Artisans, facing continued proletarianization, also championed anticlericalism and the ideology of
small family enterprises. The moderates, on the other hand, drew
their support from the commercial bourgeoisie, some big industrialists, most *hacendados,* and many ex-government ministers and
functionaries purged by the conservative dictatorship. Purists were
directed by men like Ocampo, Juárez, and Ponciano Arriaga, while
moderates were led by men like Ignacio Comonfort and the
brothers Miguel and Sebastián Lerdo de Tejada.

In 1854, after being imprisoned for several months, Juárez
joined Ocampo and Arriaga in exile in New Orleans, Louisiana.
They decided to support an antigovernment rebellion in Guerrero,
led by the old and by-now wealthy guerrilla fighter Juan Alvarez.
They sent him a statement of principles, many of which became
incorporated into Alvarez's "Plan of Ayutla." Santa Anna was unable to stop the spread of this revolt and, when he heard that
peasants to the north and west were rallying behind it, he sailed
into exile. In August 1855 the liberals seized state power and installed Comonfort as president. His moderate administration was
soon challenged by enraged conservatives, who, distressed at its
legal decrees affecting their vested interests, set up an alternative
government backed by segments of the army.

The problem for the Comonfort government was once again an

empty treasury, and the best way to fill it quickly. The new government passed the Ley Juárez in 1855, abolishing clerical and military *fueros,* and the Ley Lerdo in 1856, forbidding any "corporation" to own property. (Both the Ley Juárez and the Ley Lerdo were then expanded and institutionalized in Articles 26 and 27 of the 1857 Constitution.) "Corporately held property" included not just Church lands but also peasant *ejidos.* The Ley Lerdo partially and temporarily exempted *ejidos,* but aggressive landlords and expanding *rancheros* feasted their eyes on Indian communal pasturelands. Once the moderates had won the votes taken at the 1856–1857 constitutional convention, the Ley Lerdo's exemptions for *ejido* lands had been eliminated. Under protection of the new Constitution, the moderates' *hacendado* backers, as well as liberal bureaucrats, ambitious merchants and moneylenders, some *rancheros,* and various land speculators were legally able to purchase or confiscate huge quantities of Indian communal land.

To make sure some funds would enter the treasury immediately, the Comonfort government promised that the Church would be paid for confiscated lands, with the government receiving a part of the transfer price and a 5 percent sales tax. The Ley Lerdo also granted the state an additional source of revenue by imposing a property tax of 4 percent on every 1,000 pesos of appraised value—clerical real estate was exempted, an initial deference to the Church from confirmed anticlericals that reflected the desperate need for funds, as well as recognition of the Church's strong economic position.

This strategy raised some monies in the short run, but only delayed the attempt to capture the most attractive financial prize (other than Indian lands) promised by the legislative acts of the Liberal Reform, the legendary wealth of the Church, estimated to range from 180 to 620 million pesos. By the time the liberals finally unified their various disentailment decrees in 1859, much of the Church's wealth had dissipated, fled, or been exaggerated in the first place. Both conservative and liberal governments and armies had used it to pay for conducting the civil strife of 1857–1859. Some of it had been rescued by Church agents through subterfuge; some was plundered and consumed by the liberal forces; and some was converted by speculators into paper—and money depreciated rapidly in the chaos of civil war and speculation. Finally, foreign interests obtained some of it through complicated loan arrangements with previous governments.

For example, the British houses of Nathaniel Davidson (representative of the House of Rothschild) and Eustaquio Barron obtained over 1 million pesos in this manner. Frenchman José Yves

Limantour, who had helped finance the liberal government during its 1857 retreat to Veracruz, obtained a medley of merchant houses in Mexico City for a half million pesos. Limantour would later become the financial wizard of the Díaz "liberal" dictatorship (1876–1911). Of 16 million pesos worth of nationalized properties sold in Mexico City in 1861 to help finance the newly elected Juárez government, only 1 million was received, the rest going to pay off credits, promissory notes, and bonds. Yet without confiscated Church wealth the liberals would have been hard put to sustain their government or make occasional concessions to the peasantry or labor.

Such concessions became a key ingredient of the liberals' strategy of expanding their support among the masses once the reeling conservatives launched a strong comeback through the assistance brought them by direct European military intervention. In 1861, with the United States bogged down in its own civil war, Britain, France, and Spain signed a tripartite agreement that divided Mexico among them. Spanish troops landed at Veracruz that same year, but did not remain long. The French took over the military operation, invading Mexico in 1862 and occupying it until 1867 to protect Mexico's most famous "emperor" since Iturbide, Archduke Maximilian of Austria. In a letter to one of his generals, Napoleon III revealed France's motives behind this bold, but risky, undertaking: "If a stable government is established there with the help of France . . . we will have established our beneficent influence in the center of America, and such influence, upon creating immediate avenues for our commerce, will procure for us indispensable primary materials for our industry."[25]

Responding both to peasant demands and to rising agrarian-export and land prices, the liberals undertook an agrarian reform. As in their confiscation of Church wealth, the liberals' agrarian policies served only to accelerate the very economic processes that had stimulated them in the first place. The 5 percent *alcabala,* or marketing tax, made it impossible for most peasants to compete against the land sharks who descended on them to legally break up "corporately held property." Land monopolization was also furthered by the "vacant lands" *(baldíos)* decrees issued by Juárez in 1863 to raise funds for fighting the French invaders. In four years, some 4.5 million acres of prime land, much of it belonging to Indians who allegedly could not prove title, passed into the hands of *latifundistas* at about $.025 an acre. Similar *baldío* laws in 1883 and 1894 accentuated the process. Criollo (and some mestizo) land-holders were thus able to achieve what not even the colonial elites had been able to do: take over the vast majority of Indian land.

An occasional purist liberal voice cried out against the deception of the agrarian reform legislation and its underlying capitalist motivation. For example, Ponciano Arriaga prophetically told delegates to the 1856–1857 constitutional convention that Article 27 would inevitably produce "monopolistic capitalism." His proposal to break up the *latifundia* was unanimously rejected by the delegates, whose votes reflected the class interests they represented. Arriaga correctly perceived that under Article 27, "laboring citizens are condemned to be mere passive instruments of production for the exclusive profit of the capitalist."[26]

Ideologically, the liberals waved the flag of antifeudalism to combat such voices of reason, but other Mexicans, including many of the constitutional delegates themselves, had long since recognized the situation as Mariano Otero had described it in 1842:

> When it has been said to us very seriously that we have an aristocracy, when we have been exhorted to bring it up to date and we have been told of the European nobility and the feudal clergy, no one has known what he was talking about; words have miserably been mistaken for things, and an error in language has brought about one in politics . . . the Mexican aristocracy was not at all similar to the European: it was . . . a parody . . . and the individuals that composed it . . . lived indolently upon capital, enjoying their profits.[27]

In fact, the liberals had a credo that extended beyond their sanctimonious antifeudalism and incorporated the very ingredients of their own class interests: free labor, foreign immigration, free noncorporate land, private property, private industry, freedom of religion, free secular education, and freedom of trade and investment (which furthered the bourgeoisie's embrace of foreign capital). Here too Arriaga voiced a realistic warning:

> Upon decreeing freedom of trade, industry, and other franchises, great concessions are made to foreigners, scarcely reflecting upon the impossibility of our industry and crafts competing with the foreigners, given three centuries of delay, monopoly, and servitude that have weighed upon the Mexican people.[28]

The cloaking of the new onslaught on Indian land in the liberal rhetoric of agrarian reform and "family farming" suggests the extent to which the peasants' class struggle against *latifundismo* had become a serious threat to Mexico's landed elites. "Land to the tiller" movements had spread throughout much of the nation since the peasant uprisings of the 1840s and early 1850s. Moreover, radical priests, former military officers, and leftist agitators had penetrated the ranks of the rebellion and lent it leadership.

Yet, during the civil war years, the peasants, like other social classes, were far from unified, much less allied in an organized fashion with other groups. Some peasants were sincere Catholics seeking redemption of their land under the banner of the Virgin of Guadalupe and easily led by either conservative clerics or radical priests. Others were sympathetic to the anticlerical and nationalist appeals of the liberals, taking up arms to drive out the haughty priests and even haughtier French. Many raised reformist demands and, with the restoration of liberal federalism, won some of them in some states—for example, the Querétaro state legislature passed a minimum-wage law for rural *jornaleros,* and the San Luis Potosí legislature confiscated a few haciendas, delivering them to the peasants.

An immense urban subproletariat of street vendors, beggars, migrants, vagabonds, semiemployed and unemployed—colloquially called by the elites the *léperos* and, with seasonal rural workers, constituting a majority of the labor force—was readily recruited by both liberals and conservatives to fight the civil war. Many were economically and spiritually tied to the Church, which had an elaborate system of taking any monies they made and doling out charity. Some subproletarians became highway robbers, who did a lucrative business during the war years, adding to the lack of stability needed for capitalist development. They often protected humble muleteers or artisan produce while directing their blows against foreigners and the rich.

Doubly challenged by their own civil war and the social turbulence of the lower classes, Mexico's elites were more than willing to seek outside economic and military support. Conservative oligarchs played a key role in inviting and supporting the French military occupation. For his part, Juárez, the most nationalist leader to appear on the scene since Morelos, in 1858 offered to cede the United States passage through Tehuántepec and Baja California in exchange for recognition of his government (the McLane-Ocampo Treaty). Then, in 1865–1866, Juárez's anti-French army recruited some 3,000 Union veterans of the U.S. Civil War with offers of good pay and land bonuses. Even as the nation's elites had learned well the colonial lesson that to govern is to pillage, so their embrace of foreign aid and manners was part of their colonial heritage. Ever since the days of the Bourbons, and even more so during the French occupation, many members of the upper class were known as *los afrancesados,* or "the Frenchified," because of their adoption of French customs and putting on airs.

The French occupation marked history's first modern experiment in what emergent imperialist powers would later develop into a fine art—"counterinsurgency warfare." An elite troop of French soldiers was trained and equipped to put down the guerrilla war of resistance being conducted by peasants and workers. French strategy included all the modern counterinsurgency political devices of pseudo-agrarian reform, democratic proclamations, and cultural changes in education and science. Indeed, the crowning irony for conservatives was that Maximilian carried out what amounted to the liberals' program insofar as education, land, property, and freedom of press and commerce were concerned. The French validated the confiscation and sale of Church property. They promised the restoration of Indian *ejidos*—to the horror of *hacendados*. Moreover, since liberals led the anti-French liberation movement, the liberals' cause became equated with national independence. This left conservatives worse off than they had been before inviting the French takeover.

Wherever feasible, Juárez assigned regular army officers to lead the peasant-worker war of national liberation—men like Brigadier General Porfirio Díaz, who gained his liberal and "nationalist" credentials through his leading role in the Mexicans' first major victory, the Battle of Puebla, May 5, 1862. But many peasants were fighting a class war as well, and could not be "pacified" either by French counterinsurgency or by the policies of scorched earth and deportation practiced by occasional liberal army officers.

To help finance the war, Juárez decreed the confiscation of the property of those Mexicans supporting the French, on the grounds that they were "traitors to the fatherland." At least two hundred leading bourgeois families suffered expropriation, reducing the strength of the conservative wing of the criollo bourgeoisie and increasing that of the liberal wing. Landlords, *rancheros*, industrialists, and petty-bourgeois radicals also gained from these and related measures of the Juarista state. Bourgeois families who accepted state authority had their properties protected. Many big merchants and some industrialists conformed to the Juarista movement only at the last moment—under the double pressure of people's liberation war and threatened expropriation.

Although it cost fifty thousand Mexican lives, the people's war against forty thousand French soldiers finally triumphed in early 1867. Maximilian surrendered, was tried by court-martial, and on June 19 was executed by a firing squad (his wife Carlotta had by then lost her mind). Juárez had rejected international pleas for clemency for Maximilian's life, noting that the "emperor" had decreed and implemented the death penalty for all captured Juárista soldiers.

The defeat of the French left the most reactionary segments of the bourgeoisie isolated. Most of the clergy and military officer corps, together with some more traditional-minded *hacendados* and entrepreneurs tied to them, found themselves on the losing side against an insurmountable liberal tide led by a handful of military officers and a massive number of landholders, small and medium-size manufacturers, artisans, professionals, and various big money-lenders, merchants, miners, and industrialists. The many years of internal and international war thus ended in the establishment and consolidation of a well-defined nation-state, victorious in war and firmly committed to "freedom"—that is, freedom for unchecked capitalist development.

The Liberal Reform was more than an aggression by parts of the landlord-merchant-industrial bourgeoisie against Church properties and traditions (tithes, *diezmo*, etc.). It also delivered a telling blow to artisan corporations (guilds), accelerating the separation of artisans from their means of production and their incorporation into the textile industry's wage-labor force. Most significantly, the Reform laid the basis for the final reduction of the peasantry, dispossessing them of their lands and converting them into "free" wage laborers or debt-peons. It thus laid the foundations in both urban and rural areas for a speedier development of capitalist forms of production.

After the French military withdrawal in 1867, the Juarista state continued to be based on an alliance of many classes—but it was the agro-export fraction of the bourgeoisie that emerged dominant. Commercial *hacendados*, manufacturers, miners, and much of banking-merchant capital held hegemonic class power—all forces favoring modern capitalist development and anxious to associate themselves more and more with the trade and foreign capital of the more industrialized countries, their "natural" allies.

Much of the success of the Juarista movement against the clergy and the French derived from its building class alliances and offering possibilities of advance for elements of nonelite groups—small farmers, artisans, workers, mestizos, professionals, and so forth—at least in the arena of democratic rights and the chance to organize. Article 9 of the 1857 Constitution guaranteed the right of workers to "associate" and Article 5 forebade unpaid labor. Many professionals (most were lawyers) took sides not out of conviction but out of job hunger *(empleomanía)* and a devotion to the benefits of the corrupt system of political payoffs.

Artistans had organized into "mutual-aid" societies in 1853–1855, and in 1861 consolidated their Gran Familia Artística, which, with members' dues, guaranteed medical care. Tailors, small-scale merchants, carpenters, typesetters, hatmakers, seamstresses, brick-layers, stonecutters, silversmiths, and others formed similar organizations in the 1860s. Workers' banks and credit unions were organized. Producers' co-ops shared the capitalist ethos of private property but opposed the big bourgeoisie, which stood in the way of the creation of a society of small and equal producers. The co-ops rallied to the mine pickmen's strike at Real del Monte in 1872 and the hatmakers' and textile workers' strikes of 1875. By 1880, there existed 100 such mutual-aid societies in Mexico City, most of whose members were artisans, whose families constituted a sixth of the capital's population of 300,000.

As industrial and mining production and transportation works expanded during the second half of the nineteenth century, so did the proletariat. The cotton textile industry doubled its installed capacity between 1854 and 1879. A rough estimate of the economically active population in 1861 showed 61 percent to be *jornaleros* in agriculture and mining and another 2.5 percent to be stably employed in factories or artisanal workshops. By 1877, similarly rough estimates showed the regularly employed proletariat to include approximately 100,000 mine workers, 100,000 muleteers, 25,000 textile and tobacco workers, 60,000 urban artisans, 12,000 railway workers, and thousands of other wage and piecework laborers in industry or construction—a total of about 9 percent of the adult work force.

In spite of such expansion in wage labor, much of the proletariat still experienced preindustrial or semi-industrial forms of exploitation. Many resided in miserable barracks provided by capitalist employers and were tied by debts to the company store *(tienda de raya)*. All were subject to sudden layoffs and replacement by the immense reserve army of labor queuing up at factory gates, mineshafts, or other labor recruitment centers for a day's work. Sons and daughters of peasants increasingly migrated to the cities in desperate quest for a means of survival. Up to a third of urban women were employed as domestic servants. Unemployment still hovered around 50 percent. Almost all the proletariat were superexploited. Worst off were the thousands of women and children employed in industry (over a third of the textile labor force) or mining.

The slowly expanding proletariat, working long days at low wages in mining, transport, and construction, or in the textile, paper, glass, sugar, liquor, wheat, tobacco, soap, rope, and other factories and mills, gradually began to organize at the local level with the help of the artisans. Between 1872 and 1880, various local workers' organizations united nationally into the Great Circle of Workers, the Great Confederation of Workers, the Workers' Congress, and similar organizations incorporating thousands of members. These organizations espoused mutual aid, workers' defense, and a range of radical ideologies (Christian humanism, liberalism, utopian socialism, workers' internationalism, and anarchism), plus a few conservative ones, although in their practice they were generally reformist.

Working-class struggle throughout the nineteenth century was sparked by artisans, miners, railway workers, and textile workers. But it suffered the contradictions of the petty-bourgeois consciousness of many of its artisan leaders, who also organized against manufactured imports, a demand shared by those textile industrialists whose modernizing factories were contributing to the inviability of artisan workshops and the proletarianization of the artisans themselves. Further, many of the workers' demands were aimed at eliminating such backward conditions as the company store, fines, night work, fifteen-hour workdays, or child labor, while advocating public secular education as the road to proletarian advancement.

In their early years, some workers' organizations received donations from the liberal state, as part of a political trade-off for their having backed the liberals against the conservatives in the civil war. Others remained independent of the state and, in elections made possible by the Liberal Reform's introduction of male universal suffrage, gained political positions and even hegemony in the local governments of various municipalities. The Great Circle of Workers often acted as mediator between the state and protesting workers.

The debates nurturing an evolution toward what were to become more class-conscious, revolutionary programs and militant strikes on the eve of the Mexican Revolution of 1910 filled the pages of artisan, anarchist, and worker radical tabloid newspapers: *The Workers' Voice, The International, The Socialist, The International Worker, The Child of Labor,* and so forth. Dozens of these papers began circulating in the 1860s and 1870s, often with abbreviated life spans, or underground because of the stepped-up repression suffered by the nascent proletarian movement. Most advocated autonomy for municipal governments, workers' control, free peasant villages, women's rights, and one or another form of a universal social republic.

The modern Mexican capitalist state dates from this period of the liberal-conservative civil war and its immediate aftermath. The forerunner of the strong state interventionism of President Lázaro Cárdenas in the 1930s was the state-expropriation policy of Juárez against the Church and uncooperative bourgeois property holders. Similarly, precedents for the modern state's "protection" and regulation of the activities of peasants and workers were written into the 1857 Constitution. The modern state as a national entity constitutionally enshrined above the interests of traditional corporations or privileged oligarchies (the ancien régime) and supposedly oriented toward the "public good" rather than toward any special-interest group (or class) was ideologically conceived and juridically consolidated by the Liberal Reform and anti-French war of national liberation.

Such an ideological definition of the state is capitalist—and in Mexico reflected the class hegemony of the bourgeoisie in its triumphant fractions. Because the establishment of this state was rooted in internal class war against reactionary segments of the elites and certain traditional noncapitalist forms of appropriation of wealth (Church, artisan guilds, and Indian communities) and external war against foreign invaders, Mexico's new state had considerable popular legitimacy and ample options for controlling the rebelliousness of the masses, advancing capitalist accumulation, and consolidating the triumphant liberal bourgeoisie's "natural" alliance with foreign capitalists—at the expense of the lower classes and the Church and to the joint profit of domestic and foreign (increasingly U.S.) capital.

Now firmly established, the Mexican state was to assume both bourgeois-democratic and oligarchic-dictatorial forms.[29] From 1867 to 1880, bourgeois freedoms flourished, as urban citizens enjoyed an unprecedented range of free expression. But they were increasingly to lose this privilege as both the modernizing bourgeoisie and the traditional *hacendados* found it necessary to call on stronger state repression to contain the class struggle.

Final resolution of Mexico's civil war and defeat of the French army by no means put an end to peasant resistance. Examples of the continuing radicalization of the class struggle in the countryside included the following:

—From 1836 to 1910, the state of Veracruz was the scene of almost constant peasant revolt.

—Between 1857 and 1881, an agrarian rebellion led by Manuel Lozada (the "tiger of Alica") in Nayarit spread to Jalisco and engulfed both states.

—After 1868, Julio López's Chalco revolt spread to peasant communities in the states of Hidalgo, Tlaxcala, México, and Puebla before Benito Juárez had López executed in 1869. López's final words were reportedly, "Long live socialism!"[30]

—In 1869, to the south, a messianic movement of Chamula Indians in Chiapas erupted.

—Between 1877 and 1881, the Sierra Gorda peasant movement was renewed, incorporating a detailed program of agrarian socialism.

—Between 1877 and 1883, the Cuidad del Maíz region of San Luis Potosí experienced peasant revolt.

—In 1879, a rebellion led by socialist Alberto Santa Fé in San Martín Texmelucan, Puebla, proclaimed a "Law of the People" inspired by utopian socialism, provoking further agrarian revolts in Morelos, Guerrero, and San Luis Potosí.

In the face of this type of social unrest, only a ruthless dictatorship could sustain the class rule of Mexico's bourgeoisie.

Unlike the first half of the nineteenth century, the last two decades would be marked by the stability of a clearly defined state serving the interests of the agro-mineral export and industrial-financial fractions of the bourgeoisie, together with foreign capital. Commercial capital's role in stimulating expanded production and a transition toward modern capitalism would continue, but with changes in the forces and relations of production permitting more than mere "original accumulation" of capital. An era of domestic and foreign monopolistic enterprises exploiting cheap wage labor for capital accumulation on an extended scale was getting underway. Yet far from being a uniform process, Mexican capitalist development would continue in an uneven manner, combining various forms of labor exploitation and production. This process would reflect itself in both the state and the class struggle that followed. In a sense, Mexico's internal and external wars were just beginning.

3
Dictatorship and Revolution, 1880–1920

De los campos los burgueses se adueñaron
Explotando los veneros que en el subsuelo encontraron
Mientras tanto los millones de pesos al extranjero
Se llevaban los patronos con escarnio verdadero.

The bourgeoisie took over the countryside
Exploiting the subsoil lodes
While the owners took abroad
Millions of pesos with true disdain.
> —Mexican revolutionary song

It is better to die on one's feet than to live on one's knees.
> —Saying attributed to Emiliano Zapata
> on eve of 1910–1920 Revolution

The liberals' bourgeois-democratic state was soon superseded by an oligarchic-dictatorial one. In 1871, the liberals split into three feuding camps, with Juárez seeking a fourth term as president against the candidacies of Sebastian Lerdo de Tejada, brother of the author of Ley Lerdo, and Porfirio Díaz, an army commander who had won fame in the war against the French. When no single candidate won a majority of votes, the Congress, dominated by Juaristas, declared Juárez the winner. On July 19, 1872, President Juárez died of a heart attack, and a special presidential election in October became a two-man contest in which Lerdo defeated Díaz. In 1876, Lerdo decided to seek reelection, but the liberals underwent further internal divisions, providing the military with an opportunity to assert its leverage. Proclaiming the slogan "No Reelection" and rallying dissident officers, Díaz seized power in November 1876.

There followed a period of political crisis during which no single fraction of the bourgeoisie was able to achieve hegemony. The United States withheld recognition of the new government until it obtained a number of concessions, including indemnities for damages incurred by U.S. property owners during Mexico's recent wars, the right to own property in Mexico, extension of "free" trade along the border westward from Tamaulipas (where its practice had been legalized since 1861) all the way to Baja California, and permission to send its troops across the border in pursuit of hostile Indians such as the Apache. These concessions were granted in 1877. The United States then proceeded to substitute for its 1840s' strategy of physical conquest of Mexican territory one of economic domination through mining, oil, agricultural, and rail investments—and expanded trade.

U.S. capitalists wanted government contracts for construction of Mexico's railroad grid, and Díaz was willing to cooperate. Before leaving office to allow Secretary of War Manuel González to become president (1880–1884), Díaz got the Mexican parliament to authorize contracting U.S. companies to build the main rail lines from Mexico City to the border towns of Ciudad Juárez and Nuevo Laredo (work completed by 1891). González continued Díaz's policies in this regard, extending government subsidies to U.S. construction firms of up to $9,500 for each kilometer of track laid.

Meanwhile, Díaz cultivated key regional *caciques* and military figures in an effort to build a national network that could be centralized when he resumed office, as he fully expected to do, thereby reducing the chance of recurrences of internal strife or challenges to his power. González, unable to meet the fiscal challenges faced by the still heavily indebted state, stopped payment on the salaries of many government bureaucrats, and cries for his removal became widespread. Díaz handily won the 1884 election and began the transition to a "constitutional" dictatorship, first having the Constitution reformed to permit his reelection in 1888. He immediately set about patching up old wounds among the nation's elites, granting state favors to big landowners, merchants, and industrialists regardless of their past positions in the liberal-conservative civil war. (In his personal life, he had begun this process earlier, in 1881, when he married Carmen Romero Rubio, the daughter of Manuel Romero Rubio, a prominent pro-Lerdo political statesman.) This set the stage for Mexico's most sustained period of economic growth since the end of the previous century, made possible in great part by the political stability engineered by an oligarchic-dictatorial state headed by Díaz.

The Porfiriato: Dictatorship, Capital Accumulation, and Class Formation

Díaz's thirty-five year reign of tyranny (1876–1911), known as the Porfiriato, was the most concentrated period of political centralization and economic development that Mexico had yet experienced, with the greatest advances in production and trade concentrated in the single decade of the 1890s. It was also a period in which foreigners, with U.S. entrepreneurs at the forefront, took over much of the economy. The state did not merely submit to foreign pressures on the debt: it threw open the doors to foreign investment in an attempt to marshall sufficient capital and technical expertise to generate significant economic growth for the benefit of domestic and foreign monopolies. Until the late 1890s, almost all bourgeois and large-landholder interests prospered from vast increases in production and trade: merchants, new bankers and industrialists, miners, liberal military and civilian politicians (who had become rich during the Liberal Reform period), *hacendados* employing wage or debt-peon labor, former "conservative" opponents of the Reform, and even the Catholic Church, which reasserted its economic and social influence over daily life.

In healing liberal-conservative wounds and reconsolidating elite interests along their preferred capitalist development path, the Díaz dictatorship institutionalized a repressive apparatus and an ideological system emphasizing political stability, science, technology, and material progress as alternatives to the preceding years of "chaos and idealism." No group at the state level created this climate as well as the so-called Científicos, Díaz's brain trust of Positivists and Social Darwinists who emphasized that everything in politics and economics must be done according to the rules of "science" and sound administration, rather than those of "metaphysics" or "religion." The slogans "Poca política y mucha administración" (Little politics and much administration) and "Orden y progreso" (Order and progress) expressed the mood. Inspired by the ideas of evolutionary progress and "survival of the fittest" made popular by Auguste Comte and Herbert Spencer, the Científicos were a group of intellectuals, professionals, and entrepreneurs who had gained wealth and status from the Liberal Reform measures taken against the Church and the *ejidos*. They were enamored of the virtues of foreign capital and culture, and had ties to French capital, which, of all foreign capital, was the most involved in the development of the home market. Their role in politics, in the formation of economic policy, and in education furnished the bourgeoisie with the kind of ideology and state support it needed to develop and believe in itself and its mission; and this happened at a time when the elites, exhausted after fifty years of internal and international war, were responsive to the need for organization and discipline for economic growth.[1]

The Científicos and other prominent liberals defended the

"benefits" of foreign economic influence. In 1890, Lerdo's former Treasury Minister Matías Romero expressed his satisfaction to the Chamber of Deputies "on seeing foreigners as owners of high finance, of credit institutions, of the electric power plants, of the telegraphs, of the railroads, and of all those things which signify culture and the progress of Mexico."[2] Education, which was for the elite (by 1911 illiteracy still plagued 84 percent of the population), included teaching of English because, in the words of educator Ezequiel Chávez, "it was believed necessary . . . given the growing union between the Anglo-American people and our people."[3] Justo Sierra, minister of public education, encouraged the "saxoni-zation" of Mexico—including more immigration—to develop the nation's culture and economy. A national normal school was created in 1887, and from then until 1919 almost all Mexican textbooks became the private business of Appleton Publishing Company of New York, and were written by U.S. authors.

After renegotiating the foreign debt, Díaz introduced a new commercial code (1884) that eliminated duties on many imports, and began to modernize the banking system. Finance Minister José Ives Limantour, a leading Científico, got French capitalists to help establish a central bank, the Banco de México; the banking groups of Puebla and Monterrey got their start at this time. Between 1887 and 1892, new mining codes were introduced that permitted private capital, of whatever nationality, subsoil rights. By 1894, the nation had its first balanced budget. By 1896, all the local marketing taxes (*alcabalas*), which had constituted the economic base for the regional oligarchies, had been eliminated, and the growth and unification of the home market, as well as the centralization of economic and political power in Mexico City, were able to proceed more rapidly. *Caciques* were still encouraged to function, but now in greater coordination with the center of political power in the capital.

In agriculture, industry, and commerce, large-scale units of production were best able to monopolize markets, control job and wage conditions, and assure rapid economic expansion. They put small-scale producers, individual artisans, traders, the peasantry, and the proletariat in an increasingly disadvantaged position when it came to competing or obtaining better wages. Real wages remained practically constant; malnutrition remained common, and the average life expectancy was about thirty years. In spite of this, the population grew—from an estimated 8.7 million in 1874 to over 15 million by 1911—a rate of increase not to be reached again until after World War II, when the next major period of economic growth would commence. Here was the labor force for the economic expansion.

The construction of more than 19,000 kilometers of railway—before that there had only been the 700-kilometer Veracruz-Mexico City line, completed in 1873—reduced the cost of transport more than fifteen times, and was nearly completed by 1900. The new lines, built by Indian wage labor and owned by foreign capital, linked the rich mining areas of northern and central Mexico to key gulf ports, Texas border towns, and industrial centers like Chicago and Pittsburgh, facilitating the export of raw materials and labor power. Mexican migrant laborers began to move north in large numbers. The rail grid also connected regional markets and helped create a national home market.

This revolution in the means of transport was accompanied by the large-scale import of modern manufacturing and agricultural machinery. Industrial production almost tripled and agricultural and livestock production almost doubled. The textile and beverage industries were modernized, and new industries, such as iron and steel, began to develop. In the mines, steam power was replaced by electricity, air compression drilling was introduced, the cyanide and electrolysis processes were instituted, and manganese largely replaced mercury as the transforming agent for silver. All these revolutionized mining: immense piles of tailings could now be tapped for additional silver, and huge quantities of the mineral could be processed in a single day. Much of the labor force could be laid off, particularly from among the 40 percent employed as carriers and the 25 percent employed as pickmen—obviously a great saving in wages. The cheaper, more efficient transport system provided further savings. Mine profit rates shot up by 200 percent between 1876 and 1911, as mineral and metallurgical production increased tenfold.

Mexico became the second largest producer of silver in the world. (Mexican silver remained the chief medium of trade with the Orient, even after the institution of the gold standard in 1905.) Other mineral production also expanded, and by 1910 copper, iron, and zinc had replaced silver in tonnage produced.

Throughout the entire Porfiriato, the value of all exports increased an average of 6 percent a year, and mining's share of export value tapered off—from two-thirds in 1889 to less than half by 1911, in part because of a drop in silver prices in the early 1900s. This in turn provoked a serious balance-of-payments problem and a permanent transfer of value out of Mexico in silver exports and higher costs for imports. Mexican capitalists responded by shifting some of their investments into domestic manufacturing, which, together with the blow suffered by bankers during the financial panic of 1907, strengthened the growing industrial fraction of the bourgeoisie in comparison with the mining and financial fractions.

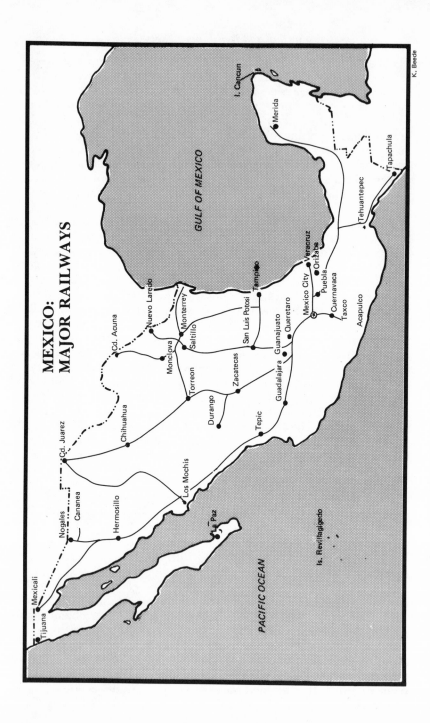

MEXICO:
MAJOR RAILWAYS

K. Beede

Agricultural production also benefited from modernization. Hydraulic pumps, electric motors, reapers, tractors, and combines were introduced. U.S. wheat interests, which needed "binder twine," and producers of agricultural machinery such as International Harvester rapidly converted the Yucatán economy into one based on the production of sisal, or henequen, a fiber from the agave plant. Trading firms like the Olegario Molina Company signed long-term contracts with International Harvester stabilizing the price of henequen and assuring mutual market access.

While the economy of the Yucatán has been called "wage-debt slavery" because Indians, hacienda peons, and small peasants were housed on, or hired by, the plantation-haciendas and tied to a company store, and while such a system existed elsewhere in Mexico as well, in many areas the process of transition from peonage to wage labor went much further. Villagers and peasants, forced off their land, had to sell their labor power on a temporary or seasonal basis. Throughout the nineteenth century such new commercial crops as chiles, coffee, chicle, maguey, tomatoes, and chickpeas *(garbanzos)* had been introduced, converting many local economies into agro-export areas and the labor force into wage labor. Cotton production increased to meet the needs of the expanding textile industry. According to the 1910 census, 80 percent of the population depended on agricultural wages and worked for 20,000 landholders, while 96.6 percent of rural households held no land whatsoever.

Out of necessity, therefore, masses of wage-oriented peasants began moving from harvest to harvest and from farm to factory, over huge expanses of territory. Many reached the United States, where they increasingly replaced Chinese and Japanese immigrants as a principal labor force in mining, railroads, industry, and, above all, agriculture. The number of Mexicans residing in the United States tripled between 1880 and 1910.[4]

The same processes that occurred in agriculture and mining occurred in sugar production, where the introduction of electric motors and metal (instead of wood) grinders and investment in irrigation works more than quadrupled production. The labor force was paid in money wages or in "chits" (coupons) that were used as currency. Morelos in particular—the home state of Emiliano Zapata, a small-scale landholder who lost his acreage to encroaching capitalists and became a leader of the 1910–1920 Revolution—became one vast network of rural sugar factories, and, after Hawaii and Puerto Rico, was the most productive sugar-cane region in the world.[5] By 1908 the seventeen owners of the twenty-four modern sugar factories and thirty-six sugar-producing haciendas owned over 25 percent of the state's land area.

Hacendados and land speculators benefited from state policies. For example, between 1881 and 1906, as a result of *baldío* (vacant-land) legislation, nearly a quarter of the nation was surveyed by private companies, which received up to a third of the land surveyed in payment; they often profited by selling it to the *hacendados*. In addition, a federal waters act increased the number of waterways classified as state property, and the state then leased or sold use rights to *hacendados*—further dispossessing peasants and Indians, who were also refused access to water or pasture lands for their animals.

In spite of this generalized capitalist monopolization of the means of production and the consequent conversion of most peasants into a wage-earning or unemployed proletariat, rural Mexico was characterized by regional variations and complex internal social stratification involving "capitanes" (labor contractors), field foremen, transport workers, *rancheros,* sharecroppers, and full- and part-time wage laborers, including millions of *jornaleros* (day laborers). *Rancheros*—small and medium-scale landholders infused with a peasant culture—constituted a rural petty bourgeoisie sympathetic to the ideology of agrarian reform, with its talk of "middle-size" farms.[6] Sharecroppers and allotment-holding workers on haciendas farmed minuscule plots of land alloted them by *hacendados* and sometimes hired wage labor from the ranks of other dispossessed peasants. They were also generally wage workers themselves, since they could not survive on their own production alone and had to raise the capital necessary to make their allotments productive.

Díaz and his advisers were well aware of what was happening and saw it in capitalist terms. They spoke of "capitalist agriculture" farmed by a "rural proletariat," and toward the end of the Porfiriato Lauro Viadas, director of the ministry of agriculture, summed up the situation in what seem very modern terms:

> Agriculture is, before and above all else, a business, and in every business the amount and safety of the profits are what determine the character of the enterprise. . . . Large-scale agriculture asserts itself and excludes small-scale family agriculture; it takes possession of the land, attracted, and I would say strongly attracted, by economic advantages that spring from the two following causes: (1) The high price of the means of livelihood. . . . The high price of these goods leads first to a high profit for the growers and subsequently, a high price for arable land, which places it within the reach only of capitalist entrepreneurs. (2) The cheapness of labor, which reduces, relatively if not absolutely, the cost of production and produces, thereby, the above-mentioned effect of raising agricultural profits.[7]

Capitalist agriculture and a rural proletariat were two aspects of the development that took place during this period. A third, as noted earlier, was the increasing foreign penetration of the economy. The United States predominated. By 1897, U.S. investments in Mexico totaled more than $200 million and exceeded such investment in the rest of Latin America, in Canada, in Europe, or in Asia. In the next fourteen years, this figure quintupled, and by 1911 U.S. investments were estimated to be greater than those of the Mexican bourgeoisie and double those of all other foreign investors. Eighty-three percent of U.S. investment was in rails and mining, with Anaconda, Phelps Dodge, and U.S. Mining, Smelting, and Refining in the lead in the latter. In fact, by 1911 some 90 percent of all fixed investment in mining was foreign, and 80 percent of this was American. In oil, an American named Edward L. Doheny, aided by loans from Mexican banking and commercial interests, created the Mexican Petroleum Company, which was later absorbed by Standard Oil. Approaching it from the export end, by 1911 the United States was receiving 74 percent of all Mexico's exports.

British interests were second to those of the United States in mining and metallurgy, and toward the end of the Porfiriato the government granted the most valuable petroleum concessions to a British firm, El Aguila. By 1911 foreigners owned between 14 and 20 percent of Mexico's land surface, and most of the eighty largest commercial and industrial establishments. Of these, twenty-one were American and twenty-three British; only six were Mexican. The rest were French, German, Spanish, or a combination (including sixteen with Mexican participation).

Rapid income growth for some and impoverization for others was producing a nation of stark contrasts, but these were not the result of "feudalism" or "traditionalism," as some writers have assumed. On the contrary, they were the result of the development of modern capitalist forms of production combined with dictatorial social and political forms of control over a restive population. A strong army, streamlined from a sprawling, officer-heavy, ill-equipped mass of 100,000 in 1875 into a well-equipped and more disciplined force of 40,000 by 1911, guaranteed political stability. To forestall possible military revolts and suppress those among peasants and miners, Díaz also created an elite rural police corps ("Rurales"), which became a veritable praetorian guard for private capital and the state. Massacres, rapes, whippings, and starvation became the sanguine underside of civilized "order and progress." The countryside resembled not so much the feudal manor as the company store, and Mexico as a whole not so much a nation as a company country.

It might seem that Díaz, and the policies he advocated and instituted, were well entrenched by the early 1900s. But seeds of discord were evident at all levels: in conflicts within the bourgeoisie over the advantages of ties to foreign capital as opposed to the advantages of greater independence; between the agro-export and industrial-financial fractions; in restiveness on the part of petty-bourgeois traders and producers ruined or blocked by the forces of monopoly capital, and of intellectuals and professionals left out of power by an authoritarian regime; in rising discontent among peasants over their loss of land; and in increasing unrest among urban proletarians over miserable working conditions and wages.

Estimates of the size of the industrial proletariat (including miners) in 1900 range from 8 to 15 percent of the adult labor force. Using the statistics gathered by the Díaz government, Colegio de México researchers and labor historian Jorge Basurto have calculated that there were 107,000 mine and 624,000 manufacturing workers. These figures reflect the fact that free wage labor for the purposes of capital accumulation on an extended scale was becoming more common as the nation's economic transformation progressed.[8]

The first two decades of the Porfiriato had been marked by a division in the urban workers' movement into two sections: the first included most artisan "masters" and better-paid workers, backed by moderate intellectuals, who wanted to work out a modus vivendi with the Díaz dictatorship; the second, more radical, section included members of the industrial proletariat and employees in artisan workshops, supported by radical intellectuals, who began to seek more revolutionary and proletarian solutions. Throughout the Porfiriato there were 250 strikes, mainly in textiles, tobacco, railways, mining, and bakeries. During the first decade of the twentieth century, when stepped-up production in the textile, beverage, cement, brick, mine, printing, and cigarette industries was dealing the final blow to all but a minority of independent artisans, the reduced artisanry together with growing numbers of the industrial proletariat began to assert revolutionary demands. Dozens of industrial, mining, and rail strikes, from 1906 to 1908, sparked by the illegal Partido Liberal Mexicano (PLM), were put down at great cost of human life. Nevertheless, these strikes broke the regime's stability and claims to legitimacy.[9]

Officially organized in 1905, the PLM had its roots in the hundreds of "Liberal Clubs" launched at the beginning of the century by disgruntled bourgeois liberals and intellectuals from the intermediate classes upset by the regime's authoritarianism and concessions to the clergy. PLM leaders, like the anarchists Ricardo and Enrique Flores Magón and Antonio Díaz Soto y Gama (later to be a major political spokesman and ideologue for the Zapata peasant movement), radicalized the democratic anticlericalism of these clubs and moved their demands in a peasant-proletarian direction. The PLM first raised the cry "Tierra y Libertad" (Land and Liberty), later to become the slogan of Zapata. This lost them some bourgeois members and speeded up the pace of their suppression by the government, but it also attracted increasing numbers of workers and peasants.

In 1906 the PLM turned itself into a political-military organization and proclaimed a revolutionary ideology opposed to imperialism and in favor of workers, peasants, and progressive elements of the intermediate classes and bourgeoisie. In the same year, and again in 1908, the PLM launched a series of armed revolts and strikes in the northern states and in the industrial and rural zones of Veracruz. It announced a program—a significant part of which was to be incorporated into the 1917 Constitution—that called for, among other things, an eight-hour day, a minimum wage, an end to child labor, an end to *latifundismo*, "land to the tiller," protection of Mexican migrants in the United States, an end to U.S. interference in Mexican affairs, and only one term for the president. Its underground newspaper, *Regeneración,* financed mainly by worker donations, reached most areas of the country and achieved a circulation of 30,000 by 1906. It was a particular target of the Díaz forces, who had its editors jailed, exiled, even killed, and the presses shut down—but it always found the means to continue.

Though few in number, women in the opposition—especially journalists—moved to its front ranks. They included poet Dolores Jiménez y Muro, Sara Estela Ramírez of *La Corregidora,* and the cofounders of the 1907 Mexico City group "Mexican Socialists": Juana B. Gutiérrez de Mendoza and Elisa Acuña y Rosete of *Vesper.* Women workers, particularly in the textile and cigarette industries, were militant participants in the strikes.

Capitalist forms of labor exploitation were most developed in the north, where much of the bourgeoisie was encouraging U.S. capital and where investment in mining, iron, steel, and agriculture had stimulated wage-price inflation and mass migration from the interior to better-paid work places further north and in the United States. In Mexico, workers began demanding pay equal to that of U.S. workers, or promotion to positions held by Americans. In 1906 the PLM led a strike against an Anaconda subsidiary at the Cananea mine in Sonora, and made this a central issue. U.S. troops were sent across the border, and some 275 armed U.S. volunteers under the command of six Arizona Rangers temporarily occupied Cananea, before being replaced by Mexican troops. Nearly 100 workers were killed.

The PLM constituted the backbone of the "Precursor Move-

ment" of the Mexican Revolution of 1910–1920. Most of its leaders
were forced into exile in the United States between 1900 and 1910.
There they organized Mexican migrant workers, who had long
been active in the U.S. southwest, where the word "huelga" was
heard before "strike." The U.S. government and Pinkerton detec-
tives systematically harassed them, beating and jailing them or
keeping them on the run as illegal immigrants, as well as opening
their mail and coordinating intelligence operations with the Mexican government. Ricardo Flores Magón, the PLM's main leader,
who would eventually die under mysterious circumstances at Fort
Leavenworth Prison in 1922, and other Mexican political exiles
received considerable support from the Mexican communities of
the southwest. U.S. and Mexican migrant workers in the surging
anarchist and socialist movements, led by people like Emma Gold-
man and Eugene V. Debs, rallied to defense campaigns for PLM
leaders like Ricardo Flores Magón whenever they were incarcerated. The PLM's principled "internationalist" cooperation with
U.S. trade-unionist radicals like the "Wobblies" of the Industrial
Workers of the World led to spurious accusations by the Díaz government that the PLM was "anti-Mexican" or—because of its 1906
and 1908 armed revolts; subsequent military actions in Chihuahua,
Coahuila, and Veracruz; and armed liberation of Mexicali, Baja
California in January 1911—a group of "filibusterers."

In spite of its importance, the PLM lost some of its members
after declaring, in June 1908, its total commitment to an anarchist
ideology. Debs and many U.S. socialists ended their support in
early 1911 when they decided to back the revolutionary movement
of the 1910 anti-Díaz presidential candidate Francisco I. Madero, a
prominent bourgeois political figure.

The Mexican bourgeoisie became severely divided on political
questions after the onset of a depression in 1907, which had been
triggered by a Wall Street panic. Trying to stop a run on the banks
and a major credit crisis in 1908, Finance Minister Limantour
started calling in loans from *hacendados,* thereby alienating many in
the Porfiriato's political network of landlords-*rancheros-caciques.*
Food shortages caused by crop blights and the Porfiriato's increase
in agricultural exports deepened the crisis; banks were overex-
tended, more loans were called in, mineral production plummeted,
industries began to close, and unemployment quickly surpassed the
50 percent mark.

Northern financiers, industrialists, and landholders blamed
Limantour and the Científicos, as well as the senile, ingrown
character of the dictator and his entourage, for the nation's problems. Throughout his reign Díaz had been forced to grant greater

autonomy to governors in the northern states, where the elites were moving increasingly into industrial production and financial and political power. In San Louis Potosí, for example, of about twenty elite families, thirteen were active in industry, and two of these industrialists were governors for all but six years of the Porfiriato (during which time a *hacendado* held office).[10] Madero, the 1910 presidential candidate, was a northerner whose family had interests in commerce, banking, ranching, cotton production, wine distilleries, mining, refining, iron and steel, and the guayule (rubber) and textile industries. The Madero family was said to be 8 million pesos in debt to Mexican banks in 1910. The financial fraction of the bourgeoisie was firmly entrenched in the north's largest city, Monterrey. Entire northern states were practically "owned" by a few families, the most notorious case being that of Chihuahua, where the "liberal" Terrazas-Creel clique owned most of the state's cultivable land and had large investments in livestock, cotton, banking, textiles, and other manufacturing industries.

Northern agricultural production as well, particularly in the northwest, had been profitably commercialized and was based on wage labor. The termination of the wars against the Apaches had made landholders less dependent on a peasant soldiery, while rebellious Yaqui Indians in Sonora had been militarily subdued or forcibly moved to the Valle Nacional region of Oaxaca to harvest tobacco crops. Sinaloa had become a major exporter of *garbanzos* (chickpeas) and other vegetables to the U.S. market.

Much of the northern bourgeoisie got behind the Democratic Party movement of 1908–1909, which called for the presidential candidacy of General Bernardo Reyes. His early backers included future presidents Madero (1911–1913) and Venustiano Carranza (1917–1920), lawyer Luis Cabrera, agrarian reformer Andrés Molina Enríquez, Díaz's personal physician, Dr. Francisco Vázquez Gómez, and Científico theorist Manuel Calero. Díaz, who in early 1908 had told U.S. journalist James Creelman that he would not run for reelection in 1910, was torn between throwing his support to Reyes and the industrial-financial bourgeoisie or to Vice-President Ramón Corral, who represented the dictatorship's underlying political network of landlords-*caciques*. He knew that Reyes and the urban-based bourgeoisie lacked a *cacique* base capable of assuring stability, but he also knew that the old landlord-*cacique* network was less and less able to do so itself, so bankrupt had it become in the eyes of most Mexicans. He finally decided to send Reyes on a military study assignment to Europe and to accept the renomination for president himself.

At that point, most of the urban bourgeoisie threw its support to the northerner Madero. Although he was a personal friend of both Díaz and Limantour, Madero had been an early financial backer of *Regeneración*, the PLM paper, and had subsequently become critical of both the PLM and the government. He was then an ideal representative for the bourgeoisie in its hour of need. He epitomized the ingenuity and idealism of the bourgeois-democratic vision that saw civilian rule, civil law, and civil behavior—backed by adequate military force—as key components of the orderly process of "democratic" politics. He had important friends inside and outside of government, at home and abroad. Like Díaz, he was a high-ranking Freemason. His year of studying agricultural technology at the University of California at Berkeley and his brother Gustavo's ownership of stock shares in Standard Oil (which reportedly helped finance his election campaign in 1910)[11] indicated a leaning toward cooperation with the United States that could forestall further U.S. intervention. Indeed, U.S. capitalists viewed Díaz as "tilting" toward European capital in his final years in office, and the U.S. government was gradually throwing its support to Madero behind the scenes, while continuing to court Díaz.

Madero's 1910 presidential campaign was based on Díaz's old slogan, "Effective Suffrage and No Re-election." In the few campaign speeches he was allowed to make before Díaz had him arrested and thrown in jail, Madero opposed the Liberal Reform laws on the grounds that they violated political freedom and that religious interests were no longer a threat. He made only vague promises to the peasants, while informing workers that there would be no reductions in work hours or increases in wages but "only freedom, because freedom will let you conquer bread . . . the people do not ask for bread, they ask for freedom."[12] The PLM considered Madero's electoral politics "a crime, because the malady that afflicts the Mexican people cannot be cured by removing Díaz and putting in his place another man. . . . Our electoral ballots will be bullets from our guns."[13] On October 5, 1910, Madero escaped San Luis Potosí's prison and fled to exile in the United States, from where he issued his call for armed insurrection known as the "Plan of San Luis Potosí." He set the date of November 20 for a national uprising. He was well aware that his call might unleash a revolutionary tide that would topple not only the Porfiristas but the entire bourgeois state apparatus and replace it with a proletarian (peasant-worker) one. The PLM, the only experienced and organized political-military party on the scene, was advocating precisely that.

Indeed, the response to Madero's call for an armed uprising was instantaneous. In the numerous armed battles launched against the dictatorship, the most significant military forces in the north came from the ranks of the PLM and the armed groups led by Chihuahua's Pascual Orozco, Jr., and (to a lesser extent) by Francisco "Pancho" Villa, while those in the south came from the peasant army led by Emiliano Zapata in Morelos. Madero was a leader without an army, sitting things out across the border. Meanwhile, PLM troops won a major battle at Casas Grandes, Chihuahua (December), and went on to capture Mexicali, Baja California (January), and Guadalupe, Chihuahua (February). In need of a military victory, Madero reentered Mexico on February 14, 1911, and went to Guadalupe, where he was given an "abrazo" by PLM commander Prisciliano G. Silva. Madero brought with him reinforcements in the form of fresh PLM troops under the command of Lázaro Gutiérrez de Lara, with whom he had struck a secret deal. Thus it was that Madero declared Silva his prisoner; Gutiérrez de Lara betrayed the PLM; and the struggle against Díaz became severely divided. Still seeking a military victory, Madero went with his armed followers to engage in battle at Casas Grandes, Chihuahua, where he was defeated (March 6). The decisive battle against Díaz's army was conducted in early May at the border city of Ciudad Juárez, Chihuahua, and was won by Orozco's troops, many of whom had fought side by side with PLM soldiers in earlier engagements.

These military losses forced Díaz to arrange a compromise with Madero, enshrined in the Ciudad Juárez peace treaties of May 17–21, 1911. The deal allowed Díaz to go into exile, named an interim president, and provided for new presidential elections in October, which Madero would handily win. But this would not bring peace, bread, or freedom. The Mexican Revolution of 1910–1920 was just beginning.

The 1910–1920 Revolution, Class War, and Imperialism's Intervention

One of Madero's first acts after the Ciudad Juárez peace treaties was to order the various revolutionary guerrilla bands and armies, including his own, to turn in their weapons. Many, trusting Madero's assurances that the national army would return to the barracks now that "democratic elections" had been scheduled, obeyed the order. Sensing the opportunity presented by a disarmed people, diehard followers of Díaz proceeded to initiate efforts at launching an armed counterrevolution. For his part, Zapata met with Madero in the summer and explained that his peasant troops could not lay down their arms without assurances that there would take place an agrarian reform. Madero said that once the arms were turned in, an agrarian reform could begin. In August 1911, the army's General Victoriano Huerta was sent to Morelos to oversee the Zapatistas' delivery of arms. Once most of the peasants had tossed their weapons into a pile, Huerta ordered his troops to open fire on them. In response to this treachery, and to the lack of any signs of agrarian reform, Zapata issued his "Plan de Ayala," calling for continuation of the revolution until land was returned to the peasants and a regime of social justice introduced. From this point in November 1911 forward, the class war of armed peasants and workers against the bourgeoisie was unleashed in all its fury.

In the south, the Zapatistas rearmed and assaulted major centers of sugar production, commerce, communications, and government administration. To the north, the PLM, which had never turned in its arms, took over northern Baja California and governed it largely on anarchist principles from January to June 1911, but, because of internal splits and the drawing away of key leadership to Baja, lost momentum in the rest of the nation. Other, larger mass movements were emerging to challenge Madero and the bourgeoisie. For example, in March 1912 Orozco declared his revolutionary opposition to Madero with a program incorporating many of the class demands of the PLM (the Terrazas-Creel clique opportunistically backed Orozco). And there were other class-based uprisings throughout the nation.

The driving social force of the revolutionary upheaval of 1911– 1916 was the rural peasantry and proletariat. To the dispossessed peasant, small *ranchero,* Indian *comunero,* or rural proletarian, the enemy—the landlord-capitalist—was still very much in evidence. To these people the solution was simple: take back the land and water, seize the mills, provide for self, family, and community rather than for the boss. And this is what thousands of *jornaleros* and peasants did. Their actions sparked a prairie fire of revolt, as peasant armies, federal troops (the *federales* that became so maligned in the popular folksongs of this period), and even *cacique-* led bands spread across Mexico in a veritable dance of bullets.

The most active revolutionaries among the peasantry were the landless wage-labor workers and *jornaleros,* rather than the share-croppers, tenant farmers, or allotment-holding farmers. The latter, like the poorest of the former, were prevented by the practical problems of feeding themselves and their families from practicing revolution on a regular basis. Some of those most under a *hacendado's* authority (the so-called *acasillados*) did not even hear of the events shaking Mexico. And if an army—revolutionary or counterrevolutionary—drove out the previous ruling elements, the *acasillados* still had to obey, work, and survive—and follow whichever general was in power. The rural proletarians (regular wage workers, *jornaleros*, and migrant farmworkers), on the other hand, did not have this problem. As agrarian-reform advocate Luis Cabrera explained to the Chamber of Deputies on December 3, 1912:

> The rural population needs to complement its salary (which is abysmally low); if it had *ejidos*, half a year it would work as *jornaleros* and the other half it would devote to cultivating and harvesting the *ejidos* on its own account. Not having *ejidos*, it is forced to live six months off day wages and the other six it takes up the rifle and becomes Zapatista.[14]

Women revolutionary *soldaderas* accompanied their menfolk on the long military campaigns, and many children were known to take up the gun. It was a time of fierce loyalties, mixed with much abuse of women, in which a curious combination of license and respect emerged for these "women in arms." An ex-tortilla maker named "La China" led an entire combat unit of Zapata's army; women were also numerous in the "red batallions," made up of urban workers who joined the civil-war battles, after the revolutionary forces divided in 1915.

Many of the battles were encounters between disciplined armies; others were guerrilla actions. The toll in human life and suffering was incredible. An estimated 1 to 2 million Mexicans lost their lives between 1910 and 1920, almost 10 percent of the population; many others were wounded. A large number of deaths resulted from inadequate medical care or sanitation, as well as from invoking the death penalty for captured soldiers, a precedent established in 1913 by landholder-capitalist Venustiano Carranza, the self-proclaimed "First Chief" of the loosely unified revolutionary forces fighting the man who betrayed Madero and helped mastermind his overthrow in 1913, General Victoriano Huerta.

While class war raged, Madero's "parliamentary democracy" drifted, and General Huerta became increasingly impatient with the socially unproductive debating of the Congress and the army's inability to stabilize the situation. When on February 9, 1913, dissident army officers, backed by artillery regiments and military cadets, released Bernardo Reyes and Félix Díaz, Porfirio's nephew, from prisons where they had been detained after their respective and abortive revolts of December 1911 and October 1912, Madero made the mistake of appointing Huerta to command loyalist forces. The dissident officers attacked the national palace, but were repulsed; Reyes was killed in action. There followed ten days (the *decena trágica*) of artillery bombardment and gunfire exchanges between dissidents and loyalists in Mexico City during which thousands of civilians were killed. In the midst of this bloodbath, on February 18, U.S. Ambassador Henry Lane Wilson—who had long favored U.S. business interests and clamored for repression of progressive anti-Madero revolts such as those of Zapata in the south and Orozco in the north—summoned to the American Embassy Rodolfo Reyes, son of Bernardo, Félix Díaz, and Huerta. There, they drew up the "Pact of the Embassy," designating Huerta provisional president.

That same day Huerta dispatched General Aureliano Blanquet to the national palace to arrest Madero. Within half an hour Vice President José María Pino Suárez and most of the cabinet were also placed under arrest. In the evening Huerta secured official resignations from Madero and Pino Suárez. With only five members dissenting, Congress made Minister of Foreign Relations Pedro Lascuráin president, and he in turn appointed Huerta minister of interior; he then resigned, leaving Huerta constitutionally next in line for the presidency. This he assumed shortly before midnight. Huerta's betrayal culminated three evenings later when Madero and Pino Suárez, on being transferred from the national palace to the Federal District penitentiary, were assassinated in the tradition of the *ley fuga*—murder of prisoners on the pretext of their "attempt to escape." Who gave the orders for these senseless murders remains a mystery, but the Mexican public now perceived Huerta as a "usurper" and "counterrevolutionary," not realizing that his administration would introduce more social reforms than Madero's had ever attempted.

Most Mexicans responded to the apparent counterrevolution by taking up arms to oppose it. Peasants and workers rushed to join such already established revolutionary contingents as that of Zapata in the south or to new units such as that being led by Francisco "Pancho" Villa in the north. A large, roughhewn working man with a strong streak of *machismo* and its corresponding values of valor, loyalty, and violence, Villa had been a fanatical admirer of Madero ever since the martyred president had helped save his life in 1912, when General Huerta had almost had Villa executed. Villa welcomed anyone into his camp who could claim Maderista credentials, and his army and staff absorbed much of the Madero government bureaucracy. (Subsequently famous novelist Martín Luis Guzmán served as a secretary in Villa's camp.) Others joined the armies of ex-Porfirian governor Venustiano Carranza in the north and prosperous *garbanzo* farmer and exporter Alvaro Obregón in the northwest. The Carranza-Obregón forces became known as the Constitutionalists, in symbolic representation of their leaders' defense of constitutional norms and democratic legitimacy. For a brief time, Mexico's revolutionary forces, led mainly by Zapata, Villa, Carranza, and Obregón, united in a military campaign against the common enemy: Huerta and the detested *federales*.

Huerta turned immediately to the British for aid—Lord Cowdray, chairman of El Aguila, floated a loan that helped keep him in power. Huerta was leery of the new U.S. president, Woodrow Wilson, who assumed power at about the same time. Wilson returned the disdain, claiming the United States had to stand up for democracy and assist the anti-Huerta forces. What was really at stake, of course, was not the competing imperialist powers' investments in democracy—their long support for Díaz belied that—but their desire to grab Mexican oil. Mexican reserves were large and production was increasing: it shot up from 10 million barrels in 1910 to almost 200 million in 1920, and by 1921 accounted for almost one-fourth of world production. The United States controlled 70 percent of Mexican oil production; Great Britain, 27 percent.

President Wilson recalled U.S. Ambassador Henry Lane Wilson and sent in his stead John Lind as his confidential agent in Mexico. Lind tried to make an accommodation with Huerta, suggesting that U.S. bankers might provide an immediate loan in exchange for new elections. Huerta, now allied with British oil interests, balked. President Wilson then withheld recognition from the Huerta regime and proceeded to establish a financial blockade and an arms embargo against Mexico. Secretary of State William Jennings Bryan cabled U.S. representatives in Mexico on November 24, 1913, that U.S. policy was "to isolate General Huerta entirely, to cut him off from foreign sympathy and aid and from domestic credit, whether moral or material, and to force him out," resorting, if necesssary, to "less peaceful means to put him out."[15]

Huerta's federal troops faced three separately commanded armies: Zapata's in the south, Villa's in the north, and the Constitutionalists (Carranza and Obregón). Each had distinct social characteristics and programs, and they were further separated by geographical barriers and regional differences.

Zapata emphasized "land and liberty," that is, restitution of stolen lands and water and pasture rights and the restoration of village democracy. Not that the Zapatistas lacked a proletarian consciousness—on the contrary, they seized all the means of production: fields, mills, railway stations, and distilleries. They set up liberated zones, basing themselves on communal traditions of village self-government. Zapata's was a classic "people's war," fought in guerrilla fashion, and his forces enjoyed great popular participation and support. First Díaz, then Madero, then Huerta, and eventually the Constitutionalists launched scorched-earth campaigns of terror against the Zapatistas, indiscriminately killing any civilians in their path, but so long as their charismatic leader lived, the Zapatistas resisted the demoralization that these barbarous attacks sought to provoke.

In the north, Villa's forces were less homogeneous than those of Zapata. In addition to former bureaucrats of the Madero regime, who helped administer the immense expanses of territory liberated by Villa's army, the top ranks of Villa's followers included more cowboy caudillos *(vaqueros* or *charros), rancheros,* and petty bourgeois storekeepers than it did communal peasant farmers; the foot soldiers were usually miners, migrant farmworkers, railway workers, and the unemployed. The aims of the Villistas were thus more worker-oriented or petty bourgeois than they were pro-peasant: as foremen of large estates, *vaqueros,* or independent ranchers, cowboy caudillos had commanded peasants but had not experienced land hunger at first hand. Workers were more interested in gainful employment than in farming for themselves. Thus lands seized by Villa's army were held by the state, not given to the peasants. Villa expropriated many of the landholdings of the Terrazas-Creel clique, but other of their industrial-financial interests survived and they were able to reassert their power after 1920, when they recognized the new "revolutionary" state and intermarried with some of the "new revolutionaries" (today, the Creels are a leading industrial group). Further, most U.S. properties in Villista areas paid taxes to Villa (including American Smelting and Refining and those owned by William Randolph Hearst) and were thus protected from the peasants: Villa depended on the United States for guns and ammunition, obtained in exchange for cattle and cash.

The combined Constitutionalist forces of Carranza and Obregón included many intermediate-class professionals and prosperous farmers, *rancheros,* and even landlords who shared the class background and goals of the leadership. Many proletarian and peasant foot soldiers also joined their ranks, believing such propagandistic promises as the one Carranza made before a rally in Sonora on September 23, 1913: "Once the armed conflict called for by the Plan de Guadalupe [program of the Constitutionalist revolution against Huerta] is over, the formidable and majestic social struggle will have to begin, the class war, whether we ourselves want it or not."[16]

Obregón realized the importance of being open to the Left and rallied around him many left-leaning intellectuals and nationalists with strong Jacobin tendencies. Carranza was shrewd enough to take Obregón's advice and decree progressive labor and agrarian reform laws in late 1914 and early 1915, which helped attract further proletarian support. He did not, however, wish to form an open alliance with the working class.

Obregón, on the other hand, understood that such an alliance was necessary if the political project of the modernizing industrial-financial fraction of the bourgeoisie was to succeed. The socialist and anarcho-syndicalist ideas of the urban workers' Casa del Obrero Mundial (House of the World Worker)—which was closed down by Huerta in May 1914—boded no evil for him. He believed that socialism could be an instrument of stabilization and regularization, permitting the ongoing accumulation of capital by capitalists. As he put it, "The principal purpose of socialism is to extend a hand to the downtrodden in order to establish a greater equilibrium between capital and labor."[17] In other words, it could be coopted for other than its avowed purpose.

Another Constitutionalist radical of the time was Salvador Alvarado, a former owner of a small business in Sonora who introduced socialistic measures as governor of Yucatán in 1915–1917. A statement he made in 1919 further illuminates the bourgeois character of the Constitutionalists' "socialism":

> Today there is a formula for the collective good, namely, the socialization of the state . . . [under a socialized state] the capitalist will be able to dedicate himself to business in peace, without the anxieties that today disorder his hours. Capital, which is only accumulated labor, will be in perfect accord with real and effective labor, because each needs the other as an unquestionable basis for the good of all.[18]

In Yucatán, Alvarado was backed by 7,000 troops, peons whose debts were pardoned, workers who were allowed to organize, and second-level *hacendados* who were appointed to administer the state agency that regulated the henequen market and prospered from the threefold increase in world henequen prices stimulated by the outbreak of World War I. Money from henequen contracts with International Harvester also helped finance the Constitutionalists' war chest.

The Constitutionalists readily obtained financial and military aid from the U.S. government and U.S. oil interests determined to replace the pro-British Huerta with a government sympathetic to them. Worried that Huerta's occasional social reforms might prolong his stay in power, President Wilson lifted the arms embargo on February 3, 1914, in order to rush in military aid for the anti-Huerta forces, particularly Carranza and Obregón. At the same time, U.S. oil tycoon Edward L. Doheny was providing Carranza with nearly $1 million in credit and military equipment and refusing to pay taxes to Huerta. In April 1914, claiming that it had to prevent a German munitions ship from landing and delivering cargo to Huerta,[19] the United States sent Marines and bluejackets (sailors) to occupy Veracruz. Hundreds of Mexicans perished during the invasion. Attempting to mediate the U.S.-Huerta conflict, Argentina, Brazil, and Chile persuaded the two governments to send delegates to an international conference at Niagara Falls. President Wilson wired his delegates that should the conferees fail to reach a pro-democracy solution, "then the settlement must come by arms, either ours or those of the Constitutionalists."[20] All these activities, but particularly the U.S. occupation of Veracruz, had grave economic consequences for Huerta: as Edith O'Shaughnessy, married to the U.S. chargé d'affaires in Mexico City, noted at the time, "With the taking of Veracruz, through whose customs a full fourth of the total imports come, Huerta is out a million pesos a month, more or less. We are certainly isolating and weakening him at a great rate. 'Might is right.' We can begin to teach it in the schools."[21]

With Huerta thus cut off from needed revenues and military supplies, all his enemies began converging on Mexico City, with Zapata and Obregón in a race to see who could seize the seat of national power first. In light of Huerta's transfer of troops and munitions from Mexico City's northern approaches toward Veracruz in the east, in anticipation of a possible U.S. military advance on the capital, the U.S. invasion of Veracruz had the effect of allowing Obregón to beat Zapata in the race for Mexico City. Blaming President Wilson for his troubles, Huerta resigned on July 8, 1914.

The U.S. invasion redounded to the advantage of the Constitutionalist camp in other ways. Carranza became an outspoken champion of "throwing out the Yankee invaders" and "national sovereignty." When representatives of all the anti-Huerta forces met in October 1914 at the Aguascalientes Convention to debate the future of the Revolution, their loose alliance fell apart, leaving two governments claiming power: that of the convention, backed by Zapata and Villa, and that of the Constitutionalists' "First Chief" Carranza, backed by various revolutionary generals, among whom Obregón stood out. The U.S.-occupied Veracruz area became a sanctuary for Carranza, who pulled his forces back into the city to regroup and take over control of the customs houses. Carranza "saved face" by claiming credit for the U.S. troop withdrawal that promptly followed.

The Aguascalientes Convention proved a tumultuous affair. Villista and Zapatista soldiers lined the packed convention hall with guns at the ready. Debaters from all camps outlined positions that well reflected the Constitutionalists' bourgeois biases and the Zapatistas' identification with the downtrodden. At one point, former PLM militant Antonio Díaz Soto y Gama, a radical lawyer high up in Zapata's group of advisers, threw the convention into wild confusion by crumpling the Mexican flag in his fist and asserting that it symbolized "the lie of history" since "our independence was no independence for the native race, but for the criollos alone," a sensational challenge that brought leveled pistols before his chest.[22]

The class lines separating the Zapata-Villa forces from the Constitutionalists remained foremost in the minds of the "Centaur of the North," as Villa had been called by the bourgeois press, and the "Attila of the South," as Zapata had been described. In December 1914 their followers, many of whom had met for the first time at the Aguascalientes Convention, set up a meeting between them at Xochimilco on the southern outskirts of Mexico City. Observers recalled how nervous each man seemed. But mention of middle-class Constitutionalist leaders triggered a sudden dialogue:

Villa: "They are men who have always slept on soft pillows."
Zapata: "Those *cabrones!* As soon as they see a little chance, well, they want to take advantage of it to line their own pockets! Well, to hell with them!"[23]

Zapata and Villa agreed to fight the class enemy—represented in their eyes by the Constitutionalists. Each returned to his respective stronghold to prepare for the assault that was to follow.

Obregón and Carranza were similarly mobilizing for civil war. Realizing the need to split off urban workers from their previous allies, the peasants, Obregón finally convinced Carranza of the need to accept worker support. The key was the 50,000-strong Casa del Obrero Mundial, based in Mexico City but with regional affiliates spreading throughout the nation. It included industrial workers in shoe factories, printshops, breweries, smelters, mills, and various small and medium-size industries, and it had led strikes in urban areas. The Casa had moved from its anarchist ideology into a medley of ideas combining anarcho-sindicalism with the many strands of socialism then being espoused in Mexico.

In early 1915, Obregón offered Casa members food, money, buildings, printing presses, and supplies, and agreed to meet their basic demands. In exchange, he asked that the Casa organize "red battalions" to help fight Villa and Zapata. Casa debates on the offer were tempestuous, but in February the majority finally accepted it—even while realizing that this decision would pit industrial workers against peasants and workers in the revolutionary armies.

The decision—a turning point in the Revolution that sealed the doom of the peasant-worker war against the bourgeoisie—was the result of several factors. The Casa was physically isolated and desperately needed supplies if it was to continue its work. In addition, strong cultural differences separated urban workers from peasants, and Casa members were not favorably impressed by the Zapatistas' seeming religiosity, their carrying the banner of the Virgin of Guadelupe through Mexico City's streets, or by the Villistas' ransacking of homes. In later explaining his own role in opting for the red batallions, which he helped organize and lead, Casa member Rosendo Salazar pointed out that in difficult conditions, the Casa had allowed itself to be "bought out" by Obregón,[24] thereby undermining its previous autonomy and leading to its suppression in August 1916.

But for the moment the alliance between the urban working class and the bourgeoisie gave urban workers a new opportunity to spread their movement and consolidate their position. The Casa's six red battalions numbered 7,000 workers and played an important part in the string of Constitutionalist military victories in 1915. Villa was forced back to northern Chihauhua, near the U.S. border, where his army, reduced in size, was isolated. A wedge was driven between the Villistas and the Zapatistas, who were unable to help Villa from their Morelos stronghold hundreds of miles to the south. In addition, some of the red battalions moved against Zapata, failing as others had done before them to put an end to Zapata's guerrilla hit-and-run attacks but nonetheless helping to keep them restricted to the south.

This opportune alliance between the urban working class, with its leftist ideas and record of militant strikes against capital, and the enlightened bourgeoisie as represented by Obregón, with its willingness to make concessions to the proletariat when necessary, broke the back of the heretofore relatively unified workers' and peasants' thrust of the Revolution. From 1915 to the present, organized labor in Mexico has remained closely associated with the state, and the state has put forward a rhetoric and inconsistent practice of what Arnaldo Córdova has called the "politics of masses."[25]

A typical expression of this new politics was the swift settlement of a Casa-sponsored general strike in May 1916, when the government granted most of the workers' demands. One of labor's leaders signing the agreement, who derived the corresponding lesson that close cooperation with the state was in labor's interest, was Luis Morones, who in 1918 founded the Confederación Regional Obrera Mexicana (CROM), a pillar of support for the bourgeois governments of the 1920s. Yet in February 1916 the Casa's headquarters had been closed down by the government, its regional directors jailed, its affiliates repressed. The "politics of masses" was obviously one of an iron fist in a velvet glove.

This was shown in the course of the Casa's next general strike, called in the Federal District to protest a fifty-fold devaluation of the peso, which had hit hard at workers' real wages and ability to buy food. The strike lasted from July 31 to August 2, 1916, and was ruthlessly crushed by troops acting under state orders. The 90,000 members of the Casa shut down all normal activities in Mexico City, but were attacked, jailed, and dispersed. "First Chief" Carranza dusted off an 1862 Juárez statute that decreed the death penalty for anyone "disturbing the public order," and what remained of the strike's momentum dissipated.

As the class lines separating Carranza from Villa and Zapata became clear, the United States provided Carranza's faction with arms and, in October 1915, granted its government diplomatic recognition. As U.S. Secretary of State Robert Lansing wrote in his private notes, Carranza was the least of the evils and could be won over with dollar diplomacy, whereas the others might be more intransigent: "The real problem Carranza will have to face is financial. He has no credit; his paper money is worthless; his source of revenue uncertain; and his soldiers without pay. We can help him in this."[26]

Mexico had been in default on its bonds—most of which were held by U.S., British, and French investors—since 1913. The U.S. State Department huddled with Thomas W. Lamont, senior partner of J. P. Morgan and Co., investment bankers, and worked out a plan for an international bankers' committee to handle the negotiations with Mexico that would reschedule debt payments and work out future loan guarantees. According to instructions from the State Department, the bankers' committee was to be "under the leadership of American bankers and the policy of the United States Government regarding Mexico [shall] be the dominating influence in the operations of this group." As Leon J. Canova of the State Department's division of Mexican affairs put it, "We hold the whip handle at the present time. We are the bankers of the world."[27] President Wilson, noting that "the masters of the government of the U.S. are the combined capitalists and manufacturers of the U.S.," was more blunt in recognizing U.S. emergence as a world imperialist power:

> Do you know the significance of this single fact that within the last year or two we have . . . ceased to be a debtor nation and have become a creditor nation? . . . We have got to finance the world in some

important degree, and those who finance the world must understand it and rule it with their spirits and with their minds.[28]

The United States cut off arms to Villa and Zapata. Its support had never been great, but it had momentarily had the effect of blurring the differences among the anti-Huerta factions. For one thing, many workers and salaried peasants, who had joined Villa's army because of their own class demands, were treated simply as paid soldiers, and this had the effect of converting many class-conscious proletarians into just one more professional army growing accustomed to taking orders. In retaliation against the U.S. action, Villa launched attacks on U.S. citizens in Mexico. One of these brought him across the border into Columbus, New Mexico, on March 9, 1916. The United States responded with a large-scale military buildup along the border, followed by a 6,000 man invasion force led by General John J. Pershing that penetrated deep into Mexican territory. Villa's guerrilla tactics ran circles around the frustrated general, and the U.S. invasion was a flop. The Pershing expedition pulled out of Mexico in January 1917. But its main purpose was largely accomplished: it kept Villa fighting on two fronts and made real the threat that another U.S. invasion might be launched against Zapata.

As far as the Zapatistas were concerned, the U.S. threat of armed force intimidated many of them, some of whom laid down their arms and sought amnesty from Carranza.[29] Meanwhile, a pro-Carranza agent infiltrated their ranks and on April 10, 1919, lured Zapata into a trap, in which he was ambushed and assassinated. This left the Zapatista movement divided and without a leader. Carranza suffered a similar fate in May 1920 when, after he tried to keep Obregón out of power by naming his own successor, a pro-Obregón member of his personal guard assassinated him. Villa, still isolated in the north, accepted a government peace offer and settled on a hacienda given him by the government. Assassins' bullets cut him down in 1923.

Villa's military defeats in 1915–1916 and Zapata's increasing isolation in the south made it possible for the Constitutionalists to convene a constitutional convention at Querétaro in late 1916. The constitution finally agreed to was a triumph for the liberal wing of bourgeois democracy, as the so-called Jacobin forces loyal to Obregón were able to win many, though by no means all, of the debates—the reason the document contains a number of progressive articles. For example, Article 3 severely limited the powers of the Church; Article 27 provided for agrarian reform and the nation's ownership of all minerals and subsoils, including oil; and Article 123 gave labor various guarantees, including the right to form trade unions and to conduct "legal" strikes, with arbitration boards having equal representation from workers, employers, and government. Nevertheless, the constitution vested ultimate authority in the "nation," whose only representative is the executive power of the state—the president. Thus the strong executive of the days of Juárez and Díaz became the law of the land, legitimizing the capitalist state's power to govern and control the country.

Carranza wisely signed the constitution, even though he opposed most of its progressive articles: not to accept would have meant renewed civil war. As constitutionally elected president from 1917 to 1920, he ruled with a firm hand. He failed to implement any serious agrarian reform and spent less on social measures than either Madero or Huerta had done, so that the long years of class war produced only token gains for peasants and workers, not a successful social revolution. Indeed, the results of the bloodshed were pitiful: a defeated peasantry, a crippled labor movement dependent on the state, a wounded but victorious bourgeoisie, and a paper triumph, the 1917 Constitution.

The outstanding characteristics of the Revolution of 1910–1920 were its explosive class confrontation between peasants and proletarians, on the one hand, and big landholders and capitalists on the other, and its heavy antiforeign and anti-imperialist overtones. Although the bourgeoisie was divided, with the more "modern" industrial-financial fractions trying to assert hegemony over the more oligarchic, traditional ones, this intra-class conflict was secondary to the need on the part of both to fight off the peasants and workers and prevent their defeating the class as a whole. In this sense, there was no social revolution, only a political one, and even that was less complete than is often claimed.[30]

The fact that the workers and peasants split into many warring factions only made the bourgeoisie's task easier. Nevertheless, their combined struggle, however beaten back and ultimately divided, undermined the oligarchic-capitalist state and won them rights they had previously been denied. It was their struggle that made possible the limited democratic concessions and social-political reforms that characterized the bourgeois-democratic part of the Revolution. And it was their struggle, through its repeated denunciations of foreign bourgeois overlords, that was the force behind the Revolution's nationalism and anti-imperialism. The energy of their fight prepared the terrain for the 1920–1940 reconsolidation of a capitalist state along lines conducive to a politics of masses—at first in rhetoric but eventually with controlled concessions to peasants and workers—that would no longer exclude the legitimacy of what Carranza in 1913 had termed "the class war, whether we ourselves want it or not."[31]

The Revolution also forced the bourgeoisie to share power in the new state with a number of military caudillos, regional *caciques,* labor leaders, small business owners, intellectuals, and bureaucrats—the petty bourgeoisie. Their reception of state favors, administrative posts, and the chance to forge policies favorable to a capitalist program of development reinforced traditions of corruption in high places and of eluding announced reforms (agrarian reform, labor agreements, etc.). Since these people gained status, wealth, and power by thus cooperating with, and benefiting from, the new state, a growing convergence of class interests began to occur, increasingly tying the top and middle ranks of the petty bourgeoisie to the bourgeoisie proper.

Ironically, the ideology that would legitimize this bourgeois project was that of the "glorious Mexican Revolution," particularly as embodied in Carranza's anti-imperialist statements, in the rhetoric of agrarian reform, and in the call for all Mexicans to unite and avoid renewed bloodshed. As liberalism was the ideology of the bourgeoisie in the nineteenth century, so revolution became the ideological banner legitimizing bourgeois class rule in the twentieth.

In terms of the key interests of peasants and workers, the Revolution of 1910–1920 did not succeed; nor was it aborted or "interrupted."[32] It was *defeated.* But since the revolutionary project of the proletariat was a historic one, preceding 1910 as well as following 1920, we cannot say that the workers and peasants lost the war. They lost a battle, but the war has continued, now peacefully, now violently, ever since.

This is not how the Mexican Revolution is always seen, however, and since the differences are important for understanding how future developments are interpreted, it is important to outline them here. Many authors analyze the Mexican Revolution through a lens that sees it as a true social revolution, or as one that overthrew "feudalism"; others explain the defeat of the peasants and workers as a product of their political underdevelopment, or of the lack of leadership in the form of a vanguard party. All of these interpretations are historically flawed.

For the first, there is no doubt that some bourgeois elements wished to cleanse the landscape of haciendas and debt-peonage in order to advance capitalist agriculture and "middle-size" farms, even as a few had sought to do half a century earlier. But the notion of a bourgeois revolution against feudalism oversimplifies a much more complex reality, including the actual dominance of the capitalist mode of production prior to 1900. Nor can the Revolution be reduced to one aimed at replacing "original accumulation" of capital with accumulation of capital on an extended scale, since the latter had already commenced. The Revolution simply helped eliminate obstacles to its continuation.

For the second, to say the proletariat was "underdeveloped" as a class is both condescending and distorted. Perhaps the massive penetration of foreign monopoly capital affected the so-called underdevelopment of the Mexican bourgeoisie, but it had a contrary impact insofar as the working class was concerned. It concentrated and centralized thousands upon thousands of workers in factories, mines, railyards, and mills, thereby objectively forming a modern (for its time) proletariat—not an underdeveloped one.

Subjectively, this growing proletariat expressed itself, however erratically, in a militant way and with typically proletarian ideologies (anarchism, anarcho-syndicalism, socialism, etc.). Its massive strike activities in Cananea, Puebla, San Luis Potosí, Veracruz, and elsewhere hardly reflected its underdevelopment as a class. Indeed, precisely because of its *development*, its members were often massacred, as they were when strikers were put down in Río Blanco, Orizaba, and Cananea in 1906–1907, and this same development helps explain the ferocity of the class war that became so sanguine during the 1910–1920 Revolution. Among the proletariats of the world at the start of the twentieth century, the Mexican was one of the most militant and advanced in its class outlook. Yet there were many peasants and workers whose class consciousness remained incohesive and confused. In the rural areas, the mixed consciousness of the stratified peasantry reflected the fact that many forms of economic development were combined—from large-scale capitalist agriculture with modern machinery to traditional subsistence farming. Peasants who acted to seize the means of production might thus also yearn for the restoration of their land rights.

For the third, Mexico had a vanguard political-military organization—first in the PLM (until 1911) and then in the Zapatista "army of the south." Even as the Paris Commune foreshadowed the future of proletarian power in Europe at the end of the preceding century, so the "commune of Morelos"[33] embodied the future of peasant-worker power in Latin America at the beginning of the present century. It was other factors, including the limited character of the vanguard organizations, that caused the defeat of the peasant-worker uprising. These were the peasant-worker split of 1915, geographical regionalism, personal leadership rivalries, and, not least of all, the failure of the Morelos "commune" to reach out beyond the liberated zones of the Zapatistas and offer a concrete revolutionary program—sensitive to workers' and not just peasants' demands and built on class alliances—

capable of transforming the entire social structure of Mexico. Likewise, the short-lived Aguascalientes Convention government of late 1914 and early 1915, which united the Villista and Zapatista forces, lacked a clear and specific multiclass revolutionary program. The question that arises, of course, is what would have happened during the 1911–1915 phase of the Revolution had class-conscious peasant and worker leaders actually coalesced into a vanguard party with a national revolutionary program unmarred by the anti-state and antiorganizational tenets of anarchism. For then, as more successful revolutions elsewhere in the world later confirmed, the bourgeoisie might well have been defeated in its effort to divide and control the revolutionary forces.

Finally, if these formulistic explanations of the 1910–1920 Revolution and its results are misleading, so too is the romantic belief that the class struggle today is the same as that of yesterday—the notion that the Mexican Revolution is "permanent." Without denying the historical roots of contemporary class struggle, we must recognize that Mexico has changed considerably since 1910—and even more since 1940—and that these changes are due precisely to the 1910–1920 Revolution, with all its political and partial results, and from the consequent alteration and intensification of the anti-imperialist class war during the 1920s and 1930s. The class struggle of peasants, workers, and progressive intermediate-class elements today is against a corporative capitalist state that implements a politics of masses and depends to a significant extent on the forces of imperialism (transnational corporations, international loans, etc.). Today's struggle is not the same as that of 1910–1920, when the obstacle to democracy and the well-being of the masses was an oligarchic-dictatorial state that implemented a politics of the elite.

Thus the Mexican Revolution is not permanent. Yet the class struggle continues, necessarily adjusting itself to the new conditions of the present and learning from the lessons of the past. Perhaps the most important historical lesson can be learned from the error of allowing an antagonistic division to occur between the urban working class and the rural proletariat and peasantry. Contemporary class struggle in Mexico makes use of the historical struggle of its predecessors, as it must. But in drawing inspiration from the militancy and heroism of the peasants and workers of 1910–1920, today's proletarians and peasants, like their historians and ideologues, can only err on the side of romantic historicism if they delude themselves into thinking that the earlier revolution, in its totality, provides a model or into conceiving their struggle as the linear continuation of a revolution erroneously called "permanent" or "interrupted."

4

The Roots of the Modern State, 1920–1940

Cárdenas es como el sol:
Brilla sobre todo
Pero calienta a nadie.

Cárdenas is like the sun:
He shines upon everyone
But warms no one.

—Mexican saying

From 1920 to 1940, the triumphant segments of the bourgeoisie extended their political project of reconsolidating the capitalist state along new lines and at the same time fought off rivals within their class and within the Church who were seeking to restore the old oligarchic order; they also faced challenges from peasants, workers, and intermediate-class radicals who were demanding implementation of reforms promised by the Revolution. Because of continued economic chaos and renewed power struggles among rival political figures and military caudillos, state policy until 1934 was inconsistent, at one moment economic nationalist, at yet another subservient to foreign economic interests. In spite of the chaos, the industrial-financial bourgeoisie of the north (the so-called Northern Dynasty, still influential today) gradually asserted itself into state circles. Employing a revolutionary rhetoric to coopt the masses and state repression to smash the most militant or leftist elements, they were able to begin introducing modernizing measures that would encourage a type of development favorable to the growth of monopoly capital—including state financing of the economic infrastructure, termination of unproductive haciendas; a readjustment to, or modification of, the domination of foreign capital, especially in petroleum and mining; control over peasant and worker movements; and subjugation of the reactionary wing of the Church.

This task was at first made difficult by Mexico's continued class tensions. For example, there were 1,289 strikes between 1920 and

115

1924, when the "social pact" between the urban workers' CROM and President Obregón finally took hold, guaranteeing labor peace. The split and defeat of the peasant-worker challenge of 1910–1915 and the subsequent state tutelage of labor and support for capitalism provided sufficient opportunity for various leading bourgeois elements of the Díaz period (bankers, industrialists, landlords, etc.) to recover and expand much of their economic strength. Indeed, such contemporary economic powers as the "Monterrey group" and the private Banco Nacional de México group, whose roots went back to the Porfiriato, benefited from the situation.[1] The most reactionary members of the Monterrey group, the Garza and Sada families (famed for their development of "white company unions," which to the present have kept even government-sponsored unions out of Monterrey), diversified their brewery and glass industries into banking and commerce, and by 1936 had consolidated into the VISA and FICA holding companies. The Banco Nacional de México group, headed by the Legorreta family, was less reactionary, tolerating or supporting radical social-reform measures; it helped negotiate Mexico's huge foreign debt, and in later decades helped place Mexican bonds in U.S. and European markets.

In addition, some "revolutionaries" became big capitalists during this period. Typical of the pattern was Aarón Sáenz, pioneer of today's influential "Sáenz group." Holding several cabinet posts in the governments of the 1920s, Sáenz, a former staff member of Obregón's army, expanded his construction-company interests with state aid into sugar refining, tourism, pulp and paper, food products, steel, and banking, achieving by 1970 a business empire worth $150 million.[2]

In spite of such capitalist success stories, the immediate postrevolutionary situation was one in which no major social class could assert total or clear-cut hegemony—a period characterized by what Italian Marxist Antonio Gramsci called "catastrophic equilibrium."[3] This boosted the influence of the military caudillos, who directed much of the state apparatus, enabling them to convert themselves and many of the petty bourgeois lawyers, intellectuals, and labor racketeers who joined their governments into political bureaucrats waxing fat from state favors. The capitalist structure of the economy conditioned state policies,[4] with the result that decisions were taken that facilitated capitalist development—and the corresponding enrichment of bureaucrats and caudillos, who were often able to join the ranks of the bourgeoisie on leaving government.

Foreign Interference, State Centralization, and Political Manipulation of the Class Struggle, 1920–1934

After Carranza's assassination in May 1920 by one of his own guards, a loyal Obregonista, the armies of Sonora led by Obregón, Plutarco Elías Calles, and Adolfo de la Huerta, supported by armed workers of CROM, were able to stabilize the situation sufficiently to permit the election of Obregón to a four-year presidential term. The United States, however, refused to grant the new government recognition, fearing the expropriation of its oil interests under Article 27 of the Constitution. U.S. and British oil companies were still draining the nation of its largest source of wealth, ruling Gulf Coast oil towns with their own police forces, or "white guards." Moreover, as recent archival research has shown, from 1919 to World War II the United States was drafting contingency plans for unilateral military intervention to secure access to oil resources. One version of the "Special Plan Green" (for Mexico) was over eight inches thick and, in language perhaps relevant for today, called for "protection of U.S. citizens and interests along the border; seizure of the Tampico oil and coal fields south of Eagle Pass; blockade of principal Mexican ports; advance on Mexico City from Veracruz; advances south from the border along railway lines; and occupation and replacement of U.S. troops by a native Mexican constabulary under U.S. leadership and control."[5]

Obregón assured the United States that Article 27 was not retroactive and therefore would not affect properties already granted to foreign oil interests, but Washington wanted the guarantee in writing. Thomas W. Lamont, a member of the international bankers' committee established during the Revolution, helped pave the way for a settlement by negotiating an agreement with the Obregón government concerning Mexico's external debt, estimated to be three times what it had been in 1911 (not counting an additional $1 billion in private foreign claims). Finally, in 1923, the two countries signed the Bucareli Agreements, which reaffirmed the nonretroactive clause Obregón had applied to Article 27 and obliged Mexico to pay compensation for damage to U.S. property incurred during the Revolution. The United States promptly followed with diplomatic recognition.

This proved convenient for Obregón, whose power was being threatened by rebellious generals incensed at his cost-saving cuts in the army's budget and nominally led by his former treasury minister, Adolfo de la Huerta. Igniting the revolt was Obregón's choice of his minister of interior, fellow Sonoran Constitutionalist general and ex-schoolmaster Plutarco Elías Calles, to run for president in the 1924 elections (the Constitution barred Obregón from succeeding himself). Fearing that Calles was a genuine radical, many conservatives, *hacendados*, and Catholic leaders took de la Huerta's side, as did some intermediate-class democrats shocked at the personalist and arbitrary character of the presidential succession. A number of nationalists critical of the Bucareli Agreements and some independent labor organizations unattached to the Obregón-CROM alliance also joined the de la Huerta revolt—many workers were growing resentful of the strong-arm tactics of CROM's corrupt labor boss Luis Morones, who routinely ordered the assassination of rival labor leaders while protecting himself in a bullet-proof Cadillac.

For a few months, battles raged between rival military forces, costing the lives of 7,000 Mexicans. Three things tipped the military balance to Obregón and saved his government: U.S.-supplied war matériel; the support of militant peasants, whose interests were represented in parliament by the Partido Nacional Agrarista (led by people like former Zapata brain-truster Díaz Soto y Gama); and the support of CROM, which formed peasant and worker brigades to help crush the revolt. The United States further intervened on Obregón's side by sending a cruiser to blockade the port of Tampico and prevent the anti-Obregón forces from receiving arms from unnamed external sources. On June 12, 1925, Secretary of State Frank B. Kellogg made clear what the price for this was:

> It must remain very clear that this Government will continue maintaining the present government in Mexico only so long as it protects American lives and the rights of Americans and lives up to its international agreements and obligations. The Mexican government now stands in judgment before the world.[6]

Although de la Huerta's revolt was defeated and the Bucareli Agreements were presumably still in effect, the oil issue was not resolved. Calles was elected in 1924 and proceeded to try to legitimize his power by appealing to nationalism and ordering oilfield owners to exchange their titles for fifty-year leases, dating from the time of acquisition—a clear violation of the Bucareli Agreements. The oil magnates clamored for U.S. military intervention. But U.S. public opinion was lukewarm after the military humiliation Villa had dealt Pershing and in light of the more recent Teapot Dome scandals, which had given a bad name to such leading U.S. oil figures in Mexico as Doheny and Albert B. Fall. Moreover, after the bloodshed of World War I, the United States was not anxious to embark on another military involvement. It sought more diplomatic means to checkmate Calles.

Thus in 1927 President Calvin Coolidge dispatched a new ambassador to Mexico, Dwight Morrow of J. P. Morgan and Company. Morrow was an astute diplomat. He outfitted his home in Cuernavaca with Mexican handicrafts and commissioned the prominent muralist Diego Rivera to paint a fresco in the local town hall, thereby appealing to Mexican national pride.[7] (In this he was taking a page from the Mexican government's own book, for in the early 1920s Minister of Education José Vasconcelos had subsidized a tremendous mural, sculpting, and literary renaissance that helped legitimize the new state and its nationalist rhetoric even while successive governments were failing to implement more than token agrarian reform and were gradually reasserting the class oppression of the past.) Morrow and Lamont, old business partners, made an effective team. Finance Minister Alberto Pani had set up the Banco de México in 1925 and encouraged talk of controls on foreign capital. Pani explained that this represented no "utopian socialistic leveling" but was rather intended to stimulate private enterprise and the "formation and encouragement of an autonomous middle class."[8] The Lamont-Pani Agreement of 1925 set the spirit for renewed U.S.-Mexico cooperation in capitalist development. The foreign bankers accepted the new bank while Mexico promised to return the railways, partially nationalized in the final years of the Díaz dictatorship, to private management—a clear signal that the new state bank was supportive of private enterprise. By 1926 foreign companies once more dominated mining, metallurgy, the textile industry, and major areas of commerce.[9]

Ambassador Morrow huddled frequently with Calles, not only to negotiate the oil issue but to discuss related issues of economic development. The results were swift and revealing. In 1927 the Mexican Supreme Court declared the fifty-year-oil-lease legislation unconstitutional, ruling that foreigners who had acquired subsoil rights before 1917 were entitled to perpetual concessions. In 1928–1929 Mexico's foreign debt was renegotiated on amicable terms.[10] Morrow and Calles clearly agreed that domestic stability, guarantees for private property and investment, and cooperation between foreign and Mexican capital represented the key to Mexico's future prosperity. Calles proceeded to assert publicly that Mexico's interests "can be satisfied only within the limits set up by the present so-called capitalist system" and to promise "to safeguard the interests of foreign capitalists who invest in Mexico." By 1930, he was announcing that the previous decade's limited experiments in agrarian reform were a "failure."[11]

While U.S. and Mexican financial and political elites thus
wheeled and dealed, militant proletarian pressure from below continued. CROM, which played a significant role in the strikes of the
early 1920s, organized the Mexican Labor Party and promised that
it would be transformed into a "class party." It sought state guarantees of a minimum wage, health care, safe working conditions,
vacations, and so on. Then in 1925, it proposed legislation—which
eventually became incorporated into the Labor Law of 1931 still
largely in effect today—that gave the state a deciding vote on the
labor-conflict arbitration boards and thus gave it the power to permit or deny a strike request and to oversee, as CROM's proposal
put it, "an equilibrium between the diverse factors of production,
which harmonizes the rights of workers and employers." This
marked a turning point in CROM's relationship with the state, as
established labor leaders now no longer took seriously the idea of
forming a class party. Through its "social pact" with the state,
CROM established not a class party but class collaboration. In return for its agreement to put the brakes on strikes, it was allowed to
participate in cabinets and received government license for its unionizing activities. The number of strikes declined precipitously,
from 300 a year in the early 1920s to 71 in 1925 to only 12 in 1928.
In addition, CROM looked the other way—and sometimes even
actively assisted—when the government repressed independent
labor actions, such as the 1926 strike of railroad workers, among
whom communists were strong.

In the countryside, the peasants organized themselves into unions and agrarian leagues, constantly pressuring the state for
agrarian reform and for arms to defend themselves against the
hacendados' hired gunmen. Obregón and Calles sought to bring the
peasants under their tutelage by granting the demands of some of
the more militant villages and by tying them into a system of state
credits for seeds, fertilizers, and tools. On the other hand, they
launched repeated attacks on more independent peasant groups
led by socialists, communists, and anarcho-syndicalists, such as the
League of Agrarian Communities in Veracruz.

More significant than these occasional concessions to the peasantry, however, were those that aided the development of an agrarian
and commercial bourgeoisie. Commercial *hacendados,* particularly
those producing for export, were protected from agrarian-reform
legislation and favored by credit policies. To move militant peasants away from these capitalist operations, the state encouraged
"colonization"—the establishment of new small and medium-size
farms in previously uncultivated areas. Occasionally a nonproduc-
tive hacienda was broken up, the peasant beneficiaries usually be-

ing less militant as a result. In 1926, the state established an agrarian credit bank, an ejidal credit bank, and an irrigation commission, all of which favored private landholders, large and small, and encouraged the growth of the agrarian bourgeoisie—augmented by former army officers or civil servants rewarded for their services with state-distributed lands.

Many peasants recognized the manipulation and deception being practiced by the state's bureaucrats. Those in the Bajío region west and north of Mexico City grew particularly distrustful. The Church, long opposed to agrarian reform of any kind, stirred them up against the "communists" in government. Many became soldiers in the "Cristero Revolt" of 1926–1929, led by enraged clerics dissatisfied with Calles's enforcement of anticlerical provisions of the Constitution, especially obligatory secular education (Article 3). Others took up arms to help the government put down the revolt, which was not ended until Ambassador Morrow intervened to negotiate a settlement easing the enforcement of the anticlerical measures. But the renewed national hysteria on the question of church-state relations ended the role of one dominant figure of the period—in 1928, shortly after being elected president, Obregón was assassinated by an obscure Catholic fanatic.[12]

In the midst of these upheavals, Calles was the only figure commanding sufficient national prestige to maintain the relative political stability that he and Obregón had introduced in 1924. Unable to succeed himself as president, he ruled behind the scenes, a wealthy and powerful man whose abuse of power transformed him into one of the nation's largest landholders. After Obregón's assassination, Congress appointed a Calles supporter, lawyer Emilio Portes Gil, former governor of the northern state of Tamaulipas, to the presidency until new elections could be called in 1929. To further stabilize the situation, Calles and his backers organized early in 1929 the National Revolutionary Party (PNR—today's PRI), the first national political party. Claiming to represent "the Revolution," and all social forces and factions, the PNR was able to draw together most rival parties, military officers, and caudillos—to give cohesion to the political, civilian, and military bureaucracies.

From this point forward, the "official" political party of Mexico would control all national elections and run the central government. For example, an obscure PNR party functionary named Pascual Ortiz Rubio won the presidential election of 1929 against the more experienced and much better known José Vasconcelos—who ran under the rubric of the National Anti-Re-electionist Party—by the incredible margin of 1,948,848 to 110,979. Ortiz Rubio governed until 1932, when he dared to disagree with Calles on minor policy questions and was forced to resign. He was succeeded by millionaire banker Abelardo Rodríguez (1932–1934), a more faithful Calles puppet. Indeed, the entire 1928–1934 period during which the PNR political machine became entrenched was known as the "Maximato" after Calles's unofficial title of "Jefe Máximo."

But the central state, despite its increasing power, still faced problems with workers and peasants dissatisfied with the tactics of corrupt leaders and state bureaucrats in coopting and disciplining them. In 1926, Calles had warned militant independent unions to fall into line with the new reality of "official" labor unions under state tutelage ("The advancement of industry and the actual functions of the state," he had declared, "impose certain obligations and consecrate specific rights for labor and capital")[13]—and the pact with CROM was also supposed to keep the peace. But in 1928 CROM, seeking to face up to its class failures and win back disillusioned members who were departing in droves, withdrew from the pact, and in 1929 the state retaliated by cutting its funds and briefly throwing support to some of the revolutionary-left unions. Armed battles soon erupted between these and CROM. The government, satisfied at seeing CROM's strength thus reduced, now acted as Carranza had done in 1916, turning against the leftist unions in a ruthless campaign of goon-squad attacks and repression. In more than a few instances, communist and anarcho-syndicalist leaders were murdered. Thus, although unionization was growing and the onset of the world depression was placing workers in ever more difficult economic and political conditions leading to increased radicalization, the stepped-up state repression meant that the number of officially recognized strikes did not pass 60 until 1934 (when there were 202). On the other hand, the number of documented "labor conflicts" tripled between 1929 and 1933.

Within CROM, which despite its decline still accounted for a majority of the unions, a "radical" wing emerged under the leadership of Vicente Lombardo Toledano, who had been active in the teachers' strikes of the 1920s. Although he opposed the Communists—blaming them for introducing "politics" into the "apolitical" labor-organizing drive—Lombardo Toledano claimed to be a "Marxist" and advocated an eventual "socialist transformation of the bourgeois regime." But, he advised CROM followers in 1932, "We cannot proclaim or praise the dictatorship of the proletariat . . . because we are living during a period of organized capitalism."[14] Morones attacked Lombardo Toledano, who reluctantly resigned from CROM, taking many militants with him. In October 1933 Lombardo Toledano's dissidents met in a national labor convention to found the Confederation of Workers and Peasants of Mexico (CGOCM).

Communists, other leftists, and Lombardo Toledano's CGOCM (which by 1934 included over half of the nation's organized workers) showed particular strength in such basic heavy industries as mining, petroleum, electricity, textiles, and railroads. Even as Morones had earlier emerged as the new "revolutionary" state's alternative to the radicals of the Casa del Obrero Mundial, so Lombardo Toledano now began to emerge as a potential state ally and alternative to the renewed labor militancy of the early 1930s—in which he himself had played an outstanding role.

The rural proletariat, Mexico's most numerous class, also stepped up its demands for reform—at the very time Calles and Morrow were seeking to cut back social welfare expenditures in order to reduce the budget deficit. The suffering of the peasants and workers intensified in 1931 when Mexico went off the gold standard and the value of the peso declined, to the advantage of U.S. capitalists. In 1932–1933, the Communist-influenced League of Agrarian Communities in Veracruz was severely attacked; its peasant militia was disarmed. By 1934, peasants and workers were at a boiling point.

The Presidency of Cárdenas, Intensification of Class Struggle, and the Corporativist Base of the Modern State, 1934–1940

The escalation of class struggle in the early 1930s was in part a desperate response by workers and peasants to conditions generated by the worldwide depression. Depending on the United States for 69 percent of its imports and 60 percent of its exports (mainly raw materials, minerals, and agricultural products), Mexico suffered badly from the effects of the sudden slowdown in U.S. economic activity. The number of Mexican unemployed, mostly laid-off workers, tripled between 1929 and 1933. For those who were lucky enough to work, the minimum wage did not cover even a third of the average family's basic necessities. In addition, the U.S. government blamed Mexican migrant workers for the high unemployment plaguing the U.S. work force, rounding up and deporting more than 300,000 workers and their families, thereby aggravating Mexico's unemployment and social unrest.[15]

Under such difficult circumstances, the ruling PNR held its party convention at Querétaro in December 1933. There it entertained recommendations for social and economic reform advanced by younger party leaders anxious to step into positions occupied by aging members of the post-1920 political elite. These "young Turks" rewrote the Six-Year Plan, which Calles had submitted in an attempt to shape the policies of the next president to be nominated at the convention. Overall, the rewritten plan emphasized reducing Mexico's dependence on foreign markets and mineral and agricultural exports, promoting agrarian reform and small and medium-size industry, and developing Mexican enterprises rather than foreign ones (including a national oil company). Outgoing President Abelardo Rodríguez, a tool of Calles' political machine, found it expedient to implement some of the progressive parts of the Six-Year Plan before leaving office, as in the case of the 1933 minimum-wage bill.

Following Calles' advice, the convention delegates nominated for the presidency a respected and socially progressive candidate, General Lázaro Cárdenas, a brigadier general during the 1910–1920 Revolution and governor of Michoacán from 1928 to 1932. Calles had little doubt that he could control the forty-year-old Cárdenas the way he had controlled previous presidents. After all, as minister of war in early 1933 had not Cárdenas done his bidding in ordering the disarming of Veracruz's peasant militia? (In doing so, Cárdenas practically assured his nomination for president, since his chief rival's social base was among Veracruz's militant peasants.)[16] As a state governor, Cárdenas had established a model for his presidential campaign: he had walked among Michoacán's people, listening to their grievances and implementing a modest agrarian reform; he had encouraged the development of peasant and labor organizations and had opened one hundred new rural schools. In his presidential campaign, he promised to do the same on a nationwide scale. In a major speech at the end of his campaign, he sanctioned collective bargaining, an increase in the minimum wage, renewal of agrarian reform, and other welfare measures commonly recommended in more industrialized capitalist countries at the time. Emphasizing the protection of private property, he said he would favor small private landholdings over communal ones. He also acknowledged the existence of the class struggle—"an essential within the capitalist regime"—and promised support for the working class.

Calles had thus already accepted the idea of reform. Moreover, a reformist government had taken power in the United States under President Franklin D. Roosevelt, whose ambassador to Mexico, Josephus Daniels, arrived before Cárdenas took office and talked of social reform, education, the welfare of the masses, and Mexico's indisputable right to develop an ideology of social revolution. The 1934 silver purchase program, which enabled the United States to buy huge quantities of Mexican silver, helped Cárdenas finance his economic development plans. In spite of earlier U.S. intervention in Mexico's Revolution, Cárdenas did not expect U.S. hostility: "The United States will not intervene in our internal affairs," he said in December, 1935, "first, because of its Good Neighbor Policy . . . and second, because it is profoundly concerned with meeting the problems that have arisen within its own territory."[17]

The political question for Cárdenas was how much power Calles was willing to surrender to him and the younger reformers he was incorporating into his administration. If Cárdenas was to become, in modern parlance, "his own man" or "captain of his own team," he would have to challenge the powerful Calles machine, with its control of the national political party and bureaucracy, its connections with big business and old-guard labor leadership (CROM), its friendships among the foreign investment community, and its influence in the army (although here Cárdenas also had some support). So Cárdenas started his administration by making sweeping changes in the PNR and the government bureaucracy and in the military. He raised military salaries and benefits, improved army education, courted and won rank-and-file soldier support, promoted junior officers, and gradually maneuvered the generals into a position of neutrality. He then set about healing the long rift between the government and the Catholic Church. In his second cabinet, he appointed the pro-Catholic General Saturnino Cedillo minister of agriculture and declared the "era of Church persecution" at an end. For his part, the new archbishop of Mexico, Luis María Martínez, issued a pastoral letter urging the clergy to be more sensitive to the economic welfare of all workers.

Education, long a sticking point in Church-state relations, proved a particularly controversial issue. A constitutional reform of October 1934 (two months before Cárdenas took office) had made public education "socialistic." Traditionally, in Spanish and Latin American thought, socialistic education meant "rational and secular" as distinguished from "religious and clerical." Cárdenas reassured the Church that its interests were not threatened and discouraged antireligious fanaticism in the schools. In addition, he augmented the education budget, leading to a reduction in illiteracy of about 7 percent. Government documents from this period clearly conceived socialistic education as "education to community responsibility." The principal aim of the reform was to develop a better-trained work force. As Cárdenas stated in a circular dated June 30, 1934, "It is necessary to stimulate utilitarian and collectivist teaching which prepares pupils for production, which foments the love of work as a social obligation."[18] Socialist rhetoric in education, as in other areas, was intended to win over the most radical revolutionaries then active in strategic parts of the society, including the schools, whose teachers had a long tradition of labor militancy and social concern. The one consistent ideological theme of the Cárdenas administration was the creation not of a socialist regime but of a government that would be "liberal, democratic, and nationalist."

In what other ways could Cárdenas lay the groundwork for carrying out a reformist program free of a potential Calles "veto"? Historically, new leaders had turned to organized labor—Obregón to the Casa del Obrero Mundial in 1915 and to CROM in 1920, and Calles to CROM as well. As it happened, the rapidly growing CGOCM was available to Cárdenas.

CROM had lost many of its major unions (printers, iron and metalworkers, and textile workers), as rank-and-file workers had become disillusioned with the corruption of its leadership and the failure of Calles to pay off in social-welfare benefits. In the first year of the Cárdenas regime (1934–1935), a rash of strikes broke out against such companies as the Mexican Tramways Company (Canadian owned), Huasteca Petroleum Company (Standard Oil), San Rafael Paper Company (Spanish-French capital), and the Mexican Telephone and Telegraph Company (American Telephone and Telegraph's allied company, in which Calles held a large number of shares). These strikes were in the tradition of continuing labor militancy against foreign capital, which dated back to the eruption of anti-imperialist strikes under Porfirio Díaz and showed once again that the Mexican proletariat was not underdeveloped when compared with Mexico's weak bourgeoisie.

As early as February 8, 1934, CGOCM used its most powerful weapon in the class struggle, the general strike, in support of three other strikes occurring at the time. In July it launched its first nationwide general strike to protest the state's siding with employers in the decisions of the labor arbitration and conciliation boards. CGOCM's moral example and fighting spirit in leading the struggle for more jobs and decent wages resulted in its incorporating more than half of all Mexico's organized workers by the end of the year. Strikes were widespread, rising according to official figures from 13 in 1933 to 642 in 1935 (one unofficial estimate put the number at more than 1,000 for the first half of 1935 alone). In the Laguna district in north-central Mexico, where half the nation's cotton was produced, there were 104 strikes by unionizing farmworkers in 1935.

Mexico's Labor Code, the federal labor law passed in August 1931, granted concessions to the workers then pressing for better conditions but also laid the basis for state regulation of labor by granting the state the right to declare strikes legal or nonexistent and to recognize or ignore the elections and directorates of all labor unions. The capitalist state was thus in a position to carry out its class role of being an organ of one class (the bourgeoisie) over another (the proletariat), of being responsible for "law and order" that legalizes and facilitates class domination, and of creating the appropriate agencies for the amelioration or resolution of confrontations between classes. Under these circumstances, the labor movement did not rush to embrace Cárdenas. On the contrary, it launched a series of strikes, thereby making the situation precarious for social stability and political order.

The combination of this heightened class threat from below and the new president's need to find additional support if he were to carry out a program of social reform and economic recovery without Calles's intervention led Cárdenas to back the main organizing force behind labor unrest, CGOCM. By recognizing labor's right to strike and by abetting the development of CGOCM (with government assistance and juridical decisions against recalcitrant private corporations), the Cárdenas administration extended the state-labor alliance begun by Obregón and Calles. In February 1936, CGOCM, with Cárdenas's support, became the officially recognized national labor movement and was renamed the Confederation of Mexican Workers (CTM). Under its general secretary Lombardo Toledano, CTM joined together some 3,000 unions and 600,000 workers.

Yet Cárdenas's handling of labor was highly complex, assisting here, restraining there—and in the long run continuing the state's role of controling labor. Committed to the reform of capitalism rather than its destruction, Cárdenas could not side completely with labor without risking such a shift in class power that the capitalist system itself might be called into question. Similarly, rank-and-file workers might take advantage of unlimited presidential support to marshall a full-scale attack against the bourgeoisie and for state power, regardless of the alliance of their leaders with government. On the other hand, if Cárdenas sided too completely with the owning classes against labor, labor's leaders might defect from their alliance with the government, also aggravating the danger of a direct proletarian attack on the bourgeoisie and the state. Cárdenas chose to steer a middle course and avoid a bloody class war.

Cárdenas's actions throughout his regime ranged from approvals of socialism to denials that he sought it; from outright support of workers on strike to declaring strikes illegal; from appearing at worker demonstrations to sending troops to quell them. This constituted political entrepreneurship, with Cárdenas employing a policy of carrot-and-stick toward labor in order to consolidate a state-regulated and state-supported capitalism.

He was aided in this by the political line taken by organized labor's most popular leader, Lombardo Toledano, who argued that if capitalism were to be abolished it would happen only in a distant future after the break with "feudalism" and "imperialism" necessary to establish Mexico's economic and political freedom. This line was even more influential when it became part of the Popular Front tactics pushed by the Communist International in its opposition to the rise of fascism, represented in Mexico by a growing threat from organized forces of the extreme right known as "Sinarquistas" and, in their paramilitary appendage, the "Gold Shirts."

Thus, prevailing conditions in Mexico were such that no single class or class fraction was in a position to get its way easily. Even though many rural oligarchs had interlocking urban investments, the bourgeoisie had conflicting landed and industrial interests. It also included numerous *comprador* elements whose interests were closely tied to those of foreigners, and these were in conflict with the more independent-minded "nationalist" industrialists.

With the misnamed "national" bourgeoisie weak and divided, other classes seemingly had a good chance to eliminate once and for all its partial hegemony. But these too were weak. They included a relatively directionless petty bourgeoisie, and the workers and peasants whose dependence on the state undercut the autonomy of their threat. In such a situation, with no class or class fraction able to assert hegemony, the state emerged as a natural arbiter and central power.

This was in fact welcomed by modernizing sections of the bourgeoisie, which had been engaged in their project of reconsolidating the capitalist state on a new basis since 1920. These elements needed to allow some of the demands of the masses to be met through state-directed social reforms in order to avoid a revolutionary challenge from below potentially as serious as that of 1910–1915. Many industrialists and bankers welcomed increased state intervention, and even social reform, if they would control the class struggle and if the bourgeoisie would gain an ally in its effort to maintain capitalism and achieve hegemonic power.[19] Any recalcitrant bourgeois fractions could be broken, or at least disciplined, by developmentalist and reformist currents within the state bureaucracy and national political party so long as the worker and peasant movements were not crushed. But the use of the state as the key power resource, rather than the use of a single, united class (either the proletariat or the bourgeoisie), combined with the dependence of the Mexican economy of the 1930s on external conditions—accumulated foreign debt, agreements with foreign bondholders, world depression—meant that there could be neither an independent "nationalist-bourgeois" industrialization program for autonomous economic development from above nor a thoroughgoing revolution from below. The state could only introduce sufficient reforms to keep the class war under control.

Cárdenas's administration set about supporting the most modern and patriotic segments of the bourgeoisie, those most rooted in nationally controlled areas of production, at the expense of *comprador* and imperialist groups. It sought increased state regulation of the economy so that the depression might be eased and private ownership preserved. Cárdenas encouraged private enterprise by allowing the government's major development corporation, the Nacional Financiera (founded in 1934), to borrow from the Banco de México to underwrite private investments and to provide initial capital for industrial enterprises. As historian James Wilkie has noted, "The basis for rapid industrialization was firmly established when Cárdenas left office. In fact, the volume of manufacturing production increased about as fast during the Cárdenas era as it did during the [succeeding Manuel] Avila Camacho epoch."[20] Moreover, by doubling the amount of federal expenditure going to economic development between 1934 and 1937, the Cárdenas administration did indeed pull the country out of its economic slump. Between 1929 and 1933, the Gross National Product (GNP) had dropped an average of 2.7 percent a year, but from 1934 to 1940 it increased at an annual average rate of 4.5 percent.

In responding to the demands of the workers, Cárdenas at first hedged on the right of either workers or the state to take over factories with idle productive machinery or those in which owners disobeyed labor laws or court decisions. Militant elements in the working class grew impatient and in 1934–1935 stepped up the pace of strikes and mass mobilizations, forcing Cárdenas to form, for a time at least, an anti-imperialist alliance with the proletariat, the peasantry, and the anti-*comprador* segment of the bourgeoisie and to encourage the mass mobilizations in order to counterbalance the forces of the rest of the bourgeoisie, including Calles loyalists and the resurgent political right.

In the midst of this heightened social and political unrest, on June 11, 1935, Calles reentered the political arena to denounce all strikers as engaging in unpatriotic behavior equivalent to treason.

He red-baited union leaders, especially Lombardo Toledano. He then challenged Cárdenas to restore order or suffer the consequences. Cárdenas responded on June 13 with a statement midway between labor's demands and Calles's adamant opposition. Cárdenas viewed many of labor's demands as reasonable and claimed that by meeting some of them the economic situation might be made more stable, assuming that concessions to labor were granted "within the economic possibilities of the capitalist sector." To reassure business, Cárdenas warned that "in no case will the President of the Republic permit excesses of any kind or acts that involve transgressions of the law or unnecessary agitations."[21]

The working class—led by the strikers, independent unions like those of railway workers and electricians, and new leaders like Lombardo Toledano—responded to Calles's attacks by threatening another general strike, branding Calles a traitor to the Revolution, and forming the National Committee for Proletarian Defense (which was soon to be reconstituted as the CTM). This new labor coalition applauded Cárdenas's June 13 statement, and from that moment on "the labor movement was wedded to Cárdenas, and he, in turn, to the labor movement . . . but the government kept, always, the upper hand."[22]

Meanwhile, reactionary segments of the bourgeoisie in the cities and countryside sought to stem the reformist tide through factory lockouts and sending armed goon squads against peasants seizing lands or state bureaucrats seeking to implement agrarian reform. The focus of the urban attack became Monterrey, the nation's largest industrial center and a veritable hotbed of bourgeois reaction. In February 1936, when striking workers immobilized the city, Cárdenas took the occasion to issue his famous "Fourteen Points"—the statement that best reflects his populist and corporativist strategy. It was a broad appeal to almost all social classes and groups, particularly those with any kind of real or potential power, in order to bring them under state regulation.

Cárdenas's Fourteen Points encouraged workers to form a "united front," which the government would deal with, "to the exclusion of minority groups which might choose to continue" (e.g., CROM). He warned industrialists that should they cease production in the factories "because of the demands of the unions," the factories could rightfully be turned over "to their laborers or the government" (a warning against the employers' use of the shutdown and lockout). On the other hand, he also encouraged employers "to associate in a united front"—which many of them rapidly did, forming chambers of commerce and industry in cities across the country. Cárdenas applauded the further growth of industry, since the government "depends upon its prosperity for its income through taxation." And he urged capitalists "not to continue provoking agitations," because "this would bring on civil warfare."[23]

All of this formed another part of Cárdenas's strategy to divert the class struggle into safe channels under state regulation. By encouraging a multitude of organizations—workers, peasants, bureaucrats, big business executives, owners of small enterprises, teachers, and so forth—to bargain with the state and (where feasible) affiliate with the national political party, and yet by keeping them separate from each other while granting them state recognition as legal entities, Cárdenas was able to consolidate the institutional corporativism that had been the political project the wounded but triumphant bourgeoisie had initiated in 1917.

Throughout 1936, Cárdenas continued to reassure the big capitalists (mainly those in Monterrey) that he had no intention of nationalizing industry. He told a delegation of bankers and industrialists that even in the most extreme cases of uncooperative behavior by big business, "the most that could happen would be that certain branches would be withdrawn from the sphere of private interest to become social service."[24] Occasionally Cárdenas spoke of the need to "socialize the means of production," but by this he meant only the regulation of privately owned productive property, the kind of regulation being introduced in many more industrialized capitalist countries during this period.

Throughout the class turbulence of 1935 and early 1936, many political figures previously loyal to Calles noted the changes in the army and the favors being offered pro-Cárdenas *políticos* by the state. They grew increasingly awed by the sight of tens of thousands of workers marching in the streets, threatening a general strike in support of Cárdenas. They understood the shift in the political balance when they saw the president arming 100,000 peasants and lesser numbers of workers to form peasant and worker militias in the name of resisting armed reactionaries and "imperialist threats." They knew that such militias were under the control of the ministry of defense, and could be used to check any attempted army revolt. And they pragmatically shifted their support from Calles to Cárdenas.

Overcome by the deterioration in their own ranks and by the newly fashioned labor-government alliance, Calles and CROM's Morones were put to rout, or, more precisely, deported (in April 1936). Once again, a new political leadership had met the rising demands of the workers part way, and in so doing had replaced the older, more recalcitrant political leadership—as Obregón and Calles had done against the Carrancistas in 1919–1924. Once again it was the actions of the working class, through large-scale strikes and demonstrations, that had precipitated the change. And once again the new government moved in to help meet some of labor's demands and to bend the labor movement back—in Cárdenas's words—"within the economic possibilities of the capitalist sector."

Among the changes Cárdenas introduced during this tumultuous time were federal price controls and the appointment of federal agents to manage some of the enterprises resisting worker demands or disrupted by strikes—for example, the railroads, electrical installations, and selected factories and farms. He gradually nationalized the railroads and established the Federal Electricity Commission (CFE), which became a powerful state force in the electrical industry. All these measures meant an increase in the influence of workers and peasants on key economic institutions. Such proletarian influence naturally raised concern among the bourgeoisie that the workers and peasants might eventually gain political hegemony. This was unlikely, however, since Cárdenas was also increasing state regulation of the proletarian movement. He introduced reforms in agriculture and industry that sometimes permitted workers' increased involvement in the management of select enterprises. But this involvement was short-lived, since he also took care to appoint state bureaucrats to manage and control the reforms in order that workers might be disciplined and production increased. Once strikes ended, business could resume as usual.

Cárdenas's agrarian-reform policies, which laid the basis for today's state-supported capitalist agriculture, typified the pattern. In the late 1920s and early 1930s, much of the countryside had become engulfed in violence, with peasants engaged in a fierce war against the "white armies" of the *latifundistas*. Often the peasants' only allies in demanding implementation of agrarian reform both before and after Cárdenas's assumption of the presidency were the schoolteachers, more than 200 of whom were shot down by the large landholders' hired *pistoleros*.[25] Cárdenas was sensitive to these problems. His administration distributed over 20 million hectares of land to the peasants, more than twice the amount distributed by all previous post-1917 regimes combined.

Based on Article 27 of the Constitution (which protected private property), Cárdenas's land program provided for state credits and aid to small private farms and to productive *ejidos*. *Ejidatarios* increased their irrigated holdings fourfold, or half their allotments. The agrarian reform facilitated the expropriation of many of the *latifundistas'* unproductive or idle lands, although here the government had to tread lightly. Even though some of the nation's *hacendados* had been killed during the 1910–1917 civil war or had gone into exile, many had survived to rebuild or expand their estates, their ranks swelled by the so-called revolutionary landlords— military officers and politicians who, with state encouragement, had amassed immense amounts of land for themselves. Cárdenas allowed large landowners to keep 150 irrigated hectares or the equivalent and to retain the upper hand in matters of credit, technical inputs, wages, and marketing. Not untypically, when distributing land to rural proletarians—as in the case of the prolonged worker-employer conflict in the prosperous sugar-growing area of Los Mochis, Sinaloa, in 1938—Cárdenas left the properties of the principal producers (in this case the United Sugar Company) untouched and refused to concede any wage increases to the workers. On the other hand, he did not hesitate to send in federal troops when regional *caciques,* allied with conservative and foreign oil interests, tried to stop his allegedly "atheistic, Bolshevik reforms," as in the case of the swiftly repressed revolt of mid-1938 led by General Saturnino Cedillo in San Luis Potosí.

Similarly, in the areas of the most radical land distribution, the Laguna and Yucatán, where labor unrest was intense, many of the largest landholdings and productive installations were also protected from expropriation. In fact, the best one-third of the Laguna lands, with more than two-thirds of the artesian wells, remained untouched by the agrarian reform; the most productive land remained in the hands of twelve corporations, 70 percent of which were foreign-owned. In the Yucatán, Cárdenas left the henequen-processing plants in the hands of the second-level *hacendados* established by Alvarado in 1915 as managers of the henequen trade, and they were thereby able to retain control of most of the area's peasants.

But Cárdenas also used agrarian reform to avoid impending agricultural paralysis and peasant disruption, as in the troubled Laguna region, which was selected for an ambitious state-sponsored project of collective production on *ejido* lands. Nationally, however, less than 10 percent of all *ejido* farmers worked on a collective basis; most farmed individual small parcels with an *ejido.* Only in the Laguna, Yucatán, and northwestern Mexico, where *ejidos* received the strongest state support, did production for export increase, contributing to a subsequent boom in capitalist agriculture in the adjacent better-equipped private properties of commercial farmers. Elsewhere, there remained widespread unemployment, partially caused by ongoing mechanization of production and the corporate capitalists' near monopoly on fertile land, water, credit, and technology, forcing the *ejidatarios* to hire themselves out as peons and even to rent their land out to the private farmers and then work it for them. Despite the entrance of the state-sponsored ejidal bank, meant to help alleviate their economic plight, many *ejidatarios* continued to obtain credit from private corporate farmers or moneylenders, however exploitative and usurious their rates of interest—the ejidal bank's employees often had worked for the old private banks or were in sympathy with the *latifundistas;* in addition, the bank was widely known for its corruption.

Consistent with his corporativist-style politics, Cárdenas took care to prevent peasant organizations—which he initially had helped develop by political appointments at every level—from affiliating with the official labor organization CTM, as he did with the bank employees' unions, the public employees' unions, and the teachers' unions. As historian Lyle Brown has pointed out:

> There was no doubt that Cárdenas desired separately organized labor and peasant confederations that would look to him for support and over which he could exercise such control as might be necessary to keep them functioning in harmony with the objectives of his administration. . . . Both the Communists and Lombardo Toledano spoke of the importance of uniting peasant and labor groups in a great proletarian organization, but Cárdenas was too shrewd a politician to allow such a development.[26]

The largest agrarian organization was the Mexican Peasant Confederation (CCM), formed initially to support Cárdenas's presidential candidacy. Incorporating most of the peasant leagues, it was renamed the National Peasant Confederation (CNC) in 1938, by which time it claimed to represent 3 million peasants and rural workers. Many of its militants fought the iron-fisted control of *caciques* and government bureaucrats and sought to create an independent movement, but the influential Communists chose to go along with Cárdenas and to "bore from within" CNC.

In reality, Cárdenas's agrarian-reform policies—which in any case were curtailed in 1936 when the combined turmoil in the countryside and cities led food production to plummet and prices to skyrocket—while arousing the enthusiasm of hundreds of thousands of Mexicans and granting the peasant a dignity not felt since the days of Zapata, were intended and served primarily to preserve and stimulate the private system of farming for commercial profit. In May 1938 the government opened the Office of Small Property, which could issue certificates of exemption from seizure. Between 1930 and 1940, the number of privately owned farms increased by 44 percent. Some 800,000 people were still living on haciendas in 1940, when the government acknowledged that Mexico continued to be fundamentally a country of great estates—more than half the cultivable land consisted of estates of more than 5,000 hectares in size. Over 60 percent of the peasants eligible to receive land had either inadequate parcels or no land at all. It is no coincidence that *neolatifundismo,* the current form of monopoly agriculture in Mexico, flourishes in precisely the most prominent areas of Cárdenas's much-disputed agrarian reform. Ultimately, civil war and disruption were avoided by agrarian reform, while capitalist production increased manyfold.

The Cárdenas administration's failure to maintain the pace of land distribution after 1937, together with runaway inflation, urban and rural labor's questioning of corruption among bureaucrats, and Cárdenas's own increasingly ambivalent policy toward strikes, put the government in a difficult political situation. Sinarquismo's neofascist ideology began making inroads among those peasants relatively unaffected by agrarian reform, among intermediate-class people suffering inflation, and among ultrareactionary clerical and business figures. By 1940 the Sinarquistas numbered nearly half a million, some of them organized into paramilitary units. A long-term intermittent strike by oil workers from 1936 to 1938 once more pitted organized labor against foreign capital, and talk of "imperialist intervention" filled the pages of the newspapers. The striking oil workers were demanding that the government annul all previous contracts and insist on a higher wage scale, and by early 1938 they were calling for a nationwide general strike to force nationalization.

Many observers wondered if Cárdenas might not terminate his populist program altogether or else face a power play by conservative army generals. The time was thus ripe for a bold government action against a long-time common enemy, the foreign oil interests. According to noted Mexican historian and economist Jesús Silva Herzog, a close presidential aide at the time, "Had General Cárdenas not carried out [oil] nationalization, his government would not have been able to stay in power."[27]

For the most part, the oil companies had stopped exploring for new wells and worked out the old ones—production had peaked in 1921, and by 1937 Mexican oil accounted for only 3 percent of Standard Oil of New Jersey's world production. The companies' prime concern was the example nationalization might set in more critical oil areas of the world and in other investment sectors in Mexico itself. Cárdenas, who accepted the oil companies' final wage proposals to the striking workers, was insulted by their insistence that it be in writing and by their refusal to accept a guaranteed share of Mexico's oil output. Apparently the companies wanted all or nothing. So, on March 18, 1938, Cárdenas expropriated the foreign-controlled oilfields.

The companies retaliated with a "blockade" of oil sales to the United States, England, and France. England broke off diplomatic relations, and the Roosevelt administration terminated the silver agreement. Immediate indemnity was demanded, and foreign loans were withheld or delayed. Until negotiations on an indemnity agreement were completed in 1941 (Mexico was eventually to pay more than $200 million to the companies), when the oil boycott was lifted, these and other economic pressures forced Cárdenas to devalue the peso and turn to the Axis powers as an outlet for Mexican oil.

There took place a massive outpouring of public support for Cárdenas's act of economic independence, including approval by the Church. Millions of people contributed whatever they could to a national indemnity fund that had been created to pay off the oil firms. Cárdenas seized this time of national unity to further consolidate a corporativist model of social and political organization. The national political party was renamed the Party of the Mexican Revolution (PRM—today's PRI). It incorporated the major mass organizations, grouped into four "sectors": labor (CTM), peasant (CNC), "popular," and military. The popular sector consisted of teacher and state employee unions excluded from CTM, small farmers outside CNC, professionals and other groups outside CTM or CNC, youth and women's organizations, and so forth. In 1940, the military sector merged with the popular sector.

At the same time, Cárdenas assured foreign investors that the oil case was exceptional and that their investments would be protected as long as they served the national interest and conformed to Mexican law. Cárdenas had no intention of going any further than necessary in resolving these crises, or of undermining long-run developmentalist goals "within the economic possibilities of the capitalist sector," as was swiftly proven by his antilabor actions following the expropriation. The distribution of land to the peasants, as noted, ground to a halt. A mineworkers' sit-down strike, directed mainly against the Anaconda Copper Company, was broken, and the mining companies were assured that further expropriations would not occur. In fact, despite Cárdenas's "anti-imperialist" and economic reforms, by 1940 Mexico depended more than ever on foreign trade, particularly with the United States, which accounted for 87 percent of its foreign commerce.

The number of workers involved in strikes declined drastically, from 145,000 in 1935 and 113,885 in 1936 to 61,732 in 1937, 13,435 in 1938, 14,486 in 1939, and 19,784 in 1940. In 1940 the oil and railway workers were still on strike, however, and their continued militancy led Cárdenas to refuse their demands and expound on "the necessity of ending extreme situations which would endanger the collective interest."[28] The oil workers, objecting to Cárdenas's plan to reorganize the industry's work force along state-controlled corporativist lines, then pulled out of CTM. Cárdenas responded by sending federal troops to break a strike at the Azcapotzalco refinery. This broke the back of the strike movement but not the militancy of the workers.

Cárdenas, like Calles, could not run again for the presidency. He selected the moderate General Manuel Avila Camacho, his minister of defense, to run in 1939–1940, counting on him to carry out the next decade's industrial development program—or, as he put it in his last major public address, the task of "unification, peace, and work." Incoming presidents have echoed these themes ever since.

The selection of Cárdenas's successor, however, was not without conflict. Conservatives, most state governors, much of the military, and powerful capitalists favored Avila Camacho, but various labor unions and peasant leagues backed General Francisco Múgica, who had gained a "radical" reputation in the Cárdenas administration for his defense of labor's causes and advocacy of petroleum expropriation. Nevertheless, the CTM and CNC leadership came out for Avila Camacho in early 1939, and their preference was imposed on the membership. The PRM likewise imposed party discipline on its dissidents and carried out a well-financed nationwide campaign to make sure Avila Camacho would win. The retreat from radicalism was consolidated when the billowing clouds of war in Europe and Asia led to an ideological shift by most progressive groups away from an emphasis on continuing the reform process and maintaining the anti-imperialist posture to one of urging unity among all democratic forces against fascism—and, therefore, support for the PRM's Avila Camacho.

Nonetheless, the difficult economic conditions caused a sizable number of Mexicans from all walks of life to rally behind an opposition candidate, General Juan Andréu Almazán, one of the new "revolutionary millionaires." Almazán drew predictable support from Monterrey capitalists and the recently formed conservative National Action Party (PAN). But he also had the backing of old Calles loyalists, including former CROM leader Morones, and many workers fed up with the state's corporativist management of their lives. National and foreign business groups helped finance the campaigns of both Almazán and Avila Camacho, with U.S.

interests tilting slightly toward the latter, apparently preferring political continuity and stability to the probable social unrest an Almazán presidency might provoke in view of his Monterrey capitalist backers' desire to dismantle the Cárdenas reforms. Both candidates campaigned on similar platforms, aimed at winning over the national and foreign bourgeoisies: protection for Mexican and foreign investment, class conciliation, law and order, and support for private enterprise, including small family farms in preference to *ejidos*. After a campaign marred by violence and claims of fraud, Avila Camacho predictably emerged the victor by the little-believed count of 2,476,641 votes to 151,101.

As Part II of this book examines in detail, the 1940 election in the final analysis represented a victory for the combined interests of the domestic and foreign bourgeoisies. In political scientist Nora Hamilton's words, "The conservative alliance again controlled the state, with the difference being that the state itself had been strengthened through its control, via the new government party, of the working class and peasantry, and through the revolutionary legitimacy given the state by the Cárdenas government."[29]

Even Cárdenas's historic anti-imperialist act against the oil companies in 1938 did not seriously jeopardize the overall pattern of capitalist development, with its heavy dependence on foreign capital. Indeed, it sufficiently rallied peasants and workers around the government so as to permit the finishing of the political project of the modernizing fraction of the bourgeoisie—the consolidation of the national political party; the final steps of the corporativist practice of organizing separate constituencies tied to the party and dependent on the state (CTM, CNC, etc.); the limiting of populist reforms and periodic declaration of their "end"; and the establishment of a strong state to aid in capitalist development in collaboration with foreign capital behind the mask of nationalism.

While unduly harsh on Cárdenas, who evoked tremendous affection from most peasants and workers, the bitter statement of a railway brakeman in Mariano Azuela's novel *La nueva burguesía* undoubtedly reflects the feeling of many Mexicans, then as today: "Isn't it true, Campillo, that the only thing that Mexico has to thank Cárdenas for is that the cost of living is five times higher than it was when he came into power? . . . and how many thousands are dying of hunger because there is no work?"[30]

It is useful to end the first part of this book with a brief observation about historical continuity in the development and evolution of Mexico's state, class struggle, and patterns of capital accumulation. The entire 1880–1940 period of capitalist economic development was structurally the same, based on agro-mineral exports and a strong insertion into the relations of world capitalism. In 1940 Mexico's population was only 19.6 million, 70 percent of it still rural and two-thirds of it still illiterate. The estimated number of haciendas was 11,470, perhaps more than in 1910, while the portion of national territory controlled by large-scale landholders was 42 percent, down from 60 percent in 1910. And although political alliances had undergone changes and massive revolutionary upheavals had occurred—in 1910–1920 and again in the 1930s—none of the political forces managing the different governments doubted the validity of the pro-capitalist role of the state, established in the 1857 Constitution and strengthened in the 1917 Constitution.

The period from 1940 to the present is marked by changes in the forces of production and by such strong state support of capitalist development that Mexico is today a relatively industrialized country. But it is a capitalist country of a special kind. Dependence on foreign capital, domestic capital's reliance on cheap labor, and other forces already noted have contributed to the great divisions between rich and poor that characterize Mexico today. Equally, the corporativist state, which had its origin in the pre-1940 period, is a critical factor in Mexico's current uneven and oppressive pattern of both rural and urban industrial development. It is useful, then, to summarize the nature of this state, which is to play such a crucial role in the years to come.

"Corporativism"[31] is employed here to describe a political system that relies for its legitimacy and perpetuation on a politics of masses, where the capitalist state provides modest concessions to popular movements and ties their mass organizations to its tutelage and where those resisting such incorporation are usually repressed by state force. The official party serves as an administrative committee of the affairs of the mass organizations in the matters of national and local elections. Political actors are not individuals or members of organizations but these party and mass organizations, which function from the top down. For the purposes of politics and state decision making, what exist are organized entities; anything not organized does not, in that sense, exist. With the official party holding a monopoly within the mass organizations, no other political party, old or new, has any significant political effect. Even though Mexican anarchists, socialists, communists, and other leftists have played a pivotal role in organizing peasants and workers since the final decades of the nineteenth century, the corporativist state and its party have defined them as "subversive," thus keeping them in a continuous minority status. The corporativist system is one in which class organizations obtain periodic concessions from the state or capital on the one hand, and the state is an instrument of political control over the toiling masses on the other.

The fight against state-supported corporate capitalism and imperialism, therefore, necessarily becomes one for a genuine labor unionism representative of workers' or peasants' interests, a struggle to establish a mass organized base for an urban and rural proletarian movement capable of seizing state power and transforming the economic structure. This is an arduous task in any circumstance, but it is made more difficult by the ease with which a strong state can divert it from its ultimate goals through cooptation, repression, and the practice of "populism"—a program and movement advocating pro-people and relatively classless egalitarian demands.

Most writings on populism tend to confuse three overlapping areas: ideology, class alliances, and social movement (i.e., ideological and political practice of a class or of a class alliance).[32] In any of these cases, populism tends to prevail only under certain historical conditions, and in capitalist societies has generally emerged as the program of an ascendant fraction of the bourgeoisie in its battle against class rivals from within and without. In Mexico's case, these rivals for hegemony were the landed oligarchy, the *comprador* fraction of the bourgeoisie, intermediate-class radicals, and workers and peasants. Any class or class fraction may use populism as a program, for its use is always geared toward specific class ends. The proletariat uses it to win reforms; the ascendant bourgeois fraction uses it to gain hegemony and to limit proletarian class demands to reforms instead of revolution. As the 1920–1940 period of Mexican history—and particularly the Cárdenas reforms—so clearly reveal, the modernizing fraction of the bourgeoisie was able to achieve its goal of growth and prosperity under just these circumstances, with the assistance of a populist movement, class alliances, and a strong state.

As we saw in earlier chapters, populism in one form or another has existed in Mexico for a long time, first under the ideological rubric of Independence, then under the rubric of Liberal Reform, and finally under that of the Mexican Revolution. Sociological theorist Ernesto Laclau believes that current forms of populism emerged with the collapse of the Madero regime and prevailed in the subsequent "long process of the Mexican Revolution."[33] By this logic, modern populism has existed since at least 1913, and will continue to do so until the Revolution is completed—it is seen by Lachau as permanent in Mexico. In a rhetorical sense, of course, this is so, but if populism is perceived in such a propagandistic sense, the concept loses its specificity and usefulness.

It is more useful to view populism as a specific phenomenon prevailing only at certain historical moments—in particular, the Cárdenas period, where it clearly took center stage in Mexican political reality. The historical conjuncture helps explain why. Imperialism was weakened and distracted by problems at home; interimperialist rivalries were heightened; class agitation from below was rising rapidly; and the Mexican bourgeoisie was divided. Whoever the president is—and no Mexican president has failed to utilize populist appeals—the degree of populism varies directly with the state of the class struggle and the relative strength of imperialism.

Thus while, as we shall see, the economic structure of Mexico underwent radical changes after 1940, changes that had a direct impact on the character of the class structure and class struggle, a historical continuity remained at the state and ideological level. That continuity is embodied in the practices of corporativism and populism, which still continue to one degree or another and make intelligible the apparent "stability" of the Mexican state, today as for the past half century.

II
Mexico After 1940

5

The Transformation
of Agriculture and Industry

The state and private enterprise are, at bottom, the same thing.
—Agustín F. Legorreta, director of the
private Banco Nacional de México

Because of the more solid social foundations provided by the Cárdenas reforms of the 1930s, capital accumulation on an extended scale after 1940 was able to proceed in an atmosphere of unusual political stability. It transformed the entire nation, producing powerful groups of monopoly capitalists at one extreme and millions of proletarians and immiserated subproletarians at the other. Introduction of modern, often imported, technologies in agriculture and industry—tractors, reapers, fertilizers, hybrid seeds, and assembly-line production of automobiles and various durable and nondurable consumer goods—generated unprecedented economic growth and sharpened class cleavages between workers and owners.

The post-1940 growth of the capitalist monopolies and of foreign investment and their domination of Mexican society were furthered by the intervention of an authoritarian-technocratic state. The government and official political party took the major initiative in economic planning and politics. The state's central role derived from the relative weakness of the bourgeoisie, the corresponding strength of workers and peasants in the class struggle, and the illegitimate character of imperialism's power over Mexico. The state appeared to be above the classes, the ultimate arbiter. It negotiated directly with the bourgeoisie, with foreign capital, and with the imperialist states, whose advice it usually took and applied to overall economic policy. Since the nature of any state corresponds to the nature of the class forces dominating the system of economic production, the Mexican state's role was not to take the place of private capital but rather to assist it, stimulate it, and complement it. This it did by using the corporativist organizations consolidated by the Cárdenas regime as mediating apparatuses to stabilize the class war—and by contributing 40 percent or more of total investment in every decade (except the 1950s).

Each successive government sought to reduce the costs and to increase the sales of private capital. Since private capital, even in the most industrialized countries, finds it difficult to afford the large investments demanded by the modern scientific and technological revolution, the Mexican state also budgeted money for research, development, and production of improved technologies—although not nearly on the scale of its importation of foreign machinery and "know-how." In the technology area too, the state investment facilitated capital accumulation in the private sector but only rarely helped to service the daily needs of human beings.[1]

The state's ability to govern in an atmosphere of relative political stability from 1940 until the massive public demonstrations sparked by students and other dissidents in the late 1960s and early 1970s was due in part to its success in presenting itself as the defender of "revolutionary" ideals for which peasants and workers had made great sacrifices and achieved at least some advances. By invoking the figures of Hidalgo, Morelos, Juárez, Madero, Villa, Zapata, Carranza, Obregón, and Cárdenas, the state was always able to accuse its opponents of being unpatriotic or "against the people." After the student revolt of 1968, even the flaming anarchist revolutionary Ricardo Flores Magón was admitted to the pantheon of national heroes, in spite of the bourgeoisie's previous denunciations of his proletarian internationalism as "anti-Mexican." Meanwhile, the very state responsible for the deaths of assassinated peasant leaders like Rubén Jaramillo of Morelos, killed in 1962 by federal troops, erected busts of their heads in village plazas.

The revolutionary heritage of peasants' and workers' struggles was taught at every level of society—not just in the schools, where 75 percent of the population over twenty-five still has attended for less than four years, but in the press, in political and social organizations and block clubs, in workshops, and on farms. Everywhere, working Mexicans were told about their contribution to the creation of a strong "independent" nation. At the same time, the bloodshed and violence that their contribution had entailed was emphasized, leaving them with the belief that another outbreak of civil war must be avoided at all costs. They were assured that, however gradually, the earlier popular goals were still being sought and that they would be attained if people worked hard and maintained peace.

For decades the state spent immense sums propagandizing the normative model of "democratic" politics that had emerged under Cárdenas and become institutionalized in the three-sector makeup of the official political party. For many years peasants, workers, the expanding intermediate classes, and segments of the poor felt that they had at least token representation in their respective sectors of the party (rural labor's CNC, urban labor's CTM, and the "popular" sector), even though actual power rested with the party's twelve-member national executive committee.

A key technique used by the ruling class and the state to maintain social peace was to channel divisions among people, wherever possible, into organized "competing constituencies" along corporativist lines. This in turn was legitimized by the ideology of nationalism, "directed democracy," "revolutionary heritage," "effective suffrage and no re-election," "autonomous" state universities, "Indianism" *(indigenismo), "machismo,"* and so on. Workers, peasants, Indians, women, students, and immiserated groups were kept as separate as possible, while class/race/sex divisions were blurred by the ideologies of populism, national unity, and class harmony.

In the cases of oppressed Indians and women, the ideologies of *indigenismo* and *machismo* played a particularly insidious role. *Indigenismo* consisted of an officially proclaimed respect for the nation's Indian heritage—one of the few, though contradictory, accomplishments of the Revolution of 1910–1920. New statues of the Indian martyrs Cuitlahuac and Cuauhtémoc were erected in many cities (hardly any monuments to Cortés or even Moctezuma were left standing), and an ugly expression, *malinchismo,* after the name of Cortés's Indian mistress and translator, Malinche, was used to denote treason. Yet there is no evidence that Malinche meant to become a "traitor"—she and tens of thousands of others rose up against Aztec tyranny and had little reason to believe that a small group of outsiders unfamiliar with the terrain and speaking a foreign tongue would later subdue them. (What they could not imagine was their own biological decimation, to be caused by imported diseases.) Moreover, if Malinche "betrayed the nation," then "the nation" was not mestizo but Indian—yet the plaque at the national monument in Mexico City's Plaza of Tlaltelolco (also known as the Plaza of Three Cultures), glossing over the Spanish massacres of 1519, asserts that "the Conquest was neither a victory nor a defeat; it was the painful birth of the Mexican nation, the Mexico of today." And even though today's nation is predominantly mestizo, the official celebration of the fusion of the races often backfires, as illustrated by the "battle of the bones," which erupted in 1946. Pro-Spanish and pro-Church conservatives claimed to have discovered the bones of Cortés and paid homage to them. Radical and anticlerical elements, for their part, sallied forth with claims of having uncovered the bones of Cuauhtémoc, and likewise paid homage. Considerable research and disputation over "the bones" has continued off and on ever since.[2]

More profound than these anatomical expressions of class and ideological struggle in the definition of the nation, however, has been the contradictory and hypocritical use of *indigenismo*. Every assertion of Mexican nationalism retains a historical animosity toward the Spaniards and often pretends defense of Mexico's original inhabitants. Such defense is often expressed as championing "the poor" *(los pobres)* and "the humble ones" *(los humildes)*. It is used by those seeking hegemony in a most cynical and opportunist way. It runs as a common ideological thread through the Wars of Independence (1810–1821), the post-Independence wars between liberals and conservatives, the Liberal Reform of 1857, the Revolution of 1910–1920, the mural renaissance of the 1920s, the Cárdenas reforms of the 1930s, and the 1968 student revolt.

In fact, *indigenismo* has served the purpose of destroying Indian culture and integrating Mexico's surviving Indians into the national economy. As an ideology and practice of integration, it became institutionalized in 1936 with the creation of the Department of Indian Affairs, which in 1948 was incorporated into today's low-budget National Indian Institute (INI). This agency serves to tie Indians more closely to the national economy. In effect, it either masks or legitimizes the exploiting and cheating of Indians routinely carried out by *caciques, neolatifundistas,* merchants, moneylenders, migrant-labor recruiters, agribusiness henchmen, and private or state factory and workshop owners. Marcela Lagarde points out that INI programs are "directed and planned by anthropologists who proclaim themselves to be for the Indian, but whose end is that he cease to be one," while anthropologists Ricardo Pozas and Isabel H. de Pozas assess the "true content" of *indigenismo* as being that of "expediting the exploitation of those human conglomerates most easily exploitable."[3]

As observed in Part I, throughout Mexican history the extreme exploitation of Indians and their participation in the class struggle has been paralleled by that of women. *Indigenismo* has its subtle partner *machismo*, which elevates women to a pedestal while successfully keeping them "in their place." In Mexico as anywhere else, women have different class positions and political or other convictions. Because of sexism, they have a double relationship to the capitalist mode of production: first, as themselves, depending on what they do (nonwage labor, farm or factory work, teacher, clerk, etc); and second, through their families or menfolk, whose activities usually determine their class situation, status, and values. But in their main economic relation of production, as nonwage labor generating and reproducing on a daily basis capitalism's most important commodity—labor power—most women constitute a distinct social group. In this specific sense they share labor's reproduction with other groups—for example, unpaid subsistence farmers and family artisans, many of whom are also female. Women's assigned role in labor's daily reproduction is constantly reinforced because of the need of capitalists to minimize the costs of labor power and its maintenance in their relentless drive to accumulate.

To keep women in this situation the Mexican state has helped organize and reinforce the value system of patriarchy and *machismo* and its practice (e.g., woman beating), while simultaneously converting women into commodities for the capitalist marketplace as potential wage labor and as sex objects. Since the 1950s, imperialism has exported to Mexico the accoutrements of sexism and the corresponding ideological message packaged in television programs, comic books, cheap romances, and other cultural wrappings. The double message consists of women as beautiful objects (passionate yet passive), mothers, homemakers, cheap labor, and upholders of the wholesomeness of family life.

While hardly unique to Mexico, sexist forms of *machismo* are particularly virulent and institutionalized there. Few women dare to confront it head-on, and many have internalized its value system. The double standard is applied in all social classes, and the nation's president is honored for the number of lovers he has. Obviously unaware of problems faced by U.S. women, a Mexican migrant worker who had recently returned from California once told me that "there the woman beats the man instead of the man beating the woman!" Hearing this, his wife looked skeptical. A male wage laborer's socially condoned license to completely dominate his *mujer* (woman or wife) serves as a kind of compensation for the exploitation he suffers at work. This reinforces the ability of capitalists to dominate both male and female labor.

Many Mexicans of whatever class, race, or sex see through the ideological manipulations of the state. So, whenever they begin to surmount their divisions and create even a semblance of popular unity, whether for reformist or revolutionary change, the state responds with violent repression and the corresponding ideological justification of "defending the Revolution and the nation against foreign plots, communists, terrorists, etc." Thus, for example, workers on strike or peasants seizing lands are repeatedly accused of being unpatriotic or disruptive of the "harmony between business and labor."

Even the late Oscar Lewis's books on the "culture of poverty" in

Mexico elicited the bourgeoisie's call for banning Lewis from the country, since he clearly reflected "Yankee biases," was "anti-Mexican," and failed to realize that "we've had a revolution here." This use of Mexico's history of revolution and nationalism to deny the possibility of grave internal faults, combined with the institutionalized practice of making the central government, especially the presidency, sacrosanct and therefore beyond criticism, produced the phony kind of "intellectual freedom" that so many observers of Mexico have noted. One is "free" to denounce economic injustice and to call for revolution in other Latin American countries, but one must refrain from attacking the Mexican government.

As if to symbolize the state's stability and the socialization of the public to the ideals of social harmony and national unity, President Manuel Avila Camacho (1940–1946) started his administration by repealing the "socialistic" reform of education and becoming the first president since Díaz to declare himself a believer in the Catholic faith. Then, on Independence Day, September 16, 1942, he gathered all the living ex-presidents of Mexico on the reviewing stand before the National Palace to observe a parade and pledge their support for his June 1 declaration of war against the Axis: Cárdenas, Calles (home from exile), Portes Gil, Rodríguez, Ortiz Rubio, and, at the podium, General Avila Camacho himself, telling the public that no one would rock the "independent" ship of state. A year earlier, the Law of Social Dissolution had been passed, presumably to defend the nation against any "subversive" endeavors by fascism. It established long jail sentences for anyone attempting to "dissolve" society. The law lasted for three decades and was repeatedly invoked to intimidate or repress left-wing reformist and revolutionary dissidents. Also during World War II, Avila Camacho had the Labor Code revised to introduce provisions making it easier to fire workers and restricting the right of public employees to strike. Finally, in early 1946, the new spirit of "stability" instead of "revolution" was invoked by renaming the official political party the Institutional Revolutionary Party (PRI).

From 1940 to 1960, what became known as Mexico's "economic miracle" took place: a 120 percent jump in industrial production and a 100 percent increase in agricultural output. Stimulated initially by increased U.S. demands for food and raw materials during World War II and the Korean War, and aided by an abundant labor supply made possible by rapid population growth—from 19.6 million people in 1940 to 35 million in 1960 to an estimated 72 million in 1982—the Mexican economy showed substantial GNP growth rates, particularly between 1950 and 1970, when 6 percent a year was frequent. The outbreak of World War II sufficiently distracted the major imperialist powers from attending to Mexico's internal affairs to permit Mexico to undertake the first steps of its industrialization program on its own. With its northern neighbor unable to export the usual quantity of manufactured goods, Mexico increased protective tariffs for its manufactures and engaged in intensive import substitution; industrial production jumped 35 percent. The United States purchased copious amounts of silver to help finance its war production, as well as other minerals and varied foodstuffs. Mexico's exports doubled during the war. The United States also advanced large credits for Mexico's industrialization program, and a number of private investors, fleeing U.S. wartime price regulations and high taxes, invested in Mexico as well.

Immediately after the war, U.S. capitalists increased their investments and began purchasing many of Mexico's new industries. U.S. direct investment in Mexico started to rise sharply in 1946, doubled in the 1950s, tripled in the 1960s, and quadrupled in the 1970s. The large amount of foreign and state investment made possible the installation of ever newer technologies, and industry and agriculture experienced an unprecedented degree of concentration as scattered productive units, artisans, workers, and peasants were moved into modern factories and onto large farms. The greater productivity and higher level of profits generated by this process facilitated centralization of capital (monopoly) in the hands of the big bourgeoisie and foreign capitalists. Dispossessed peasants trekked to the cities, and by 1960 Mexico was 50 percent urban (defining "urban" as communities of more than 2,500 inhabitants).[4]

Until the late 1960s, when signs of economic crisis and social unrest became unmistakable, Mexico's industrialization program was dubbed one of "stabilizing development." While economic growth did occur, it was far from stabilizing; it did, however, make Mexico more industralized than most other Latin American countries. Mexico's industrialization achievements were made possible by its not becoming bogged down in a colonial and neocolonial "enclave economy," which characterized most of its production and trade from the Spanish Conquest to the 1938 nationalization of oil. During those earlier times, Mexico had produced mainly mineral and agricultural goods for export and imported manufactured goods and raw materials for production, which often occurred in foreign-controlled "enclaves." The 1910–1920 Revolution and Cárdenas' reforms, however, had sufficiently loosened foreign controls over the economy to permit the Mexican bourgeoisie and state to begin to assert some influence or control over key parts of the economy, especially in minerals, tourism, light industry, and economic infrastructure.

In the launching of Mexico's modern industrialization program, an unbalanced class structure and uneven income distribution (still today more unequal than that in India or Puerto Rico), together with the existing demand structure and the character of the bourgeoisie and state, resulted in concentration on the development of Department II goods—consumer goods, mainly for the high-income market—instead of Department I goods—capital goods, the means of production. For its part, foreign capital increasingly shifted its activities into heavy and intermediate industry and the financial sectors of the economy, with the result that it came to play a preponderant role in the nation's economic growth, both in agriculture and in industry.

The postwar administration of Miguel Alemán (1946–1952, the nation's first full-term civilian president since Juárez), typified the new spirit of collaboration with foreign capital that Mexico's bourgeoisie and its partners in the state were undertaking. The long-standing unwritten rule that those in top government posts may filch public money without risk of serious reprisal was reaffirmed in the most blatant ways. Where before bureaucrats on the lower rungs had to be careful, under Alemán everyone used the same excuse: "President Alemán leads and I follow." Alemán himself, having made a fortune from graft and deals with U.S. capitalists, including partnerships with hotel magnate Conrad Hilton, left office in 1952 a millionaire—but only after placing a thirty-foot statue of himself at the entrance to the Universidad Nacional (a generation later, indignant students toppled it). In 1981, Alemán was still the major official in the nation's tourism industry, so critical in obtaining foreign exchange needed to help offset Mexico's perennial trade deficit. While not as blatant, Alemán's successors to the presidency—Adolfo Ruiz Cortines (1952–1958), Adolfo López Mateos (1958–1964), Gustavo Díaz Ordaz (1964–1970), Luis Echeverría Alvarez (1970–1976), and José López Portillo (1976–1982)—upheld this colonial and postcolonial tradition.

State corruption and collaboration with private capital reached new heights in the countryside under Alemán, who modified the legal basis for agrarian reform. He reinstated the so-called law of *amparo* (a kind of writ of appeal) to protect all private landholders from undue confiscation. He extended the legal size of landholdings to a range of from 100 to 300 irrigated hectares, or up to 50,000 hectares of arid grazing land—enough to maintain 500 head of cattle. He also supported the parcelization and privatization of *ejido* lands, while offering private farmers state subsidies and incentives for improving their technology and productivity. Federal troops and the traditional "white guards" (private armies) of the *latifundistas* were dispatched to disband progressive peasant organizations. The preservation or creation of small landholdings and highly parcelized *ejidos* served to maintain the appearance of an ongoing agrarian reform and to deflect the rural class struggle into reformist channels. The function of the *ejido* and *minifundium* (a small subsistence parcel) has since that time been, in sociologist Roger Bartra's words, to act as a "shock absorber" for the social violence inherent in the rapid expansion of capitalist agriculture.[5] A Mexican book published in 1968 highlighted the role of peasant labor, foreign investment, and the monopolization of landholdings in this process:

> The impact of foreign demand appears clearly in the following statistics: in 1940 agricultural products were about 10.3 percent of total exports, whereas in 1945 this proportion was nearly 21 percent. . . . After 1940 when, during the war, American demand for Mexican agricultural products increases again: (1) Agricultural development depends more an external forces (demand and supply of inputs) than on the domestic market; (2) the best lands, the irrigated ones, and other resources like capital, labor, credit and physical inputs, become concentrated in certain regions and in the hands of a few owners; (3) that growth opens the doors to foreign capital, which begins the process of control of national agriculture. It is necessary to emphasize, then, that the *minifundium* really constitutes 86 percent of the units of production. . . . In 1960, 2 percent of the farms accounted for 70.1 percent of all sales. To get an idea of the acute degree of concentration suffered in agriculture, it is well to note that in the United States 10 percent of the farms generate 40 percent of sales, and it is said that this already constitutes a high degree of concentration.
>
> This means that agriculture is a wonderful business for a very few people, while the vast majority of the working population lives under extremely poor conditions. . . . *Neolatifundismo* is simply the natural result of the present power structure, that is, of the class structure.[6]

In terms of the nation's politics and class structure, the old *ejido* bureaucracy and network of *caciques*, commercial intermediaries, and state technocrats became mediating forces that effectively allowed the banking, agrarian, and industrial bourgeoisies to expand their economic power and rule the nation without total revolt in the countryside. The state further stimulated and guided the process of rapid capitalist expansion by maintaining one of the lowest corporate tax rates in Latin America, procuring international loans, offering state credits and tax incentives to private industry, and allowing relatively free remittance of profits abroad for foreign

investors. The state also invested heavily in economic infrastructure: electrification, from 629,000 kilowatts installed capacity in
1937 to 13 million in 1977; highway construction, from 10,000
kilometers in 1940 to 200,000 in 1977; irrigation, from 5 percent of
cultivated land federally irrigated in 1940 to 60 percent in the
1970s; fuel and energy, a $3 billion subsidization of private com-
panies from 1953 to 1972 through lower prices offered them by
the Federal Electricity Commission (CFE) and the state petroleum
company, Petróleos Mexicanos (PEMEX); public education, halv-
ing the illiteracy rate between 1940 and 1970 and creating high
schools and universities for the intermediate and upper classes;
culture, sponsoring the arts, cinema, sports, publishing, tourism;
and so on and on.

Most important of all, however, was the state's enforcement of
strict labor discipline and a low wage scale. From 1939 to 1946, the
manufacturing worker's real wage dropped 50 percent; it did not
recover its 1939 purchasing power (when it was particularly low
because of runaway inflation) until 1968.[7] A 1963 survey revealed
that 65 percent of average expenses for an urban family and 84
percent for a rural family went for basic food supplies, in either
case an indication of grinding poverty. The state turned a blind eye
to illegal work conditions and maintained a low level of social security and related social-welfare investment.

A paramount mechanism in the state's role in capital accumulation was its control over labor. Leaders of urban labor's CTM and
rural labor's CNC lined up with the official political party not only
to obtain political benefits or influence, but because they recognized that the party had the state behind it—and the state was a
pivotal source of whatever economic benefits were to be granted to
either labor leaders or rank-and-file proletarians. Most CTM unions deducted a sum from membership fees as a "contribution" to
the party; those funds not so invested and not simply stolen by
corrupt union leaders were often invested in state and private industry. The state financed all the political manipulations and programs of the party and, when necessary, the repression of left-
leaning labor militants.

Immediately after the social upheaval of the 1930s, when the
state was anxious to implement its renewed policy of "class harmony," such repression became necessary. On September 23, 1941,
when the Union of Workers in War Industry marched to Avila
Camacho's luxurious home in Chapultepec Heights demanding to
be heard, presidential aide Colonel Maximaiano Ochoa ordered
troops to open fire, killing nine and wounding eleven. In 1943 and
1944, spontaneous strikes spread across the nation to protest the

wartime slash in wages, a 300 percent rise in prices, and corresponding superprofits piling up for big business. In spite of much repression of this continued labor militancy, leftists and antifascists remained influential among certain key industrial trade unions after the war, leading Avila Camacho's successor, Alemán, to complete a withering purge of progressives from organized labor in the spirit of "McCarthyism" spreading on both sides of the U.S.-Mexican border. In 1948, the militant National Railway Workers Union had its leadership replaced by the state-imposed Jesús Díaz de León, alias "El charro." His alias swiftly spread throughout the labor movement, spawning the term "*charrismo*," common parlance for violence, corruption, anticommunism, and antidemocracy on the part of official union leadership. Among opposition groups, only the fascistic Unión Nacional Sinarquista grew noticeably during the war years, claiming a membership of 800,000 by 1946. Alemán outlawed the Communist Party and then denied registration to the Sinarquista political party.

Today's corrupt and wealthy CTM boss Fidel Velázquez, who had replaced Lombardo Toledano in 1938, typified the official anti-Left union leadership that remained after the witch hunt. It increasingly tied itself to state favors, class collaborationism, and upper-class aspirations and values. In exchange for sending hired thugs to murder or maim labor dissidents and for guaranteeing labor discipline, labor leaders received personal luxuries that elevated them into the living rooms of the bourgeoisie. In addition, they periodically obtained institutional payoffs for their organizations. For example, a 1962 profit-sharing law was passed to cool out rising labor unrest; after union leaders took their cut, few of the shared profits actually reached rank-and-file workers.

Under Velázquez, CTM joined the notoriously anticommunist Inter-American Regional Organization of Workers (ORIT, founded 1951), whose use of "dirty tricks" to help imperialism topple progressive governments in Latin America has since become legend. Once ORIT became discredited, the AFL-CIO's anticommunist leadership got together with transnational corporate executives and the U.S. government to found (in Mexico in 1962) the American Institute for Free Labor Development (AIFLD), the actual power behind ORIT (which exists only nominally today).[8] Funded largely by the U.S. government's Agency for International Development (AID) but also by transnational corporations and AFL-CIO membership dues, AIFLD works closely with the U.S. Central Intelligence Agency (CIA) against progressive governments and labor unions throughout Latin America, protecting foreign capital in the region.[9]

State tutelage of organized labor left little room for Mexico's working classes to act on their own. Whether to obtain and keep a job, to enjoy the social benefits written into a union contract, or simply to get on a waiting list for seasonal or part-time work, a worker routinely became entangled in a web of *mordidas* (bribes) and fees to *charros* and their lackeys, often other workers. This humiliated and separated workers, enriched the *charro* network, and discouraged protest. Since the unions played a major role in the job market and were the workers' only legally recognized representatives, few could afford not to pay their union dues and follow orders. Ritualistically, CTM and CNC membership "approved" the leadership imposed from above by the self-reproducing labor and political bureaucracy. Rarely did they democratically choose their own leaders, make their own decisions, or conduct the class struggle on an independent basis. When they did, they faced swift repression.

In labor-capital relations, labor discipline was guaranteed by the union itself, the supposed protector of labor's interests. Labor contracts were renewed every one or two years, and official union leaders did little more than arrange these—usually demanding just enough to keep labor quiet but rarely obtaining economic gains sufficient to improve the membership's lot. In a practice that continues to the present, whenever a new branch of a transnational corporation or a joint Mexican-U.S economic venture was about to be established in one of the new state-sponsored "industrial parks" near a metropolitan area, the branch manager or joint venture's representative promised the CTM local that any workers would be from the union. In exchange, the local CTM leader guaranteed that all contract negotiations would be completed promptly and without worker protest. The CTM leader also guaranteed protection for the employer in case of labor conflict outside the factory gates or on the shop floor.[10]

Laws governing labor's conduct were heavily weighted in capital's favor. For example, the conciliation and arbitration boards could make one of three rulings on strikes: the action was "legal," "illegal," or "nonexistent." Since the last two resulted in state intervention and also prohibited restitution of pay for days lost in the action, and since the boards could delay for weeks or months before coming to a decision, dissatisfied workers often postponed action or settled matters peaceably. If they did decide to strike, they frequently obtained government approval—sometimes tacit, sometimes explicit—before acting.

As a result of deliberate state and *charro* policy, most unions were limited to a single plant. Consequently, the number of unions grew much more rapidly than did union membership, furthering the atomization of organized labor. By 1970, about 42 percent of all employed industrial workers were concentrated in the Federal District (greater Mexico City), and CTM accounted for at least 75 percent of those unionized.[11] In light of the power of economic monopolies and of the state over both urban and rural workers, it is not surprising that Mexico's "economic miracle" was accomplished largely on the bent backs of superexploited peasants and the low-paid urban work force they helped supplement. Two-thirds of the population received no share of the benefits of the economic growth its labor helped generate.[12]

This chapter analyzes all these trends through 1970, while succeeding chapters explore the consequences in class formation, economic crisis, heightened class struggle, and domestic and international politics, primarily since 1970. To avoid breaking up statistical tables and to reveal the continuity of basic trends in spite of the onset of crisis in the later 1960s, some data in this chapter extend beyond 1970, a date chosen because of the richness of 1970 census materials and the clear exhaustion of the stabilizing development model.

Transnational Corporations and U.S. Influence

From 1945 to 1978, U.S. companies and banks invested an estimated $150 billion abroad, creating an overseas commercial empire that by 1980 was generating half a trillion dollars in sales, $20 billion in profits per year, and one-quarter of the world's GNP. Latin America's share of this investment grew to about 20 percent, most of it in the manufacturing and financial sectors. Brazil, Mexico, and Venezuela accounted for over half of Latin America's share. The 18.3 percent rate of return on investment in Mexico remains the highest in all Latin America.[13]

This export of capital by the more industrialized countries has not been without effect in Mexico. According to a study completed in 1970 by economist José Luis Ceceña, of the 2,040 companies with the largest incomes in Mexico, foreign (mainly U.S.) capital controlled 36 percent of the income of the largest 400 companies and strongly participated in another 18 percent, while Mexican private capital controlled only 21 percent and the Mexican government 25 percent. Of the largest 100 industrial firms, 47 percent were foreign, 40 percent were private Mexican, and 13 percent were state.[14] Foreign capital concentrated in the fastest growing areas of the economy, particularly the capital goods and basic intermediate goods industries.

"Mexicanization" legislation over the years, a series of laws permitting 51 percent Mexican control of any industry and requiring it in such strategic areas as mining, did not discourage foreign investors. Many firms remain 100 percent foreign-owned— General Motors, Ford, Chrysler, Volkswagen, General Electric, Kodak, Sears, Anderson-Clayton, and Dow Chemical—but even "Mexicanized" industries are frequently foreign-dominated. Many Mexicans have loaned their names to front for foreign investors (*prestanombres*), disguising foreign penetration and takeover of the economy. Another factor strengthening foreign control of Mexicanized companies was the concentration of stock ownership in the hands of one or two foreign corporations and the dispersal of Mexican participation among a larger number of very junior partners. Corruption, bribery, and economic pressure applied by foreign investors and creditors further diluted the effect of Mexicanization. And, as a *New York Times* article of September 19, 1971, pointed out, "Mexicanization is now seen as guaranteeing foreign investors against expropriation." Foreign capital's participation in joint enterprises also allowed it to borrow more easily from Mexican banks and to diversify into other lines of business. Indeed, in booming areas like appliances, food products, and industrial chemicals, some 153 foreign companies in the late 1970s chose to sell a majority interest to Mexicans.

The United States was the prime investor. By 1970, U.S.-based transnational corporations (TNCs)[15] had come to obtain the following percentages of control of key sectors of the economy: automotive, 57 percent; petroleum products and coke, 49 percent; paper and cellulose, 33 percent; rubber, 76 percent; mining and metallurgy, 53.6 percent; copper and aluminum, 72.2 percent; tobacco, 100 percent; industrial chemicals, 50 percent; food and beverages, 46.8 percent; chemicals and pharmaceuticals, 86.4 percent; electrical machinery, 50 percent; nonelectrical machinery, 52 percent; transporation equipment, 64 percent; computers and office equipment, 88 percent; commerce, 53.4 percent; construction materials, 38.9 percent.[16] The areas of most rapid growth in U.S. investment were petroleum, petrochemicals, transport equipment, and machinery. Of the top 500 U.S. manufacturing concerns ranked by sales, 277, or 55 percent, had Mexican operations in 1977. Of the top 100 U.S. companies, 71 percent had Mexican manufacturing investments.[17] U.S. firms also dominate television programming, tourist hotels, and related services. In addition, foreign capital dominates the cement, synthetic fibers, and communications industries, and has influence in such sectors as textiles, iron and steel, and agriculture.

Most significantly, TNCs are located in those sectors of industrial production having the highest levels of capital concentration. According to economists Fernando Fajnzylber and Trinidad Martinez Tarrago, by the early 1970s almost two-thirds of TNC investments, compared with less than one-third of Mexican investments, was located in sectors with more than 50 percent concentration (i.e., the four largest firms in the sector accounted for over half the sector's total production).[18] These monopoly sectors also tended to be the most dynamic ones, veritable engines of capital accumulation and major contributors to Mexico's high GNP growth rates in the 1950s and 1960s. Since they also tended to be capital-intensive, they did little to resolve Mexico's unemployment problems.

Consequently, when in 1964 the United States terminated the *bracero* program, which had legally contracted up to 450,000 Mexican workers a year for seasonal farm labor in California, Texas, and other states since 1942, Mexico introduced its Border Industrialization Program of labor-intensive assembly plants *(maquiladoras)*. The Mexican government allowed the *maquiladoras* to import parts duty-free, while the U.S. government allowed the return of assembled products in like manner. By 1972, nearly a third of the value of *all* U.S. components sent abroad for assembly went to Mexico, and by 1977 more than $1 billion worth of *maquiladora*-assembled products was being returned to the United States every year. Mexican workers received wages far under those paid U.S. workers in the same industries, worked longer days, and produced more per hour at greater risk to their health—for example, women performing electronic assembly operations with the naked eye and producing 25 percent more than their U.S. counterparts using microscopes. One Mexican minister of industry and commerce said that the goal was "to offer an alternative to Hong Kong, Japan, and Puerto Rico for free enterprise."[19] Besides traditional U.S. manufacturers like GM, Dupont, Dow Chemical, and so on, such diversified concerns as Transitron Electronic Corp., Litton Industries, Fairchild Camera, Hughes Aircraft Co., and Lockheed Aircraft, most of them among the top twenty subsidized clients of the Pentagon, moved into Mexico. Subsequently, Mexico permitted the establishment of foreign *maquiladoras* in the interior of the country as well. By 1982, U.S. companies owned some 700 of these *maquiladoras*.

In the border area, the *maquiladora* program proved particularly profitable for U.S. interests. A TNC paid wages according to Mexican norms but sold the finished products in the United States according to much higher U.S. price norms. Moreover, sizable portions of the wages earned by *maquiladora* employees were spent on the U.S. side of the border. Of those employed by the 500 border-area plants established between 1965 and 1975, most (85 percent) were poorly paid single women between sixteen and twenty-three years of age. Whenever there was labor unrest or a recession, *maquiladoras* routinely dismissed personnel, closed down, or moved to another part of Mexico. Each new locale of such plants experienced a small economic boom until the next economic downturn. Consequently, far from being reduced, unemployment rates in those cities penetrated by the *maquiladoras* rose, boosted by the arrival of thousands of persons from nearby areas in quest of work. From 1965 to 1982, fewer than 140,000 jobs were provided by the *maquiladoras*.

Foreign capitalists like to justify their behavior in Mexico by claiming that it is, after all, "their" money that is involved. Yet U.S. corporations finance 71 percent of their direct investments with Mexican state and private capital. A 1967 Harvard Business School survey ranked Mexico the third (after the United States and Canada) most important host for 187 U.S.-based TNCs (representing the bulk of U.S. foreign direct investment in manufacturing), half of whose Mexican ventures were either acquisitions or branches of other previously established enterprises. By the early 1970s, three-fourths of all new foreign investments were acquisitions of existing companies.[20]

Tables 3 and 4 present an illuminating profile of foreign investment in Mexico between 1940 and 1980. Table 4 gives the lie to the foreign investors' claims that "they put in more than they take out." It shows that they have been taking out more than twice what they have been investing since from at least the 1960s. For example, in the two-year period 1975–1976, a time when an estimated $4 billion of Mexican private capital was "fleeing" the country because of the populist rhetoric of President Luis Echeverría and the recession that started in 1973, new direct foreign investment amounted to $594 million (twice the 1969–1970 amount), but the outflow of dividends, interests, and other payments to foreign investors added up to a whopping $1.5 billion, almost triple what came in.

Part of the U.S. TNCs' power in Mexico derived from the head start in technology and capital reserves enjoyed by the companies over their Mexican counterparts. Although in recent years the United States' technological supremacy has been challenged by Japan and Western Europe, as late as the decade of the 1960s the United States still accounted for more than two-thirds of all receipts based on patents and licenses accruing to the six capitalist

Table 3
Direct Foreign Investment, 1940–1980

Year	Total (million U.S. $)	Agri- ure	Mining and metallurgy	Manuf.	Elect.	Com- merce	Transp.	Other
				(by percent)				
1940	418	1	28	7	30	3	31	0.3
1945	583	1	28	15	23	7	25	1
1950	566	1	20	26	24	12	13	3.1
1955	919	2	19	34	20	13	6	5.2
1960	1,080	2	16	56	1	nd*	nd	5
1965	1,744	1	8	69	1	16	0.5	5.5
1970	2,822	1	6	74	0.2	15	0.3	3.5
1974	4,275	1	6	76	0.07	14	0.02	3
1977	5,643	0.2	4.7	76.1	nd	12	nd	7
1980	8,459	0.1	5	77.6	nd	8.9	nd	8.4

Source: For 1940 through 1974, prepared by Sergio Ramos G. in Peter Baird and Ed McCaughan, *Beyond the Border: Mexico and the U.S. Today* (New York: NACLA, 1979); Banco de México, annual reports; and Ministry of National Properties and Industrial Promotion (Sepafin) (1981).
*nd = no data.

nations most active in patent activity.[21] By 1970, research-and-development (R & D) funding in the United States, over half of it paid for by taxpayers' monies (even though most of its products remained within TNC hands), approached $40 billion a year, an amount far greater than most countries' GNPs and 2.5 times more than that spent on R & D by all the West European nations combined.[22] Of course, quantity did not entail quality, as any U.S. consumer can verify. U.S. TNC activity in technology was, and remains, monopolistic or oligopolistic, with the advantages quantitatively measureable but qualitatively insecure.

Classically, when dealing with weaker countries, TNCs have used technology sales to help "denationalize" strategic economic sectors, such as oil, mainly through the capitalization of technological inputs. Whether through joint-venture deals or pure licensing agreements, a TNC can stipulate that part or all of the technology furnished may be paid through "equity participation" (together with a lump-sum payment or a running royalty, usually calculated as a percentage of net sales). Later renegotiations of technological agreements may include the demand for equity participation. Or the terms of payment for technology may imply an increase of the debt/equity ratio that can lead to some sort of equity "sale" or "transfer" to the supplier of the technology.

While Mexican industrial output increased 5 times between 1940

Table 4
Foreign Investment and Income, 1960–1980
(million U.S. dollars)

Year	New direct foreign investments	Total net foreign income on investments*	Reinvested profits
1960	62.5	141.5	10.5
1961	81.8	148.1	25.2
1962	74.9	159.3	36.2
1963	76.1	182.9	34.4
1964	83.1	242.2	56.3
1965	110.1	234.9	73.5
1966	111.1	277.4	73.7
1967	105.4	321.4	105.3
1968	111.1	367.7	112.2
1969	166.3	435.5	139.6
1970	183.9	473.6	154.2
1971	168.0	339.6*	nd†
1972	189.8	403.8	nd
1973	287.3	485.6	nd
1974	362.2	556.9	nd
1975	295.0	686.0	nd
1976	299.1	816.9	nd
1977	327.1	633.2	nd
1978	383.3	707.4	nd
1979	810.0	1,073.4	nd
1980	1,622.6	1,580.3	nd

Source: Nacional Financiera, *La economía mexicana en cifras* (1970); Banco de México, *Estadísticas básicas de la inversión extranjera en México* (nd), Cuadro 5; and Sepafin (1981).
*For 1960–1970, profits remitted abroad and profits reinvested, interest royalties, and other payments; for 1971–1980, same *minus* profits reinvested (for which there are no data).
†nd = no data.

and 1965, imports of foreign (mainly U.S.) industrial or capital goods and replacement parts increased 12.5 times. This not only added directly to capital accumulation for U.S. corporations but also provided them with critical leverage for increasing their investments in related areas of the economy. U.S. companies "tied" their sales of technology to further sales and expansion possibilities, using a panoply of means, including patents, licenses, and know-how agreements. Yet Fajnzylber and Martínez Tarrago have emphasized the inappropriateness of most of the technology that was imported, both in terms of cost and labor utilization. They conclude that "fewer and fewer productive jobs have been created per unit of capital invested" and that capital has been increasingly remunerated "at the expense of workers' incomes."[23]

Starting in the 1950s, most U.S. TNCs became interested in exporting investment capital, technology, and capital goods rather than merely manufactured items, seeking abroad an outlet for their own overproduction of Department I goods and access to pools of cheap labor in order to achieve rates of profit superior to those at home. Products then manufactured in a country like Mexico were in turn sold there or exported at handsome profits. To assure ongoing reproduction of these superprofits and fend off potential nationalization or Mexicanization, TNCs used their technological supremacy as a lever. Many retained full control over factories; some opted for joint ventures; yet others preferred direct technology sales to state enterprises since they could fetch high prices. In 1970, Business International Corporation, a consulting firm for TNCs, suggested that "a new era of international investments has dawned, in which the predominant characteristic is the exploitation of technology. . . . If licensed technology and management contracts can afford sufficient income and control without equity ownership, all the better in terms of economic nationalism."[24] Consequently, U.S. Secretary of State Henry Kissinger made so-called technology transfers a key agenda item at the 1976 meeting of the Organization of American States (OAS) in Chile.

Technology sales helped increase foreign domination of Mexico's economy and enabled the foreign TNCs to evade nationalist laws ostensibly aimed at regulating foreign investment. As the manager of one U.S. affiliate in Mexico was reported in 1975 to have stated, "The use of payments for technology is the easiest legal way to transfer profits out of the country."[25] TNCs in the Mexican pharmaceutical industry, for instance, by using various tricks of internal bookkeeping, particularly "transfer pricing" whereby they underpriced exports and overpriced technology imports (sometimes using a fictitious third-party "dummy office" as an intermediary), were reported as making up to $400 million a year on transfer pricing alone.[26]

Transfer pricing and disguising profits as costs for technology imports enables TNCs to increase their capital accumulation in Mexico. By raising their declared "costs" they reduced whatever profits they declared and had to pay taxes on. They further reduced their declared profits and taxes owed by underpricing exports of goods produced by the "expensive" technology. Transfer pricing thus had the effect of partially decapitalizing Mexico in the name of capitalizing it. Such disguised parts of imperialist capital accumulation never appeared in the statistics on foreign profits, such as those in Table 4. By 1970, so-called technology transfers, through the tricks of transfer pricing, were remitting to the United

States from Mexico almost twice as much money as officially declared profits.[27]

Although the Mexican government periodically paid lip service to the idea of independent technological development, it never spent more than 0.6 percent of its GNP on R & D. Its research aims were oriented toward reproducing U.S. technology. Research for meeting the needs of the masses remained practically nonexistent. "Comparative-cost tables" were drawn up and a decision then made whether it was more economical and conducive to economic growth to import foreign know-how and entire productive installations or to invest in developing an indigenous science and technology—and the former invariably won out. Yet Mexico usually could not import a piece of machinery without importing the entire technology-and-science package insisted on by the TNCs, including know-how,[28] thereby making its economic development decisions inseparable from its approaches to such cultural questions as education.

Much of the success of imperialism's historic expansion and survival has derived not only from its maximization and maintenance of advantages in technology but also from its intellectual sources, science and education. In the 1940–1970 period, the Rockefeller and Ford foundations spent millions of dollars on Mexican educational projects, much of it going to scholarships and professional training. U.S. public and private "aid" flowed heavily into Mexican private universities and technical or business administration schools. The private University of the Americas was created on the outskirts of Mexico City (since moved to Puebla). Trained Mexican professionals often limited their services to the wealthy elite, the state, or private (often foreign) corporations. Or they emigrated. For example, between 1966 and 1968, about 20 percent of all graduates in engineering left Mexico, while from 1961 to 1965 almost 10 percent of all medical school graduates went to the United States.

Capitalism tends to reproduce itself wherever it asserts its dominance as a mode of production, and this reproduction, however uneven in practice, occurs also in the superstructural areas of science and culture. Anyone who has experienced the spread of the English language and U.S. cultural norms abroad, along with the export of Coca Cola, Donald Duck, and U.S. technology, can readily appreciate the validity of the concept "cultural imperialism." By 1960, *Selecciones del Reader's Digest* had the largest circulation of any magazine in Mexico, and U.S.-style goods and fashions, including the latest model cars or rock and pop music, were being mimicked by the bourgeoisie as devotedly as ever they imitated the French.

U.S. tourists, magazines, films, and television programs began flooding Mexico. In spite of their own nationalism and bountiful culture, Mexicans found themselves imitating and aspiring to the values and goals of the historically hated "gringo."

Thus technology sales contributed not only to capital accumulation for the seller but also to a culturally deformed and economically subordinated capitalist development for the buyer. Both the Mexican and the non-Mexican bourgeoisies, directly or indirectly, managed to accumulate capital as a result of technology transfers at the expense of the working class, which used the technology. Yet the non-Mexican bourgeoisies, being the technology sellers, accumulated far more capital and at faster rates. Consequently, in spite of Mexico's economic growth, there developed a deepening pattern of relative decapitalization, manifested in the outflow of remitted profits, payments on technology, debt amortization, trade imbalances, and so on.

Because of dependence on foreign loans, capital, and technology, because of large-scale state participation in productive investments, and because of domination by domestic and foreign monopolies, Mexico's economic system could, by 1970, be succinctly described as dependent state monopoly-capitalism. U.S. capital did not control the economy in its entirety, but it wielded sufficient influence to make a critical difference—and therein lay Mexico's structural economic dependence.

"Green Revolution," Peasant Dispossession, and Land Concentration

Mexican agricultural production increased sixfold between 1940 and 1975. Contributing to its success was the "Green Revolution," introduced to the world for the first time by the Rockefeller Foundation and Mexico's Ministry of Agriculture in 1943. By increasing yields through the implementation of a "package of inputs" (hybrid seeds, chemical fertilizers, insecticides, and systematic regulation of water), the Green Revolution served to replace many acres of traditional foodstuffs with specialized crops for export, animal feed, or food processing, setting Mexico on the road to becoming an importer of its most traditional crop, corn. The proportion of cultivated land dedicated to corn dropped from 65 percent in 1940 to 53 percent in 1960. Massive corn imports in the late 1950s, combined with state-fixed prices, led to a relative decline in the price of corn, which never recovered its 1945 level. Meanwhile, TNCs gained control of Mexico's food imports—and one, Continental Grain, began exporting Mexican corn to the Soviet Union. The Green Revolution, which soon spread to other ex-colonial countries, thus became a dream come true for modern agribusiness, as Continental joined Cargill, Cook Industries, Burge Corp., Luis Dreyfus Corp., and Garnac in obtaining control of over 80 percent of the world's grain trade.[29]

The character of Mexico's agricultural production was transformed. In 1950 the country was consuming only 3,500 tons of fertilizer a year; today it uses over 1 million tons. Some 3.5 percent of farms currently absorbs over two-thirds of such modern inputs, including irrigation and total agrarian capital investment. As early as 1957, some 60 percent of agricultural products was for export, and between 1950 and 1970 production of wheat, sorghum, and soybeans shot up sixfold. Sorghum production for the booming export-oriented animal-feed industry exemplified how the new system worked. Bank credits from the national Banco Rural and the two largest private banks, Banco de Comercio and Banco Nacional de México, financed production by *ejidatarios,* smallholders, and large-scale farmers. Through direct sales contracts to Ralston Purina, the Carretero family of Tamaulipas, the northeastern state accounting for a quarter of the nation's crop, handled 40 percent of its commercialization. Another 40 percent was accounted for by the multi-million dollar state food agency CONASUPO, which in turn sold directly to Ralston Purina, Anderson Clayton, International Multifoods, Malta, or the state-private joint venture Alimentos Balanceados Mexicanos (Albamex). In central Mexico's Bajío, the nation's traditional granary, one-fourth of sorghum production was absorbed by Ralston Purina—which, together with Anderson Clayton, currently removes 3 million tons of corn and 6 million tons of sorghum a year from human consumption for the animal-feed industry. The National Center of Agrarian Research has repeatedly acknowledged that this helps enrich TNCs, dispossess peasants, and increase hunger, but the state, complicitous in these trends, still looks the other way. As a result, from 1965 to the present food imports have approximated up to one-fifth of the balance-of-trade deficit and, together with shortages in locally produced food staples, have helped fuel Mexico's rising rate of inflation.

Such "modern" agricultural development has meant substantial investment. Only 7 percent of Mexico's cultivable land can produce good harvests without irrigation, and so, as a first priority, the government dedicated 15 percent of *all* its investments between 1941 and 1946 to irrigation projects. After the war, additional funding for the Green Revolution came from the Ford Foundation, AID, European Economic Community aid programs, and the World Bank.[30] The state further participated by channeling funds, limiting land distribution, rewriting agrarian laws, regulating certain agricultural prices, and subsidizing the social costs of production and infrastructure (roads, electrification, fuel, warehousing) in a manner favorable to the rural bourgeoisie and modern agribusiness.

Most costs and risks were passed on to the small and medium peasants. Peasant labor was regularly undervalued and often not remunerated—for instance, the work of children or poor kin went unpaid. Crops were taken to cover interest payments (of 18 to 100 percent), and there was a multitude of other swindles. These, and the low prices paid peasant producers by commercial intermediaries, represented a constant transfer of value from the peasantry to the more favored elements of society. Of the price paid for food by an urban consumer, only 15 to 30 percent remained in the hands of the peasant producer, and various studies have estimated a transfer of value out of the countryside of some $300 million between 1942 and 1961 based just on price differentials among agricultural products, manufactured goods, and services.

Based on the biased assumption that large-scale landholders were more receptive to technological change than "mere" peasants, and on the recognition that only *latifundistas* could afford new expensive inputs, the Rockefeller Foundation and the Ministry of Agriculture focused postwar agricultural development aid on select regions, especially the northern states, which had a high degree of land concentration in the hands of former Porfiristas and new "revolutionary" landlords. In Sonora, for example, the government gave wheat producers an annual subsidy of 250 million pesos ($20 million), some of which these old-time hoarders pocketed without greatly increasing production. The rest they added to federal irrigation subsidies (60 percent of which went to the northern states), sucking the water table nearly dry as they opened new lands to cultivation and maintained the federal bonanza. Today, the North Pacific region has 53 percent of the nation's irrigated surface, compared with only 1.7 percent for the south; yet the southern, largely Indian, state of Chiapas—Mexico's poorest—contains one-fourth of the nation's potential hydraulic resources. The result, according to the 1970 census, is that the northern states of Sonora and Sinaloa, together with Veracruz, account for almost 40 percent of Mexico's 91,000 tractors and 30 percent of the value of agricultural production.

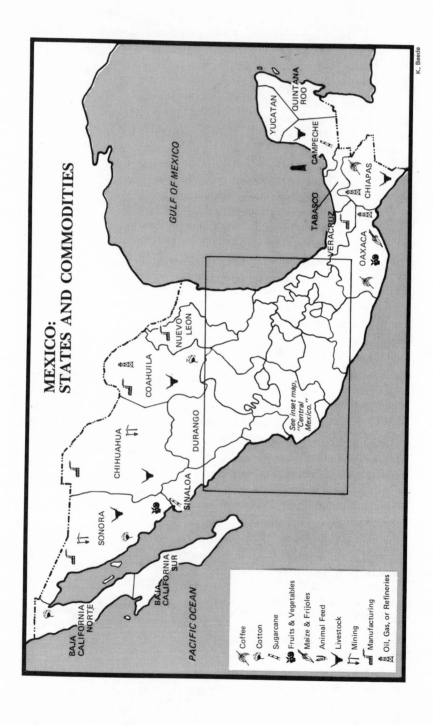

MEXICO: STATES AND COMMODITIES

GULF OF MEXICO

PACIFIC OCEAN

BAJA CALIFORNIA NORTE

BAJA CALIFORNIA SUR

SONORA

CHIHUAHUA

SINALOA

DURANGO

COAHUILA

NUEVO LEON

See inset map, "Central Mexico."

YUCATAN

QUINTANA ROO

CAMPECHE

TABASCO

CHIAPAS

VERACRUZ

OAXACA

Coffee
Cotton
Sugarcane
Fruits & Vegetables
Maize & Frijoles
Animal Feed
Livestock
Mining
Manufacturing
Oil, Gas, or Refineries

K. Beede

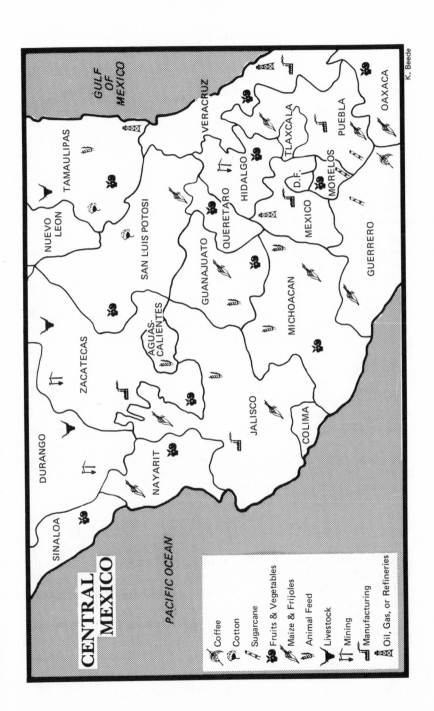

CENTRAL MEXICO

Legend:
- Coffee
- Cotton
- Sugarcane
- Fruits & Vegetables
- Maize & Frijoles
- Animal Feed
- Livestock
- Mining
- Manufacturing
- Oil, Gas, or Refineries

Labels:
GULF OF MEXICO
PACIFIC OCEAN
TAMAULIPAS
NUEVO LEON
VERACRUZ
SAN LUIS POTOSI
QUERETARO
HIDALGO
TLAXCALA
PUEBLA
OAXACA
D.F.
MORELOS
MEXICO
GUERRERO
GUANAJUATO
MICHOACAN
AGUAS-CALIENTES
ZACATECAS
JALISCO
COLIMA
DURANGO
NAYARIT
SINALOA

K. Beede

Under the effects of the Green Revolution, official credit unions, energy co-ops, and fertilizer plants swiftly turned the small-scale landholders into a captive market for supplies, charging them higher rates than those charged to the large-scale landholders, whose professional organizations carried more clout with officialdom at home and abroad. By 1965, a typical region developed by the new technology—like the Yaqui Valley of Sonora—had dispossessed 80 percent of those peasants who had received lands earlier under agrarian reform. In addition, the agrarian boom brought with it the crassest of consumerist values, which further drove smallholders into debt as they took out loans to obtain consumer goods and services. One researcher has emphasized the creation of an internal class system among the communal Yaqui Indians of Sonora through this "financing of class divisions through commercial debt."[31]

State agencies established in the name of protecting national and peasant interests normally favored the large-scale commercial farmers, often punishing smallholders for minor infractions while tolerating or encouraging the unscrupulous behavior of the landed elite. While capitalist landholders were given ample credits and subsidies, smallholders and *ejidatarios* averaged little more than 2 percent annual credit increases from 1943 to 1968. Today, 85 percent of agricultural credit goes to the top 0.5 percent of landowners. Unable to compete with these state-favored sharks, the lesser fish of the agrarian sea were steadily gobbled up. *Neolatifundismo* was the order of the day. State price guarantees also worked to the advantage of large-scale mechanized units of production with high labor productivity, further reducing the prospects of peasant producers. And CONASUPO—supposedly engaged in providing low-cost food for the masses—set decent prices for crops only to routinely cheat the peasants, while paying for many of the imported inputs of agricultural industries and for most of the nation's corn imports. Food prices eventually went up, not down.

Small and medium peasants received the new technological inputs on credit. Failure to pay on time resulted in default and the loss of land or water rights, or in their having to rent or sell their parcels outright. Article 55 of the Constitution prohibits *ejido* land from being alienated, but exceptions are permitted under Article 76 and various agrarian-reform laws allowed the leasing of *ejido* parcels. "Rent parcels?" groaned one Sonora peasant in 1963. "Why here entire *ejidos* are rented out."[32] By 1970, some 70 percent of Sonora's *ejidos,* according to most estimates, were rented; in other areas of high-profit capitalist agriculture, like the Zamora Valley of Michoacán, famed for its U.S.-controlled strawberry industry and for the provision of cheap migrant labor for California, the figure ranged as high as 80 percent. Commercial intermediaries, many in the pay of the agribusinesses, often handled the renting and were paid in kind, thus extracting the product of peasant labor for the marketplace.

Since the state could legally alter the terms of *ejido* and private lands awarded under agrarian reform, it was easy to dictate to the peasantry what to plant, even what rallies to attend. Although most incoming presidents claimed there was no more land to be distributed, the state periodically broke up a few estates, distributed new land, or settled old land claims in order to quell incipient unrest. For example, during the peak of the peasant revolt in Morelos, led by Rubén Jaramillo, the regime of Adolfo López Mateos decreed that 12 million hectares be distributed, more than the combined total of the previous three presidents. Only 25 percent was actually delivered, however. President Gustavo Díaz Ordaz decreed that 14 million hectares be distributed, but delivered only 30 percent of it. President Luis Echeverría Alvarez decreed the distribution of 11.5 million hectares, and delivered half. President José López Portillo, on the other hand, had, by the end of 1981, distributed less than 1 million hectares. Overall, between 1940 and 1976, only 25.6 million of 52.7 million hectares decreed for distribution was actually handed over. The balance was under dispute, and was often forcefully seized by the deceived peasants. On the other hand, a tiny minority of state-favored *ejidos* achieved agribusiness size, contributing to a sixfold increase in *ejidos'* hiring of wage labor (often other *ejidatarios*) in the 1960s.

In 1967, François Chevalier offered a provocative comparison between the growing plight of the peasantry now and that in the nineteenth century:

> The majority of *ejidos* possess only non-irrigated land on which essential foodstuffs are cultivated, especially the traditional crop, maize. Above all, these *ejidos* do not have access to credit, and the result is greater dependence on moneylenders. These may be capitalists from outside the *ejido*, or local shopkeepers or farmers who are more enterprising or thrifty than the others. Here the danger of seizure of the plots, even of complete ruin and elimination of the *ejidatarios*, is greater than elsewhere. The situation is comparable to that in certain ancient Indian communities which, at the end of the nineteenth or the beginning of the twentieth century, were literally dispersed or destroyed by the penetration and incursions of *mestizos* who—since they were much more economically advanced than the Indians— rapidly took over all the land.[33]

Even as the Liberal Reform of 1857 furthered the monopoly control of land and wealth by a dependent national bourgeoisie allied with a foreign bourgeoisie, so the agrarian reform of 1935–1936 resulted in strengthening the interests of modern capitalism, now with the state as a key intermediary, linking peasant producers to capitalist appropriators. Commenting on the credit mechanisms of peasant dispossession, agrarian analyst John W. Barchfield has observed:

> The more common association of the *ejidatario* with private capital owners involves one of a series of arrangements that is tantamount to rental. The *ejidatario* is paid a fee for the use of his parcel . . . and, if he is fortunate, permitted to participate as a *peon* on his own land. . . . In both cases [the state's Banco Rural and private creditors], however, there occurs a humiliating juxtaposition in which the *ejidatario* is deprived of his autonomy and subjected to the decisions of irresistible bureaucratic or commercial interests . . . which channel . . . the *ejido's* surplus . . . to the support of domestic and international industrial capital.[34]

Unemployment, induced by mechanization and peasant dispossession, became widespread in agrarian communities—and with it, alcoholism, factionalism, and violence. The average number of workdays for the rural proletariat and day laborers declined from 190 a year in 1950 to 90 in 1970. In the 1960s the average annual wage of day laborers dropped, and 3 million rural inhabitants migrated to the cities. Many of the earliest migrants were young women from thirteen to sixteen years of age seeking ways to support their impoverished families.

Despite the severe deterioration in their already abysmal living conditions, those dispossessed peasants forced to farm marginal lands still generated 40 percent of Mexico's corn production, often on steep slopes, and were forced to rent their good lands out to agribusiness interests and become wage or piecework laborers on their own land. Many displaced peasants signed up with the Mexico-U.S. *bracero* program. Initiated as an emergency wartime measure to solve the U.S. labor shortage, the *bracero* agreement was periodically reenacted and increasingly came under the direct control of modern agribusiness or its agents, leading to widespread complaints in both countries about the abuse of the *braceros,* who became virtual slaves, and whose ill treatment helped to keep the wages of other workers down. Eventually organized labor in the United States and other interests brought about the program's termination in 1964, but the migratory flow continued almost unabated—as did the abuses.

Many who did not leave the country migrated inside Mexico itself. The 1970 census showed 1.2 million migratory farmworkers, representing more than 20 percent of the rural population, following the harvests. For example, workers from Morelos and Oaxaca, after harvesting sugarcane, tomatoes, and cotton in San Luis Potosí and Tamaulipas, moved to Veracruz to cut tobacco, and then to Morelos for the tomato harvest. A new occupation emerged: that of the *lonchero* (lunch server), who picked up the afternoon meal prepared by women in town for their menfolk in the field and took it to the workers, sometimes as far as twenty miles away.

As ever larger numbers of desperate peasants were driven into urban slums in the late 1960s and early 1970s, the actual farming population declined in absolute numbers despite an annual population growth rate of over 3 percent. The waves of rural migration to the cities served to maintain a surplus labor force for industrialization, commerce, and services; to keep wages depressed; and to provide scabs for breaking strikes. Those who found steady jobs in the cities abandoned their small rural parcels, while those who did not sometimes returned to the countryside to engage in subsistence farming in little-noticed spurts of "reverse migration."[35]

Meanwhile, Mexico's low rural wage structure attracted TNCs in quest of higher profit rates than those available in their home countries. Wage differentials between Mexican and California farmworkers reveal the basis for agribusiness superprofits. Using the Mexican legal minimum wage as a point of comparison but noting that few Mexican farmworkers earn anything near it, agronomist Ernest Feder observed that by the mid-1970s California farmworkers were making eight times as much as their Mexican counterparts (or seven times allowing for cost-of-living differentials). In industry, the difference was 13 times (or 11.5, allowing for the cost of living). Feder calculated a $95 million annual difference in strawberry agribusiness profits based *only* on these wage differentials—and similar calculations could be produced for other cash crops.[36]

Foreign agribusinesses were glad to share their dominance with Mexico's *neolatifundistas,* select *caciques,* and powerful private or public merchant and banking interests because these were the ones best able to impose the required production, credit, and marketing systems on the rural labor force. These "locals" arranged for the renting of *ejidos* and parcels, and for labor contracts; also they spared the TNCs the need to tie up capital in land, risk nationalization, or take on the problems endemic to agricultural production. Employing such methods, United Brands (formerly United Fruit) and an array of small and medium TNCs known as " broker-capitalists" introduced the huge strawberry industry, which, after ruining Irapuato's human and natural ecology, moved on to Zamora, Michoacán. U.S. investors generally were able to amortize their entire investment in this industry in one year. Similarly, together with Mexican investors, Ralston Purina and International Multifoods came to control the poultry industry. Condensed, evaporated, and powdered milk became a Nestlé operation, and high-powered advertising campaigns selling infant formula as a "modern" substitute for breast-feeding in Mexico (and in other countries with impure water and little refrigeration) contributed to increased infant malnutrition, disease, and mortality. Yet today 35 percent of the population never drinks milk, and many others go for months without it. This is because the food-processing industry consumes 30 percent of milk production and many agrarian capitalists would rather raise cattle for meat export than for domestic milk sales. On the other hand, the average Mexican downs five bottles of soft drinks a week, 45 times his or her milk consumption. Coca Cola alone accounts for 42 percent of soft-drink sales, which increased 31 percent from 1976 to 1979 (compared with less than 10 percent for milk).

It was in fruits, vegetables, and food processing that foreign capital made its presence most strongly felt. Between 1965 and 1975, about 10 percent of U.S. manufacturing investment in Mexico went into the food industry, while profits doubled. Freezing, canning, jarring, and the preparation of soups and sauces, which make up 90 percent of Mexico's industrial food processing, became TNC-dominated. Much of this activity was in the form of joint ventures with Mexicans because of the 1970 law decreeing a minimum of 51 percent Mexican participation. TNCs appropriated between 25 and 35 percent of the Mexican food industry's total gross product and profits. By the late 1970s, fruits and vegetables accounted for 20 percent of all plantings, almost a third of agricultural production, and about one-half of the nation's agricultural exports (for the U.S. winter and spring market). Some twenty-five TNCs, eighteen of which were U.S.-owned, monopolized the largely intermediate- and upper-class internal market and, for occasional foods like strawberries, frozen vegetables, and certain fresh vegetables, the external market as well.

In spite of competition and state regulation, TNCs in industrial food processing spent up to 7 percent of their income in advertising for the internal market—and higher amounts for new crops like brussel sprouts and broccoli. Yet they also produced for urban elites in Central America and elsewhere. For example, Del Monte, to escape the militant unionizing labor force in California, moved its entire white-asparagus production to Mexico in 1975, and now makes over $8 million a year on it through exports worldwide.

Modern agribusiness tied peasant producers to its interests through the provision of credits and technical inputs. Del Monte developed the largest agricultural machinery complex in the Bajío, where John Deere and Ford also established thriving tractor factories. Many TNCs engaged in "contract farming," providing large growers with financial advances for everything from seeds to workers' wages, and then collecting these advances on the basis of delivered produce. This helped cement the alliance between the rural bourgeoisie and foreign capital. Large firms—especially TNCs whose diversified investment portfolios permitted them to pay better wages and to obtain higher rates of productivity than Mexican companies—further controlled rural producers by becoming the "pacesetters" in wages, prices, product selection (by arbitrarily rejecting part of a harvest), marketing, and the ultimate use and distribution of agricultural products.

TNCs also set the trends in land allocation, through their impact on yields, profitability, and demand. For instance, between 1960 and 1975 TNC investments displaced basic food staples in several states by increasing per-hectare yields in commercial crops as follows: tomatoes, chiles, and stringbeans in Guanajuato, fourfold; onions in Querétaro, sevenfold; strawberries in Michoacán, fivefold; pineapples in Veracruz, twofold; tomatoes in Sinaloa, fivefold. Correspondingly, acreage in corn declined in Guanajuato, Querétaro, Sinaloa, and Veracruz; similar declines occurred for wheat in Guanajuato and Michoacán and for *frijoles* (beans) in Veracruz and Michoacán. By 1970, TNC-dominated fruits and vegetables for foreign markets or domestic elites accounted for almost 30 percent of the value of the principal agricultural products in Guanajuato, the heartland of Mexico's traditional "food basket" and, ironically, the 1810–1821 "cradle of national independence."

Moreover, although absorbing the bulk of employed agrarian labor (almost three-fourths in 1975), agribusiness absorbed less labor per unit of production every year due to its ongoing mechanization. Because of the opportunity to exploit women at lower wages, most male labor employed by the food-processing industry was replaced with female labor, and male unemployment increased.

A good example of the prevalent U.S. influence in Mexican agriculture was Anderson Clayton, which ranked second in sales and tenth in net earnings among Mexican companies in 1967. Cotton was then Mexico's leading export, and Anderson Clayton controlled its marketing, production, and scheduling, in part by providing over $200 million annually in credits (or nearly twice the amount of all loans to *ejidatarios* from the ejidal bank, forerunner of Banco Rural. Anderson Clayton was also a major force in cotton production in the countries with which Mexico had to compete—Brazil and the United States. A one-cent drop in the world market price cost Mexico $9 million in export earnings—and Anderson Clayton periodically engaged in cotton "dumping" to remind Mexico who was in control. Then, as costs and risks rose and world demand for cotton dropped between 1967 and 1975, Anderson Clayton stopped financing Mexican cotton cultivation. Production dropped over 50 percent and nearly half a million Mexican farmworkers were thrown out of work. The Mexican government took over the financing, but Anderson Clayton still controlled processing. At the same time, it expanded its investments into production of cattle feed, chocolate, planting seeds, edible oils, chickens, and insecticides, a diversification model followed by such other TNCs as Heinz, John Deere, and Ralston Purina. In this way, Mexico's agriculture came to be dominated by foreigners—from the production and sale of machinery and fertilizers to the processing and merchandising of agricultural goods.

As early as 1967 some Mexicans were expressing concern about the heretofore unimaginable political consequences of this trend. That was the year United Fruit purchased one of Mexico's oldest food preserve companies, Clement Jacques—and Mexicans had heard of United Fruit's propensity for toppling uncooperative governments. However, they need not have worried. Mexico was not Guatemala, and United Fruit was not Anderson Clayton. About a decade later, the Cuauhtémoc Brewery of Monterrey's ALFA group acquired a controlling interest in the United Fruit concern. When the local bourgeoisie gets along so well with imperial capital, there is little need for imperialism's direct intervention.

In the late 1960s and early 1970s, as international farm commodity prices dipped, the livestock-raising and animal-feed industries became the chief arena for capital accumulation in rural Mexico. Millions of acres of cultivable land were turned over to the industries, at great human cost to the peasantry. One-third of reusable land was kept idle in the interest of the cattlemen, and a full 64 percent of the land actually in use was devoted to cattle. The number of head of cattle and acreage for grazing in Chiapas, for example, doubled between 1967 and 1976, leading to eighty-six major peasant protests by communal Indians deprived of their lands. During the same period production of sorghum (used to fatten cattle for export) doubled, and, as noted earlier, Mexico began importing large amounts of corn to feed its people, most of whom hardly ever eat meat. Meanwhile, grazing herds destroyed precious forest reserves, and imports of forest products skyrocketed.

The logical result of the Green Revolution was land concentration on the scale of the final days of the Porfiriato. The 1970 census reveals the trend: 2 percent of all *predios* (farms) were over 1,000 hectares and yet comprised 76 percent of the land; 4 percent were between 200 and 1,000 hectares and comprised 14 percent of the land; and 51 percent were under 5 hectares (half were less than 1 hectare) and controlled only 0.6 percent of the land. In other words, over half the farms were so minuscule as to represent not so much landholders as landless farmers with access to subsistence plots for supplementing whatever income they could obtain from selling their labor power to others.

Such capitalist transformation of the countryside did not help the majority of Mexicans. The world's ninth largest food producer, Mexico ranks sixtieth in life expectancy and food consumption per person. From 1967 to 1976, the average caloric intake per Mexican declined 10 percent. Animals and foreign consumers eat more basic foodstuffs produced in Mexico than do Mexicans themselves. U.N. researcher Cynthia Hewitt de Alcántara concluded her widely acclaimed study of the Green Revolution in Mexico by calling it

> waste: waste of natural resources . . . ; of manufactured agricultural inputs (and the foreign exchange needed to acquire many of them) . . . ; waste of profits generated by rapid technological change, that went into conspicuous consumption or speculative investment . . . ; above all, waste of human skills possessed by the landless workers, *ejidatarios*, and *colonos* [private possessors of state lands in agrarian colonies] whose control over their own land was taken away in the course of agrarian technification, and by the majority of dryland farmers who were abandoned for three decades to survive as they could.[37]

But it was not wasteful in the eyes and pockets of the domestic and foreign bourgeoisies profiting from it. For them, the Green Revolution and the state policies integrated with it established four cornerstones for their capital accumulation on an extended scale. First, it provided relatively low-cost food—until 1965 at least—for the urban population, thereby holding down the reproduction costs of labor and the level of industrial wages. Second, it generated a relative surplus population of displaced peasants who served as labor power for industrialization and as a reserve army of unemployed, thereby helping sustain a low wage base and limiting organized labor's social benefits. Third, it supplied inexpensive raw materials (cotton, tobacco, hemp, etc.) for industry. Finally, through increased agricultural exports, it became a principal source of foreign exchange, then used for the importation of capital goods for industrial production and of items for luxury consumption. Agricultural modernization thus proved to be a basic *condition* for the "economic miracle" of industrialization and its corresponding immiseration of millions of Mexicans.

Industrialization, Monopoly, and the State

The billions of dollars' worth of capital that foreign investors poured into Mexico after World War II penetrated the commanding heights of the economy. As noted before, they included joint ventures with Mexican private and state enterprises. This created a structural connection that united foreign capital with Mexican monopoly capital, the political bureaucracy, and the class-collaborationist trade-union leaders. The authoritarian-technocratic state that evolved did not separate public from private capital in a "mixed" economy, but rather practiced a capitalism backed by the state: the state, claiming to act on behalf of "national" capital, subsidized private monopoly capital, both domestic and foreign. State-produced energy, fertilizers, paper products, and air, rail, and truck transport were offered to capitalists at prices well below the international norm; the state also subcontracted public works projects to private firms. The federal budget allotted ever greater sums ($5 billion in 1980) for the import of capital goods and spare parts, from whose use private capital profited the most. The state also invested in activities considered by private capital to be too unprofitable or risky, and, during recessions, engaged in pump-priming investment to stimulate recovery. For example, the government stimulated a business recovery from the 1958 recession (provoked by the U.S. recession) by granting four-month tax exemptions on reinvested profits and, in 1961–1962, procuring from the United States $615.8 million worth of loans, a new record for U.S. economic assistance to a Latin American regime.

Mexico's large-scale capitalists were the first to acknowledge that their businesses could not prosper and social stability could not be maintained were it not for the state's role in the economy. Paraphrasing a Mexican banker, economist Alonso Aguilar felicitously described the state's role thus: "It is the duty of the state humbly to set the table, and the job of private enterprise to eat what it finds there."[38] Agustín F. Legorreta, director of the private Banco Nacional de México, was more blunt: "The state and private enterprise are, at bottom, the same thing."[39] State expenditures soared from only 8 percent of Gross Domestic Product (GDP) in the 1930s to 25 percent in the 1960s, 45 percent or more in the 1970s, and, with the expansion in oil production, over 50 percent today.

Table 5
Type of Manufacturing Activity, 1960–1974
(by percent, at constant 1960 prices)

	1960	1970	1974
Nondurable consumer goods	61.1	50.3	47.0
Intermediate goods	27.6	31.7	33.5
Durable consumer & capital goods	9.1	15.7	17.5
Other industries	2.2	2.3	2.0
Total	100.0	100.0	100.0

Source: Banco de México, annual reports.

Table 6
Gross Domestic Product (GDP) by Economic Activity, 1960–1979
(by percent)

Year	GDP (billion pesos)	Agri.	Industry		Con- struct.	Whole- sale & retail trade	Transp. & commun.	Other*
			Total	Manuf.				
1960	150.5	16	25	19	4	34	3	18
1963	196.0	16	26	19	4	32	3	20
1970	418.7	11	29	23	5	32	3	20
1975	1000.9	10	29	24	6	31	3	20
1976	1220.8	9	30	24	6	31	3	21
1979	2827.4	9.8	30.2	23.2	6.6	33.6	3.6	16.3

Source: U.N., *Annual Statistical Yearbook,* 1977, and Banco de México, *Producto interno bruto y gasto,* 1979.
*Insurance, real estate, social services, public administration, and defense.

Tables 5 and 6 reveal the character of Mexico's industrialization. Table 5 shows the distribution of manufacturing activity in 1960 and the slow changes beginning to appear by the early 1970s as efforts were made to confront the underdeveloped nature of Department I. By 1968, capital goods represented 50 percent of Mexican imports while raw materials for industrial production accounted for another 32 percent. Import substitution thus turned out to be import-intensive.[40] Further, those enterprises producing capital goods were dominated by foreign capital, which in 1970 received 70 percent of the income from Department I production (20 percent went to state firms and 10 percent to private Mexican companies).[41]

Table 6 shows that manufacturing industries increased their share of GDP from 19 percent in 1960 to 24 percent in 1976, at a

time when the portion of all foreign investment dedicated to manufacturing was moving from 56 to 76 percent. According to the
annual reports of the Banco de México, the share of manufactures
in total exports moved from 11 percent in 1960 to 22.5 percent in
1968 to over 35 percent in 1978/1979 (before dropping back to an
estimated 15 percent in 1981 in the face of petroleum's 72 percent
share, up from 21 percent in 1977).

Most of the manufactured exports were generated in significant
part by foreign capital, including those produced by the U.S. *maquiladora* plants established in the northern border's free-trade
zone.[42] Prior to the boom-and-bust cycles established there, however, U.S. investors had already begun exporting manufacturing
technologies—as in the 1950s when they sent obsolete, over-priced
machinery to "help" Mexico begin developing a wasteful, expensive, and irrational system of producing automobiles.[43] Soon they
insisted on newer technologies and on increasing the number of
original production or assembly plants, using reinvested profits or
Mexican capital and highly productive labor to produce and sell
finished goods for the domestic or foreign markets. From a U.S.
capitalist's point of view, why bother with taxes, trade regulations,
quotas, tariffs, and other intermediate expenses involved in exporting manufactured goods to Mexico when they could be produced right there at lower cost and higher profit? And the United
States could simultaneously maintain and even augment export
profits and favorable trade balances with Mexico by replacing the
export of finished goods with that of capital goods needed in industrial firms. Additional profits were garnered by the export of products manufactured in Mexico to other Latin American countries in
the Latin American Association for Integrated Trade, or, prior to
its demise, the Central American Common Market.

For their part, Mexican capitalists focused their investments in
light industry, banking, agriculture, services, and tourism.
Stimulated by the example of foreign monopolies establishing
themselves in the nation's technology-intensive industrialization
process, they centralized ownership in the hands of a few firms,
families, or economic groups. Between 1972 and 1977, for example, the social capital of the largest fifty private Mexican enterprises
increased 130 percent from $200 million to $456 million.[44]

Tables 7 and 8 reveal the continuing centralization tendency of
capital and the distribution of workers and wages by industrial size
according to the Industrial Censuses of 1970 and 1975. Some 84.2
percent of total production is accounted for by 4.1 percent of industrial firms (i.e., large and medium-size industry). Labor's productivity is greater there, as are wages. Big industry employs 40.7

Table 7
Centralization of Industrial Capital, 1970 and 1975

	Small industry (up to 3 million pesos*)		Medium industry (3 million to 20 million pesos)		Large industry (20 million pesos and up)	
	1970	1975	1970	1975	1970	1975
No. of firms	115,295	114,362	2,712	3,534	968	1,316
Percent	96.9	95.9	2.3	3.0	.8	1.1
Gross production (billion pesos)	44.47	74.76	53.39	107.83	108.76	290.56
Percent	21.5	15.8	25.8	22.8	52.7	61.4
Gross value added (billion pesos)	17.91	30.18	20.37	40.35	40.78	112.30
Percent	22.6	16.5	25.8	22.1	51.6	61.4

Source: Industrial Census, 1970, 1975.
*Gross fixed capital; 1 peso = $.08 (U.S.).

Table 8
Distribution of Industry by Size, Number of Employees, and Wages Paid, 1970 and 1975

	Small industry		Medium industry		Large industry	
	1970	1975	1970	1975	1970	1975
No. of firms	115,295	114,362	2,712	3,534	968	1,316
Percent	96.9	95.9	2.3	3.0	.8	1.1
No. of employees	713,368	604,362	471,837	407,391	469,969	696,166
Percent	45.9	35.4	23.9	23.9	30.2	40.7
Wages paid (billion pesos)	7.93	14.20	8.53	18.79	15.24	46.21
Percent	25.0	17.9	26.9	23.7	48.1	58.4
Average annual wage/worker (pesos)	11,113	23,503	22,942	46,122	32,438	66,380

Source: Industrial Census, 1970, 1975.

percent of the industrial labor force, with an average of 529 workers per firm; medium-size industry employs 23.9 percent with an average of 115 persons per firm; small industry employs 35.4 percent with an average of 5.3 persons per firm. The tables show that centralization of capital was accompanied by the concentration of workers in technology-intensive industry, which generated great surplus value (i.e., surplus labor, or the value of the total product of social labor beyond the equivalent of the socially necessary labor time requisite for the maintenance of the workers and their families). This process was accompanied by a dispersal of other workers in numerous smaller industries that produced far less surplus value. Both capital and labor in small and medium-size industry received lesser rates of profit or wages than was received in big industry.[45]

Labor received better wages in the monopoly sectors of the economy because there the workers organized themselves into unions, which were limited by state law to those areas dominated by monopoly or larger medium capital (as opposed to smaller capital). The 1970 Federal Labor Law, Title 7, Chapter I, Article 364, stated: "Labor unions may be constituted with a minimum of 20 actively employed workers or three employers." This effectively eliminated 80 percent of businesses, mostly small private capital, employing a quarter of the labor force, from any possibility of having labor unions and a correspondingly regularized work force.

Maldistribution of wages was only one aspect of the continued uneven development of the Mexican economy. Another was a sharp imbalance in the distribution of labor. Tables 6 and 9 reflect the neglect of the subsistence sector of agriculture and the growing importance of industry and services, which by 1979 absorbed more than 70 percent of the labor force (compared with only 34 percent in 1940). Yet a comparison of the tables shows that 28.8 percent of the work force remains in agriculture, even though agriculture accounts for only 9.8 percent of GDP. In other words, manufacturing industry, which generates 23.2 percent of GDP with only 19.5 percent of the labor force, is not absorbing workers rapidly enough to uplift the rural poor or their migrant kinfolk, who constitute the majority of Mexico's unemployed and underemployed—estimated at 40 percent in the 1950s and early 1960s and more than 50 percent today. Allowing for a shift in production from mining to manufacturing between 1910 and the present, the picture of unbalanced and unequal distribution of labor and income today resembles in its proportions that of 1910, when agriculture accounted for 67 percent of economic activity and only 24 percent of production, and mining and manufacturing 15 percent of the employed and 23 percent of production.

Table 9
Economically Active Population by Sector, 1940–1979
(in percent)

	1940	1950	1960	1965	1970	1975	1979
Total workforce (in millions)	5.86	8.27	11.27	12.24	13.18	16.6	19.17
Agriculture*	65	58	54	46	39	40	28.8
Industry	15	15	19	20	22	24	27.6
Mining/petroleum	2	1	1	1	1	1	1
Manufacturing	11	12	14	15	17	18	19.5
Construction	2	3	4	4	4	5	6.4
Electricity	0.4	0.3	0.4	0.4	0.4	0.4	0.7
Services	19	26	27	32	38	35	43.1
Trade	8	8	10	9	9	10	13.9
Trans./commun.	3	3	3	3	3	3	3.3
Others	9	11	13	17	20	nd†	25.9
Not specified	—	4	0.7	3	6	—	0.5

Source: 1940–1950, General Population Census; 1960–1970, Nacional Financiera (1974); 1975, *Primer Informe de Gobierno*, Anex I-1977; 1979, Secretaría de Programación y Presupuesto, *Encuesta continua sobre ocupación*, 1980.
*Includes livestock raising, forestry, and fishing.
†nd = no data.

The growth of monopolies has not been limited to industry and agriculture. By the early 1970s, seven private banking groups controlled an estimated 85 percent of all capital, while the two largest private banks, Banco Nacional de México and Banco de Comercio, controlled almost half of all the nation's banking resources. This powerful financial bourgeoisie retained close links to the state, as well as to other banks, insurance companies, investment houses (*financieras*), industries, and foreign corporations. For example, the state's Manufacturing Exports Development Fund, which spent up to $1 billion a year to further private export activity, channeled almost 50 percent of that money through the Banco Nacional de México and Banco de Comercio.[46]

In fact, Mexican banking capital exemplified in a vivid way the high degree of centralization of capital, as well as the continuing merging of bank and industrial capital (the union known as "finance capital") and this finance capital's alliance with the state. Evidence from the bankers' own annual reports confirms that Mexico's political economy was becoming dominated by this alliance— commonly known as state monopoly-capitalism. A series of interlocks and overlaps developed among a handful of leading private banks and the largest national and foreign industrial firms. These in turn maintained close relationships to the state banking sector, which, through its rapidly increasing capitalization and its diversification into the "mixed" (public and private) banking and industrial sectors, came to account for almost half of all credit resources in Mexico by the end of the 1970s. As economist Alonso Aguilar has pointed out:

> The recent expansion of large private mining, iron-and-steel, metal-lurgical, and petrochemical firms, many of them foreign, would have been impossible without state investment and the backing of government banks . . . state banks also are an important factor in that they maintain a low-wage policy and high rates of exploitation of workers.[47]

The state's credit and banking system, increasingly serving to grease the entire production system, was tied to the major international lending markets, headed by the International Monetary Fund (IMF) and the World Bank. Mexico's industrialization was furthered by international loans, making the country by mid-1982 the most indebted in the world ($80 billion). The use of such debts by foreign powers has already been illustrated in Part I. The role played by a developing country's debt structure in capitalist accumulation is not just interest payments or the opening up of new investment opportunities for foreign capital, however. Since labor produces the economic surplus used to meet the payments on the foreign debt, capital accumulation for foreign monopoly capital, while originating in the sphere of Mexican production, finally takes place in the sphere of international money circulation as well. Most important of all, imperialism uses a nation's debt structure to intervene in the shaping of critical national decisions.

A few examples highlight the growing integration of the state with private Mexican and foreign capital. Since its inception in 1934, the industrial development bank Nacional Financiera (Nafinsa), a "mixed" body with the state holding the majority of shares, received billions of dollars in foreign loans—well over half its resources. Most of this was U.S. capital channeled through such international loan agencies as the World Bank, the Inter-American Development Bank, and the U.S. Export-Import Bank. Among the largest lenders were Bank of America, Prudential Insurance Co., Manufacturers Hanover Trust, Irving Trust Co., Chase Manhattan Bank, Chemical Bank, New York Trust Co., Girard Trust Corn Exchange Bank, First National City Bank of New York, Bank of Tokyo, Institute Mobilaire Italiane, and Barclay's Bank, Ltd. Nafinsa cooperated with both the Mexican government, whose top financial officials were usually drawn from Nafinsa's board of directors, and private capital, including foreign investors, to whom it often made loans. U.S. bankers, through their status as Nafinsa's creditors and their purchases of state bonds issued by Nafinsa, were thus able to assert considerable influence over state economic decision making.

At first, most of Nafinsa's loans went into economic infrastructure—irrigation works and transportation. But increasingly Nafinsa shifted its loans to industry proper, especially heavy industry, where it created dozens of its own subsidiaries (often jointly with private capital), employing 100,000 workers. In planning huge investments in the petrochemical industry, Nafinsa in its 1978 annual report said that it would use "the criteria of tripartite association, that is, public sector, foreign firms providing technology, and private national investors."[48] What better statement of the integration of national and foreign monopoly capital with state banking?

The Banco de México, like Nafinsa a "mixed" body with a slim government majority, accumulated even more resources than Nafinsa and constituted the nation's "central bank." It worked closely with the IMF and followed its conservative, pro-monopoly approach to banking. Finally, the third major state banking institution, the Banco Nacional de Comercio Exterior, received 85 percent of its resources from foreign bankers (again, mainly United States.). It worked in close association with the agro-export sector of the economy and the gigantic agrarian state bank Banco Nacional de Crédito Rural.

But it was not just through its joint ventures and financial services to the private sector that the Mexican state played such a pivotal role in the monopolies' accumulation of capital. The state itself gathered the necessary resources by directly exploiting labor, including peasant labor indebted through its lending agencies. Today the state employs at least 1 million workers in its industries and banks, plus another 4 million in joint ventures and subcontracted operations. In addition the state employs 1.1 million people in federal government administration, and another 1.5 million or so in the public education system, the social-security system, the military and police forces, local government, and so on.[49]

Thus, in launching Mexico on the road to rapid industrialization, the state has come to exploit labor on a double scale: directly as the employer of a large labor force, including important parts of the unionized industrial proletariat; and indirectly, through its development of a vast, unproductive state bureaucracy, which implements and enforces labor discipline and political conformity through a complex series of institutions reaching into the remotest rural communities and most degraded urban slums. No worker, no peasant, no small businessperson, state office employee, street vendor, or aspiring student is immune from one part or another of this double exploitation at the hands of the state.

6

Classes and the State

Banco Rural is our *patron* [boss]. We're the workers and we don't even get a wage or have a labor union.
—Group of *ejidatarios*, Michoacán, 1981

Because social classes are not static entities but dynamic, evolving relationships, always in the process of forming, combining, recombining, and reproducing the conditions of their existence, a concrete and complete picture of classes at a specific moment is impossible. Both objectively (the nature of the group's relationship to the means of production) and subjectively (the group's consciousness of this relationship), classes are changing all the time. Nor are classes recognizable from income-distribution figures: although these often provide a useful overall picture, they can confuse rather than clarify a class analysis.

Under capitalism, forms of labor are continuously being transformed: from self-employment to wage labor, from simple commodity production to capitalist commodity production, from a society of scattered producers to one organized in corporate groups, "from relations between persons to relations between things" (Marx). Capitalism's ongoing transformation of labor for the purpose of extracting surplus value constitutes a conflict-ridden *process* of social class formation. Indeed, it is this process of continuous struggle between capitalism's two primary classes, the proletariat and the bourgeoisie—a struggle that involves shifting elements from the intermediate classes and groups undergoing proletarianization, such as peasants and artisans—that gives form and specific historical character to an evolving class structure. In this sense, class structure is shaped by class struggle, even as class struggle is delimited by economic structure.

This chapter analyzes Mexico's evolving class structure in terms of such a process of ongoing class formation and transformation. Underlying the last four decades of class struggle have been changes introduced since 1940 in capitalist production, a second wave of "modernization" following on that of 1880–1940. Throughout this period, the state played a larger and more complex role than it had in the "robber baron" days of the Porfiriato. The state not only regulated labor (and to a lesser degree capital), but it also helped create classes or class segments, shaped or conditioned the class structure, and affected class attitudes. Whether impoverished peasants, urban slum dwellers, unionized workers, low-paid bureaucrats, or influential technocrats, Mexico's social classes and groups grew, declined, prospered, or suffered in relation to the various programs of the capitalist state. The state thus acted as an important agent of class formation or transformation.

As in the preceding chapter, the focus here is on the 1940–1970 period. By 1970, the basic trends of class formation under conditions of the consolidation of dependent state monopoly-capitalism were already established. These trends included the proletarianization of the peasantry, as well as "re-peasantization"; labor exploitation in diverse forms, including proletarianization of the traditional petty bourgeoisie; a growing overlap between different fractions of the large-scale bourgeoisie; the growth of intermediate classes; the development of a sizable industrial proletariat, some of it unionized and most of it low paid, along with atomization of the working class as a whole; and the immiseration of the majority of the population, many of whom migrated to the major cities, which became paved with superhighways and filled with festering slums. The exhaustion of the stabilizing-development model and the onset of economic crisis in the 1960s meant the deepening of these trends. Chapter 7, using the analysis of the class structure offered here as backdrop, will examine in detail the consequent post-1968 intensification of class struggle

By 1970, Mexico was almost as sharply divided between rich and poor as it had been in 1910. In spite of an expansion of the intermediate classes, income distribution had worsened over the years. As Table 10 illustrates, only the upper sectors of the much-heralded "new middle class" managed to resist the gradual decline in share of national income that 70 percent of the population experienced after 1950. Of total disposable income, the share going to 90 percent of the population dropped from 51 percent in 1950 to 49 percent in 1969. During the same twenty-year period, the top 20 percent of the population maintained or increased its income advantage, while the next 30 percent experienced a 0.1 percent decline in its share. The bottom half of the population suffered a 4 percent drop.

To highlight the extremes of class polarization, one research team estimated that by the mid-1960s no more than 300 foreign companies and 800 Mexican ones, many of them only nominally Mexican, dominated the nation, and that within the Mexican

Table 10
Distribution of Family Income, 1950–1969
(by percent)

Deciles* (10% of families)	1950 By decile	1950 Cumulative	1958 By decile	1958 Cumulative	1963 By decile	1963 Cumulative	1969 By decile	1969 Cumulative	Avg. monthly income (1969 prices) 1950	1958	1963	1969
I	2.7	2.7	2.2	2.2	2.0	2.0	2.0	2.0	374	437	457	533
II	2.4	6.1	2.8	5.0	2.2	4.2	2.0	4.0	472	545	518	533
III	3.8	9.9	3.3	8.3	3.2	7.4	3.0	7.0	527	638	745	795
IV	4.4	14.3	3.9	12.2	3.7	11.1	3.5	10.5	610	745	865	927
V	4.8	19.1	4.5	16.7	4.6	15.7	4.5	15.0	665	880	1,069	1,193
VI	5.5	24.6	5.5	22.2	5.2	20.9	5.0	20.0	760	1,140	1,208	1,330
VII	7.0	31.6	6.3	28.5	6.6	27.5	7.0	27.0	968	1,220	1,528	1,860
VIII	8.6	40.2	8.6	37.1	9.9	37.4	9.0	36.0	1,190	1,660	2,308	2,390
IX	10.8	51.0	13.6	50.7	12.7	50.1	13.0	49.0	1,498	2,632	2,960	3,450
X†	49.0	100.0	49.3	100.0	49.9	100.0	51.0	100.0	6,790	9,560	11,615	13,540
90–95%	8.8		10.7		11.6		15.0		2,450	4,124	5,395	7,960
95–100%	40.2		38.6		38.3		36.0		11,110	14,975	17,850	19,150
Total	100.0		100.0		100.0		100.0		1,385	1,935	2,328	2,651
Gini coeffi.	0.50		0.53		0.55		0.58					

Sources: Ifigenia M. de Navarrete, "Income Distribution in Mexico," in Mexico's Recent Economic Growth, ed. Enrique Pérez López et al. (Austin: University of Texas Press, 1967); 1969–1970 family income survey with adjustments. For subsequent surveys showing ongoing deterioration of income distribution, see Banco de México, La distribución del ingreso en México (Mexico City: FCE, 1973); and Manuel Gollás, "Orígenes de la desigualdad en la distribución del ingreso familiar en México," in Panorama y perspectivas de la economía mexicana, ed. Nora Lustig (Mexico City: Colegio de México, 1980).
*Each decile represents 510,500 families for 1950; 640,510 for 1958; 732,960 for 1963; and 889,174 for 1969.
†The last decile has been divided into two parts of 5 percent each.

bourgeoisie 2,000 families constituted the industrial-financial elite.¹ Few have found fault with these estimates. Census data from 1970 and 1980, together with government statistics released between 1976 and 1982, confirm the acute labor exploitation and poverty on which the empire of the upper stratum of the bourgeoisie and its foreign counterpart were built.

On a strict comparative-income basis (see Table 10), at least 65 percent of the Mexican population qualifies as "lower class," while 10 percent qualifies as "upper class"—colloquially, the rich and the poor. About 25 percent fall somewhere in the middle and presumably constitute the intermediate classes. However, closer examination suggests that many people from the intermediate classes are poorly paid and struggling white-collar workers; that lines between classes are blurred; and that cleavages exist within classes. Nevertheless, the major gap in the social structure is between rich and poor, with many elements of the intermediate classes falling on the poorer side of the divide, even as was the case in 1910.

It should be kept in mind that such statistics underestimate the harshness of reality. For example, figures for 1960 show about one-third of the population "economically active"; for 1970 and 1980, about one-fourth. Yet in fact many economically active women, children, and aged are never counted. They work as family labor, or as shepherds, seamstresses, street vendors, carriers, messengers, servants, shoe-shiners, car washers, marketplace stall operators, and so on. Thus in reality the official rate of unionization—24 percent of the labor force—is much lower, since so many of the economically active are not counted in work-force statistics. Correspondingly, those earning less than the legal minimum wage—officially 60 percent of the labor force—constitute a much larger percentage than reported. Census categories obscure class lines, conceal unemployment, and fail to capture the complexity of economic-survival strategies undertaken by working families, village communities, or *ejidos*. The truth is that almost everyone who can, works. For most people their survival is at stake, and even when an entire family works, they often cannot make ends meet.

Polarization of social classes is what one would expect given Mexico's history. As production, distribution, and exchange became more uniform and centralized during capitalism's development into monopoly capitalism, and as imperialism increasingly integrated its economic stakes with those of the Mexican bourgeoisie and state, a clear dividing line polarizing the classes emerged: on one side of the line stood the triad of imperialism/state/domestic and foreign bourgeoisies; on the other side were much of the lower-paid intermediate classes, peasants, workers, and the general mass of underpaid, underemployed, or unemployed.

Of course, the political picture is more complex, with select elements from one polarity siding from time to time with those of the other. But the objective reality, in terms of Mexico's historical dynamic, is this one of class polarization between owners of the means of production and workers who produce or help realize value. Subjectively, class consciousness, class alliances, and social mobilization are political phenomena that alter from crisis to crisis in quite complicated ways, as was evident in Part I and as this and subsequent chapters will further illustrate.

Rural Class Structure: Proletarianization, yet "Re-peasantization"

Gross differences in the standard of living between the city and the countryside have led one scholar to refer to Mexico's "lopsided revolution."[2] In the countryside, schooling averages 1.3 years, medical services are minimal, 62 percent of the people lack potable drinking water, 80 percent of adult workers suffer malnutrition, and 75 percent of the work force receives a total annual income well below the equivalent of the legal minimum wage. Two-thirds of the unemployed reside in rural Mexico. Further, within the countryside there exist great regional disparities in wealth as well. Ten states, most of them in southern and central Mexico,[3] have 80 percent of the rural unemployment and account for most of the out-migration. The central-south region (Hidalgo, Oaxaca, Puebla, Querétaro, San Luis Potosí, and Tlaxcala) accounts for 60 percent of the *minifundios* (tiny land parcels), which cultivate mainly corn. In the northwest, on the other hand, large-scale capitalist agriculture is firmly entrenched and a "permanent" rural proletariat exists (supplemented by seasonal migrant labor).

Generalizations about the rural class structure are therefore difficult at best. Notwithstanding, post-1940 technification of agriculture reached all regions. To one degree or another, peasants were dispossessed and they and their land subordinated to capital's needs. In addition, there was widespread ecological destruction, not limited to the northwest. For example, commercial agriculture severely reduced forest reserves in oil-rich Tabasco even before the recent petroleum boom. Parts of southern and central Mexico today resemble lunar landscapes.

By 1970, the rural class structure was basically bipolar: a wealthy elite and hoards of poor, mostly landless, peasants. Yet such obvious appearances disguised a more dynamic complexity. Simple formulae that emphasize "de-peasantization" or proletarianization of the rural masses, on the one hand, or the perseverance of communal, folkloric, or other peasant traditions maintaining the peasantry as a single, coherent class, on the other, fail to allow for the shifting patterns of class transformation and intraclass stratification that accompanied the stepped-up tempo of agricultural capitalization after 1940. In any process of capitalist transformation, a dialectic of dissolution-reproduction of the peasantry emerges, with the long-range trend being one of proletarianization. Capitalism's dominance, together with historical, geographical, or cultural conditions, underlies the specific forms taken by this dialectic. In Mexico's case, the process of de-peasantization was never completed, ironically *because of* capitalism's transforming impact.

In 1950, about 85 percent of the nation's *ejidatarios* earned over half their income from farming: today less than 40 percent do so. Most engage in seasonal labor as part of a low-paid proletariat. The vast majority of farms *(predios)* do not produce enough even for their own consumption. Thus most rural workers literally cannot survive in only one activity, whether as peasant or proletarian. In terms of income, subsistence farming supplements wages and not, as usually stated, the other way around. The majority of the rural economically active population, in seeking wage income where it lives or by following the harvest trail from state to state and crop to crop, from as far south as Chiapas to as far north as Michigan, is an irregularly employed rural proletariat. A minority—in 1980 an estimated 12 percent of the rural work force, or 800,000 people—constitutes a "permanent" rural proletariat, regularly salaried although underpaid; another 1.7 million workers were counted in 1980 as occasionally employed fieldhands. Many of the regularly salaried were employed on small farms hiring under five workers and were as immiserated as some of their employers who, because of the low level of technology, sometimes increased their deficits rather than their earnings because of having to pay such hired hands. Yet their only alternative was starvation.

Nearly 80 percent of Mexico's 25,000 *ejidos* and Indian communities can no longer support themselves on farming alone, even though "legally" they account for 43 percent of cultivable land. Since they are forced to rent or migrate, they, together with similarly desperate small private landholders, actually possess less than 30 percent of cultivable land—and most of that is arid, high risk, and of low productivity. More than 90 percent of *ejidos* are noncollective units composed of minuscule individual holdings. There no longer exists sufficient space for the owners' sons to receive parcels; most therefore join the rural proletariat. If this trend continues, any semblance of communal farming will probably disappear altogether.

The government's occasional efforts at preserving Mexico's fading *ejido* tradition accomplish capitalist goals with a populist rhetoric. For example, in the late 1960s and early 1970s the state implemented an internationally financed program in the Chontalpa region of the southeastern state of Tabasco aimed at making it "the granary of Mexico" to meet the food needs of the internal market. In the spirit of the neopopulism of President Echeverría, *ejido* "collectivist" traditions were to be emphasized and large-scale landlords were to be forced to "modernize." Yet, as researcher Armando Bartra discovered[4] and government sources later confirmed, the peasants put up stiff resistance against reformist state technocrats, even allying briefly with landlords and *caciques*. Local religious groups and reactionaries sparked a campaign of anticommunism against the same technocrats. The peasants protested the forced expropriation of their parcels to make way for new dams and collective farms, recognizing that collectivization was meant to strengthen centralized control over *ejidatarios* rather than to democratize the power structure. The state's intervention converted most *ejidatarios* into wage laborers; the remainder in turn hired the labor of immigrant day laborers (50,000 in 1979).

An unforeseen but predictable political effect for the region's proletarianized peasants and immigrant workers was that they carried out their resistance struggle in terms of not just labor demands but also "peasant" demands: the right to a plot of land (and its products). As for the unit of production originally targeted for revitalization, the *ejido*, the Ministry of Agrarian Reform admitted in 1980 that *ejidatarios* were discriminated against in favor of the livestock industry and were suffering a crisis in agricultural production. By exploiting *ejidatario* labor and loans at no risk to itself, Nestlé controlled the biggest dairy operation—appropriating what the peasantry produced. And there resulted more unemployment than when the new program began.

Mexico's few remaining *ejidos* with well-irrigated land—normally for export crops—are as efficient as any of their competitors. In general, however, state agencies like the Banco Rural and other credit institutions run entire *ejidos* (and some private small holdings) as state/capitalist enterprises, giving the peasant "owners" the difference between the bank's investment and the value of production (which is sometimes negative). Most *ejidatarios*—through insufficient capital, the Banco Rural's control of their lands and labor, the corruption of civil servants, the emergence of compromised *ejidal caciques* linked with outside interests, and their own poverty—have been forced to seek wage labor. Those staying on their *ejidos* often feel like proletarians themselves. As one group of mestizo *ejidatarios* in northern Michoacán complained to me in 1981, "Banco Rural is our *patron* [boss]. We're the workers and we don't even get a wage or have a labor union. We feel more exploited by the bank than if we were officially its employees. Our earnings from farming are far less than what we'd get if we were bank employees." Their irrigated *ejido* consisted of four hectares per family and used fertilizers and tractors. And it was not as badly off as most.

Worse off are the Indians, whom census takers count as 14 percent of the population according to the ability to speak one of dozens of indigenous dialects or languages; but many poor people are considered to be Indian because of their labor or economic conditions, so that some demographic estimates range as high as 30 percent. On the other hand, some prosperous mestizos consider themselves white, which increases the portion of whites from 1 percent to as much as 15 percent. Once again, class factors determine racial/cultural designation.

Eighty percent of Mexico's 9 million Indians are agricultural workers, and half of these are landless. The land they still hold is the worst imaginable and continues to experience encroachment and reduction by outsiders, especially now that oil has been discovered on much of it. In 1975, to cite but one example, Indians from the San Francisco community of Chiapas told of how soldiers from the 46th Battalion (with approval of local authorities) assaulted them, burned their homes, and drove them from their land—which was then handed over to non-Indians with political connections.[5] Most Indians are dominated by a system of external *caciquismo,* mediated through coopted community leaders. Indians are excluded from the government, although in 1980 the official political party and the Communist Party each had an Indian deputy in Congress. The INI and the CNC, in spite of Indian resistance, normally impose pro-government candidates in elections for the National Indigenous People's Council, which claims to represent the Indian population, a third of which knows no Spanish. Only a quarter of Indian children attend school, and a recurrent Indian demand focuses on what little education they do receive: the need for more schools, for an end to teachers beating children who do not understand or speak Spanish adequately, and for more teachers from the Indians' own linguistic communities.

Whether Indian or mestizo, women also suffer a special kind of exploitation, especially in the countryside. Wages paid rural or urban workers by capitalists supposedly cover basic necessities for maintaining workers and their families—ongoing reproduction of labor power. Unpaid household tasks performed by women necessary for labor's reproduction are, in effect, being "purchased" by the capitalists when they pay workers wages. The part of the workday's total product equivalent to the wage is known as "necessary labor," while the part beyond that equivalent is known as "surplus labor" and is the surplus value appropriated by the capitalist. In a sense, then, women's domestic labor in the sustenance of workers and the upbringing of future laborers is part of necessary labor. Yet capitalists pay only for the labor of the hired worker at the work place, not the labor carried out at home. Indeed, Articles 168 through 170 of the Civil Code for the Federal District and Territories permit a woman to take a paid job only if she continues her legally assigned role of "taking care of the home" and if her husband feels her domestic obligations will still be met. In the countryside, as well as in the urban slums, women typically care for a few animals or a small garden plot, make or sew clothes, take care of children, prepare meals, clean house, and generally oversee family consumption needs—all without pay.

Among Mexico's women, the most exploited are peasants—5.7 million over the age of twelve according to the 1970 census. Most of them lead a cruel life, routinely subjected to beating by their men, kept to the home whenever feasible, and giving live (or dead) birth every 16 months or so. In spite of its campaigns for birth control, the government says that 10.5 percent of Mexican women have no knowledge of contraceptive methods. By law, abortion is prohibited except in cases of rape or to save a mother's life. Yet there occur an estimated 1 million abortions a year, most of them botched backroom jobs ravaging the lives of thousands of impoverished women. Peasant women's work in child rearing, food preparation, farming, handicrafts, and so on exceeds the labor performed by men. Since so many of their male kin migrate, they are often heads of family without the social rights associated with that role. Most Mexican men, whether rural or urban, are unable or unwilling to conceive of any alternatives for women other than those deriving from patriarchy and capitalism's ongoing reproduction of it.

In addition to this double exploitation of Indians and women, Mexico's peasants suffer the consequences of landlessness, *minifundismo,* and inadequate job opportunities. Of 6.5 to 7 million rural adult workers, about 3.5 to 4 million are permanently landless and must sell their labor power or remain unemployed. Three-fourths of a million hold less than 1 hectare of land, and an equivalent numbers hold under 5 hectares. Less than a fourth of private smallholders make family farming their principal activity. Most of these private smallholders and about 2 million *ejidatarios,* plus lesser numbers of *colonos, nacionaleros* (occupiers of state lands whose status has not been regularized), and *avecinados* (squatters accepted by the community) work their own lands either on behalf of renters or for themselves as subsistence parcels to supplement income earned seasonally as day laborers or in domestic crafts, petty trade, mining, or other activities. In effect, then, the common estimate of 6 million landless peasants is realistic. A minuscule percentage of the rural populace benefits from the impressive production statistics of Mexico's booming agribusiness and *neolatifundismo.*

While all statistics are subject to error, and while considerable crossing over occurs between nonbourgeois groups in the countryside, the figures in Table 11 reflect both class proportions and the continued proletarianization within the rural class structure. If the peasantry is broken down into "rich," "middle," and "poor," then rich peasants constitute about 1 percent of the rural population, middle peasants about 4 percent, and poor peasants, pauperized and semiproletarian, about 33 percent. If we add the poor peasants and rural proletariat together, as most researchers do, then over 92 percent of the rural population are proletarians (including unpaid family labor, mostly minors, who are future proletarians). The poor peasants are often worse off than the landless wage workers and day laborers; they are sharecroppers, tenant farmers, *aparceros* (partners in small plots, private or *ejido*), and landholders whose wage labor accounts for most of their income and whose wages finance the inputs for their subsistence parcels.

All of rural society is highly stratified, with each layer tending to exploit the layers immediately below. For example, middle peasants are generally at the mercy of the bourgeoisie for credit, supplies, and political and social status, and they in turn exploit less prosperous peasants and *ejidatarios,* who often become their labor force at planting and harvest time. They then have a direct and clearly antagonistic relationship with the rural bourgeoisie and less serious conflicts with poor peasants and rural proletarians—with whom they share a class hatred for bourgeois overlords. Similarly, the tiny number of properous *ejidatarios* and private small landholders seek control over middle peasants and also exploit the more pauperized elements of rural society. And even though they are less clear and antagonistic, a series of contradictions—of race,

Table 11
Social Classes in the Countryside

	1960	1970	1960	1970
	(in thousands)		*by percent)*	
Proletariat	3,400	3,030	57.4	59.3
Peasantry	2,500	1,950	42.2	38.2
Bourgeoisie	20	130	0.3	2.5

Source: 1960 and 1970 census data, rounded figures, as presented in Roger Bartra, *Estructura agraria y clases sociales en México* (Mexico City: Era, 1974), p. 172. Nonbourgeois landholding, sharecropping, or tenant elements have been included in the category "peasantry," even though most of them gain over half their income from proletarian labor activities; of prosperous landholders, only capitalist-landlords are included in the bourgeoisie. Figures for 1980 will be based on the 1981 economic census, the results of which were unavailable when this book went to press.

language, and regional customs—separates millions of immiserated rural inhabitants, thereby further complicating the class struggle. Moreover, such contradictions many times become highly antagonistic, as in the land squabbles between different communities of similar Indian groups (e.g., among Michoacán's Tarascas).

Of those peasants who still own land, whether a tiny parcel of an *ejido* or a small private plot, at least 85 percent qualify as impoverished *minifundistas*—down-and-out subsistence farmers unable to produce enough to feed their own families. Big capital's monopolization of land, machinery, credits, and markets has determined the conditions of smallholder production. Few peasants can prosper even as "kulaks," and the movement of property-possessing rural producers continues to be into subsistence production or the proletariat or both, with only a handful rising into the lower ranks of the rural bourgeoisie. It is this immiseration of the rural masses and their recourse to working a subsistence parcel, hiring themselves out as fieldhands, and using community or kinship networks for mutual support that leads sociologists to see most of the rural work force as simultaneously proletarian and peasant. Although there is a continuum from traditional small peasant to full-fledged modern proletarian, most rural laborers engage in both kinds of activity. Even though income from labor (i.e., proletarian activity) is in the majority of cases a more important component of individual, family, or group survival than subsistence farming or other forms of peasant domestic "self-exploitation," the fact remains that the combination of such activities defines these workers as a class in a manner distinct from either a traditional peasantry or a completely modern proletariat. Therefore, when the term "peasant" is used here, it incorporates this twofold activity of most rural workers and recognizes that—given the high cost of technical inputs for producing for the modern market and the lack of availability of year-round paid work—they have to emphasize traditional peasant-type demands for land simply to reproduce themselves as a class. As Arturo Warman has observed, "To be 'modern' and propagate grafted fruit trees, use chemical fertilizers, harvest products which are too expensive for themselves to consume, the peasants have had to make themselves more 'traditional.'"[6] In other words, to make ends meet rural people have had to revert to artisan production or subsistence farming—for which they need adequate raw materials, land, and water.

Re-peasantization has thus accompanied de-peasantization. One rural sociologist describes the majority of those engaged in such domestic peasant activities as "proletarians disguised as peasants."[7] The reason is that they are part of a larger capitalist context that generates both their exploitation as low-paid farmworkers *and* their recourse to self-exploitation as subsistence farmers or domestic handicraft producers for the purposes of survival. This double exploitation, as we shall see, extends to the urban subemployed and some of the regularly employed as well. Many factory workers augment their abysmal wages by weekly gifts of food supplies from relatives in rural areas. In what the French anthropologist Claude Meillassoux has called "domestic economies,"[8] the self-production of food, primitive shelter, articles of clothing or furniture, and other necessities by rural and urban workers offers up to capital quantities of labor power for which capital has never had to pay a living wage, or offers pitiful wages to employ when convenient. In Mexico, the high levels of self-sustenance engaged in by workers in general help fulfill functions that capitalism and its state avoid or barely address, particularly the function of social security.

One result of the combined process of proletarianization and re-peasantization is that peasant demands are increasingly being matched by proletarian ones. For example, in May 1978 some 5,000 farm laborers led by a regional peasant federation successfully struck some of Sinaloa's agribusinesses. Similarly, women workers in the booming food-processing industry, most of them from peasant families, started fighting for their proletarian rights in the 1960s, when they won the right to unionize. After CTM stepped in to enforce labor discipline, productivity increased, thereby offsetting the companies' periodic state-imposed reductions in food prices. But the women renewed their struggle in the early 1980s, launching a wave of strikes at Kellogg's, General Foods, and Coca Cola against the CTM-TNC alliance. These proletarian demands are related to the rural workers' need for productive land. In a case study of the Mezquital Valley of Hidalgo in central Mexico, sociologist Luisa Paré found that 72 percent of those seeking land or water were rural proletarians, as were 68 percent of those demanding wage hikes, steady work, or improved working conditions.[9] Paré found the proletarians' struggle for land to be a rational way of assuring a source of employment or of finding a more fixed source of income. Similar attitudes were encountered by university researchers in 1981 when they interviewed Michoacán peasant families whose male adult members migrate annually to the United States for lack of sufficient land or jobs.[10]

The fight for productive land, then, reflects not a persistence of traditional peasant customs or of a simple commodity mode of production (subsistence farming, artisanry), but rather a reaction to the forces of modern capitalism that have uprooted earlier forms of small-peasant or community agriculture only to recreate them on a new basis. An abundant labor supply recruitable at much less than the national average wage is obviously in capital's interest. Through its control over marketing networks, capital (or the state serving capital's goals) also appropriates any surpluses produced by *ejidatarios*, subsistence farmers, sharecroppers, and tenant farmers. Moreover, capital converts nonwage laborers and the irregularly employed into "modern" consumers, making it economically impossible for them to revert to precapitalist production as such since they have to buy some of their basic necessities and sell whatever surplus they can generate in a market that, however remote from them, is connected to a national and international process of capital accumulation. Whether buying refined white sugar, soft drinks, the preservative-loaded breads of Pan Bimbo (a subsidiary of International Telephone and Telegraph's Wonderbread), or packaged tortillas, peasant producers and their impoverished urban relatives are paying more for less quality, when in previous generations they consumed the healthier "panela," ground corn, or milk. To do this they need more money income. Thus the reproduction of subsistence-farming peasants (and, as we shall see, of the urban poor), through multiple economic activities, is imposed by capital's dominance.

Moreover, representatives of monopoly capital foster these trends even when recognizing that their development strategies (like the Green Revolution) ultimately produce hunger and revolt among rural producers. For example, in the late 1960s the World Bank, leader of the cartel of international development enterprises sponsored by monopoly capital, and AID began advocating as a solution to the agrarian problems that they helped to generate the delivery of more technical inputs to subsistence farmers—once again choosing Mexico as the pilot project. Now, instead of dispossessing peasants and incorporating them as free labor into the overflowing ranks of the rural and urban proletariat, the aim was to keep them producing on their small parcels as supervised unfree labor. As World Bank Director of Agriculture and Rural Development Montague Yudelman explained, "The traditional, small-farm sector will have to become the producer of an agricultural surplus rather than the provider of surplus labor, as it has been in the past."[11] In this way, subsistence farmers and domestic handicraft producers were expected to serve as cheap commodity producers for capitalist monopolies and as key nonwage reproducers of the labor force. (Actually, by the bank's own testimony, rainfed, unirrigated subsistence parcels already generate about half of Mexico's total agricultural product, while providing food for 87 percent of all peasants.) This represents, then, an increasing emphasis on obtaining surplus food production by controlling the market, sale of seeds, fertilizers, insecticides, machinery, and provision of credit, in order to maintain peasants producing on the land. The goal, again in the World Bank's words, is "to draw farmers from subsistence to commercial agriculture . . . in the form of increased trade in farm produce and in technical inputs and services."[12] It seeks to prevent the "leakage" of technical inputs and resources to large enterprises, the better to build a kulak class of "family farmers," and to maintain a "dynamic balance" of different types and sizes of agricultural units—which the bank hopes will mitigate class polarization and defer revolution.

The commitment of the World Bank, the Mexican government, and other development agencies to "investing in the poor" in rural Mexico has been mammoth. The 1980 figures included the following amounts: World Bank, $300 million; a U.S.-Europe-Japan banking syndicate led by Bank of America, $320 million; Mexican Department of Agricultural and Hydraulic Resources, $800 million; Mexican Ministry of Commerce, $3.5 billion. In early 1981, the World Bank authorized an additional $275 million and the federal government $506 million in credits for unirrigated subsistence parcels for the year 1981 "to eliminate the abandonment" of such parcels. Following the trail blazed by the World Bank, the Inter-American Development Bank promised it would destine half of its 1981–1982 resources "to the poorest sectors in Latin America."

Even the least recognized segment of the poor—women—is encouraged to produce more by this new strategy on behalf of monopoly capital. As an unclassified AID document puts it:

[Women's] contribution to production must be enhanced. . . . The
U.S. recognizes that women in developing countries already have
skills in agricultural production, processing, and marketing which
provide a broad and relevant foundation on which to build. . . . The
U.S. . . . [favors]: fostering labor-intensive economic activities to provide more income-earning opportunities; increasing productivity
through the introduction of appropriate technology, credit and other
inputs; . . . giving people control over their own reproduction.[13]

More than likely, the control over reproduction envisioned by AID
is birth contraception (or sterilization, so often financed by AID)
and *not* control over the means of production and reproduction as
such. Indeed, despite a 1978 Food and Drug Administration ban
on Depo-Provera (a synthetic form of the hormone progesterone)
for contraceptive use in the United States, AID is a major funder of
birth-control injections of Depo-Provera in Mexico and other
Third-World nations. The injection inhibits ovulation for three to
six months, but experiments on animals have shown that it leads to
cancer and other fatal side effects.

In cooperation with Mexico's Río Papaloapan Commission, the
World Bank launched its first full-scale pilot project implementing
this "investment in the poor" strategy in the early 1970s. Called
PIDER, it aimed at capitalizing a remote area in Oaxaca, Puebla,
and Veracruz by harnessing the energy of the Papaloapan River
and the labor of 1.5 million hillside peasant families. PIDER established fruit, vegetable, and sugar agro-industries to process crops
harvested by peasant labor. Yet despite its promises to benefit the
poor, the majority of peasants resisted the engineers' pressure to
grow new crops and use new technical inputs, not because they
were traditional or "backward" but because they soon learned that
the consequences were heavy debt, financial loss, and the reduction
of their lands. When sabotaging the plans failed to stop their implementation, many peasants withdrew into their previous hillside
farming, where at least they knew how to survive. A vicious circle
resulted: the World Bank, local banks, insurance companies, CON-
ASUPO, provincial elites, and modern agribusinesses successfully
commercialized the region; most peasants were ultimately drawn
into the scheme as laborers or food producers; and immense quantities of cheap foodstuffs were generated, but the peasants were left
worse off—having to increase their subsistence farming just to sustain themselves. A select minority, however, became prosperous
kulaks, while the network of petty-bourgeois technocrats, merchants, and middlemen expanded.[14]

Thus, the strategy of investing in the poor perpetuates re-
peasantization precisely because—in German sociologist Veronika

Bennholdt-Thomsen's words—"it is not the lack of market integration, rather its increase, which leads to the immiseration of the peasants and to a retreat to (not persistence in) self-consumption."[15] The participation of the Mexican government in such schemes ties peasants to state apparatuses, prevents their self-organization, and intensifies their division of labor, thereby raising their output and extending the scope of potential labor-capital conflict between the two.

Not coincidentally, the presence of permanent wage laborers is today concentrated not only in the northwest but also the supposedly backward southern areas that have drawn this new infusion of state and international capital: Puebla, Oaxaca, Campeche, Tabasco, Yucatán, Chiapas, and parts of Veracruz, Morelos, and Guerrero—all falsely reputed to be bogged down in precapitalist peasant economies. In the coffee sector, for example, where small or medium-size landholders traditionally handle much of the growing, a state coffee institute has failed to ameliorate the superexploitation suffered by pickers and marginal growers. The institute and a network of TNCs, big coffee exporters, the medium-size agrarian bourgeoise, some capitalist landlords, and commercial intermediaries keep the majority of the coffee workers (many of whom are Indian women) in abject poverty. Some 25,000 Tzotzil, Tzeltal, and Mame Indians harvest the German-owned coffee plantations of Soconusco, Chiapas, while a like number of Nahuas, Totonacos, and Otomís of Puebla's northern sierra pick the crop of La Unión on modernized farms of 100 hectares each. Meanwhile, this sizable labor force is supplemented by 30,000 "undocumented" workers from Guatemala and El Salvador who are paid $2 for 13-hour days. While Nestlé and General Foods dominate the domestic market for instant coffee, Folgers (Procter & Gamble), Coca Cola, and Anderson Clayton account for one-sixth of Mexico's huge coffee export trade (because of the Brazil frost in the late 1970s, Mexican coffee gained second place behind oil in exports).

Nationalization of the tobacco-processing industry in the 1970s likewise has done little to alter the exploitation of growers and cutters by commercial and foreign interests, with whom the new state enterprise is seen as being in cohoots. Mestizo *ejidatario* tobacco growers in turn exploit Indian and other migrant fieldhands who do the cutting at harvest time. Similar patterns exist in the state-dominated henequen and sugar industries of Yucatán, Morelos, and other southern and coastal states.

Such forces of modern capitalism have helped convert the Mexican countryside into a scene of immiseration and violent class struggle, heightened by the unscrupulous behavior of state bureaucrats and commercial intermediaries who exploit the peasantry. Not uncommon are cases of a middleman (or "coyote," as he is known) buying corn from a subsistence farmer at a price well below the federal minimum and then, during a time of scarcity, returning to sell it to the same peasant at up to 200 percent above what he first paid for it. The most immiserated are driven to stone-age conditions: women with their children hunting small animals or collecting wild fruits and herbs on mountain slopes, or, when migrating to cities, seeking food in garbage dumps where entire communities have built shacks, mingling with the scavenging dogs and rats.

In many respects, the poverty, violence, migration, and class warfare in rural Mexico are as intense today as they were at the end of the Díaz regime. Peasants continue to mass and invade the land in an attempt to ensure their own survival, and the army or the landholders' hired *pistoleros* (gunmen) continue to drive them back. A number of peasant movements have had a forty-year record of ongoing militance. For example, in 1943 and again in 1953, Rubén Jaramillo, who in his youth had ridden with Zapata, rose in guerrilla war in the south-central state of Morelos. Jaramillo was both an ordained Methodist minister and a member of the Communist Party. With the Bible in his hand and a rifle on his shoulder, he preached revolution. In 1962, after he had met with President Adolfo López Mateos, army soldiers yanked him, his pregnant wife, and their three sons from their home in Xochicalco and massacred them. The land-for-the-tiller movement continued in his name and in the late 1960s came to encompass most of the nation. In an effort to reduce post-Jaramillo peasant-guerrilla efforts in Morelos, the state placed a sculpted bust of Jaramillo in the center of one of his favorite towns. Commented a disgruntled peasant: "Take a close look at that bust: even in supposedly honoring him, his assassins had to cut off his arms and legs."[16]

For another example, pockets of peasant militants throughout the nation, who since the late 1920s have been known as *agraristas,* have repeatedly rallied to national movements drawing together progressive elements from diverse social classes. In the early 1960s many *agraristas* joined the nationwide but short-lived Movement for National Liberation (MLN). The MLN represented a vigorous attempt to unite Marxists, disenchanted intellectuals and artists, workers, peasants, and prominent progressive *políticos* like ex-President Lázaro Cárdenas into a broad-based movement for revitalization of the Mexican Revolution. It fell apart when Cárdenas grew disenchanted with the pro-Fidel Castro leanings of younger militants and the state escalated its dual policy of repression and cooptation. Nevertheless, many ex-MLN peasants continued their struggles locally. In the southwest state of Guerrero, they were led by schoolteacher Genaro Vázquez, from a local peasant family, who formed an armed guerrilla band that continued active after his death in battle, February 2, 1972.

Since the 1960s, much of the rural class struggle has been directed against the traditional mediating process of *caciquismo*. Earlier in the twentieth century *caciques* had been used as intermediaries in the introduction or spread of capitalism, and after the 1910–1920 Revolution "good" *caciques* were expected to deliver the benefits associated with agrarian reform. Struggles to replace "bad" *caciques* with good ones became commonplace, but they were usually in vain. Then leaders of the so-called Northern Dynasty, men like Obregón and Calles, laid the foundations of the national political party that brought together warring regional military caudillos and integrated local *caciques* with the official party and other organizations of the corporativist state. Although some good *caciques* emerged, particularly during the Cárdenas presidency, *caciquismo* and its corruption inexorably became institutionalized—both in political practice and in most people's daily lives. *Caciques* involved themselves in various commercial and financial activities. Whether wealthy regional magnates or simply local bosses with a little more political clout or money than anyone else, they became astute at providing loans and using money as a means of making friends among the people. Only a few rose to prominence by supporting honest leaders instead of corrupt ones. One aging rural *cacique* told a team of rural sociologists, "Of humble background I do everything to serve the people." He had held various political offices, including national ones, and was leading a "humble" bourgeois life.[17]

Rather than being the result of a lack of popular participation in national politics, *caciquismo* is its basic cause. Marked by populist rhetoric and paternalistic content, *caciquismo* has always been characterized by a universally recognized streak of violence, capable of being called on at any moment, with the help of private armies or the national armed forces. Thus *caciquismo* both applies control with armed terror and legitimizes control with unarmed (and disarming) celebration—such as inauguration of a new school, clinic, or road. *Caciquismo* is also linked to *patronazgo* (the patronage and godfather system) and to religious or cultural ceremonies. These customs are in turn economically beneficial to merchants and local *caciques*, as "folklore" becomes "business," not just in the traditional manner of squeezing funds out of the poor to provide for ceremonial rituals but in the modern mode of national and international tourism. Poor Indians often identify with their rich Indian *cacique*-exploiters, who use their traditional dances to collect money from tourists, rather than unite with their impoverished mestizo peers, who in turn sometimes support local mestizo *caciques* or entrepreneurs selling tourists their wares. In this and other ways, *caciquismo* blurs class consciousness.

Caciquismo and its system of bribes, payoffs, and control has thus served to disguise or divert the heightened stratification and conflict within the rural population it buttresses. For instance, in a case study of workers and peasants involved in a regional center of sugar production, Paré found that the contradiction between agrarian capitalists (and the state), on the one hand, and peasant producers and rural proletarians, on the other, was diffused by systems of *caciquismo* and internal stratification that often pitted *ejidatario* producers against proletarian cane cutters, often fellow *ejidatarios* who were paid directly from credits advanced by the mill or the state. The capitalists and some of the *ejidatarios* shared a common interest in keeping wages low and worker productivity high. Most day workers in the fields referred to the *ejidatario* "bosses" as *patrón*. In this way, the *ejido* became a camouflage for the mill, even though the internal differentiation among *ejidatarios* was steadily sharpening. With increased state participation in the sugar industry, both as *patrón* and in the form of rural labor-union or peasant-organization *caciques,* the main contradiction between capital and labor sharpened while at the same time a complex economic and political patronage system was reinforced.[18]

In addition, *caciquismo* has served to reinforce peasant susceptibility to following state tutelage or to being coopted. Peasant organizations are easily coopted once their leaders are, since they typically have a shortage of personnel who can become effective leaders; and with their authoritarian organizational structure, coopted leaders can bring the membership with them. On the other hand, the state lacks sufficient resources to pay off large numbers of coopted peasants without carrying out genuine and massive agrarian reform, which leads to a leadership pattern of rebellion-cooptation-rebellion. For instance, radical peasant leader Jacinto López, a member of the late Lombardo Toledano's Popular Socialist Party (PPS, which ordinarily cooperated with the official political party), was one of the first to organize landless peasants into a mass movement in the 1960s; he was coopted with a seat in Congress. Then, in 1969, either because of his followers' disillusionment or his own dissatisfaction with wasting time in a do-nothing Congress, López resigned from the PPS to lead an independent agrarian movement. He died shortly thereafter.

A somewhat different course was followed by Alfonso Garzón, who in the early 1960s helped create the now sizable Independent Peasant Confederation (CCI), often in opposition to CNC and the state. According to post-Watergate revelations, the FBI cooperated with the Mexican government in harassing CCI. Yet today Garzón and CCI are arms of the state they once opposed, often more useful and effective than CNC. Garzón too speaks of "serving the people."

As a result, achievement of immediate reformist goals or longer run radical social change on behalf of peasants and rural workers has come to depend more often than not on leaders from the nonpeasant classes or class fractions. To become leaders, peasants need either personal charisma or outside resources. The most honest are often jailed or assassinated; others are too easily coopted.

Just in case leadership cooptation does not totally decapitate the peasant struggle, a subtle ideological control has become institutionalized: the daily lip service to the "law." Since so many abuses in the countryside are in fact illegal, everyone—whether an upwardly mobile good *cacique* or a down-and-out peasant seeking justice—talks of "carrying out the law" or of making progressive changes "within the law, of course." When the law itself is used as a means of oppression and the legal system appears as a maze without exit for poor people seeking survival, rural social movements and their leaders become entrapped in the bizarre language and practice of "peaceful, legal protest." Peasants or rural workers still express their faith in the law and defer to public functionaries with honorific titles like *patrón* or even the colonial "Don." This manifestation of a paternalistic culture is necessary to daily survival, as well as to obtaining any local improvement, such as potable drinking water.

Yet in spite of these obstacles, peasants do recognize and combat—now subtly, now directly—the oppressive character of the *cacique* system. And in *class* terms, the immediate enemy served by the *caciques* is not so difficult to spot. The rural bourgeoisie's insolent attitude toward peasants and workers is legendary. Scarcely having had to lift a finger to accumulate capital, the rural bourgeoisie has developed as a doubly parasitic class: living off both state subsidies and the cheap labor of the producers, while investing in land and agricultural production, commerce, regional banking, construction, urban real estate, speculative ventures—and conspicuous consumption. In great part it has become integrated with urban bankers and industrialists, foreign agribusiness people, state and international credit institutions, exporters-importers, or real-estate interests. Far from being a bunch of lazy *latifundistas* living off land rent, the leading elements of the rural bourgeoisie are men on the make, accumulating capital on an extended scale. But they depend on forces greater than themselves—mainly domestic and foreign finance capital (i.e., the merger of bank and industrial capital) based in the cities—for their capital and markets, and they share their regulation of the countryside's daily life with a medley of second-level bourgeois and petty-bourgeois groups essential to their own aggrandizement. Consequently, it is most useful for analytical purposes to view the rural ruling class as a power bloc made up of two broad layers—the large-scale agrarian bourgeoisie and a second-level bourgeoisie—with each layer in turn consisting of three segments. The large-scale agrarian bourgeoisie is made up of capitalist-landlord, agro-commercial, and agro-industrial segments, all of which are ultimately linked to one another through their dependent connections with urban-based finance capital. The second-level bourgeoisie is made up of a medium-scale agrarian segment, a commercial segment, and an agro-political segment, some of whose more successful members graduate into the ranks of the large-scale agrarian bourgeoisie.

The capitalist-landlords base their wealth on the accumulation of capital and land ownership. Though including a few inefficient *latifundistas* interested only in continuing the "original accumulation" of capital, they are for the most part oriented toward the accumulation of capital on an extended scale, even if often in speculative ventures. Some capitalist-landlords are nouveau riche who made it big after World War II, while others have descended from the *hacendados* of the past century. A number are former officials of the state bureaucracy. Almost all retain some aspects of the old-fashioned paternalistic populism linking landlords to *caciques*, state bureaucrats, or commercial intermediaries in a mutually advantageous alliance that demagogically claims to have the peasantry's best interests at heart. Typical of these capitalist-landlords are the eighty-five growers who control one-fourth of all irrigated land in Sinaloa, where commercial agriculture is highly advanced, as well as those engaged in monopoly-capitalist agriculture in Sonora and other northern states. All have close ties to U.S. agribusiness interests, and some own distributorships for U.S. farm equipment, automobiles, or insecticides.

The agro-commercial segment of the large-scale agrarian bourgeoisie derives its wealth not from land ownership but from commerce and, occasionally, industry. With state cooperation, this segment controls the market for agricultural products and finances much agricultural production. It includes large-scale *arrendatarios de tierra,* who rent land from peasants or *ejidatarios* and market their produce. Closely tied to the state and foreign agribusiness, this segment is strong in such leading sectors as the animal-feed industry, which in 1980 accounted for 8 percent of the value of all food production.

The agro-industrial segment derives its wealth from industry and to some degree from commerce, but not from land ownership. Linked to production either directly or through purchases from members of the agro-commercial bourgeoisie, the agro-industrialists own the mills, breweries, and food-processing plants. For example, Monterrey's ALFA group, together with TNC beer firms, controls the prices, production, and commercialization of barley. Both the agro-industrial and agro-commercial segments of the large-scale agrarian bourgeoisie, more than the capitalist-landlord segment, are concerned with modernizing the overall agro-political structure of the countryside.

The medium-scale agrarian bourgeoisie, the first of three segments of the second-level rural bourgeoisie, is mainly a product of the agrarian reform. It consists of small and medium-size independent private farmers, occasional *ejidatarios,* and the modern *rancheros* who formed the backbone of the relatively self-sufficient period of Mexican agriculture between 1940 and 1960. They are organized into regional political organizations of small proprietors, which in fact incorporate many *neolatifundistas* or their agents. Representing only 1 percent of the rural population, the medium-scale agrarian bourgeoisie nonetheless constitutes a significant political force in the rural bourgeois power bloc. Although generally a conservative defender of private property, the medium-scale agrarian bourgeoisie does include some neopopulist elements trying to renovate and modernize *caciquismo* in order to foster their own position (it also includes some inefficient elements who are gradually disappearing from the agrarian scene).

The second segment of the second-level rural bourgeoisie is the commercial bourgeoisie, which feeds on rural misery at intermediate and lower levels of production and exchange than those dominated by the agro-commercial segment of the large-scale agrarian bourgeoisie. One rural sociologist calls this segment the "rural commercial-usury bourgeoisie."[19] Its members include moneylenders; *acaparadores* who buy up indebted peasants' products below their value and resell at a profit; a wide range of intermediaries involved in commerce between agriculture and industry; and merchants trafficking in bottled drinks, furniture, plastics, and similar items in the provincial urban centers that have sprung up as a result of the growth of the home market. A relatively dispersed group of small capitalists, the rural-commercial bourgeoisie has a large network of personal relations among the peasantry and introduces capitalist relations by serving as intermediary between the countryside and big merchant and finance capital or the state. The rural commercial bourgeoisie is thus part of the older system of political and economic corruption, as well as the agent and beneficiary of the explosion in commerce stimulated by modern agribusiness and industrialization.

The final segment of the second-level rural bourgeoisie is the agro-political bourgeoisie. This consists of the upper ranks of the rural bureaucracy, and incorporates high-level local and federal bureaucrats, congressmen, regional political *caciques*, officers or heads of military zones, regional presidents of the official political party, presidents of important *municipios* (administrative units of towns or communities), and the like. Some, by means of corruption, have become agrarian capitalists in their own right. Most are quick to seize a share of the economic surplus marketed or appropriated by the state. Because these important officials help the rural bourgeoisie obtain surplus value from agricultural production, they must be viewed as part of the bourgeois power bloc and rural ruling class.

As in the case of other rural social classes, the intermediate classes in the countryside are internally differentiated. Only a small portion—mainly commercial intermediaries, bureaucrats, and *caciques*—can be called affluent. They are usually mestizo, not Indian, and have connections with foreign or Mexican capitalist employers or government banks and regional political machines. The more acquisitive among them make it into the ranks of the agro-political or rural commercial bourgeoisies. On the other hand, ever larger numbers—from lower-level bureaucrats to small-scale businesspeople to modest farmers to schoolteachers—live under austere conditions. Political attitudes among these intermediate groups thus vary from adherence to the official political party as an avenue of security or occasional upward mobility; to right-wing, often religious-based, opposition; to more leftist-oriented antistate positions, as in the case of unionized, low-paid schoolteachers who periodically join regional movements against unrepresentative union leaders and for decent salaries. A minority of the intermediate classes—such as farm administrators or labor recruiters hired by the agribusinesses—though rarely well paid, enter into direct class conflict with the rural proletariat.

However complex the evolution of Mexico's rural class structure has been, it has generated three transparent problems that promise sooner or later to explode in the face of the triple alliance forged by the state with the bourgeoisie, TNCs, and global lending agencies: (1) excessive unemployment; (2) inadequate food production to meet the minimal nutritional needs of the populace; and, as the next chapter shows, (3) renewed worker-peasant insurgency. Jointly with the exhaustion of the stabilizing-development model and with the emergence of political protest movements in urban factories, schools, and slums, the rural class struggle has become fundamental to the economic and political crisis of contemporary Mexico.

Urban Class Structure: Bourgeoisie and Intermediate Classes

The urban class structure after 1940 continued to be conditioned by Mexico's close economic relationship with a foreign metropolis, the United States. By 1970, Mexico's bourgeoisie was in practice neither autonomous, nationalistic, nor progressive—in the sense of trying to achieve the economic development of the nation for the benefit of the majority of its citizens. Known popularly as the "oligarchy," the bourgeoisie was, like the "revolution" it championed, so misdeveloped as to constitute, together with the state, the most effective force for smoothing Mexico's way to continued economic dependence on the United States and to an ever greater maldistribution of income and social benefits.

The modern Mexican bourgeoisie gained its status and power more by means of industrial production, commerce, and banking than by land ownership. It exercised its power inside Mexico through its influential role in select industrial sectors, in the distribution of goods and services, and in the networks of national and regional political power. Single families or clusters of families came to hold national or regional monopolies; most became loosely grouped into bourgeois fractions, which have more uniting than separating them.[20] Some of the fractions are recognizable by type of economic activity and organizational affiliation. For instance, by state law, industrial capitalists are organized into the Confederation of Chambers of Industry (CONCAMIN, founded in 1918), and commercial capitalists are grouped into the National Confederation of Chambers of Commerce (CONCANACO, founded in 1917). As obligatory state-corporativist entities used to assure bourgeois "representation" in state decision making, both CONCAMIN and CONCANACO maintain close ties with the government and draw some of their membership from business-minded (or corrupt) *políticos* who prosper from the informal partnership between state and capital. This corporativist organizational method permits government bureaucrats to retain a certain autonomy vis-à-vis capital but also to maintain a direct link to it for the sake of their own accumulation of wealth. For its part, the bourgeoisie has its interests within the state guaranteed, and uses CONCAMIN, CONCANACO, and the state bureaucracy—not its own (class) political parties—to achieve its political aims. Moreover, the bourgeoisie is assured an independent voice through such nonobligatory organizations as the Mexican Bankers Association (ABM, founded in 1928) and the Mexican Employers Confederation (COPARMEX, founded in 1929), a national business group led by capitalists from Monterrey.

These capitalist organizations are not "pressure groups," but form an integral part of the governing bloc. They are connected to the state through their members' circulation in and out of government. Until late 1982 the director of the Banco de México and the minister of finance routinely delivered the "second" annual state-of-the-nation report to ABM; similar interchanges occur throughout the top echelons of government and private capital. Weekends and vacations at exclusive country clubs and resorts informally seal the alliance.

Until the 1950s, there were two sectors within CONCAMIN representing distinct ideological emphases. Small and medium-size manufacturers, grouped into the National Chamber of Transformation Industries (CANACINTRA, founded in 1941), defended high protective tariffs against foreign competition and benefited from the import-substitution program of the 1940s. Other industrialists, representing larger firms—often "mixed" enterprises with foreign capital—opposed import controls, instead encouraging foreign penetration of the economy and handsome profits for those capitalists who cooperated. In 1945, CONCAMIN signed a pact of mutual cooperation with CTM. This helped to maintain low wages and hold strikes to a minimum, as well as to institute a regressive tax system that hurt some of the intermediate classes as well as all of the lower classes while barely touching the wealthy. (Of all Latin American countries with a population over 7 million, Mexico has the lowest tax revenue as a percentage of GDP.) Most of those among the bourgeoisie who in the 1930s had tolerated or encouraged a populist alliance with unionized workers against foreign monopolies and had begun to develop a viable manufacturing base of their own were subsequently bought out or partially absorbed by more affluent and technologically better-equipped foreign capitalists, or became big capitalists in their own right, sharing the goals of monopoly capital of any nation.

Thus, since the 1950s these ideological differences have given

way to a shared rhetoric and practice in which nationalistic sentiments are ritualistically expressed while an informal alliance with
foreign capital is carried out. One bourgeois economist has approv-
ingly described this as an "alliance for profits."[21] The differences
among Mexico's bourgeois fractions or between them and the state
receives little publicity except in moments of crisis (as was the case
earlier—under Cárdenas, for example). Even in these instances,
however, with the exception of parts of the Monterrey group, the
bourgeoisie does not sever its links to the state.

Commentators usually describe the Monterrey group as big capital's leading voice of reaction. Its resistance to Cárdenas reforms
was described in Chapter 4. In the early 1960s it opposed López
Mateos's nationalization of the foreign-dominated electric companies and campaigned against the state's free school textbook program. Yet the Monterrey group is by no means a cohesive unit. Its
most reactionary wing is led by a secondary group of capitalists,
whose most prominent spokesman is Marcelo Sada. A notorious
critic of "socialist" tendencies in the state and a rabid anticommunist, Sada is the director of Celulosa y Derivados, S.A. (CYDSA), a
chemical group that includes the nation's second largest chemical
firm. Less reactionary but more powerful is the fraction called *el
gran capital financiero*. The core of this fraction consists of the brewery group VISA and big steel's ALFA, both linked to SERFIN, one
of Mexico's four largest financial groups. Though in competition
with foreign capital after World War II, Monterrey's *gran capital
financiero* gradually established links both to this and to state
capital. Consequently, its reactionary tendencies became tempered
by a sense of economic and political pragmatism. Although statements continue to be made by Monterrey's bourgeoisie that are
critical of state intervention in the economy and espouse ultracon-
servative values, it must be kept in mind that such propaganda is in
the interests of all monopoly capital in the sense that it shifts the
terrain of debate enough to the Right that *any* reform begins to
seem "revolutionary." Like the rest of Mexican monopoly capital,
the Monterrey group as a whole normally does pledge its support—however critical—to the state.

In many ways it is misleading to view the Monterrey group as
either omnipotent or limited to one city. The "Guadalajara group"
of capitalists rose to a position of almost equal strength during the
1960s, and Monterrey's capitalists have spread their investments
throughout the nation and abroad (obtaining, for instance, control
over Spanish-language television in the United States). They have
joint ventures with foreign firms like Coca Cola, invest heavily in
central Mexico, and share holdings with the so-called Puebla frac-

tion of the bourgeoisie. Yet their ALFA group had to declare many of its enterprises bankrupt in 1982 and undertake a major program of refinancing and reorganization.[22]

In addition to the Monterry group, there are two other cohesive fractions of the Mexican bourgeoisie that call the shots: the "central fraction" and the so-called "1940s group." The central fraction, which is based in Mexico City, is primarily big finance capital, a fusion of banking and industrial capital with some elements of commercial capital, and has considerable political clout through its strong financial role in public and private economic activities. It is the single most important voice in financial capital's ABM which traditionally has been linked to the state's main development bank Nafinsa and to the Banco de México, two of whose long-time chief advisers have been the heads of the largest private banks—the central fraction's Banco Nacional de México and Banco de Comercio, each of which has ties to foreign capital. It includes the Mining and Mercantile Bank group, a group of capitalists independent of foreign capital with roots in the breweries and department stores of the Díaz period who are in turn linked to Banco de Comercio (a fusion of thirty-five banks and much of the chemical industry).

The "1940s group," so named because most of its members became industrialists and financiers with the assistance of the post-1940 state industrialization programs, is the fraction of the big bourgeoisie that has the strongest links to the state bureaucracy. It is difficult to distinguish between the bureaucrats and private entrepreneurs in this group: ex-president Alemán, former Obregón cabinet member Aarón Sáenz, and 1981 Federal District *jefe* (boss or mayor) Carlos Hank González have not only used their high state positions to accumulate capital but have also invested it in such powerful financial groups as those of Carlos Trouyet (banking, manganese, steel, cellulose, cement, paper) or Bruno Pagliali (steel, aluminum, real estate, finance). Members of the "1940s group" are also very influential in CONCAMIN and CONCANACO.

While most intrabourgeois divisions are neither major nor widely publicized, the division between the big bourgeoisie and established businesspeople of the petty bourgeoisie is recognizable on economic grounds alone. The small simply cannot compete with the big. Nevertheless, each needs the other for economic and political reasons. For example, small and some medium-size capital undertakes all kinds of "risky" investments that monopoly capital is reluctant to try until it can be assured of the growth potential. Those that succeed are then bought up by monopoly capital, while those that fail do so at the expense of smaller capital alone. Simultaneously, smaller capital depends on big capital and the state for loans, technical assistance, transportation, marketing, and the like. And all capital is in fundamental opposition to the disorder, "anarchy," "communism," "rabble-rousing," and rebellious tendencies of the working classes. Thus the state recognizes and encourages regional and national organizations of small and medium-size businesspeople in much the same manner it does those of big capitalists, even though it grants them fewer concessions.

After World War II, Mexico's intermediate classes entered a phase of remarkable growth. This was reflected in the statistics for those engaged in tertiary labor activity (the so-called services sector): from 19 percent of the economically active population in 1940 to 43 percent in 1979, according to the Ministry of Budget and Planning. While it is true that this figure includes many small traders, salespeople, servants, and temporary laborers, the fact is that it reflects a real demand generated by capital's rapid growth and centralization. Tertiary labor activity fulfills important administrative and related functions associated with the realization (as in commerce or sales) and appropriation (as in banking) of surplus value by capital. As the late Harry Braverman observed:

> The more productive capitalist industry has become—that is to say, the greater the mass of surplus value it extracts from the productive population—the greater has become the mass of capital seeking its shares in this surplus. And the greater the mass of capital, the greater the mass of unproductive activities which serve only the diversion of this surplus and its distribution among various capitals.[23]

Thus many intermediate-class people serve capital yet exist in antagonism to it or the state. Their labor power is purchased and the use values they produce in the performance of necessary administrative or social services are appropriated by either private or public capital.

This growth in the service occupations was accompanied by monopoly capital's gradual destruction of the artisanal basis of production and of the craft sectors of the traditional petty bourgeoisie (owners or possessors of their own means of production). Pettybourgeois merchants and shopkeepers were likewise driven to the margins of viability by big capital's supermarket and department-store chains, as police, tax, and licensing officials regularly harassed them. Figures for the traditional petty bourgeoisie are misleading. For example, the National Chamber of Small Commerce claims there are 1.25 million small commercial enterprises, yet many of these are simply marketplace operations engaged in by the urban poor. As Chamber president Juan Rodríguez Salazar puts it: "He

who is without work immediately engages in petty commerce."[24]
According to 1978 figures released by the Ministry of Budget and
Planning, 80 percent of such enterprises can be characterized as
"traditional and atomized commerce," but they account for only
9.6 percent of invested capital, 6 percent of total sales, and 7 percent of "value added"—while employing 46.4 percent of the 2.5
million people working in the commercial sector. More often than
not, these people's lives are enmeshed in a subproletarian reality
with a petty-bourgeois appearance and so are discussed in this
chapter's final section on immiseration.

Among the urban intermediate classes there has developed a
significant gap in status and income between upper-level bureaucrats, select professionals (doctors, engineers, clergy, etc.), and
prosperous small businesspeople on the one hand, and the vast
majority on the other—mostly bureaucrats, low-paid schoolteachers and paraprofessionals, clerks, shopkeepers, and struggling small businesspeople. As Salvador Hernández has pointed
out:

> Although individual mobility is permitted, mobility as a group is not,
> because such mobility in Mexico would radically alter the shape of the
> political pyramid. Consequently, if any group pressure begins to
> build up anywhere in the politico-economic system, sharp measures
> are taken in order to counteract those trends.[25]

Normally employing servants and living off the redistributed
surplus produced by labor, the better-off layers of the intermediate
classes have come to expect a life-style that contrasts sharply with
the poverty around them. They tend to blame their declining economic condition on salespeople or peasant producers rather than
on the forces of big capital. Economically squeezed, they are ripe
for proto-fascist appeals and authoritarian solutions, and right-
wing political parties find them good recruiting ground. On the
other hand, the Left recruits from these classes as well. Traditionally strong in the schools and universities, where the sons and
daughters of the intermediate classes went in large numbers after
1950 (by 1972 there were over 300,000 university students and
600,000 pre-university "Preparatoria" students, only 3 percent
from peasant background and 7 percent from the working class),[26]
the Left has politicized many students. Militants of the national
union of university students have frequently linked up with elements from radical or independent labor unions and the working
class.

As among others of the middle layers of the intermediate classes,
a handful of public school teachers have been drawn into the

affluent layer, while most have been reduced to proletarian living conditions. Traditionally a respected profession, teaching has become a waged trade, and teachers have little voice in the educational process. Much "teaching" activity consists of supervising overcrowded classrooms, a kind of glorified child-sitting. As agents of the state, teachers are obligated to reproduce the dominant bourgeois ideology and inculcate students with the virtues of *civismo* (good citizenship) and other values that will lead them to accept their given social position or chance in life. Yet historically teachers have earned their public "image" as defenders of social justice, and to the degree that they learn (from their students) of poor people's complaints or improve the ability of young workers to analyze critically, they become important agents in the struggle to transform society.

This was evidenced in the late 1950s when the Movement of Revolutionary Teachers arose to infuse democratic life into Latin America's largest government-controlled teachers' union. Othón Salazar led striking teachers in seizing and holding the Ministry of Public Education, and for a month the "little giant," as this silver-tongued communist was called, successfully urged the teachers to link their movement to that of railway workers on strike, his speeches echoing Diego Rivera's revolutionary murals in the ministry building. Many of the teachers were physically attacked by hired union thugs. The president broke the strike by granting them a 17 percent wage hike and slapping Salazar in jail. But two decades later the teachers launched an even larger movement for democratization of their union, infusing it with some of the feminist outcry emerging among other parts of the intermediate classes, especially university students, 30 percent of whom are women. Traditionally barred from union leadership posts, women schoolteachers (who constitute 70 percent of the union) gained up to 10 percent of the new movement's leadership positions—a herculean accomplishment in *macho* Mexico.

Illustrative of the obstacles to women's equality among the intermediate classes—besides the structural ones thrown up by the active forces of capital—have been the "feminist" manipulations of the state. The government sent Pedro Ojeda Paullada, the nation's male attorney general, to head the Mexican delegation to the International Women's Congress convened in Mexico City in 1975 ("International Women's Year"). It also passed an equal rights amendment for women that year, which it proceeded to ignore (most employed women are still paid far less than men for equivalent exertion of physical or mental labor). During his election campaign in 1976, López Portillo told a meeting of women: "The struggle for equality, of which women's equality is an exceedingly important part given that she makes up half of humanity, is a battle of our political culture against nature which has made her unequal in capacity, conditions, and function, and equal in her needs." Yet Senator Hilda Anderson, a director of women's affairs in CTM, announced in December 1980 that López Portillo's successor as president should be "a male, since males have the most political experience in the country."[27] Indeed, women from the affluent minority of the intermediate classes and from the upper class, most of whom exploit other women and expend little energy reproducing the commodity labor power, help the bourgeoisie to maintain a patriarchical system. Expected to be "good wives" and attractive adornments of the men's homes, few are admitted into the ranks of high political office or the professions. When women do reach prestigious professional positions they receive equal pay and status with men (although the sexual stereotypes are not broken). This is because of their class status. It is not uncommon, for instance, for a woman professor to chair or participate in a high-powered intellectual panel and have her views attended to—typically with a male colleague's reference to his "beautiful and charming colleague's" contribution.

Intermediate-class women are now publishing feminist magazines, of which the best known is *Fem*. Some are reaching out to oppressed lower class women, particularly those incarcerated or those who have "disappeared" for political reasons. Those belonging to left-wing political parties have mounted a campaign to legalize abortion. Some of their rallies in downtown Mexico City have drawn up to 500 people. A march for equal rights by a few hundred male and female homosexuals drew that many or more curious onlookers in 1981, and in spite of an occasional whistle or catcall they received very little heckling.

Starting in the 1950s the bourgeoisie began to share a tiny part of its power with a small but growing segment of the intermediate classes, the administrative and technocratic agents of capital and the state. These people are not high-level corporation managers or junior executives, military or police officers, or top state bureaucrats—who usually enter the ranks of the bourgeoisie rather than becoming a "new managerial elite." They come from the middle ranks of management, scientific research or technological coordination, and social control. They include a wide range of successful professionals whose labor was purchased not to produce surplus value but to participate in the overall planning, coordinating, and functioning of capital and the state. Many of them became a technocracy opposed to labor and enamored of bourgeois and foreign values. Dependent on the productive processes dominated by the TNCs, with their corresponding techniques of distribution, exchange, and education, they increasingly came to define the continued presence of such techniques as being in their *own* class interests. This was reinforced by a form of ideological, or cultural, imitation known as the "cult of technocracy,"[28] which exaggerated the importance of "expertise" and called for deference to technocratic solutions at every level of social and political organization. The cult of technocracy dominated the highest circles of economic planning and permeated the education system, thereby reproducing economic dependence. "Technocracy" rather than "bourgeoisie" is thus the appropriate term for this grouping because it includes people from a number of classes who use positions of power and authority in government to carry out the tasks of production and education.

One result of this process is that Mexico's oft-proclaimed quest for an indigenous science and technology was flawed from its inception. The goal was to close the gap between Mexico and a country like the United States, and this approach imposed on Mexico a set of already existing standards of technological efficiency, "models" for economic development, and the accompanying baggage of cultural attitudes and educational biases. The cult of technocracy so elevated and mystified technology as to make independent experimentation virtually impossible. Workers and peasants were excluded from the control over technology and made to feel "unprepared" to tackle technological questions, even at the workshop level of repairing broken parts. Furthermore, the cult of technocracy, and the technocrats who participated in and benefited from it, created a stratum of upper- and middle-level officials and bureaucrats on whom the forces of counterrevolution could rely—especially in situations where the normal supply of consumer goods or replacement parts was threatened.

This techno-bureaucracy constitutes a layer of the intermediate classes, and its members, who routinely implement bourgeois measures of capitalist efficiency, economies of scale, labor discipline, bribery, and corruption, and may move in various class directions—more often into the bourgeoisie than into the proletariat. Those who move into the bourgeoisie accumulate capital for themselves and their friends: for example, the *empresarios del estado* (high-salaried managers and directors in some thousand state enterprises) or high-level politicians or political appointees (presidents, cabinet members, governors, etc.) who use political power to accumulate funds for investment in the monopoly sectors of the economy. Many of these officials move easily from government to government accumulating capital as they go. Some ex-presidents own hotel chains; others own newspaper chains; still others retire on their wealth. It is this *cúspide* (summit) of the techno-bureaucratic and political pyramid that analytically may be described as a "bureaucratic bourgeoisie."

But this is *not* the ruling class: it is only a part of it, and a small part indeed. It is part of the bourgeoisie, and to the extent that it is integrated with Mexican and foreign private capital, it shares the general direction of capitalism and official politics—moved, and strongly so, by the forces of monopoly capital. This is not to deny the many policy conflicts that the representatives of the state and of monopoly capital have to grapple with, including conflicts among themselves; but such conflicts rarely become antagonistic, since the evolution of the corporativist political system has tended to unite, more than to divide, the interests of the state bureaucracy and those of the Mexican bourgeoisie and foreign capital.

Those who argue that Mexico is ruled by a "bureaucratic bourgeoisie"—that since the state governs and bureaucrats administer the state, bureaucrats must rule—have mistaken the *form* of political governance for the *substance* of class rule. In form the state is the "strong presidency," but in fact it is an entire web of high executive officials drawn from public and private life. Far from being an "external" force that independently "decides" to support the capital accumulation process, the state is a product of class struggle and capitalist economic development. Bureaucrats do indeed make decisions, but they are shaped by the class struggle and the power of the ruling class or its dominant fraction (bourgeoisie and monopoly capital, respectively). Moreover, the state shares more and more of its economic enterprises with private capital—one of the reasons they are known as "parastatal" enterprises. The state's takeover of the banks in late 1982, provoked by an economic and political crisis unprecedented since the 1930s, has not altered this pattern, since the state banks will continue to service monopoly capital and be staffed by many of the old bank managers—and will also be "privatized" as shares are sold back to the "public." Thus to expect the bureaucracy or its "progressive" elements to convert the state into a proletarian one is idle fancy. Similarly, to expect workers or peasants to unite with the state in their conduct of the class struggle is tantamount to class collaborationism. The state executive, far from being "sacrosanct," is—so far as the real interests of the masses are concerned—"evil." It not only represents and serves the proletariat's class enemy more than any other section of society, but it is hand in glove with that enemy. Consequently, as proletarians seek their liberation they have to oppose not only the bourgeoisie but the state itself.

While situations might develop in which workers, peasants, or progressive segments of the intermediate classes would find it advantageous to side with the state, this would be limited to cases of genuine reform or concrete anti-imperialist actions. Should the worker-peasant struggle take a quantum leap, however, the corresponding shift in the balance of power within the class struggle would manifest itself within the state. Under such exceptional conditions, we could then, and only then, expect significant change in the behavior of state bureaucrats toward either pole of the labor-capital conflict: they might engineer socialist measures or they might smash popular mobilizations with military ferocity.[29] It is well known inside Mexico that those few persons within the government who do advocate genuine revolutionary change are either overruled or gradually co-opted into more "pragmatic" positions of band-aid reformism. Their reforms simply end by strengthening the system that generates the need for reform in the first place.

The vast majority of public and private bureaucrats, technicians, supervisors, and the like form part of the intermediate classes. Many of them, in terms of comparative income and nature of work, are undergoing a gradual process of proletarianization. The paradox of gaining a better chance in life through education and access to "white-collar" jobs is that the jobs themselves have become deskilled and routinized, submitting their practitioners to the despotism of capital in labor processes that more and more resemble a proletarian assembly line. If many of these people are still "middle class" in their values, they increasingly tend to fall on the less affluent side of the polarizing intermediate classes. Their values are often mixed between self-proclaimed notions of reform and "helping the downtrodden," and a materialistic daily existence based on consumerism, status through display of wealth, fear of the "rabble," and a personal sense of belonging to the *gente decente* (an untranslatable expression roughly meaning "people of decency"). A significant number have internalized their "anticommunism." Yet the oppressive character of their labor has contributed a schizophrenic quality to their consciousness noted by many observers, which helps explain their tendency to leave their offices and join progressive street demonstrations like those of the 1968 student movement.[30]

Complicating these trends in class formation has been Mexico's system of influence-peddling, including such techniques as the following: the "*mordida*" ("little bite," or bribe); provision of government housing and social security benefits; distribution of seats in Congress and of local offices; promising promotion within the sprawling state bureaucracy; offering dissident intellectuals and professionals lucrative and/or prestigious appointments in government ministries or the education system; and providing high-status jobs in either the public or private sector with incomes adequate for employing two or more domestic servants and buying fancy consumer goods. The same corrupt system, with its myth of providing for "all the people," has penetrated the middle and lower ranks of the intermediate classes and the lower classes, but with much smaller payoffs and only limited success.

The political behavior of the intermediate classes strongly affects the outcome of the class struggle at any stage. Their behavior is characterized by a political ambivalence that corresponds to their "middle" position in the class structure—their inability to make it into the ranks of the bourgeoisie and their genuine distress at the gradual proletarianization being imposed on them by the forces of capital. Depending on the character of the larger bourgeois-proletarian class struggle and according to historical circumstances, a majority of the intermediate classes may consolidate behind one political extreme or another, and change quite suddenly. Starting in the 1950s, these conflicting tendencies were manifested in the creation of strong movements against the official political party from both the Right and the Left. Opposed to the government, they generated contradictions within the state as to the best way to handle the dissent.

At the same time, many politically concerned people, while sympathetic to the opposition movements, did not join them. They stayed on the sidelines, or expressed their politics through the official party or other state institutions. Those among the latter who were sympathetic to the Right pushed for greater repression of dissent, while those sympathetic to the Left were voices of reform; many more refused to go even this far for fear of "rocking the boat" and perhaps worsening their situation. Growing voter abstention (from 25.8 percent of *registered* voters in 1952 to 35.3 percent in 1976) and political deviation (only 33.8 percent of *eligible* voters backed the official party in 1979) reflected this spreading disenchantment. The younger, more educated people were more apt to voice their discontent. For example, graduating university students, 15 to 30 percent of whom were not able to find immediate employment by 1970, flooded the ranks of the state bureaucracy where they helped organize and expand the Federation of Workers Serving the States and Municipalities (which had 110,000 members in 1979). The federation has often petitioned for recognition of their labor rights as defined in Article 123 of the Constitution.

Officially, the so-called middle classes constitute one of the three sectors of the official political party—the "popular" sector, known as the National Confederation of Popular Organizations (CNOP), which also includes various organized elements of the urban poor. For years CNOP was stronger than the worker or peasant sectors of the party (CTM and CNC, respectively), but since the 1960s its strength has noticeably declined.[31]

Capital Accumulation: Industrial Proletariat and Immiseration

With increased industrialization and migration to the cities, the size of the urban proletariat has grown considerably since 1950. The percentage of salaried workers (with or without steady employment) jumped from 46 percent of the economically active population in 1950 to an estimated 75 percent in 1982, and the percentage employed in manufacturing reached 19.5 percent in 1979. Those working in industry were increasingly concentrated in the monopolized or foreign-controlled sectors. By 1975, almost 25 percent of all industrial employment was in areas where four enterprises accounted for more than half of production. Foreign companies increased their portion of industrial employment to 16 percent by 1975.[32] Yet that year's industrial census showed 60 percent of such employment remaining in medium-size and small industry that accounted for only 42 percent of manufacturing wages.

Less than a quarter of the urban proletariat is unionized, and most of these (some 3 million) work in large or medium-size industries. Another 3 million, most of whom do not belong to unions, work in small industrial firms and workshops. By Latin American standards, Mexico's industrial proletariat is large—about 25 percent of the economically active population of 20 million. Most of it is "superexploited"—that is, it earns wages insufficient for it to reproduce itself—since the legal minimum wage suffices to purchase less than half of what a family of five needs to maintain itself, and only 40 percent of the economically active population receives even that. Reduction of wages below the value of labor power, as Marx pointed out, "transforms, within certain limits, the laborer's necessary consumption fund into a fund for the accumulation of capital."[33] The fundamental forms of superexploitation are increase in the intensity of work, extension of the working day, and payment of labor power below its value. Mexico experiences all three. As total wages become less able to meet even the bare minimum necessary to meet the daily reproduction costs of labor power, and as the bourgeoisie and the state refuse to assume these costs, they have to be met by the larger wage and nonwage working class in its entirety.

If one recalls that national capital accumulation depends on a dynamically expanding home market, and that adequately paid workers make better consumers (an important factor in the realization and expansion of production), then Mexico's "miracle" of industrial growth is a poor example of a self-sustaining, ever-expanding cycle of capital accumulation: only 35 percent of GNP went to wages in 1970, about half the figure for the United States and less than that for many other Latin American countries. Since wages include salaries paid to corporate managers, state bureaucrats, and the intermediate classes, the actual share of GNP going to those who ultimately generate it—the workers—is far less. Further, the workers' real wage has declined over the years, perpetuating the low-wage basis of capital accumulation. After dropping to half its 1939 level in 1946, it recovered its 1939 level only in 1968; then it peaked in 1974 (up 40 percent from 1939), only to plummet downward again.[34]

As a result of these developments, male workers have increasingly adopted a multiple wage-earning "family strategy." More women have entered the labor force, and capital has welcomed them since they are easier to exploit, easier to lay off (e.g., on the grounds of pregnancy), and more difficult to organize on a class or trade-union basis. According to the Mexican government, 25 percent of the labor force is now female. Two million are employed in services and one million in commerce—but of these, one-third are subemployed or intermittently unemployed. Growing numbers—about a million—are employed in industry, principally textiles, food processing, electronics, and the TNCs' *maquiladoras*. Consistent with the family-strategy (and *macho* tradition), a woman wage earner, even if heading a household, distributes her earnings to the "responsible" male authority: a father, an uncle, an unemployed husband, even a brother. Money she keeps for her own necessities or diversion is usually pocketed on the sly. Moreover, at her work place she is bullied into working harder and faster, while often being expected to provide sexual services to her male superiors during breaks or after hours. Because and in spite of such abuses, the women *maquiladora* employees began forming labor unions in the late 1960s and early 1970s, encountering such strong repression that in order to preserve their organizational achievements they allowed CTM locals to incorporate them.

Mexico's failure to maximize labor utilization and remuneration for the purposes of expanded social production and consumption is reflected by the fact that only 27 percent of the population is described by census takers as economically active (compared with 39 percent at the start of the century). This figure is lower than that for many other Latin American countries. Mexico has never tried to absorb this labor force since the bourgeoisie has always preferred to have available a large reserve army of unemployed in order to keep wages low. According to the Ministry of Labor in 1981 there existed 8.5 million subemployed persons. CTM boss Fidel Velázquez claims there are more than 2 million unemployed by the government's own testimony. In other words, some 10.5 million Mexicans or 52.5 percent of the work force lack sufficient employment. Just to keep unemployment from rising, 800,000 new jobs a year have to be created—and Mexico is not achieving that. The 1980 census shows 42.6 percent of the population to be under 15 years of age. Tens of millions of these youngsters will be entering the job market in the 1980s.

It is against such miserable conditions of remuneration and employment, reinforced by the *charro* union bureaucracy and—when necessary—military repression, that the unionized industrial proletariat has repeatedly rebelled. For example, between 1958 and 1962 there were up to 60,000 strikes a year, ignited by the railway strike of 1958–1959, which sparked strikes among workers in petroleum, communications, education, and agriculture. Members of the railworkers' union voted to disaffiliate from the official political party, and for eight months the union experienced genuine internal democracy. The government broke the strike with troops and jailed its Communist leaders. Renowned Communist muralist David Siqueiros was thrown into prison for four years, strike leaders Valentin Campa and Demetrio Vallejo for more than a decade. Telephone, oil, educational, and other workers or peasants who attempted to back the rail strikers or to assert democratic demands of their own were attacked and arrested. Two decades later David Vargas Bravo, a key protagonist in the installation of *charrismo* in the railworkers' union in the late 1940s, publicly detailed the authoritarian and unconstitutional steps taken by the López Mateos administration to quell this labor unrest—as well as similar practices since (the 1964–1965 doctors' and nurses' strikes, the 1968 student strike, etc.). Nonetheless, this unrest helped inspire the growing labor agitation of the 1970s and early 1980s, which in turn helped gain the release of the imprisoned leaders.

Moreover, organized labor's resistance caused capital to shift its investments from disrupted sectors of the economy to new ones, setting the stage for new labor organizing drives and strikes. Because of the 1959 railworkers' rebellion, investments in railroad equipment dropped, while those in the automotive and air transport sectors skyrocketed. By 1980 Mexico had the world's fifth largest infrastructure in air transportation (airports, etc.). Its TNC-

dominated automotive industry became the nation's fastest growing industrial branch (13 percent annually in the 1970s), so that
today it is a veritable motor of the economy, producing yearly half
a million vehicles for the home market, 2 million car engines for
export to the United States, and various parts and services, while
employing 140,000 workers, most of whom are unionized. Chrysler, Ford, and General Motors (GM)—in that order—account for
60 percent of its sales. Chrysler may be flirting with bankruptcy in
the United States, but it is making millions in Mexico. The reason is
not hard to discover. A U.S. auto worker earns an average of $14
an hour, while a Mexican one makes $3.90 an hour (1979). And
when Mexican auto and electrical workers ignited organized labor's
revolt of the mid-1970s and early 1980s in much the same manner
as railroad workers had done in the 1950s, the TNCs fled the
Federal District the way they abandoned Detroit, now to convert
northern Mexico into the newest zone of automotive "development." Wages at GM's new plant in Ramos Arizpe are one-
fourth to one-fifth of those in the Federal District, and "white"
company unions are more common in the north. Chrysler is moving its assembly plants to Saltillo, Coahuila. Ford is investing with
Monterrey's ALFA group in an engine plant and with Monterrey's
Vidrio group in a windshield-wiper plant, also in the north. In the
northern states of Nuevo León (capital, Monterrey), Tamaulipas,
Coahuila, and Chihuahua, the auto companies are consolidating
their engine plants and auxiliary production plants for steel parts,
electric parts, and replacement parts for vehicles. State and private
steel and electric companies are taking charge of much of the production.[35]

In part to rationalize the organization of labor and in part to
check the recurrent signs of insurgency, CTM and the state have
repeatedly sought to centralize all industrial workers' organizations
into a so-called unity bloc. In 1955 they organized the Bloc of
Worker Unity (BUO); in 1960 they founded the National Central
of Workers (CNT); and in 1966 they merged these two organizations with some of the unions nominally outside their control to
form today's umbrella Congress of Labor (CT). In effect an arm of
the official political party, CT includes leaders from thirty-two
labor-union confederations or unions, and is dominated by oc-
togenerian labor boss Fidel Velázquez, the archtypical *charro.*

The nonunionized, on the other hand, have generally lacked the
political consciousness of the unionized workers, although they
share a sense of class resentment and even organize at their work
places from time to time. The class struggle in small and medium-
size industries is often more brutal and personal than that in big

industry. The lives of workers and the conditions of the enterprises are more problematic, job security is rare, and there is little opportunity for the worker to achieve more than token wage increases—usually parallel to inadequate inflation-related adjustments made in the legal minimum wage. In urban slum areas many capitalists have begun establishing factories that employ fewer than 100 people, thereby avoiding the constitutional stipulation of housing and other benefits. Case studies reveal that the owners of these factories prefer to hire recent migrants from the same rural region (TNC *maquiladoras* in the border area also tap select rural regions), often contributing funds to the migrants' hometown churches and becoming godparents to their children. Foreign capital is involved in many of these factories; or, if it is not, it soon steps in to buy out the more successful ones. Susan Eckstein has described the two largest such factories she researched, a canning operation and the nation's largest chocolate factory, before and after their sale to U.S.-owned TNCs in 1971; wherever possible, the foreign firms modernized administration but retained the old hiring patterns and paternalism.[36]

Unable to afford inflated rents, many of the nonunionized urban employed reside near, or in, the slums that house the unemployed. Their houses are recognizable by their better construction; their fear of being permanently submerged in abject poverty haunts them. They are torn by two opposing desires: to hold on to the little they have and perhaps improve their lot, or to risk engagement in organized actions against their employers, even against the system itself, in order to change their lives and those of their children. In spite of the anticommunist propaganda that surrounds them, they are open to appeals by radical union organizers or friends. Yet, as in the case of the unionizing women *maquiladora* employees, when they do struggle and achieve victories the most practical way to preserve them in the short run is to affiliate with CTM or other corporativist structures, which are always ready to absorb them.

Every decade greater numbers of wage earners have moved into and out of the ranks of the unemployed or subemployed, reducing the barriers separating unionized from nonunionized workers. This has been particularly true in construction, where the owners like to rotate their labor force or use new migrant labor in their "crews." Mexico City's labyrinthian subway system, which is still expanding, has been built by a mixture of urban proletarians and subproletarians and peasants—some of whom commute between the city and their subsistence farms weekly. Similarly, in the nationalized petroleum industry, whose work force has grown from approximately 18,000 in 1938 to 150,000 today, more than

70 percent of the workers are hired on a temporary basis, and only two-thirds of these are unionized. But they are strategically placed, carrying out 60 percent of all activities directly related to phases of production (exploration, extraction, refining, petrochemicals). Whether unionized or not, temporary oil workers have to *buy* their job contracts on a monthly basis from union or private labor contractors. A system of *caciquismo* flourishes in this flesh market, to the extent that inter-*charro* quarrels over the spoils have frequently led to assassinations. Temporary oil workers have increasingly organized and rebelled: they launched angry militant anti-*charro* street demonstrations in Mexico City in 1967 and 1975. Even some permanently employed, unionized oil workers (among the nation's best-paid proletarians), in spite of their tradition of looking down on the temporaries, are becoming fed up with the *charro* gangsterism running their own lives and have begun to express support for their temporarily employed brethren.

It has become fashionable to refer to the urban semiemployed and unemployed as "marginalized." This is misleading, because it implies that they constitute a separate class (or "mass") on the margins of society, removed from the main social and economic process of capitalist accumulation and class struggle.[37] Far from being marginal, these hungry and overworked millions form a vast fraction of the working class and are the product of an ongoing process of immiseration, the other side of the coin of capital accumulation. The uprooting of people from the countryside, their separation from the means of production, their crowding into the towns and cities, all constitute a fundamental part of the capitalist mode of production, which fosters the labor pool it needs for its expansion. Yet as industrial production becomes more capital-intensive, fewer rural migrants to the cities can find stable or adequate wage labor and instead wander from job to job, working for a pittance as street vendors, lottery ticket sellers, household servants, laundresses, subcontracted seamstresses, carpenters, irregularly employed factory hands, small-scale workshop employees or owners, messengers, and so forth. While technically unemployed or underemployed, most are in fact "overemployed," often working more than one job per person and at least two jobs per adult couple per family. Children and the aged work when and where they can. Through their extended workdays and the so-called independent labor performed in family subsistence activities (self-exploitation), they contribute to the capitalists' extraction of surplus value by helping to meet the costs of the reproduction of labor. Thus, the most important commodity they produce for capital is labor power.

The overwhelming majority of these people constitute a subproletariat in a double sense: first, as a relative surplus population or part of the reserve army of labor; second, as a sector that moves in and out of the agrarian, industrial, and service/commercial working class. In drawing on the labor of this expanding pool of job-hungry workers, the TNCs internationalize capitalist relations of production, reorganizing the basis of exploitation and conditions of employment and unemployment. This international division of labor is an old process deriving from imperialism's creation and distribution of surplus labor on an international scale—with national differences in wage levels relating in part to the power advantages accruing to imperialist nations over time. From this historical process there has evolved the so-called new international division of labor utilized by the TNCs to further their accumulation of capital. As capital and production transcend national boundaries, becoming transnational, labor also becomes more mobile, crossing national frontiers—*but at a slower rate* than does capital. For the monopoly capital that is based in the more industrialized countries, this permits access to a growing reserve army of labor and a higher rate of surplus value abroad. However, the completion of the internationalization of capitalist relations of production is barred by countervailing forces, including anti-imperialist wars of national liberation, interimperialist rivalries, and uneven development patterns within capitalist nations. All of these are but forms, or partial expressions, of the underlying contradiction that fuels capitalism's expansion, international competition, internal decay, and external threats: the contradiction between labor and capital.

It was Karl Marx who defined a relative surplus population as a "condition of existence of the capitalist mode of production." Industrial capitalism, he pointed out, "depends on the constant formation, the greater or less absorption, and the re-formation of the industrial reserve army of surplus population, independently of the absolute growth of the population."[38] In this sense, the roots of immiseration of millions of Mexicans have little to do with population growth as such and everything to do with the nature of capitalist production and its penetration into the remotest areas of the countryside.

Whether the relative surplus population takes the floating form (as in modern industrial centers, now employed, now laid off), the latent form (low-paid, subemployed agricultural labor, ready to migrate to town or city), or the pauper form (the unemployed, orphans, poor children, demoralized, mutilated, or sickly workers), it grows in rough correspondence to the increase in social wealth, functioning capital, labor productivity, and the absolute mass of the proletariat. In his trenchant way, Marx expressed this dialectical process as follows:

> The same causes which develop the expansive power of capital, develop also the labor power at its disposal . . . the surplus population forms a condition of capitalist production. . . . The more extensive, finally, the lazarus-layers of the working class, and the industrial reserve army, the greater is official pauperism. This is the absolute general law of capitalist accumulation. . . . The law by which a constantly increasing quantity of means of production, thanks to the advance in the productiveness of social labor, may be set in movement by a progressively diminishing expenditure of human power, this law, in a capitalist society . . . is expressed thus: the higher the productiveness of labor, the greater is the pressure of the laborers on the means of employment, the more precarious, therefore, becomes their condition of existence.[39]

In modern times the antagonistic character of capitalist accumulation—"accumulation of wealth at one pole, accumulation of misery, agony of toil, slavery, ignorance, brutality, mental degradation, at the opposite pole"[40]—has, through its immiseration of millions of people in imperialist-dominated countries with weak bourgeoisies accustomed to relying on undervalued labor, generated contradictions that Marx could not foresee. Among these are the social problems generated by mass misery (disease, crime, drug addiction, gang warfare, etc.); the growing tendency of large numbers of the poor to organize themselves, gain political consciousness, and resist or revolt; and the expenses incurred in maintaining a degree of stability and regulating these impoverished masses, whether through public services or policing. An example of police costs is the Radio Patrols Battalion of the State of Mexico (BARAPEM), an elite paramilitary assault squad founded to drive out "land invaders" in greater Mexico City. Its violent attacks have led to a campaign among the poor by leftist-influenced political coalitions to have it dissolved. (In late 1981 the newly elected state governor promised to disband it, but other elite paramilitary units are being developed.) Thus the immiserated masses are both functional and dysfunctional for capitalist accumulation. Increasing amounts of capital and energy have to be channeled out of the accumulation process in order to provide state-run food stores (CONASUPO); minimal health care (IMSS-Coplamar, introduced in the early 1970s and covering 15 percent of the population but leaving 42 percent without any organized form of obtaining health care); housing; sanitation; and military or police control over ever larger slums, which in Mexico are known as "lost cities" or *colonias proletarias*.

These slums account for half the population of the metropolitan area of Mexico City, which contains about 18 million people or one-fourth the nation's populace and to which arrive 10,000 new residents every day. The largest one is Netzahualcóyotl (in Nahuatl, "fasting coyote"), commonly known as "Netza." Founded near the international airport in the late 1940s by some 3,000 *ejidatarios*, Netza has mushroomed into an unmanageable urban jungle of 3 million—the nation's third largest "city." Of its land area of 150 square miles, 95 percent houses people who still lack state-recognized legal title. Only half its residents are employed, and some 80 percent of them work outside the area. To its north and west on the outskirts of Mexico City is another such lost city of almost equal demographic character, the "Gustavo A. Madero Delegation"—and many smaller slums dot the capital. A study of one such *colonia proletaria* found that 89 percent of heads of family were proletarians (only half of them received a stable wage), 10 percent were in the petty bourgeoisie, and a mere 1 percent were "lumpenproletarian."[41] Through their frequent though irregular employment in factories and their living next door to regularly employed proletarians, many of the slum dwellers pick up a more proletarian consciousness and integrate themselves into a larger *class* culture (not "subclass" or "national" culture, although this also exists).

The various jobs undertaken by the immiserated further integrate them with capital's accumulation process either through their direct production of surplus value or through their role in the circulation, distribution, and servicing of commodities. A good example of their production of surplus value is their widespread operation of sweatshops in the interior of Mexico. In the Federal District alone there are 300,000 *maquiladoras de ropa*—workshops that assemble clothing. In the shoe industry, where they are known as *picas*, there are many more such slum workshops across the nation. These cobbling operations produce over half the nation's shoes (including $36 million worth for export in 1979), using modern imported machinery as well as imported leather and synthetic materials. The surplus value produced goes to the tanners and shoe companies. Hundreds of thousands of other such workshops produce furniture, housing parts, leather goods, various automotive parts or supplies, and so forth, for the profit of capitalists.

To illustrate the character of these sweatshops and their petty-bourgeois disguising of a proletarian reality, the clothing workshops may be considered. The individuals (sewing at home) or the workshop owners (who hire a few laborers to work in their homes) own part of the constant capital, often modern sewing or cutting machinery they have purchased on credit or with their savings.

However, they are dependent for raw materials (textiles, pieces, etc.) on the capitalists, who often, like the traditional "jobbers" on New York City's Lower East Side, subcontract the work to them. When the workshop owners attempt to purchase the raw materials outside the monopolized market, prices are increased beyond their ability to pay, or the purchase is simply denied them. Recent case studies have estimated that the rate of surplus-value appropriation by capitalists employing this type of productive labor, most of which is female, is more than double that of large-scale clothing factories hiring regular proletarians.[42] Even the workshop owner who exploits the labor of poorer neighbors fails to appropriate a portion of the surplus value thereby produced. In fact, he or she usually makes more when not having to hire other laborers, since the "wage" paid in self-exploitation is normally half or less of that paid a hired worker (and this is in turn less than half the legal minimum wage). Moreover, workshop owners are generally recent rural migrants who have not engaged in this type of activity before—and are easily victimized by capitalist jobbers.

Since the number of slum workshops in various industries has risen dramatically in recent decades—in part because of the working class's feverish attempts to compensate for its inadequate earnings or employment—these cannot be viewed as precapitalist modes of production that are destined to disappear. On the contrary, these workshops are a product and tool of modern capitalist accumulation. Viewed from the capitalist's vantage point, they are profitable because the wages are substandard or nonexistent, there is no problem of labor unions, strikes, or state-enforced labor benefits, and some of the costs of constant capital are paid by the workshop owners. Moreover, the rate of recuperation of the cost of constant capital is rapid, once the capitalist recuperates the cost of raw materials with the sale of the finished product, but it is low for the workshop owner, whose overhead and machinery payments are spread over a much longer period.

Capital accumulation is furthered in less direct ways. It is furthered politically, by the belief of many slum workshop owners that they are not proletarians since they own part of their own means of production. This is a false belief, however, since in terms of their overall relations of production they are disguised proletarians whose ownership of a humble workshop masks their insertion into a larger capitalist structure that appropriates the fruits of their labor. Similarly, the workers hired by such sweatshop "owners" often tend to view their immediate *patrones* (bosses) as the "enemy," more than the actual appropriators of their surplus value, the capitalists who reside elsewhere.

It is often assumed that most of the immiserated gain their employment in the rapidly expanding services or tertiary sector of the economy, but case studies indicate otherwise. While it is true that many poor do become involved in services of various kinds—for example, one of every five employed women in Mexico City is a domestic servant, and there are over 60,000 girls from eight to fourteen years of age engaged in low-paid household labor—a much larger percentage becomes involved in either productive activities like sweatshop or factory labor or in ostensibly "independent" commercial activities for the purposes of capital accumulation (but not their own). Once again, now as shopkeepers, stall "owners," or street vendors (3 million street vendors in the Federal District, 1980), a petty-bourgeois appearance masks a subproletarian reality.[43]

For example, one study of *misceláneas*—as one-room stores selling tobacco, soft drinks, cookies, oils, and so forth, are called—found that about one-third of their products were of foreign origin and over two-thirds were delivered direct from the factory; that prices were universal throughout the Federal District (i.e., fixed pricing); and that the average local "merchant" worked fifteen hours a day and earned 45 percent less than the minimum wage.[44] Bribes are routine, and a gangland network of fake health inspectors parasitically feeds off the hundreds of thousands of such stores, typically marked by Coca Cola signs. The state charges a series of small taxes, and the merchant is also obliged to pay dues to the National Chamber of Small Commerce. The millions of subproletarians engaged in petty commerce of this or other types are dependent for their "business opportunities" on the Coordinating Federation of Small Industrialists and Merchants, a part of the official party's "middle-class" CNOP.

A personalistic network of low-level officials of various state organizations makes sure that these store operators and vendors pay them off or appear at party rallies, and failure to cooperate can lead to the takeover of a store or a route by the local official, or to his placing another poor person in front of the store or stall, selling one of the products at a lower price. There are less tactful means of enforcement as well.[45] The process is similar to the labor bureaucracy's control of the wages and jobs of those who seek employment in TNC *maquiladoras*.

It is not only in the production or distribution of commodities that the immiserated contribute to capital accumulation. It is in the consumption of goods as well. The slums offer a vast, teeming market for capitalists large and small—for the sale of furniture, wood products, school and stationery supplies, soft drinks, liquor, tobacco, processed or packaged foods, construction materials, and sundry domestic articles, almost all of which encompass significant portions of foreign or Mexican monopoly-capital investment. Slum dwellers, unable to travel elsewhere to obtain commodities at reasonable prices, are a captive market that will pay exorbitant prices for everything from tortillas to rent. Even when the poor produce clothing at home or in domestic *maquiladoras* they normally save neither money nor time. Instead, they sweat, produce, distribute, and, without getting a cent of surplus value for their labor, end up buying that which they produce at inflated prices.

Thus, whether in the production, distribution, or consumption of commodities, the immiserated are scarcely "on the margin of," or removed from, the national and international system of capital accumulation. Further, the capitalist mode of production *supplants* noncapitalist modes of production; it does not "preserve" or "combine with" them. At the same time it restructures many of their forms of economic activity, in both rural and urban areas, for the purpose of capital accumulation on an extended scale. Noncapitalist forms of production and distribution offer capital raw materials, certain necessities of life for labor's reproduction, and even finished products. While in the countryside a de-peasantization process is disguised by peasant production for markets and subsistence, thereby limiting the completion of proletarianization in the modern sense, in the cities a process of proletarianization, subproletarianization, and immiseration is often disguised by pettybourgeois forms of economic activity that actually generate surplus value or realize it on behalf of capitalists. Superexploitation of labor develops and creates anew these noncapitalist forms of production and distribution, thereby helping to combat the declining tendency of the rate of profit inherent in capital-intensive industrial production,[46] while also absorbing some of the unemployed and inculcating them with what Sol Tax has called a "penny-capitalist" ideology.[47] The resultant widespread immiseration of many that accompanies the proletarianization of some into a modern industrial work force denies the benefits of proletarian status (social security, unionization, etc.) to millions while limiting those benefits won in hard-fought battles by the industrial proletariat.

It is for such reasons that a notable part of monopoly capital's strategy to overcome the recent crisis in accumulation is to fortify the relation between itself and village- or neighborhood-based "domestic economies." This is reflected in the World Bank's programs for "investing in the poor," as illustrated by its new emphasis on financing subsistence farming and "independent" neighborhood enterprises. On September 26, 1977, World Bank President Robert

McNamara (former Ford executive and U.S. Secretary of Defense during the Vietnam war) outlined the urban component of this World Bank strategy. He said that the bank planned to create and aid independent producers in the development of artisanal operations, domestic workshops, small grocery stores, and so on. Tying some of the urban poor to international credit systems is one further step toward integrating them with monopoly capital, which in turn accumulates new dividends in its realization of surplus value through marketing of artisan products and sales of its own goods in the new stores established.

That the immiserated are both central to the capitalist productive process and a critical force in the struggle to replace it with a revolutionary socialist one is clearly recognized by the imperialists, who pour hundreds of millions of dollars into research projects designed to control or win over the "marginalized" and into armaments for repressive state apparatuses, including the most sophisticated military technology for "crowd control," "counterinsurgency," and the maintenance of "internal stability." Recent developments in the national and international accumulation of capital have generated a corresponding need for state intervention on many levels—increased repression, militarization of the society, and the technocratic bureaucratization and organization of social groups. All these tendencies are evident in Mexico.

The Mexican government plays a salient role in regulating the immiserated, concentrating them in certain areas, organizing their political behavior, and channeling their economic activity. It does not enforce tax or labor laws on the sweatshops; it tolerates a high degree of graft, deception, brutality, and police complicity in migratory flows to the cities and especially to the United States. When not driving squatters off the land, it encourages a mock "petty-bourgeoisification" of the poor by organizing them into petty-trade networks, regulating their markets, and introducing land-distribution schemes and a minimal degree of public services—to confirm them as "home owners." It sponsors or assists in occasional squatters' self-help, training, or services programs. For example, "training centers" have been established for Indian women who migrate to Mexico City (the so-called Marías) in which their home-craft skills are exploited to produce rag dolls, clothes, kitchen accessories, and the like. They are paid token wages, but if they ask for more they are reminded that they are "students" being taught "skills" by their "professors." Their hand-crafted products are then sold to the residents of luxury suburbs like San Angel and Polanco.

The growing numbers of immiserated and their energy and sense of moral indignation often generate a spontaneous rage that, if politically channeled, could provoke revolutionary consequences. However, of all social movements, those of the immiserated are the least stable, consistent, or predictable. Their political direction often depends on the social movements and political character of other groups in the society, particularly the employed proletariat and the petty bourgeoisie.[48] They are susceptible to religious superstition and mystification, and yet they also respond to the ideas and practices of the theology of liberation. In Netza, for example, priest-led Easter processions supporting the guerrillas in El Salvador pass by "holy roller" Baptist reunions. On the other hand, their economic vulnerability makes them subject to a range of political responses, from militant land grabs to easy recruitment into the armed forces, police squads, and terror groups that the state or employers use to repress strikes and progressive political movements (something that many Mexicans can personally verify).

We noted earlier how the state uses populism and paternalism to channel movements among the peasantry and urban poor into a fixation on owning a parcel of land or a dwelling in order to keep them as dependent as possible on state favors. The subproletariat thus has a tendency to support the status quo, and to tolerate or even support capitalist or reactionary values. Eight years of literacy, co-op, and political work in Netza showed Jesuit-socialist priest Martín de la Rosa that "the values of bourgeois ideology have been profoundly incorporated in the consciousness of a large portion of the popular classes."[49] His and others' interview data suggest that almost all people engaged in petty commerce and many workshop owners see their situations as determined by larger class, social, and political forces beyond their control, but still have consciousnesses that mix petty-bourgeois profit-making (or debt-paying) goals with subproletarian ones of rebellion against oppression. Referring to the "irony of organization," political scientist Susan Eckstein concludes that many of the immiserated have shown great will and ability to organize only to find that their various organizations, through cooptation or government regulations, end by serving to "legitimate a regime, extend a government's realm of administration, and reinforce existing social and economic inequities."[50] When cooptation fails, repression is used: from the burning of squatters' cardboard hovels to the assassination of leaders, including priests (as in Torreón and Chihuahua during the 1970s).

Yet cooptation is a tricky business. Francisco de la Cruz, a coopted leader of Mexico City's oldest and most politically conscious, self-organized, and self-policed *colonia proletaria*, "2 de octubre" (created in 1969 by land invaders), claimed he was arrested in March 1981 because the official party (which he had joined years earlier) had asked him to become a congressional deputy "in exchange for selling out my people." Most progressives thought he had already sold out: the "2 de octubre" colony was rife with corruption he had fostered and organizational disintegration. More ominous was what happened on the night of de la Cruz's arrest. Thousands of heavily armed police and military groups, many on horseback, stormed the colony in the early dawn hours and razed it to the ground. Sleeping women, children, and old folk were crushed in the melee, then herded off to temporary camps pending "resettlement" of some of them in state-provided housing in another neighborhood. The raid itself was not new—for years the state has sent troops and elite units like BARAPEM to militant *colonias proletarias* to kill, wound, or intimidate their residents, reflecting the intensity of the class war raging in the daily lives of millions of impoverished Mexicans. But the savagery of the dawn raid on "2 de octubre" was a clear and symbolic escalation, serving to warn all politicized slum dwellers that they could be next. Shortly after the raid, Nuevo León's governor publicly threatened Monterrey's independent slum-based Land and Liberty Front with a similar action—"2 de octubre"-style.

Recognition of the potential for political consciousness among the immiserated masses does not negate the reality of the many obstacles to politicization in a corporativist, controlled, and regimented social formation like Mexico's, particularly those obstacles within classes differentiating distinct fractions, groups, or individuals. Most of the day-to-day organizational networks among the immiserated masses are not politically progressive: petty crime syndicates; extended kinship systems dominated by *macho* males even when they are unemployed; dependence on religious or social institutions like the *compadrazgo;* deference to *el patrón* and related informal patron-client systems; and so on. Almost all these forms of social organization constitute blocks to the political organizing of people for progressive change. Nonetheless, the potential for politicization must be pointed out precisely because so many scholars and writers have emphasized only these "quaint" or "fascinating" mechanisms of social cohesion, which in fact are integral parts of the larger oppression holding millions of people down.[51]

From the viewpoint of slum dwellers, whose social movements have usually been limited to struggles for public services, jobs, elections of local officials, and the like, perceiving themselves as marginalized from society instead of integrated into the proletariat involves serious political and human consequences. Similarly, those self-sacrificing organizers who attempt to instigate or support slum political movements on the basis of a theory of marginalization are unlikely to achieve more than temporary goals based on charity, self-help, and mutual aid. Only when both the working poor and concerned organizers recognize that the role of the immiserated is not merely that of a reserve army of labor but that of an activated arm of capital accumulation can the burgeoning mass movement of the immiserated be linked to the fundamental dynamic of class struggle in Mexico: capitalist owners versus urban and rural proletarians.

7

The Crisis, 1968–1977

When stabilization programs, justified by transitory conditions, are perpetuated, greater injustices result than those supposedly being corrected. Fatally, salaried workers' wages are restricted; capital centralizes; and the state's room for maneuver is reduced. The state's capacity to resolve conflicts is annulled, its possibility of governing cancelled.

—President José López Portillo,
Third State of the Nation Address,
September 1979

If guerrilla violence succeeds [in El Salvador] the killing will increase and so will the threat to Panama, the canal and ultimately Mexico.
—President Ronald Reagan, speech to the
National Association of Manufacturers, March 10, 1983

Although today the crisis of the Mexican state appears to be its insolvency caused by the oil boom's "overheating" of the economy and a sharp fall in oil prices in the early 1980s, in actuality it is both a political and an economic crisis rooted in the problems described in the preceding chapters: weak patterns of capital accumulation and dependence on foreign loans; exhaustion of the stabilizing-development model; and, above all, the class contradiction between the producers and the appropriators of the nation's economic surplus. This chapter examines these patterns from 1968 to 1978 and the strategies introduced by the state to replace stabilizing development with rapid development of Department I of production (means of production, heavy industry) and a new stage of industrial expansion and employment to be fueled by oil production. Some of the failures of these strategies, as well as the state's efforts to defuse a new labor insurgency and a rising tide of anti-imperialist protest through an "independent" foreign policy, are described up to late 1982, but the internal class and political consequences are examined here only through 1977.

The strategies themselves constituted a response to the class struggle, which intensified so greatly after 1968 that the state had to resort to unprecedented extremes of repression, first against the student revolt of 1968 and then against workers, peasants, and

237

students in the mid-1970s. In response to the heightened class war, the bourgeoisie had to regroup and close ranks, entering into more direct participation in state affairs. The social movements of peasants, the urban poor, industrial workers, and students became less sporadic and isolated, as national, independent networks of their organizations began to take form. By 1977 the state and the bourgeoisie had to impose on the masses a new lid of political repression and economic austerity, causing Mexico's class struggle to become more difficult and yet more polarized than it had been at any time since the 1930s. The post-1977 phase of class struggle and state crisis, together with such international factors as emigration and the Mexican community residing in the United States, is examined in Chapter 8.

To comprehend the political character of Mexico's state crisis, it is necessary to recall that the high GNP growth rates and monopoly-capitalist nature of Mexico's "miracle years" of industrialization generated new needs in the economy, including needs at the state level. In order to control the masses, the state increasingly had to affirm its legitimacy through costly programs of limited social reform; yet its legitimacy was undermined by ongoing military/police repression of organized popular protest. This type of contradiction permeated every major apparatus of the state. When one speaks of state contradictions one is, in a sense, uttering a tautology. The capitalist state by its very nature is a contradictory institution. The mere fact that the Mexican state must represent *all* the fractions of capital—as well as parts of the working class and peasantry—while pretending to speak for all Mexicans plunges it into a series of contradictions over which compromises have to be made on a regular basis.

As has become evident, these compromises are conditioned by the state's serving of monopoly capital and by its own economic interests within the state areas of production. This pro-bourgeois, antilabor tendency on the state's part continuously creates friction even with class-collaborationist labor leaders like CTM boss Fidel Velázquez. The *charros,* after all, are more directly connected than the state to the proletariat and so have to "deliver the goods" to the workers in some minimal degree. As rank-and-file workers in revolt against *charrismo* began once more to organize themselves in the late 1960s and early 1970s, it became necessary for the *charros* to address not only their economic demands but their political ones as well. For example, in mid-1977, Velázquez momentarily withdrew CTM's commitment to a 10 percent ceiling on wage increments and demagogically spoke of the need for "greater democracy" inside CTM. Although this was an opportunist maneuver to reassure CTM members of their leader's sensitivity to their demands, it nonetheless exemplified the kind of pressures that have to be mediated repeatedly within all state apparatuses.

Mexico's economically dominant forces, in spite of their receiving favored treatment by the state, never find it a merely routine matter to assert their class hegemony inside the government. The foreign bourgeoisie is excluded, since it is not Mexican. Indeed, historically, in its U.S. form, foreign capital and its political and military representatives constitute the only external enemy Mexico has ever had to take seriously.[1] For its part, the Mexican bourgeoisie has always been too weak vis-à-vis other internal and external forces to manipulate the government as an instrument of *only* its interests. Nonetheless, for decades the most important weapon in the Mexican bourgeoisie's political arsenal has been the authoritarian-technocratic state. For this reason, many of the traditional democratic tasks of earlier bourgeois revolutions, such as the creation of credible free elections, the guarantee of basic civil liberties, the freedoms to organize, demonstrate, dissent, and the like, have fallen on the shoulders of the intermediate and lower classes. Democratic demands in Mexico, like other reformist demands, derive their social force and political impact from the working classes and disaffected intermediate classes, which express such demands, rather than from the bourgeoisie, which advocates their suppression or else their diversion into "safe" (i.e., state-regulated) channels.

As we saw in Chapter 6, popular pressures began building up against the authoritarian character of the state in the late 1950s and early 1960s. We say "the state" and not the official party because the PRI is only a part of the state; other state apparatuses include the increasingly influential military and the techno-bureaucracy of the executive branch. Yet part of the rigidity of Mexico's political system is the inflexibility of the PRI itself. Every new attempt at democratizing the PRI fails. For example, in the early 1960s incoming PRI president Carlos Madrazo sought to introduce party democracy by phases, only to be promptly removed from his position. Old PRI officials never forgave him, accusing him of backing the 1968 student uprising (shortly afterward he died mysteriously in a plane crash). So bankrupt is the PRI's democratic mythology that large numbers of dissidents no longer consider entrance into the party a politically viable alternative. Given Madrazo's failure and the growing rigidity and old age of the political system, much popular protest has had to be expressed through direct action in

factory, field, and school, as well as in the streets. The principal
contradiction of proletariat/bourgeoisie has thus erupted in the
socioeconomic arena and not just in the political one.

This eruption was first sparked not by workers or peasants but by
students, long a politically volatile element in Mexican society. The
gigantic democratic movement they found themselves igniting in
1968 started out as a minor affair involving military and police
repression of some street fighting between students from two rival
high schools in Mexico City (a vocational school and a preparatory
school) on July 22 and 23, 1968, during which students and
teachers were beaten and one student died. Separate student
marches protesting this incident and celebrating the 26th of July
(the anniversary of Fidel Castro's 1953 attack on the Moncada Barracks) were similarly repressed, leaving four students dead and
hundreds more injured and arrested. By week's end, indignant
students from the vocational schools and the National University's
preparatory schools had seized school buildings, constructed barricades, and engaged in pitched battles with the elite riot-squad
granaderos and police, returning the fire of bazookas with their
molotov cocktails. The week's toll was from ten to thirty dead,
hundreds of injured and arrested, and some "disappeared." The
separate vocational and preparatory school student organizations
united with the more leftist student organization of the National
University (UNAM) to form the National Strike Council (CNH)—
and a chain reaction of student strikes and military repression
swept the nation, leading to a massive rally on August 27 of nearly
half a million people in Mexico City's great Zócalo plaza. Soldiers
and riot police dispersed the militant remnants of this demonstration near the presidential palace in a predawn raid the following
day. By September 19, 1968, army troops had invaded UNAM and
taken several thousand prisoners (including teachers, staff, and
parents of students); CNH had gone underground; and Mexico
City was lit up with fires from overturned buses and street barricades.

Moreover, significant portions of the less affluent layers of the
intermediate classes had begun participating in the mass marches,
as the student movement widened to protest state authoritarianism, corruption, and repression. Besides objecting to their having plateaued at too low a level of prosperity to meet their
expectations, the civil servants among them were indignant and
bitter at the dislocation caused by the state's preparations for the
1968 Olympic Games—the spectacle of "their" government spending huge sums of money for the pleasure of foreigners, the price
increases, and the government's refusal to allow them to take days

off during the forthcoming games. For their part, students from the vocational schools and the more prestigious UNAM felt their education was not rewarding them with decent jobs, and that the one-party political system was shutting off avenues for redressing legitimate grievances. For UNAM students, there was not sufficient rotation of elites to permit them all to join the already crowded upper branches of the establishment; for graduates of the vocational schools, the poor pay and rising cost of living, combined with unfulfilling jobs, led to their mass discontent. Peasants, slum dwellers, and workers, all harboring long-standing grievances, also began to join forces with the student militants, forcing the government to take decisive action—and before the Olympics opened.

On October 2, 1968, just ten days prior to the start of the games, student organizers scheduled a mass rally in downtown Mexico City at the Plaza of Three Cultures (Tlatelolco), the site of a high-rise housing development. Anticipating trouble, rally leaders decided to cancel the main march to the plaza, but could not: too many student delegations had already congregated. As feeder marches of peasants and workers began to arrive, the army and police opened fire with automatic weapons. Six CNH members were killed in the ensuing indiscriminate massacre. The next morning 300 coffins appeared in the UNAM plaza, and unpublished photographs of old women impaled on bayonets and children with their heads blown off were circulated by students throughout the city. Conservative estimates put the number of dead at 49 and wounded at 500, but most observers estimated 500 dead, 2,500 wounded, and 1,500—mostly students—arrested. Not since the days of Porfirio Díaz had a massacre on such a grand scale taken place. Mexico's boasted political "stability" had come to a bloody and tragic end; a new era of crisis was beginning.

The New Labor Militancy

Underlying the student revolt in 1968 and the spread of its democratization goals to other sectors of the population then and afterward was the clash between the ideal of a "three-sector democracy" within the official party and the undemocratic reality of authoritarian-technocratic decision making, political patronage, *personalismo*, and physical repression of dissidence. As the secrecy of PRI's internal workings and the certainty of its electoral victories became ever more obvious, growing numbers stayed away from the polls. Mexicans grew cynical about their political institutions and the widespread corruption that they encouraged in everyday life. The 1968 examples of people from different walks of life momentarily breaking free from their cynicism and repeatedly marching en masse to the seats of state power in a show of unity raised popular expectations that not even the "dos de octubre" massacre could dampen. Fearful of the contagion of the students' democratic demands, the CTM leadership struck a deal with the government during the 1968 student strike whereby they obtained improved wages for CTM members in exchange for not protesting or interfering with the repression. But this did not silence the workers, and when economic hard times set in a few years later there erupted a new labor militancy that proclaimed democratization as its main goal.

There are at least three reasons that the state's system of ideological persuasion has proven less and less effective. First, the socialization process contains within it a number of revolutionary sentiments that contribute to the gap between the normative model and what people see all around them. Second, the traditional techniques of cooptation have been exposed and criticized, as has their stop-gap nature.[2] Third, state institutions increasingly have been unable to pay off their constituents at a level commensurate with popular expectations.

The 1968 crisis was an example of this. What united the young people, including students from different class backgrounds and types of schools, as well as growing numbers of young clergy, workers, and peasants, was a shared value system—including a sense of an international community of youth—that exalted honesty, freedom, and sharing, and opposed hypocrisy, authoritarianism, and selfishness—the values of the social system in which they lived. Socialized in an inspiring nationalist mythology of Morelos, Júarez, Zapata, and Cárdenas, these youth saw their leaders "following policies which are diametrically opposed to the professed ideals. . . . The trouble with the students is that they believe in the ideals they have been taught, and many of them want to rescue these ideals from their 'safe' entombment as statues, names of plazas and boulevards, and neon-lit slogans on walls."[3] In a personally freer situation than were the workers or peasants, and conscious of the dangers of cooptation, the students were less easily coopted. The political ideologies of 1968 varied from rather traditional reformism to a rich blend of Flores Magonista, Zapatista, Marxist, Leninist, and Guevarist revolutionary ideas. The new consciousness rejected bourgeois values, life-styles, and practices; its proponents wanted to forge a worker-peasant-student alliance. In the long run, of course, this would have meant confronting the ruling class and state directly. Before this could happen, the state responded with its own confrontation—the "dos de octubre" massacre—for which the responsibility ultimately rests with President Gustavo Díaz Ordaz and his Minister of Interior (Gobernación) Luis Echeverría, the man who became president in 1970.

During the first year of the Echeverría government, the new president promised a "democratic opening"—*apertura democrática*—a choice of words that recognized the authoritarian character of the state. Nevertheless, when on June 10, 1971, thousands of students and workers marched in the streets of Mexico City to demand basic political rights and the release of all political prisoners, a combined armed attack of police and a right-wing, state-financed terrorist group known as "The Hawks" *(los halcones)* led to the murder of 11 demonstrators and wounding of over 200—and the "disappearance" of another 35. The parallels to the 1968 massacre were obvious, except for one thing. The government was now encouraging an overtly fascistic group that it recruited from among "lumpen" elements, trained in the most savage techniques of beating, torture, and killing, and given free reign to terrorize the populace. Operating with impunity throughout the Echeverría *sexenio*, the Hawks and other paramilitary right-wing goon squads were suspected of being assisted by the CIA, as were other such groups in Latin America that emerged as exceedingly strong and ruthless forces during the same period. These suspicions were reinforced when, in February 1977, the *New York Times* reported that Echeverría had accepted money from the CIA when he was Díaz Ordaz's minister of interior.

Reacting to this unleashing of the extreme Right, disenchanted students—many of whom had read Che Guevara and were trying to revive a program for land reform—and frustrated peasants attempted guerrilla warfare, beginning in the mountains of Chihuahua and Sonora and spreading to southern states (other than those already affected by the armed actions of Rubén Jaramillo and his successors). But they had little success, and their efforts were repeatedly repulsed by the armed forces. In the southwest state of Guerrero, Lucio Cabañas, a former student from a peasant background, escalated the level of guerrilla struggle while winning over students to his Party of the Poor; he was betrayed and killed in 1974. Five years later the government claimed to have killed "El Güero" (Florencio Medrano Mederos), a guerrilla leader in Oaxaca who had fought with Cabañas and earlier with Genaro Vásquez Rojas, a southern guerrilla leader killed in action.

Between 1969 and 1975 a dozen urban guerrilla groups carried out spectacular actions—airplane hijackings, bank robberies, bombings of buildings, kidnappings, and police ambushings. Military intelligence was given the task of hunting them down, and by 1975 the urban armed struggle was broken. Both the rural and the urban guerrilla movements, though unsuccessful, momentarily radicalized political struggle, especially among poor peasants and urban slum dwellers. In 1974, for instance, the Land and Liberty Settlement of San Luis Potosí extended its urban land occupations into Tamaulipas, Zacatecas, and Veracruz. Its leader, Eusebio García, was assassinated in 1976, but it has continued to be active.

President Echeverría felt the social volcano rumbling beneath him and responded with a program of neopopulism that called for a "New International Economic Order" (approved by the United Nations in 1974) and generally advocated social reform. He ranted against TNCs, levied some taxes on the rich, promised to close loopholes in the Mexicanization legislation, funded the collectivization of a few select *ejidos,* and steered a small part of the nation's trade toward Europe and Japan. But his modest reforms were hampered by the lack of an adequate class base (and thus support) among the masses, a dishonest and inefficient bureaucracy, and a fiscal crisis aggravated by the international recession of 1973–1975 and foreign pressures to reduce the state debt. Moreover, any anti-imperialist democratizing project ran the risk of releasing too much popular energy and opening the floodgates to increased mass demands—and even to an open fight for socialism and the demise of bourgeois power. In any case, workers and peasants took the opportunity to push for more rights; some on the Left were taken in by the rhetoric and rallied to Echeverría's side; and the government sought to stabilize matters by strengthening its alliance with CTM and yet subsidizing commerce, importers and exporters, and organized industrialists to the tune of an estimated $3 billion.

Meanwhile, some of the business community, particularly Marcelo Sada's *mano dura* (hard-line) fraction of the Monterrey group, the large landholders, and the forces of U.S. imperialism, took Echeverría's rhetoric seriously and mounted a "destabilization" campaign against his government. FBI documents obtained through the Freedom of Information Act indicate that FBI director J. Edgar Hoover believed Echeverría to be "soft on communism." Operating through the office of the legal attaché in the American Embassy, the FBI carried out counterintelligence operations inside the trade unions, left-wing parties, and the Echeverría government itself, infiltrating the ministries of interior, foreign affairs, national defense, public education, and the attorney general's office. At one point, Hoover wrote the legal attaché of his "pleasure at the wave of night machine gunnings to divide subversive leaders" and congratulated him for the "detonation of strategic and effective bombs." Echeverría's attempts to build bridges with Mexican communities in the United States by currying favor with prominent Chicano leaders were partially countered by the FBI's routine planting of cocaine or other drugs in the leaders' cars in border areas. Mexico's military and police forces had long-standing links to their U.S. counterparts, including the CIA, which continues to maintain one of its largest Latin American operations in Mexico; some 900 military and police agents have been trained by U.S. security forces to combat and conduct terrorism. During the Echeverría years, the Drug Enforcement Administration (DEA) helped train Mexican police and often served as a cover for CIA agents. From 1973 to 1977 the Mexican police received $47 million from the DEA, much of it to purchase hardware for use against political dissidents. In the Sierra Madre of the northern states of Sinaloa and Durango, for example, 7,000 soldiers aided by 226 DEA advisers fought a "special war" against Indians and peasant land occupiers under the pretext of destroying marijuana fields. Herbicides of a type used in the Vietnam war were used to kill food plants, causing starvation among the Indian population.[4]

Aggravated by such destabilization tactics, polarization between Left and Right increased. Thugs armed with clubs or pistols (and sometimes heavier weapons) were given free reign to assault the Left. Known as *los porros*, they still operate at universities, schools, public demonstrations, workers' strikes, village community centers—wherever their intimidating presence and violent acts can sow fear and terror among people seeking to organize themselves and change the country (a group of such thugs known as the National Patriotic Anti-Communist Front currently claims credit for various armed attacks on progressive meetings and threats on the lives of leftists and their families). Prominent establishment figures warned of the danger of Mexico's becoming engulfed in a process of gradual "Argentinization," and the secretary general of UNAM's center for political studies reported a struggle within the PRI between proto-fascist and democratic elements. During the final days of the Echeverría regime, rumors that tanks were moving in the streets of Mexico City in preparation for a military coup were taken seriously—a clear sign of the gravity of the state's crisis.

Scores of peasants, workers, and students have been killed by *los porros*, the police, and the army, either in isolated incidents or, more commonly, during periods of public agitation for democratic or economic rights. Hundreds have been kidnapped and have disappeared. Families of many of the disappeared banded together in

1977 to demand that the government return over 800 of their loved ones. Subsequent amnesties led to the "discovery" and release of some of these people, as well as a number of political prisoners. Close to 200 of the disappeared have been reported dead, while some of those remaining have been seen in the inner confines of Mexico City's Military Camp No. 1, where their incarceration has been censured by Amnesty International and other respected international human rights groups.

Yet the practice of seizing dissidents and later reporting them disappeared continues, especially in the strife-ridden countryside where the pace of peasant land takeovers rose dramatically in the mid-1970s. Disappearances, killings, and torture of mestizo and Indian peasant militants have become commonplace in impoverished states like Oaxaca, Chiapas, Guerrero, and Hidalgo. The army patrols in many rural areas, and massacres are not uncommon. On orders from local *caciques,* some 500 Triquis of Oaxaca were murdered in the 1970s, and a similar reign of terror was imposed on the Indian majority of the population of the southern border state of Chiapas. For most of 1977 a state of seige existed in Juchitán, Oaxaca, in an attempt to enforce the delivery of 25,000 hectares of *ejido* land to private owners. That same year police killed 29 *communeros* trying to seize a municipal office in Oaxaca. In Hidalgo, where *caciques* allied with big landlords rule with an iron hand, quarreling peasant groups united themselves into the Regional Union of Hidalgan Huasteca Ejidos and Communities (URECHH) and began taking back their lands, leading to army occupation of over thirty communities; from 1976 to 1980 alone, over 200 protesting peasants of the Huasteca disappeared or were assassinated. Peasants who refused to join the pro-government CNC or CCI were routinely packed off to jail. Hidalgo's *cacique* violence with state cooperation has since been reluctantly acknowledged by the Ministry of Agrarian and Hydraulic Resources, and international investigative bodies have condemned the violations of human rights in the region. For the nation as a whole, the International Federation of Human Rights reported in January 1981 a dropping off in human rights abuses directly attributable to the government—with the notable exception of "clandestine paramilitary and uniformed military bands intervening in detentions with political motives . . . and accused of torturing detainees."

The character of peasant demands and tactics varies with the nature of peasant activities. Farmworkers strike for better wages and working conditions, while small producers organize for better and fairer prices for their products. In 1975, for example, peasants demanding higher prices for their sugarcane and an end to such abuses as inaccurate weighing or bookkeeping manipulations occupied sugarmills in Veracruz and Morelos. Besides repossessing their lands by armed force, peasants typically occupy and even dynamite municipal offices, take hostages, go on long marches (as far as Mexico City), and disrupt production. Peasants also mobilize against state authorities to demand the release of political prisoners, the punishment of assassins, the breaking up of paramilitary goon squads, an end to the misuse of public funds, and the removal of *caciques* or venal functionaries. A number of new independent peasant organizations like URECHH emerged in the 1970s, and they began to form alliances with other sectors of the population— immiserated urban squatters (known in the countryside and cities alike as *paracaidistas* or "parachutists" for their sudden seizing of a piece of land), rank-and-file labor militants, teachers, students, and left-wing political organizations. These alliances often proved shaky, however, because of differences over goals and tactics.[5]

In an attempt to divide or coopt the independent peasant organizations, the Echeverría administration increased the state's involvement in the peasantry's land and wage struggles. In 1975 it launched the Pacto de Ocampo, which brought together under the hegemony of CNC such major independents as CCI, the Mexican Agrarian Council (CAM, founded in the 1970s), and the General Union of Workers and Peasants of Mexico (UGOCM, founded by PPS in 1949) in order to support its modest land-distribution program and limited experiments in "collectivization." Although Echeverría's successor, López Portillo, bypassed the Pacto de Ocampo to bring all land reform once more under the centralized aegis of the Agrarian Reform Ministry and the Ministry of Agrarian and Hydraulic Resources, most of the coopted peasant organizations remained loyal state supporters.

The peasant land movements were accompanied by unionization drives among farmworkers in response not only to the proletarianization of the peasantry but to the start of independent union-organizing achievements by the workers themselves and to the state's desire to stabilize the chaotic situation in the countryside. In 1967 CTM, with the approval of CNC, first decided to incorporate *jornaleros* into its ranks, and by 1981 it claimed to have enrolled over 200,000 of them. CNC began unionizing a few salaried rural workers in the late 1970s. Similarly, in 1975 CCI renamed itself CIOAC in order to reflect its intent to incorporate agricultural workers as well as peasants.

That same year, the Coalition of Yaqui and Mayo Valley Ejidos forced Echeverría to expropriate a *latifundio* of the daughter of ex-President Calles and led the occupation of many other lands in the

area. In the final month of his presidency, Echeverría responded to
these pressures with his most significant neopopulist land-reform
measure—the return of some of the lands held by Sonoran land-
sharks to their original owners. The land that was handed over did
not include that controlled by flourishing agribusinesses; the is-
suance of restraining orders (writs of *amparo*) against the expropriation and a "lockout" by the rural bourgeoisie and the *mano dura* of
the Monterrey group further diluted the impact of the reform.
The incoming López Portillo administration paid handsome
indemnities to the affected landlords, declared future land invasions a federal crime, and in general conformed to the bidding of
the agrarian bourgeoisie. Nonetheless, rural protest activity continued and efforts to "nationalize" the struggle escalated. In 1977
the Coordinating Center of Independent Revolutionary Peasants
was launched, and within two years it had expanded into the National Plan of Ayala Network (CNPA), whose rallying cry of "Land
to the tiller!" has since galvanized peasants throughout the nation.

More serious than these peasant mobilizations against capital and
the state however, has been a new insurgency among urban workers that began to appear in the late 1960s and—since the mid-
1970s—has become the principal target of state repression. The
roots of the militancy lie not in the general post-1968 disenchantment with the system, but in the failure of the post-1950 industrialization process. As official union leaders were able to meet
legitimate economic demands only part way, and as they increasingly sold out striking militants in the course of labor-capital confrontations, the workers became much more responsive to
demands for union democratization. Organized labor protest was
most strident among the best-paid workers—those in the automotive, air transport, electricity, metallurgy, steel, petroleum, nuclear
energy, telephone, and other industries where CTM was strongest
and yet the left-wing and reformist opposition was able to make
deep inroads. The proletariat's political consciousness rose with the
spread of the democratic ideals of the 1958–1959 railworkers', telephone workers', and teachers' strikes and the 1968 student strikes.
It also deepened as monopoly capital concentrated, disciplined,
and unified immense numbers of industrial workers in single workplaces, where the labor-capital conflict is experienced in a direct
way. In addition, younger workers became more open than the
previous generation to Marxist ideas, militant protest, solidarity
with other sectors in revolt at home and abroad, and radical social
change. A new type of worker began to emerge in those areas of
industry having a high capital investment and a small but relatively
well-paid labor force. Tens of thousands of these workers have

found that their wages do not suffice to advance themselves. They work five and a half or six days a week, are repeatedly laid off, and perform demeaning unskilled tasks; industrial accidents are frequent. And their avenues for improving working conditions are blocked by their *charro* leaders, who are allied with their employers. As a result, especially after the onset of the 1973 recession, they have engaged in countless slowdowns, strikes, and street demonstrations, and—in order to achieve their economic and political goals—have sought to replace *charro* leadership or go "independent" of CTM.

For example, starting in 1973, "independent" union organizers began making great headway among automotive workers. Unions at DINA (diesels and trucks), General Motors, and NISAN (Datsun) broke with CTM that year and affiliated with the Independent Worker Unity (UOI, founded in 1972). In less than a decade, UOI gained control over four big autoworker unions and 80 percent of the aviation industry's unionized workers. It also established "workers' commissions" (radical caucuses) in the rail, petroleum, metallurgy, steel, telephone, and electrical workers' unions. But the evolution of the new labor militancy has not been so unilinear or simple, and it is best understood in terms of two distinct phases: 1973 through 1977, examined here, and 1978 to the present, taken up in Chapter 8.

In the first phase there occurred about 3,600 strikes and "labor conflicts" involving between 1 and 2 million workers (because "illegal" and "nonexistent" strikes are only roughly estimated, figures vary widely). They were a response to layoffs, unemployment, rising inflation, and dissatisfaction with *charrismo*. In 1974 alone, workers struck firms in construction, textiles, automobiles, glass, metals, machinery, and transport. University students, bank employees, and doctors also went on strike. These actions continued into the next year, as the movement spread into shoe, chemical-pharmaceutical, metallurgical-mining, electrical, rail, and agricultural enterprises.

It was during this period that independent unions began to emerge, gradually breaking with the official unions and the PRI. This struggle was marked by intense conflict between *charros* and rank-and-file workers and by considerable violence. For example, the 120-day strike of more than 600 workers at the Spicer auto-axle plant was crushed by army troops and CTM goons; the strikers were fired. Despite such repression, the independents had some successes, and began to form regional *centrales*, links with the independent peasant movements, and plans for a national organization. At the same time, however, the majority of anti-*charro* elements—led by the radical wing of SUTERM, the largest electrical workers' union—preferred to continue the struggle within CTM; they became known as the "Democratic Tendency" (DT). The DT program called for nationalizing TNCs, "redirecting the course of the Revolution," abolishing *charrismo*, and incorporating other independent unions and workers' commissions into a broad coalition known as the Revolutionary Trade Union Movement (MSR).

In November 1975, DT *electricistas* sparked a street demonstration of a quarter of a million people in Mexico City, the largest such protest march since 1968 and the most important show of labor strength since the 1959 rail strike. Large delegations participated from the Revolutionary Railworkers Movement, government employees, telephone trade unionists, university employees advocating a single union of teachers and workers, and public school teachers. Many of the banners were addressed to "*señor presidente*," in the hope that the president would protect the unionists against the attacks of the *charros*.

But the *charros* fought back, through layoffs and physical assaults (including assassinations and disappearances) on militants. They expelled from SUTERM the charismatic DT leader (Rafael Galván, who died in 1980), along with dozens of regional leaders. Nonetheless, the new militancy spread to more unions and into the ranks of students, urban squatters, and peasants. On the eve of their largest strike action, in 1976, the *electricistas* brought together the university unions and over 300 organizations to form the National Front of Labor, Peasant, and Popular Insurgency. This attempt at unifying different sectors of the population represented a more serious threat to the state than did the student-led mass mobilizations of 1968, because now industrial workers were in the forefront. Testing President Echeverría's reformist rhetoric, the *electricistas* then launched a nationwide strike—and on July 16, 1976, *señor presidente's* "protection" was starkly illustrated by the army's invasion and occupation of all major electrical installations, public and private, to forcibly break the strike. Hundreds of strikers were subsequently fired. A year later, troops invaded UNAM to break a major strike by university employees that was also attracting thousands of supporters from the rest of the insurgent labor movement. These and similar acts of repression dealt a severe blow to the new militancy, especially its reformist DT wing. In 1977 the remaining *electricista* "democrats" inside SUTERM dissolved their DT caucus into MSR. That same year the government granted CTM labor boss Velázquez effective control over the National Housing Institute and the new Workers' Bank in exchange for his promise to cooperate with a 10 percent ceiling on wage hikes imposed by incoming President López Portillo at the behest of the IMF.

These setbacks did not deter labor militants from conducting some 300 strikes in 1977 and mounting 80 public demonstrations in Mexico City—but these figures were lower than those for the preceding years. Rather, they caused organizers to emphasize more than ever the need for greater solidarity with other sectors of the population. A telling example was the long strike in Monclova (Caohuila), which shook the joint state-private steel complex Altos Hornos de México. Responding to the massive unemployment, these steelworkers, among the nation's best paid, insisted that there be more job openings for their unemployed comrades. Many of their economic demands were met. Similar tendencies showed up in 1977 during the sixty-two day strike at General Motors and other strikes at General Electric, Empresa Panam de México, Volkswagen, Ford, Unipac, and so forth. In other words, far from behaving like a spoiled "labor aristocracy," some industrial employees of the state and monopoly capital voiced a *class* solidarity and attempted to show leadership in the larger proletarian and political struggle to democratize Mexico.

Indeed, the new militancy has not been limited to trade-union members but has extended into the ranks of the urban poor—many of whom are the last hired and first fired by both big and small industry. For example, temporary workers constructing the Tula oil refinery walked off the job in 1976, and those building the Cactus petrochemical plant in Chiapas sustained a militant strike in 1977. In the mid-1970s there were unusually large numbers of protest actions and strikes in small and medium-size industries—including a particularly long and militant strike conducted by textile workers in Cuernavaca in 1977.

In the ranks of the nonunionized employed segment of the urban proletariat there has developed a seething anger, mixed with confusion and incipient politicization. People in the lowest ranks, together with millions of urban unemployed and underemployed, contribute to the rising social tension that threatens modern Mexico with spontaneous explosions not unlike the *tumultos* of colonial times. For that reason, and because political activism has emerged in all these strata, the state pays close attention to them. It is increasingly sending CTM organizers into their work places and representatives of other state institutions into their neighborhoods in an effort at control. The PRI network is omnipresent. Religious groups and right-wing political parties make strong pitches to the nonunionized proletariat. Nevertheless, these elements can—in spite of many obstacles—be organized for progressive causes. A case in point is the example of the nonunionized and temporarily employed oil workers already mentioned.

The issue has gained particular relevance since the onset of the 1973 recession, when the international crisis in accumulation of capital provoked new efforts by U.S. monopoly capital to restructure its industries at home and augment its investments in areas of cheap labor abroad, like Mexico. Mexican capital also intensified its use and exploitation of easily replaceable labor. Consequently, the industrial productive process today is marked by strong fragmentation of the work force; deskilling of work and its division into limited, simple tasks; degradation of labor; "feminization" of the work force; and termination-rotation of workers.[6] By making most of the industrial process consist of interchangeable tasks performable by anyone, capital is contributing to an atomization and decomposition of the political and trade-union organization process of the working class. The division, dequalification, and rotation of labor end by separating workers economically, socially, and politically.

On the other hand, by attracting (even if temporarily) new elements into the industrial process of work, including women and rural migrants, the same capitalist industrial restructuralization serves to concentrate socially thousands of persons whose backgrounds are usually individualized (the home, the village, etc.). The new shared social and work experiences these recruits to the industrial work force undergo create a social-political base for the organization of a rapidly growing fraction of today's working class. For example, women workers in northern Mexico's *maquiladora* plants formed many unions in the 1970s, and although plant managers there still resist their efforts to organize and constantly rotate the labor force, some companies have accepted the inevitable and welcome the CTM-controlled unions as a means of keeping order on the shop floor.

By the end of the first phase of the new labor militancy, DT had regrouped itself into MSR and reaffirmed its reform-minded commitment to "defend the nation and the presidential institution." DT leaders thereby blurred the class nature of the democratic insurgency and reinforced the bourgeois ideology that slanders progressives and independent labor militants as "antinational" or "communist" deviants who lack respect for the presidency. The minority independents, on the other hand, vowed to defend the working classes and extend their nascent networks of antibourgeois solidarity. Both wings of the new insurgency geared themselves for a period of economic austerity and continued state repression.

For its part, the state was still not out of its crisis. The sharpened labor-capital conflicts of the 1970s were producing among both the workers and the bourgeoisie a critical questioning of the traditional forms of state populist posturing, *charrismo, caciquismo,* and state-bureacratic management of corporativist institutions. Capitalist groups like those in Monterrey saw that the *charro*/rank-and-file conflict was reducing labor's productivity, while growing numbers of proletarians saw *charrismo* as an obstacle to their advance. The political "class" that traditionally mediated conflicts between classes could no longer easily control these forces. It found its demagogic politics of masses challenged by both major classes.

The Roles of the Oil Card and Foreign Policy in the Crisis

The crisis of the Mexican state is a crisis of Mexican capitalism. It is rooted in the uneven and incomplete industrialization process that the bourgeoisie and the state carried out after World War II with their stabilizing-development strategy. As we have seen, this approach called for state financing of the economic infrastructure, heavy infusions of foreign capital, and the centralization of capital, resulting in the creation of a system of dependent state monopoly-capitalism. In spite of achieving rates of industrialization and economic growth superior to those of most of the rest of Latin America, Mexico did not emerge into autonomous sustained growth. The economic causes of this failure—and that of the new development strategies introduced in the 1970s—are located in the weakness of Mexico's patterns of capital accumulation and the economy's dependence on foreign capital. Since the Mexican government still has not confronted these causes except at the rhetorical level and, in part, through its foreign policy measures, this analysis will extend beyond the 1968–1977 period covered by the rest of the chapter.

As the previous chapters have illustrated, Mexico's process of capital accumulation has relied since late colonial times on an abundant supply of cheap labor, accompanied in recent decades by the preservation and refunctionalization of noncapitalist forms of economic activity in order to maintain the reproduction of the labor force at minimal cost to the employer. The most mechanized, productive, and dynamic sectors of the economy have been able to attract labor from, and expel it back to, the more traditional sectors and the reserve army of labor, thereby stemming wage advances even in the most capitalized industries and in the face of labor unrest. The bourgeoisie, able to rely on cheap labor, has thus never had to attempt total industrial transformation, while the modern industrial sectors have, through their accumulation of capital, not been able to complete the transformation of the economy as a whole.

Under capitalism, capital accumulation on an extended scale depends on continuous and growing value transfers from traditional areas of production to the modern industrial sector, development of which in turn depends on a vigorous Department I of production (the means of production) and an ample home market of adequately paid consumers. Mexico lacks both. Since 1950, the traditional areas of production (food, textiles, etc.) have not transferred value out but instead have *received* value from the other sectors of the economy, while the modern industries (metallurgy, industrial manufacturing, etc.) have failed to continuously receive value. Only agriculture, forestry, fishing, construction, electricity, transportation, and services have continuously transferred value— and this they have sent to *both* traditional and modern areas of production. Moreover, since wages have been higher in the modern industrial sector than in the traditional one, the *rate* of surplus value has been less in the modern sector—and the rate of profit overall for both sectors has been sticky at best since 1950. Even an advance in the profit rate in the early 1970s failed to achieve the levels of 1960.[7] One result has been lower productivity of Mexican industry, which in turn means that Mexican products are seldom able to compete with those of foreigners, at home or abroad. This has only served to reinforce the Mexican bourgeoisie's dependence on cheap labor, the root cause of the nation's weak accumulation pattern.

The traditional source of this labor supply has been the countryside. Not surprisingly, therefore, Mexico's industrial crisis is symbiotically linked to its agrarian crisis. In 1965 the average rural wage was more than a small-parcel farmer could earn through self-exploitation, and in the next decade more than 2 million hectares of rain-fed farmland was abandoned, much of which had provided the bulk of the food staples for the provincial centers and the big cities. In addition, wholesale food prices failed to keep pace with the peasants' cost of living (agrarian tools, seeds, and other inputs). Consequently, land monopolization and agribusiness expansion continued to dispossess peasants in ever-growing numbers; the number of landless workers doubled in the 1970s. As day labor became harder and less well paid, and as the average number of workdays per year for rural wage earners dropped from 90 in 1970 to 65 in 1980, migration to the cities and to the United States escalated. A 1979–1980 drought compounded the problem, and in 1980 Mexico was importing a quarter of its nutritional needs, mostly from the United States. By 1981, agricultural imports (about $3 billion worth of corn, grains, *frijoles*, sugar, and edible fats and oils) were greater than agricultural exports, thereby undercutting the state's financial ability to provide for the new migrants. In addition, the quadrupled investments of TNCs in the 1970s elevated the level of capital needed for the creation of each new job. Since all productivity comes from *activated* labor power, Mexico's productivity disadvantages correspondingly deepened with this growth in its surplus population.

Mexico's self-reproducing pattern of limited capital accumulation has thus been aggravated by the continued inability to create employment, as well as by the consequent absorption of millions of the unemployed and subemployed into the petty economic activities described earlier. These activities in turn have retarded poor people's development of a more organized political or class response to oppression, thereby helping to perpetuate the cycle of low wages, low social productivity, noncompetitiveness of Mexican industry—and imperialism's economic power in Mexico.

The Echeverría administration attempted to correct the problem by supplementing import-substitution industrialization with the development of heavy industry (Department I). During an international congress on science and technology in Mexico City in 1973, it was suggested to some of Echeverría's top advisers that Mexico's technology development plans coincided, consciously or not, with those of U.S. imperialism. TNCs were committed to a new export drive euphemistically called "technology transfer" (i.e., technology sales) as a means of solving the cash liquidity crisis—since most technology sales are paid for promptly with cash transfers through international credit institutions. Because of rising production costs at home, TNCs were also committed to a strategy of selling more industrial installations abroad, particularly to such low-wage areas and expanding home markets as Mexico. Such technology commercialization and capital export constituted the fastest growing means of capital accumulation for U.S.-based TNCs, and had become crucial for their survival and growth. U.S. imperialism was momentarily on the defensive after the Vietnam setback; the dollar was no longer hegemonic on the international money market; the terms of trade had stiffened due to the activities of OPEC and similar cartels; there was a recession at home and "stagflation" (high unemployment with inflation), as well as intensified interimperialist rivalries and the rise of revolutionary governments and liberation movements throughout the world. Thus Mexico was one of the first test cases for U.S. imperialism's strategy to displace part of its own crisis onto the backs of the working classes in the so-called Third World.

President Echeverría's advisers responded that the 1972 Law on Registration of Technology Transfers, implemented through CONACYT (National Council on Science and Technology), would provide government oversight and forestall such a "sacking." Yet they conceded there was no adequate way to discipline the TNCs short of opening their accounting books, which would require a revolution. Three years later, CONACYT publicly acknowledged the failure of the 1972 law—and the previous thirty years' development strategy in general. The savings derived from registering technology sales had been insignificant; the registering had been irregular and only after contracts were negotiated.

Yet the state stuck to its strategy, and from 1976 to 1980 the importation of production goods tripled—despite state development plans that demagogically called for Mexico's becoming a capital goods *exporter*.[8] Of all capital goods developed in the 1970s, more than 80 percent were imported, strengthening foreign capital's domination of heavy industry. The state cooperated by offering such incentives as the elimination of all *ad valorem* import duties on raw materials and components and of 75 percent of them on machinery; 75 percent cuts in sales taxes; 15 to 20 percent cuts in income taxes; and increased depreciation allowances. It was estimated that for every $1.00 of new foreign investment entering the country there left some $2.50 to $3.00 in profits, royalties, other payments, and tricks of transfer pricing on technology imports—a structural basis of the economy's "dollarization" and relative decapitalization.

Moreover, since Department I development depended on increased foreign borrowing, the ninefold rise in production-goods imports in the 1970s contributed heavily to the more than sixfold increase in the public sector foreign debt (see Table 12, where the figures for imported production goods underestimate the actual costs since they represent only the value of specific goods and omit various costs associated with their importation). Of Mexico's total public and private debt in 1980, some 95 percent was in dollars, and more than half of this was owed U.S. lenders. Chase Manhattan alone had outstanding $10 billion in credits to the Mexican government or private Mexican borrowers.[9] Interest payments and amortization on the foreign debt typically absorbed—until the recent expansion in oil exports—half or more of Mexico's export earnings (see Table 13).

Table 12
Production Goods Imported and Public Sector Foreign Debt, 1971–1980
(billion U.S. dollars)

Year	Capital goods	Raw materials	Total production goods	Public sector foreign debt
1971	1.00	.80	1.8	5.55
1975	2.40	3.00	5.4	14.45
1979	3.58	7.41	10.98	29.76
1980	5.12	11.03	16.15	33.81

Source: Banco de México, annual reports, and *V informe de Gobierno, Anexo estadístico histórico* (1980).

Table 13
Debt Repayment and Foreign Trade, 1965–1980
(billion U.S. dollars)

Year	Interest & amortization	Imports	Exports	Exports as % of imports
1965	.52	1.56	1.11	71
1966	.54	1.61	1.16	72
1967	.55	1.75	1.10	63
1968	.67	1.96	1.18	60
1969	.63	2.08	1.39	67
1975	1.66	6.58	2.86	44
1980	7.68	31.42	24.82	79

Source: Nacional Financiera, *La economía mexicana en cifras* (1970); Banco de México, annual reports, 1977, 1980.

Table 14
Profits from Direct Foreign Investments Plus
Interest Payments on Foreign Debt, 1974–1980
(billion U.S. dollars)

Year	Profits
1974	1.22
1975	1.55
1976	1.84
1977	3.54
1980	5.54

Source: Banco de México, annual reports.

Mexico's continuing trade deficit is rooted in its oppressive history of colonialism and imperialism during which periods it always sold commodities to more industrialized countries relatively cheaply and "in exchange" bought commodities dear. Unequal exchange is thus a product of power relations between people in which the labor of generations of Mexican peasants and workers has subsidized the economic development of the more industrialized nations.[10] By 1980 Mexico's trade imbalance was four times what it was in 1970—and the non-oil deficit in trade was running at over $10 billion a year (or greater than oil revenues). Moreover, tourism receipts, which had often made up for the deficit, were now covering less than a third of it. At least a third of the negative trade balance derives from the TNCs' purchases of materials needed by their Mexican affiliates: for every product exported from Mexico by a TNC, eight are imported for its installations. In addition, luxury items for the wealthy constitute at least 5 percent of imports. Mexico is the world's third largest trading partner of the United States, with which it conducts 65 percent of its commerce. Mexico's perennial complaint is directed at U.S. protectionism practiced with regard to major Mexican exports—for example, shoes and tomatoes. But as oil has now become the name of the trade game, and the United States is far from in a liberalizing mood on manufactured imports given the phenomenon of U.S. "runaway shops," it is unlikely that the trends described here will alter.

The more that foreign investments flow into Mexico (70 percent of them U.S.), the more the country is sacked. In one year, 1977, declared foreign profits and interest receipts exceeded those for the entire decade of the 1960s (compare Table 4 in Chapter 5 with Table 14 below). Moreover, this trend is escalating at an incredible pace. Since 1978, U.S. direct investment in Mexico has doubled just about every year; new foreign investments quintupled in the 1978–1980 period, passing the mark of $1.5 billion a year—while in *only* the first three months of 1982 some $1.5 billion in foreign profits was being remitted abroad (78 percent of the investment is in manufacturing).

Thus, increased foreign investments and profit remittances, technology purchases, foreign debts, and trade imbalances have gone hand in hand in a sharp upward spiral, creating a "suction-pump" effect that drains Mexico of much of its economic surplus and greatly benefits U.S. capital accumulation (and to a lesser degree that of England, West Germany, Switzerland, Japan, and France, in that order of their investments in Mexico). This phenomenon is what has been baptized in the United States as the "silent integration" of the Mexican and U.S. economies. Although heavily weighted to the U.S. bourgeoisie's accumulation, the flow of capital is not just one way. By 1980, Mexican monopoly capital had established affiliated enterprises in Europe, Japan, Latin America, and the United States. Banco de México figures showed $6.45 billion leaving Mexico from 1976 to 1979 in such private ventures, an amount equivalent to new loans taken out by the public sector in 1978–1979. And although it periodically gripes about "capital flight," the Mexican state encourages the silent integration by selling "petro-bonds" and stock shares in Mexican industry in U.S. money markets, selling most of its petroleum to the United States at prices well below those of OPEC (through 1982, at least), opening up state bank branches in New York (e.g., Somex, a bank with majority state shares), and tolerating the emigration of workers and peasants to the United States.

From such economic integration comes the common saying that "when the United States sneezes, Mexico catches cold." This was illustrated when the effects of the U.S. recession hit Mexico in the mid-1970s. By late 1975, more than 32,000 workers had been laid off by border *maquiladora* managers, crippling many local economies. The impact in the interior was similar—for example, in the Federal District half a million workers were dismissed and 3,000 small companies went bankrupt in just one year (1976). In an attempt to protect desperate peasant producers, the government allowed the price of *frijoles*—the most important source of protein in the Mexican diet—to increase 265 percent, pricing half the population out of the market; tortilla prices tripled. Capital flight, noncompetitiveness of Mexican products, dollarization of the economy, and IMF pressures forced a nearly 100 percent devaluation of the peso in late 1976, almost doubling the real foreign debt (to almost $50 billion), as well as the real costs of imported capital goods—to the detriment of nonmonopoly firms and the advantage of the TNCs. Using the swollen debt as leverage, together with an emergency $1.2 billion loan, the IMF imposed on the incoming López Portillo government restrictive guidelines on the federal budget, trade policies, and wage structure. Social-welfare programs were to be cut back, federal spending reduced, wage increments limited, currency exchange rates freed, and private firms given easy access to credit—all steps favorable to monopoly capital.

López Portillo complied with the IMF's wishes, announcing a campaign against corruption in government (former Agrarian Reform Minister Félix Barra was arrested for accepting $800,000 in bribes), an "alliance for production," *topes* (ceilings) on wage increases, and measures to increase labor productivity (including speed-ups). He set and enforced wage *topes* at 10 percent (1977), 12 percent (1978), 13.5 percent (1979), and 21.5 percent (1980) but let the value of the peso and many market prices "float," leading to galloping inflation. From 1977 to 1980 inflation averaged almost 25 percent a year, wage hikes averaged 14 percent, and worker productivity increases (discounting inflation) averaged 10 percent. In other words, instead of raising wages sufficiently to augment the consumption of the masses and the expansion of the home market, the state and the bourgeoisie opted for the usual limited pattern of capital accumulation: more monopolization and higher prices. From 1978 to 1980, the buying power of all salaried Mexicans dropped 36 percent, while the stock value of 110 leading monopoly firms rose 60 percent. First and foremost, as Table 15 illustrates, those earning the minimum wage were able to buy much less than before. In residential areas with the highest working-class concentration, such as Mexico City, Guadalajara, and Monterrey, the 1980 loss in purchasing power of the minimum wage was 40 percent or more.

The state's implementation of IMF recommendations letting prices move ahead of wages (inflation in the name of combating inflation) thus permitted at least a momentary renewal of capital accumulation at the expense of fixed- or low-income groups. A newly introduced value-added tax of 10 percent—in effect a sales tax—further squeezed buyers, and was unpopular enough for it to be eliminated on some products in 1981. In 1980 the lowest 75 percent of income earners spent 62 percent of their income on food. By the end of 1982, inflation approached 100 percent.

Moreover, in spite of the huge debt, U.S. and other foreign creditors sought to prop up the economy by pouring in some $3 billion worth of *new* credit in December 1976 and January 1977. To bail out big private bankers who had been hurt by the recession, the state's leading financial agencies (Nafinsa, Banco de México, etc.) increased their foreign borrowing. Between 1975 and 1978, Nafinsa augmented its resources fivefold, to $10 billion, a quarter

Table 15
Average Annual Percent Loss in Purchasing Power of the Legal Minimum Wage, 1977–1980

1977	18.6
1978	12.9
1979	16.2
1980 (through October)	24.0

Source: National Commission of Minimum Wages, Mexico City.

of which went to service its own foreign debt. The agrarian Banco Nacional de Crédito Rural owed foreign creditors $1.1 billion by the end of 1977.[11] This saved the private banks but further jeopardized the state banks, whose dependence on foreign loans undermined the state's autonomy in economic planning; after 1980, for each dollar loaned Mexico, at least $.96 had to be returned in interest payments on earlier loans. Therefore, as we shall see in Chapter 8, the next occasion for an IMF-imposed austerity program would find the state unable to bail out the private banks in the accustomed manner.

Besides needing to protect investments and trade, U.S. monopoly capital had a new and more important reason to discipline and "help finance" Mexico's economy. On taking office as president, López Portillo had announced vast new discoveries of oil in Chiapas and along the Caribbean coast. For political reasons the announcement came three years late: in 1974 the PRI inner circle knew that Mexico was the Arabia of the Caribbean—but they also realized that once the bureaucratic pirates broke open the oil treasure chest, the ship of state, despite momentary stabilization, would soon be sacked of its cargo and drift toward the rocks. So they had locked the oil story up in the presidential cabinet and had chosen instead a rhetorical "nationalist" tack of verbally assaulting the TNCs' "looting" of Mexico. But by late 1976 U.S. imperialism and its junior partners in the Mexican bourgeoisie had destabilized the country, pulling out much of their capital in the face of the new labor militancy. Informing the public that he "found the nation on the edge of violence," López Portillo was forced to take a first step into the arms of temptation, and he dealt the PRI's trump, the oil card. U.S. President Jimmy Carter came gladhanding down for a visit, the IMF and the World Bank opened their fists with giant loans, and foreign investments flowed back into Mexico. Even employment picked up momentarily, at least in those industries affected by oil.

By 1982 Mexico's proven oil reserves were estimated at 72 billion barrels, its probable reserves at 90 to 150 billion, and its potential reserves at 250 billion, not far behind Saudi Arabia; in addition, there are 200 trillion cubic feet of proven natural gas reserves, and four times that amount of potential gas reserves. In the early 1980s, oil production fluctuated between 1.5 and 3 million barrels a day. Ranking fourth or better in refining capacity, sales, and oil and petrochemical production, PEMEX extended its exploration and technological development programs into Ecuador, Colombia, Uruguay, Nicaragua, Panama, Spain—and Cuba, which planned to obtain virtually all its oil imports of 10 million tons a year from

Mexico. PEMEX also hopes to install distribution plants for gasoline and diesel fuel in California, Arizona, and Texas.

Once more in its history Mexico is a mono-exporter, as oil accounts for 75 percent of its export earnings. Over half its GNP derives from oil, and PEMEX accounts for a quarter or more of state expenditures. Officially, the state has said it will never send more than half its hydrocarbon exports to any single country—but by the first quarter of 1981 it was sending 80 percent of them to the United States. Competing for a distant second place were Israel, Japan, Spain, and France. More than half of PEMEX's sales come from exports, 90 percent of which consist of crude oil. In the rush to produce oil for export, the amount of gas lost through flaring is equivalent to enough money to pay the minimum wage for half a million Mexicans in the Federal District. Mexico's "production platform" is slated to reach a capacity of 5 million barrels a day by 1983. Yet officially the government said in 1980 that it would not allow production to surpass 1.5 million barrels a day *throughout the 1980s* (and 300 million cubic feet a day of natural gas, considerably less than the amount already going to the U.S. consortium Border Gas, Inc.). PEMEX plans to double the nation's port capacity at Pajaritos to 2.5 million barrels a day. Another port in Tabasco (Dos Bocas) is slated to become even larger, revealing a potential port base for oil exports of well over 5 million barrels a day.

Most new investments by PEMEX are financed by foreign loans. In recent years, PEMEX's income has been half its expenditures, leading to its mid-1982 debt of $25 billion (or one-third the nation's foreign debt, another 15 percent of which is owed by the state electricity complex CFE). PEMEX export earnings do not suffice to meet the service payments on Mexico's foreign debt, as PEMEX expansion fuels the vicious circle of technology imports/debt already described. To assure foreign capital's cooperation in its expensive rush to obtain the equipment and technical know-how required for its sudden expansion of oil production, the Mexican government has relaxed its regulatory laws on machinery imports for the petroleum industry and foreign investment in petrochemicals. Additions to the Petroleum Law legislated in 1959 had already opened the door in secondary petrochemicals to U.S. concerns, and today these have twice as much capital invested in them as does the primary chemical sector; pharmaceuticals, paints, and synthetic fibers are all U.S.-controlled. By 1978, the chemical industry accounted for almost 30 percent of U.S. industrial investment in Mexico. After López Portillo's liberalization of the Petroleum Law, the petrochemical industry as a whole became dominated by foreign capital. TNC researcher Víctor Bernal Sahagún reports that TNCs now control more than 90 percent of the petrochemical industry's machinery, 80 percent of its transport and chemical-pharmaceutical production, and 70 percent of its chemical production.[12] Meanwhile, U.S. oil equipment companies have experienced a veritable boom, selling PEMEX $2 billion worth of machinery in 1981—an amount equivalent to one-seventh of PEMEX export revenues.

The López Portillo administration also undertook construction of a 780-mile natural gas pipeline *(gasoducto)* from Chiapas to Texas. A consortium of six U.S. gas producers and distributors began negotiating an offer of loans in exchange for purchase rights to the gas. Among leading contenders for the lucrative construction contracts was San Francisco's Bechtel Corporation, a veteran of quick profits in the Vietnam war years and Saudi Arabia's largest foreign investor. Eximbank, Chase Manhattan, and West Germany's Commerzbank advanced billions of dollars in credits for Mexico's oil-development plans.

There was a reaction to this, however. Thousands of professionals, students, and workers from thirty organizations launched street demonstrations in 1977 and 1978 to defend the country's natural resources. Aging one-time PEMEX director Antonio J. Bermúdez warned that the nation was allocating its "reserves for the progress of other countries, sacrificing the progress of Mexico."[13] Responding to these pressures, López Portillo announced that the *gasoducto* would not be extended to Texas. In 1977 energy czar James Schlesinger nixed a deal with Mexico for U.S. purchase of natural gas at $2.60 per thousand cubic feet, claiming the price was too high; two years later he agreed to a price of $3.62. The *New York Times* editorialized that this was "a bargain." The formula for calculating future price revisions was kept a secret, and Mexican nationalists feared that sales would not maintain their real value. Mexico's bargaining position was not helped by the sight of the world's largest oil spill from the Ixtoc I undersea well in the Bay of Campeche fouling beaches in southern Texas. A nine-month fight against the spill finally succeeded in capping Ixtoc I in March 1980, but Mexico refused to pay damages to injured U.S. interests unless the U. S. government paid Mexico for damages caused by saline water from the Colorado River flowing into Mexico from the agribusiness fields of California and Arizona in the 1960s. Later, a Texas oil drilling concern, Sedco, Inc., that had leased the rig installed by PEMEX at Ixtoc I, reportedly agreed to pay $2.14 million in damages to private U.S. businesses, fishermen, and others affected by the spill and $2 million to the U.S. government for cleanup costs.

Early in his administration, López Portillo unveiled a general plan for "rational" use of the world's energy resources for the benefit of the developing nations, promising the Mexican people that "their" state would never use its oil revenues to service its debt or to pay for corn imports. Yet by 1981 Mexico was doing just that. It no longer controlled the energy resources it owns, its oil, gas, and uranium. Such TNCs as Occidental Petroleum and Dallas's Dresser Industries have Mexican oil-related operations generating tens of millions of dollars worth of sales each year. Two other U.S. concerns, Hercules and DuPont (the latter moving strongly into the oil field when it absorbed Conoco Oil in 1981, in history's largest corporate merger), have joint ventures with Monterrey's ALFA group, which also negotiated a joint venture with Japan's biggest corporate conglomerate, Mitsubishi. In mid-1981 a group of eighty-two banks in eleven nations extended PEMEX a $4 billion short-term loan. U.S. banks lent 40 percent of the total, Japanese banks 30 percent; the loan's agent was Bank of America. In addition, industry in Mexico benefits because it buys PEMEX oil and gas products at one-third their world market value. For their part, the Mexican people experience repeated price hikes in hydrocarbon products for their vehicles and homes—in the words of a Michoacán peasant, "What do we gain from that fabulous wealth if the poor are crying from hunger?"[14]

Accustomed to exploiting the natural resources of poor peoples and to having a big voice in the formation of U.S. foreign policy, U.S.-based oil companies assume that Mexico's petroleum, gas, and uranium reserves are—in the long run—their own. Besides having roughly one-third of all U.S. overseas investments, they already account for about 65 percent of the world petroleum industry's spending (capital investment), 80 percent of its expenditure on oil exploration, and 50 percent of its fixed assets.[15] Over the years, executives, lawyers, and bankers associated with the giant Rockefeller-dominated Standard Oil of New Jersey have headed the CIA, occupied top posts in government cabinets, and determined many ambassadorial appointments. While the American Ambassador to Mexico no longer can arrange military coups as easily as in 1913 or push a button on his desk and in a matter of seconds issue a command to the Mexican president as one acting ambassador claimed to have been able to do in 1964,[16] the American Embassy remains—in countries like Mexico and, prior to its takeover by student insurgents in 1980, Iran—a main conduit for plotting imperialism's next steps.

Central to U.S. policy formation on Mexico is the Rockefeller family. Early in the López Portillo *sexenio*, David Rockefeller (for many years the president of Chase Manhattan and in the early 1970s the main founder of the Trilateral Commission, a group of political and business leaders from North America, Western Europe, and Japan that coordinates long-range economic and governmental policy for international capitalism) and his long-time aide Henry Kissinger met with leaders of Mexico's principal industrial groups to try to persuade them to have Mexico join the General Agreement on Trade and Tariffs (GATT). They hoped to "develop" Mexico through GATT in the direction of its "natural" oil-exporting advantages in exchange for increased exports of manufacturing and capital goods to Mexico from the nations represented in the Trilateral Commission. Responding to popular pressures against this scheme, López Portillo announced in early 1980 that Mexico was postponing entry into GATT, but the Rockefeller family kept pushing the idea. Rodman C. Rockefeller, David's brother, is chairman of the U.S. section of the Mexico-U.S. Business Committee, an organization of large-scale capitalists. This and similar organizations—such as the Commission of the Californias, the American Chamber of Commerce (of Mexico), and the Rockefeller-founded Center for Inter-American Relations and Council of the Americas (nonprofit, tax-free institutions influential in the formation of U.S. policy on Latin America)—have been very active since Mexico's announcement of new oil discoveries in championing closer U.S.-Mexican relations. In the summer of 1981 a new organization was introduced by David Rockefeller, the tax-free Americas Society, Inc., incorporating the Center for Inter-American Relations, Council of the Americas, and Pan-American Society and composed of heads of TNCs with investments in Mexico and the rest of Latin America. The Reagan administration expressed its intent to work closely with the new group.

In the light of this background, it surprised no one that American Ambassador Julian Nava described Mexico in 1980 as "a strategic and vital zone for U.S. interests"—standard diplomatic language for an area subject to direct U.S. military intervention. Three years earlier Secretary of Energy James Schlesinger had declared that securing U.S. oil supplies was "a military responsibility." A CIA study entitled "The International Energy Situation: Outlook to 1985" anticipated that Mexico would provide the United States 4.5 million barrels of oil a day before 1985. The proximity of Mexican oilfields to Guatemala and El Salvador is a cornerstone of the rationale for U.S. military intervention in Central America. In August 1980, in one of his last public addresses, Enrique Alvarez Córdoba, president of the Salvadoran Democratic Revolutionary Front, informed a group at the Riverside Church in

New York City that State Department officials in Washington had told him: "If El Salvador has a revolution, then the Mexican oilfields 150 miles away will be hit by revolution: we can't permit either" (three months later, ultra-rightist forces kidnapped Alvarez and other Front leaders from a press conference in San Salvador and assassinated them). On March 10, 1983, President Ronald Reagan affirmed: "If guerrilla violence succeeds, El Salvador will join Cuba and Nicaragua for spreading fresh violence to Guatemala, Honduras, even Costa Rica. The killing will increase and so will the threat to Panama, the canal, and ultimately Mexico."

A recent shift in mass-media coverage of Mexico forebodes preparation of U.S. public opinion for possible direct U.S. military involvement in Mexico. A 1980 *Gallery* magazine article described an imaginary U.S. invasion south of the border to secure oil supplies, while a 1982 CBS special portrayed Mexico as reeling on the verge of chaos and incoming president Miguel de la Madrid as a somewhat laughable incompetent. In response to the *Gallery* article, widely excerpted in the Mexican press, the Mexican army vowed "to defend the fatherland," which to date it has done by breaking up peasant protests against PEMEX's raping of their lands. Oil is greasing an increased militarization of Mexican society.

This meets the needs of U.S. imperialists, whose preferred strategy for securing Mexican oil is not direct military intervention (except as a last resort) but rather a combination of economic/diplomatic pressures and courtship of Mexico's military and police apparatuses. The U.S.-sponsored ideology of "the military coup [as] part of the democratic process in Latin America"[17] has not been excluded from Mexico. Many are the Mexican military officers who publicly declare themselves "defenders of the nation," "professional," or "constitutionalist." But that is not so unusual in Latin America among military personnel—such was the case in Chile, for example, prior to the 1973 coup against a democratically elected president. Mexican and U.S. security forces have conducted joint operations for years. Under López Portillo, the director of federal security, Miguel Nassar Haro, was the CIA's most important source of information in Mexico and Central America (in early 1982 U.S. officials arrested him for alleged involvement in a $30 million car-theft ring and then released him on bail—the CIA requested that he not be prosecuted). In October 1980 Mexico's director of police and transit announced a new agreement with the FBI "and other U.S. security agencies" for an exchange of know-how, experience, and techniques. The wide range of activities undertaken by the CIA, FBI, and DEA in Mexico with the knowledge and cooperation of their counterparts in the Mexican state give the lie to the Mexican government's claims that it is independent of the United States.

Only in its foreign policy has Mexico been able to establish a credible, though uneven and contradictory, independent stature. In part to maintain the nonintervention doctrine of the Mexican Revolution, in part to cool out leftist opposition, and in part to gain leverage in its international bargaining with the United States, the Mexican government not only protests U.S. intervention in other parts of Latin America but also lends considerable moral support to the new revolutions shaking the continent—from Cuba and Grenada to Nicaragua and El Salvador. Throughout the Caribbean Basin, Mexico has worked out multimillion dollar joint ventures with various governments; so has Venezuela. Economically, however, these plans are not completely free of U.S. interests. Through their influence in both Mexico's and Venezuela's state inputs, U.S. investors can readily use these conduits for their own economic benefit or, on the other hand, attempt to block them for the purposes of destabilizing progressive governments as in the case of Michael Manley's Jamaica (replaced in 1980 by a friend of the CIA and IMF) or the Sandinistas' Nicaragua. In 1980–1981, Mexico defined Central America as its "natural area of influence." It agreed to guarantee a $130 million syndicated loan being sought by Nicaragua from foreign banks and offered Central American nations new trade preferences, including a 25 percent reduction in import duties and new lines of credit worth $68 million for the purchase of Mexican products. Like Venezuela, Mexico has agreed to provide Central American and Caribbean countries with oil, 70 percent of which will be paid for at international market prices and the rest of which will be converted into long-term credits at low interest rates for the financing of high-priority development projects. For Mexico this offers a chance to establish an unprecedented industrial, technical, and financial presence in the region—one reason the government is willing to accept new "developmentalist" revolutions there (which appear as inevitable as Mexico's did in 1910). But Mexico sends oil to the terrorist right-wing regimes of Haiti, El Salvador, and Guatemala on the same favorable terms as it does to the Sandinistas.

Also, the Mexican military maintains close contacts with the Guatemalan military (reputed to be Latin America's worst violator of human rights) in patrolling the two nations' common border. The southern zone of Mexico and the northern area of Guatemala became in the 1960s a free-fire military theater of operations for the armed forces of Mexico, Guatemala, and the United States (including representatives of the Green Berets, or Rangers). In fact, the first major Guatemalan guerrilla leader, Yon Sosa, was killed by Mexican soldiers. The technology of the Vietnam war was introduced there, as well as the practice of massacring civilian populations. Mexico reportedly helped provide the napalm from its own napalm factory, along with tanks and other components from its burgeoning arms industry (Mexico's military and paramilitary forces have also utilized this type of counterinsurgency warfare to stamp out guerrilla bands in various parts of rural Mexico). In recent years the Mexican army has beefed up its forces along the Guatemalan border in part to crush social unrest among the Indians there. Until late 1982, when Mexico's foreign ministry issued a formal protest, the army looked the other way each time Guatemalan soldiers crossed the frontier allegedly to hunt down fleeing guerrillas. The Mexican government rationalizes its contradictory policies in the Caribbean Basin as consistent with the "evenhandedness" it views as inherent in the doctrine of nonintervention.

While economically Mexico has made only minuscule gains in diversifying its trade and sources of foreign investment (e.g., with Japan), in its foreign relations it has gained international prominence. Its joint proclamation with France in late 1981 recognizing the Democratic Revolutionary Front as a legitimate political force in El Salvador and its offer to mediate the conflicts between the United States and radical governments in the Caribbean and Central America in an effort to establish a regional peace have propelled Mexico onto center stage of international diplomacy. Its advocacy of negotiated settlements and peaceful resolution of conflicts, however much contradicted by its violent suppression of Guatemalan and Salvadoran refugees flooding into its territory (jailing or deporting most of them and cooperating with U.S. authorities' deporting them from the United States), stands in contrast to the U.S. government's portrayal of popular forces in the region as part of a massive Soviet-Cuban conspiracy.

The Mexican PRI has joined with other major Latin American social-democratic parties and the European-dominated Socialist International in convening the Permanent Conference of Political Parties in Latin America (COPPAL). The common aim of these parties, like that of the Socialist International, is to maintain political systems without violent confrontation among social classes. The International is a minority voice in the less reactionary wing of the international bourgeoisie (so-called reformists) and is under the relative hegemony of the German Social Democratic Party (it includes the Socialist Party of France, which won that country's 1980 national elections). In February 1982, COPPAL made public a general plan for peaceful resolution of the crisis in Central America and the Caribbean that was consistent with Mexico's earlier proposals. By courting the Socialist International and Nicaragua's Sandinistas, who also joined COPPAL, the Mexican state expands its space for maneuver in its relations with the United States and refurbishes its "revolutionary" traditions at home.

Nonetheless, by mid-1982 it was evident that the state's innovative foreign policy measures and desperate playing of the oil card could no longer compensate for its historic failure to confront the structural causes of its crisis. In 1981 the petro-bubble began to evaporate, and by the end of the year Mexico had to slash its oil-export prices by $8 a barrel or more, leading to a national outcry—especially among elements of the bourgeoisie and the state bureaucracy fattening off oil sales and among nationalists. To appease the latter, PEMEX head Jorge Díaz Serrano, an associate in Texas business enterprises with U.S. Vice President George Bush, was fired; to assuage the suspicions of the former over this move, the state denied electoral registration to the largest left-wing opposition party, the Mexican Workers' Party (PMT), whose principal leader, civil engineer Heberto Castillo, had sparked the earlier outcries against the *gasoducto* and the state's "giveaway" of the nation's patrimony. Behind the oil price slashes were such obvious U.S. pressures as withholding loans and investments and cancelling contracts with PEMEX. The oil companies claimed there was a world oil glut. One of the contract-breakers, Exxon, was reputed to be implementing a plan to break up the OPEC cartel by accumulating enough crude supplies for a two-year period, forcing producing nations into a price war. For Mexico, depressed world oil prices meant lost earnings of $10 billion in the first half of 1982.

U.S. pressure was also applied to have Mexico temper its "independent" foreign policy. President Ronald Reagan met with López Portillo in Washington and held firm on the U.S. refusal to attend the "North-South Summit" of fifty nations scheduled for the fall of 1981 in Cancún, Mexico, if Cuba were invited. Behind the scenes, U.S. government officials pressured Mexico to deport Guatemalan refugees fleeing the terror unleashed by the military dictatorship—U.S. generals did not want Guatemalan guerrillas to have a rear base in southern Mexico. The Mexican army responded by deporting thousands of the refugees back to Guatemala (an earlier deportation of hundreds had resulted in their all being killed). The Cuba-Cancún summit issue was defused when López Portillo met with Cuba's Fidel Castro, head of the Non-Aligned Movement, in Cozumel, Mexico, in August 1981. Cuba's absence from the Cancún summit was confirmed in terms of all participating nations

of the "South" deferring to Reagan's conditions—and U.S. loans
and investments were renewed. With a poker face, President López
Portillo informed the public and the international community: "We
are a nation which proceeds upon principles and not upon mercantile interests."[18] Shortly after this statement, the government
slashed oil-export prices and broke earlier promises by announcing
that PEMEX had signed a five-year contract to sell crude oil directly to the U.S. Energy Department for its Strategic Petroleum
Reserve (SPR)—the first such direct purchase from a foreign government agency by the U.S. Energy Department. Prices were not
made public, but it was pointed out that they could be renegotiated
every three months and that Mexico was currently underselling the
average OPEC price by more than $3 a barrel. Commented one
U.S. Energy Department spokesman: "This is a delightful thing."

But this was just the first of oil delights in the offing for imperialist interests, whose pressures on the Mexican government
intensified. In February 1982 the government devalued the peso
by 65 percent, in hopes of staving off new demands by the IMF for
yet another austerity program. To alleviate the economic impact on
the populace, it decreed wage hikes of between 10 and 30 percent
from best paid to worst paid respectively. But the decree not only
failed to compensate for losses in real wages, it was also resisted by
private employers. So the government announced a 30 billion peso
subsidy for private enterprise in the form of tax rebates, further
undermining its solvency. There followed severe federal budget
reductions. Claiming that they had uncovered a secret U.S. State
Department briefing paper that allegedly (and prophetically) said
that Mexico's economic crisis might make it "less adventuresome"
in foreign policy and lead it "to sell more oil and gas to us at better
prices," government officials assured the public there would be no
more devaluations. As they had done in 1976, capitalists withdrew
their money from Mexico (up to $100 million a day), and the inevi-
table financial panic broke—in August 1982. A two-stage 100 percent devaluation of the peso completed a tenfold decline in its
value vis-à-vis the dollar since 1976. "Petrolization" of the economy
thus produced runaway inflation and state insolvency. The public
and private foreign debt surpassed $80 billion ($66 billion public,
$14 billion private), the highest per-capita debt in the Third World,
and Mexico could not pay its debt for the next ninety days. U.S.
monopoly capital seized this opportunity to obtain more oil and gas
and a stranglehold on the Mexican economy and state.

To help bail out Mexico on its next ninety days' debt payments,
the international banking community, led by U.S. bankers and the
U.S. government, agreed in late August to roll over the debt princi-

pal for three months. The U.S. government arranged a cash-in-advance billion-dollar oil purchase for its SPR at a per-barrel figure too low to be announced. Mexico agreed to quadruple its rate of delivery of light crude to the SPR in 1983 at a price no higher than $35 and no lower than $25 per barrel, no matter what OPEC did. Put together in the offices of the U.S. Treasury with Mexican Finance Minister Jesús Silva Herzog, Jr., son of the influential nationalist behind Cárdenas's 1938 oil nationalization, the "bailout" included another $1 billion from the Commodity Credit Corporation to cover grain imports and $925 million toward a $1.85 billion "bridge" credit from the Bank of International Settlements. As part of an additional $4.5 billion stand-by IMF credit, Mexico tentatively agreed to accept a stabilization program similar to the arrangement made in 1976–1977 which, in hindsight, had only deepened the nation's economic and political crisis. Mexico also stood by its 1981 agreement to double its natural gas exports to the United States to about 600 million cubic feet a day.

All told, the international bailout of Mexico in August 1982 totaled $10 billion, in exchange for which the Mexican government practically guaranteed U.S. receipt of the bulk of oil and gas sales at less than market value for the foreseeable future. Mexico is now the United States' principal oil supplier. For the Mexican public, the message of who would pay had been delivered earlier in August, when the government announced a doubling of prices on tortillas, bread, gas, and electricity.

On September 6, 1982, Silva Herzog, Jr., announced that in 1983 Mexico would pay only the interest on its debt. The truth is that: Mexico cannot pay even the interest short of doubling its oil production to 5 million barrels a day (it has almost that capacity now). Increased oil production probably means more inflation, more foreign borrowing, and a deepening of the very crisis that triggered August's double devaluation of the peso. Indeed, by the end of 1982, Mexico was seeking a rescheduling of some $20 billion in principal payments on the foreign debt due between August 1982 and December 1984; the IMF had persuaded private commercial banks to supplement an IMF $3.92 billion extended fund facility for Mexico with a $5 billion loan; Mexico had received $2 billion worth of industrial government trade credits; and the value of the peso was down to 150 per dollar. The collapse of the oil boom, alleged to have occurred in August 1982, thus promises to repeat itself on a much larger scale later in the 1980s. In light of mass poverty, the new labor militancy, and signs of unity among left-wing parties, a natural question occurs: Is Mexico on its way to an Iran-type eruption?

With more than a million of the regularly employed laid off in the fall of 1982, an ever greater percentage of the populace is being driven into the ranks of the relative surplus population, from which capital can obtain new cheap labor to exploit for a period before discarding it again. Such is the strategy of monopoly capital to extricate itself from the worldwide recession it generated in the first place. As the manager of a Fisher-Price Toys plant in Tijuana told the *New York Times* (September 20, 1982): "Essentially, we are buying labor, and the devaluation is going to make it less expensive to purchase that labor." Augmented use of a dual labor market incorporating superexploited temporary workers, an increase in the reserve army of labor through massive layoffs, lower real wages—all are basic components of capital's immiseration strategy to stem declining profit rates and bring itself out of crisis.

But this places insurmountable burdens on the shoulders of the state, which has the contradictory mission of controlling the labor force through concessions like wage hikes and yet fomenting capital accumulation. State subsidies to the private sector add to the state's growing indebtedness and fiscal crisis, thereby eroding the state's autonomy in the conduct of public and private corporate relations. The state's ability to take on directive functions for future mediation of the class struggle and overall policy formation in national and international affairs becomes, as López Portillo put it in his 1979 state of the nation address, "annulled, its possibility of governing cancelled."

The Bourgeoisie Closes Ranks and Endorses Political Reform

The bourgeoisie's closing of ranks and the regrouping in 1975 into the Management Coordinating Council (CCE) in response to the growing insurgency among the popular classes further constrained the state's room for maneuver. Declaring the need for the bourgeoisie to participate more openly in the nation's political life, CCE brought together the heads of CONCAMIN, CONCANACO, COPARMEX, and other capitalist groups to coordinate the major fractions of the big and medium-size bourgeoisie in the process of consolidating monopoly capital's dominant influence on the state. The "central fraction" and the Monterrey group spearheaded CCE's founding, and public statements by two of their leading representatives, Agustín F. Legorreta and Marcelo Sada, respectively, reflected their mission. "Not private enterprise versus the state but private enterprise with the state," said Legorreta, "the mixed economy is the guarantee that Mexico will follow the road of democracy and freedom."[19] "Never again," added Sada, would big business assume "second-class citizen status vis-à-vis the national political environment."[20]

While maintaining the bourgeoisie's formal separation from the state, CCE sought to assure its supremacy over the summit of the techno-bureaucracy by *insisting* that the state act as guarantor of its interests. Aware of the destabilization campaign being mounted by Sada and other reactionaries, the Echeverría administration bristled at this type of ultimatum—Secretary of Finance López Portillo publicly attacked CCE and the forces of "nazi-fascism."[21] Yet he was soon forced to change his attitude, and even the 1982 expropriation of private Mexican banks (with compensation) did not break the state's alliance with monopoly capital, although—as Chapter 8 explains—it altered its form. CCE played a central role in the politicking around the presidential succession of 1976 and in López Portillo's subsequent austerity program and "alliance for production." Bourgeois figures like PEMEX director Díaz Serrano entered the López Portillo government, which, at CCE's behest, passed a "multiple banking" (i.e., nonspecialized banking) law that made it possible for the nation's 243 private banks to consolidate into 63 big ones by 1981. The top 4 banks, holding 70 percent of private bank assets, augmented their profits more than tenfold during the same period. Thus, the formation of CCE produced a more direct presence of the large-scale bourgeoisie inside the state, thereby facilitating even more than before private monopoly capital's expansion.

Most of the bourgeoisie's internal differences have been buried now that CCE calls the shots. The main visible line of division is over the best approach to the class threat from below. Some favor an intensification of repression, reduced emphasis on democratization, and a return to the "basic values" of family, religion, fatherland, and work discipline. Others, including a broad sector of monopoly capital, favor certain institutional changes and adjustments, in the hope of moving the voices of discontent into the mainstream of political life, where they can be better controlled. They believe that such measures will accelerate economic growth by broadening the ruling class's base, or by at least tempering proletarian discontent. Thus, CCE critically endorsed President López Portillo's attempt to demobilize the popular movements for democratization through the "political reform" he announced after assuming office.

López Portillo's political reform increased the portion of minor-

ity seats in the Chamber of Deputies to 100 (reserving 300 for the
PRI), legalized the Communist Party, invited opposition parties to
"join the national electoral system," and obligated the state to
finance television time for all registered political parties. Student
supporters of the left-wing opposition parties were thus given
something to do besides train for guerrilla warfare—*el presidente*
would obviously rather have them painting election slogans on
walls than bombing banks. The timing of political reform coincided
with declaration of a partial amnesty for political prisoners and the
exposure of corruption in high places, thus making it appear that
the state was ready to cleanse itself of a corrupt past and turn over a
new leaf toward "democracy" and "honesty in government." Few
Mexicans believed that the anticorruption propaganda was intended to alter the institutionalized corruption of the system; instead they recognized that the state was attempting to put forth a
"new face," so besmirched had the old one become.

Since the state's crisis is rooted in the structure of the economy
and the class struggle, why did López Portillo opt for political reform and not economic reform? Having bowed to the IMF and
CCE in 1976, the state had already surrendered much of its autonomy in the economic arena. Moreover, prevailing conditions in the
class struggle did not permit economic reforms to occur without
serious danger of worsening the economic crisis or of provoking
revolutionary changes (from the viewpoint of the ruling class). By
making the political system just flexible enough to incorporate into
its electoral practices most dissident groups, political reform was
intended to serve as a safety valve for Mexico's economic problems.
Demands being generated by the oppressed masses and discontented intermediate-class elements, particularly students, might be
channeled into the political-reform process, thereby allowing the
state to regulate them and to pursue its IMF-style policies of labor
discipline.

López Portillo thus sought, as he put it, "to legalize the fight of
the opposition"—but to legalize in a very specific way, namely in
the Chamber of Deputies and electoral arena, under state regulation. He did not attempt to do it through the official mass organizations, such as the labor unions, peasant leagues, and so on, because
these were the main basis of the PRI's power in the political arena.
In fact, since labor unions already participated in a political party,
opposition parties were not allowed to participate in the unions
because, according to López Portillo, that would violate the unions'
"freedom of decision." This amounted to a presidential attack on
the Communist Party for its influence in the UNAM strike of July
1977, a strike through which the workers had hoped to achieve
more freedom of decision making, not less.

Mexico's polity consists of a political party that is not a party and labor unions that are not unions. The PRI is in effect a small group of top union bureaucrats and the twelve members of the party's national executive committee. The unions are political arms of the PRI and the state. Thus, in a corporativist system regulated by a technocratic-authoritarian state, the governing party does not organize the class whose interests it usually serves (the bourgeoisie's CCE does that), and the official trade unions do not genuinely represent the class they nominally serve (the Democratic Tendency and independent unions of the new labor militancy do that).

In the formal political system (regular elections, no reelection of the president, and rubber-stamp legislatures), the PRI's control is now "the law of the land" because of López Portillo's political reform, which changed Article 41 of the Constitution to make political parties "entities of public interest" that "contribute to the integration of national representation." The president stated in his first state-of-the-nation address: "Elevating to the height of the text of the Constitution the political parties assures their presence as determining factors in the exercise of popular sovereignty and in the existence of representative government." Since all constitutional texts become translated into practice through the laws and policies of the state, and since the state is a capitalist one, all political parties—as entities of public interest—are constitutionally obligated to abide by the decisions in which they participate and to serve the "national interest." If certain contradictions erupt—for example, between the working class and the "national interest," or between public employees and the state—political parties are legally expected to defend the national interest against the workers. Similarly, the state's traditional anticommunist (or antiforeign) campaigns now have a constitutional reinforcement in the notion of "integration of national representation." Finally, since the laws of the political-reform program speak of "majority" and "minority" parties, the rewriting of Article 41, by subjecting all political parties to whatever "the law determines," has the effect of making constitutional the political monopoly of the PRI. The constitutional reform also permits the state to do legally what it had previously done by custom: finance the "entities of public interest," principally the PRI but now also other political parties.

Notwithstanding, the political-reform program represents a concession by the state to the mass democratic movements of 1968 and afterward. By acknowledging the existence of left-wing parties and the need to legalize them, the state has recognized for the first time in over thirty-five years that dissent is legitimate. Like all reforms, this program has its own built-in dialectic, capable of wavering between greater rigidity and more flexibility. And like most populist measures, its long-range effect is to deflect or hold back the radicalization of masses of people. Yet it provides a certain breathing space, however limited, and a certain time period, however short, for progressive forces to assert mass democratic demands within and beyond the context of the political reforms as such. It also has allowed the Left to claim a victory in its long struggle to expose the illegitimacy of the prevailing political system and its anticommunist justifications of repression (otherwise, why the necessity of reform and of recognizing the Communist Party?).

In the context of the political reforms, progressive forces have to continue to be vigilant against sudden repression (as they learned from the military suppression of the 1976–1977 strikes). Yet they can scarcely afford to reject the reforms out of hand; nor can they accept them uncritically. By providing the Left with access to public television, they offer it the following opportunities: to point out the necessity of eliminating the government's prohibitions of opposition-party activity inside the mass organizations; to call for a genuine change in election laws and electoral boards that will permit democratic competition between all parties, without *built-in* definitions of majority and minority and without continued favoring of the PRI by state apparatuses; and to escalate the fight for all democratic freedoms and political rights, so long denied in Mexico. At the same time, the Left, and the mass democratic movements that have given life to most of its political parties in the first place, are able to escalate their programmatic demands, which, in spite of certain internal disagreements, have much in common. These demands include calls for nationalizing the banks *without* compensation, and for expropriating domestic and foreign private monopolies. They emphasize sweeping economic reforms and improvements in the standards of diet, health, education, and housing of the masses, all of which can advance the capacity of workers and peasants to fight for their eventual liberation. Thus, the overall effect of the political-reform program is to present progressive forces a new context in which to conduct the class struggle while simultaneously creating a much-needed space in which the state can maneuver to defuse this struggle and attempt to resolve its crisis.

8

The Crisis Prolonged, 1978–1982

Nationalism is a phenomenon that exists throughout the world. As for the nationalism of Mexico, that nation opens its doors to foreigners, as it always has done in the past. So nationalism is no problem in Mexico.
— Henry Ford II, December 2, 1970

Imagine a mob let loose on the streets, out of control.
— Fidel Velázquez, March 24, 1982

Prolonged and deepened by the post-1977 IMF-imposed austerity program and the petrolization of the economy, Mexico's crisis has at last gained the serious world attention it merits, but without a correspondingly careful analysis of the domestic and international factors that underlie and shape its evolution. Many of these have already been discussed:—Mexico's weak patterns of capital accumulation, the heating up of the class struggle in the 1970s, U.S. imperialism's gaining a stranglehold on the economy, and the state's serving domestic and foreign monopoly capital. This chapter examines additional important elements, such as the highly influential roles of the military, the Church, and the mass media, and the resurgent controversy surrounding the seasonal emigration of Mexican laborers to the United States. Since much of the crisis derives from problems in the U.S. economy, which in turn generate increased demand for Mexican migrant labor and a publicly acknowledged danger of a world financial panic, post-1977 events in Mexico are related to the international scene. The continuation and intensification of the rank-and-file labor insurgency, the emergence of unification tendencies among antistate mass movements and political parties, and the government's desperate attempts to cope with them are analyzed from the 1978 CT national assembly to the 1981–1982 stepped-up repression of strikes, election of a new president, expropriation of private Mexican banks, and the deepening of the worst recession in over forty years.

277

The Role of the Military, Church, and Mass Media

Extensive institutionalized repression has resulted in the buildup of a complex power bloc of repressive forces, including a 135,000-member military, the police, various intelligence-gathering agencies linked to different branches of the government, paramilitary units, goon squads, and more. These forces are neither coordinated nor necessarily unified. The military retains a significant degree of autonomy, and represents a political force to be reckoned with. The nation is divided into thirty-five *zonas militares,* which receive their orders from the minister of defense, generally a military man. No state governor can give orders to the *jefe* of a military zone, who has significant autonomous power in matters of "social unrest." With a few exceptions, the head of the PRI has always been selected from the army officer corps, and in the 1950s and 1960s almost 20 percent of the presidents' cabinets consisted of military personnel. Since the 1970s it has become common for generals to run for elective office, particularly at the gubernatorial and congressional levels. In 1980–1981, talk of a military candidate for president was accepted as legitimate by the PRI and state officialdom. When asked by journalists how he defined "national security," Minister of Defense General Félix Galván López answered "social, economic, and political equilibrium"[1]—thereby confirming the military's central role in Mexican politics.

Those who believe otherwise point to the allegedly "low" military budget in comparison with that of other Latin American countries. This is misleading for a number of reasons. First, some specialized units (such as the division of rural defense, comprised mainly of unpaid peasants) are not budgeted. Second, the military received pay raises in the 1970s, an improved pension program, access to many important government jobs, and control over the customs posts along the U.S. border. Third and finally, in 1981, despite reductions in most of the federal budget, the defense budget was doubled. Yet official ideology holds that the days of army rule expired with Porfirio Díaz. Obviously, however, a lot depends on which *class* of civilians rules. The Mexican military is the armed fist of the bourgeoisie and acts accordingly. It is not surprising, therefore, that—despite the proletarian composition of its general ranks and the presence within it of most of the ideological and class forces of society as a whole—the military routinely carries out its class duty when breaking strikes or killing peasants.

A grim reminder of the military's armed strength to intervene directly in Mexican politics occurs each Independence Day, when there passes down the capital's Paseo de la Reforma a military parade featuring Mexican-produced rockets, rocket launchers, tanks, and low-flying jet fighters (to which were added in 1982 the nation's first supersonic jet fighters, seven F-5Es purchased from the United States). Besides the burgeoning home defense industry, the international weapons market (mainly the United States, France, Belgium, and Israel) arms the military to the teeth. Since 1946 U.S. military and police aid to Mexico has totaled about $100 million. A military university inaugurated in the 1970s maintains an exchange program with such U.S. military schools as West Point, and more than 1,000 army officers have been trained in the United States and Panama. Some of these officers constitute part of the elite counterinsurgency "White Brigade" (the 9th Army Brigade, based in Mexico City's Military Camp No. 1), which has been accused by human rights organizations of torture and other crimes. In addition, the United States began selling nuclear-reactor systems to Mexico after the so-called accident at Three Mile Island (when creation of new domestic nuclear-energy plants ground to a halt). Although it advocates a nuclear-free zone for all Latin America, uranium-rich Mexico has ample potential to become a nuclear power. In the late 1970s it took bids from five countries for the construction of twenty nuclear reactors whose final sale price was estimated at more than $65 billion. Although two nuclear plants were built on Indian lands in Veracruz state, further nuclear-energy projects were momentarily shelved in 1982 after Indians successfully resisted construction of a plant in Michoacán and the foreign debt almost bankrupted the state.

A force for repression far more subtle than the military—and one that appeals strongly to women—is the Roman Catholic Church. Some 90 percent of Mexico is nominally Catholic. The Church hierarchy supports the present system—from a nineteenth-century liberal's point of view, Church-state relations are obscenely harmonious. Cardinal Corripio Ahumada blesses Church-state relations as "beyond reproach,"[2] and the state welcomes papal visits with great fanfare. Minor tensions remain, as when the Church criticizes free school textbooks or is ambivalent about the state's birth-control program. On the other hand, private Catholic education flourishes, the Church and the state have mounted an enormous campaign to defend motherhood and the "virtues" of family life, and the Church backs the state's rejection of leftist proposals for the legalization of abortion.

Many Catholic conservatives would like the state to put an end to its demagogic revolutionary rhetoric, but their main quarrel is less with the "constitutionalist" clergy that accepts state posturing than with those "revolutionary" clerics who advocate and practice the theology of liberation. Illustrative of the liberation position is the following proclamation issued by the Church-affiliated Secretariado Social Mexicano:

> In our country there occur regular killings of peasants, Indians, and workers who claim their rights; but, above all, there abound slow deaths from malnutrition and lack of employment; total inequality of opportunity generates widespread inequality and oppression. This situation of misery, a collective and structural fact, is an injustice which cries out to the heavens, conspires against peace, and constitutes an institutionalized violence in violation of fundamental human rights.[3]

And Tehuántepec Bishop Arturo Lona Reyes stated in April 1981 that "violence becomes legitimate defense" in the face of antipeasant repression and widespread hunger. According to Lona Reyes, "both the government and the Church are carrying people to a new revolution."[4] A growing number of socially committed priests and nuns work alongside progressive organizations of workers, peasants, slum dwellers, and students to provide assistance to the deprived and to organize politically for radical social change. Some clergy of other faiths have also become political activists.

It is said that the Catholic Church hierarchy, while now constitutionally outlawed from involving itself in the nation's political life the way it did in the nineteenth century, nonetheless asserts its influence through the conservative political parties PAN and PDM, as well as the PRI itself. While by no means as overtly influential in state affairs as it once was, the Church still represents a powerful social force in contemporary Mexico.

Even more awesome in influencing public opinion are the mass communications media. Technically Mexico has a "free press," but the media have always been tied to wealthy and conservative financial groups. The state reserves licensing and related prerogatives, giving it the potential of interference. The Echeverría administration, for instance, dissolved the staff of the nation's most prestigious daily newspaper, *Excélsior*, in order to bring it under the control of the government. Many of the former staff members founded alternative papers or magazines, including the left-liberal daily *Uno Más Uno*.

All printed communications media, including book publishing firms, are subject to the whims of the state monopoly on paper supplies, Productora e Importadora de Papel, S.A. (PIPSA). In 1981, for instance, the leftist publishing house Nueva Imagen had to halve its publication programs because PIPSA withheld paper and the government impounded imported paper at the port of

Veracruz. In early 1982 PIPSA increased paper prices 80 percent, further undermining the viability of the opposition press; then, on "Freedom of the Press Day," President López Portillo threatened the leftist press in general and the weekly magazine and publishing house *Proceso* in particular by announcing, "We're not going to pay people to slap us around." Since the government subsidizes almost all the Mexican media, people assumed that *Proceso's* outspoken critiques of state policies had gone beyond the limits of self-censorship that journalists routinely practice. But the magazine did not tone down its criticisms and was still publishing as this book went to press. Later in 1982, after López Portillo left office, the Senate shelved a bill that would have imposed strict censorship on news outlets and silenced all nonofficial reports on governmental activities. On the other hand, the new administration proposed additions to the criminal code that would penalize the press for the crimes of "moral damage" and "disloyalty."

As only 2 percent of Mexico's population reads books, and lesser numbers consult the leftist press, the main media of communication have become television and, to a lesser degree, radio. In 1945, CBS and NBC integrated their radio interests into Radio Programas de México, and now focus on television programming and technology sales. The state runs an occasional radio station, mainly with cultural programs—such as Radio Educación, founded in the 1970s—but in general radio is controlled by the capitalists, who spread a highly commercial and conservative message. As for television, from its inception in 1955 it has been a quasi-monopoly in the hands of private capital. The state's Channel 11 (founded in 1958) has always been economically strapped; its Channel 13 provides only limited additional competition to the nation's sixty-seven commercial television stations. Even though the state has the right to 12.5 percent of these stations' programming time, it uses only a small part of it. Besides owning controlling interests in various publishing houses and in the new Rufino Tamayo Museum of International Art, Monterrey's ALFA group dominates the strongest of the nation's three television networks—Televisa. In 1982 the state cracked down on independent programming on Channel 13 and extended to Televisa financial support in obtaining control over a satellite the government had recently purchased from the United States. Televisa had already saturated the Mexican public with U.S. programs (in Spanish translation).

In any case, foreign and domestic private interests call the tune in the mass media. Madison Avenue advertising firms do a booming business for monopoly capital through the media. Whether through radio, television, records, tapes, books, tabloids, magazines, or *fotonovelas*, Mexicans for the most part are a captive audience for the message of capitalism and anticommunism. It is in this inhospitable atmosphere that progressive political parties and forces have to try to communicate their alternatives for the nation's future.

Migration and Chicanos: U.S. Capital's Attempt at Recovery

While drawing considerable propaganda advantage from the issue of the abusive treatment received by some 2 million "undocumented" Mexican workers who migrate to the United States every year (most stay less than three months), the Mexican government rarely lifts a finger to defend them.[5]* This is no accident, since it knows that more than sixty years after the end of the Mexican Revolution it has not been able to resolve the problems at home that obligate Mexicans to seek their survival abroad. From the government's viewpoint, it is better that the adventuresome, courageous, and economically desperate leave the country to seek their subsistence than that they stay in Mexico to undertake the fight for lands, jobs, and higher wages—in sum, a more dignified life. Untold hundreds die every year in the migratory passage (at least 400 in 1979, according to representatives of both nations' border consulates),[6] but the continuing economic crisis in both countries is adding to the flow of Mexican labor northward.

The main cause may be found in U.S. capital's increasing use of such labor in its attempt at restructuring the economy in order to recover from its crisis in accumulation. As *Business Week* (June 23, 1980) reports, "The U.S. will need immigrants to buttress the labor supply if the economy is to grow." According to the U.S. Census Bureau, declining numbers of young workers will be entering the labor force over the next fifteen years—some 7 million fewer in 1996 than in 1981. As the *Wall Street Journal* (June 18, 1976) observed, "Legal or not, the present wave of Western Hemisphere immigrants is already enriching and contributing to North American society . . . illegals may well be providing the margin of survival for entire sectors of the economy."

---

*The terms "undocumented" and "illegal alien" are put in quotation marks to highlight their obviously racist connotation. Needless to say, those workers without proper immigration papers stopped the most freqently by authorities tend to be nonwhite; and, as we shall see, even U.S. *citizens* of Latin American descent are harassed during periodic roundups conducted against "illegals."

About half the Mexican migrants to the United States go into agriculture. Of the other half, most are now employed in the services sector, while a rapidly growing portion are entering either industry proper or its subcontracted workshops, whether in garments, automotive parts, or electronics. This is because corporations are attempting to improve profitability by increased mechanization, cost-cutting layoffs, and recourse to more easily disciplined and low-wage immigrant workers in the course of rotating the work force. The technological revolution of computers, telecommunications, and robotics has already begun to reduce the need for mainline U.S. factory workers and increase that for immigrants, who now are finding employment in modernized production systems. Two hundred so-called undocumented, unskilled workers run the machinery for Electrosound Company in Los Angeles, which produces 25 percent of the phonograph records U.S. consumers enjoy in their homes; and twenty-five Mexican immigrants at Tigart Industries in Alahambra, Los Angeles, operate its newly introduced sophisticated machinery. The aim, in Manuel Castells' words, is to activate a "twenty-first-century technology with a nineteenth-century proletariat."[7] Although high-tech industries have more than doubled the number of their employees in the past decade, this has not been the sector creating the most new jobs. That sector has been services, particularly the restaurant, health, sanitation, retail trade, and personal services, most of which depend heavily on immigrant labor.

Capital's demand for cheap, easily exploitable labor underlies not only its increased resort to immigrant workers but also the phenomenon of "runaway shops." In both instances, U.S. capital maintains the legal fiction of the U.S.-Mexican border—long since erased in its "silent integration" of the two economies—because the border serves to justify its deportation of "unwanted illegals" (e.g., those who attempt to unionize), that is, to discipline Mexican immigrant labor, while also serving as a barrier to U.S. and Mexican workers' integrating their common struggle against capital. It also assures that the Mexican working class, through its export of human capital, subsidizes the U.S. economy. U.S. capitalists do not have to bear the costs of educating and nurturing the temporary migrants (nor in most instances do Mexican capitalists). The migrant is encouraged to come alone and to remit, by U.S. standards, small amounts home for the subsistence of his or her family. The "cost" to the U.S. economy is minimal. A 1979 Department of Labor study found that over 75 percent of undocumented workers paid social security and income taxes, while only 0.5 percent received welfare benefits and only 1 percent used food stamps.

Moreover, 60 percent of their wages was spent in the United States. Only 10 percent joined unions, further saving on costs for U.S. capitalists. This puts into another light U.S. claims that Mexican migration is a cost to the U.S. economy and a benefit to Mexico (on the grounds that Mexico is exporting "its" unemployment problem, a problem in fact aggravated—as noted earlier—by U.S. capital's presence in Mexico). Finally, the legal fiction of the border reinforces the propaganda of U.S. capitalists and their class-collaborationist partners in the AFL-CIO that the cause of U.S. unemployment rates of 10 percent and more is in main part the immigrants' taking jobs away from "Americans."

In fact, few Mexican migrants displace U.S. workers because they respond to a labor market with rules that are unacceptable to U.S. citizens. When a U.S. employer hires an illegal immigrant, he or she wants not just any worker but one who is in the highly vulnerable and exploitable condition specific to that subclass known as the undocumented.[8] According to the U.S. Labor Department, in the eight Southwest and Midwest labor market areas that experienced the greatest increase in Mexican illegal immigrant workers from 1968 to 1977, the unemployment rate was *lower* than the national average. Nor is it true that certain jobs are inherently bad or low-wage, while others are good or high-wage—the good jobs became that way because of labor's organizing and fighting to improve them.

While most of the discussion of Mexican immigrants focuses on the unskilled, a small but significant number of the migrants are trained professionals (an estimated 20,000 in 1981). The drain of income and skills caused by this out-migration contributes to Mexico's failure to develop more prosperously. Mexico suffers extreme shortages in all areas of skilled labor, from engineers to skilled workers. Further, the composite educational level of all Mexicans migrating to the United States is above the Mexican national average (third grade)—an often overlooked but not insignificant part of the "brain drain." Moreover, most have been employed prior to their migration. And as more women enter the labor force, only to be laid off after a few years, they too have begun to migrate northward, leading to a recent drop in the proportion of males (90 percent) comprising the migratory flow.

These, then, are some of the structural forces behind President Ronald Reagan's mid-1981 proposal to authorize the legal admission of Mexican workers with "guest-worker" cards. Ever since the 1964 termination of the *bracero* program, U.S. agribusiness and other sectors dependent on immigrant labor have sought to overcome labor and liberal opposition and pass an immigration bill that would create a guest-worker program. In 1982 they almost succeeded. A bill drafted by Senator Alan Simpson (R-Wyoming) and Congressman Romano Mazzoli (D-Kentucky) easily passed the Senate and almost reached a floor vote in the House. Cloaked as a defense of U.S. borders against unwanted immigrants, it combined expansion of legal admission for Mexican and other immigrant workers with such attacks on civil liberties as the exclusion from entrance of those who "are, or have been, anarchists, communists . . . or would engage in subversive activities." The racist and jingoistic attitude underlying the legislation was illustrated by Simpson's introduction: "If language and cultural separatism rise above a certain level, the unity and political stability of the nation will—in time—be seriously eroded . . . a common language and a core public culture of certain shared values, beliefs, and customs make us distinctly 'Americans.'" Senator S. I. Hayakawa (R-California) added a "Sense of the Congress" clause to the bill making English "the official language of the United States." This was intended to undercut various bilingual programs—including voters' ballots—required in many states.

Simpson-Mazzoli, like most other immigration bills aimed at assuring a cheap and regulated flow of migratory labor, threatened all U.S. workers by requiring an identification system for getting a job. It directed the president "to develop and implement a new, secure system to verify work eligibility within three years. Such a system would not be available for any other law enforcement purpose and, if it were to involve the use of a card, such card would not be required for any purpose except verification of work eligibility." Civil liberties advocates pointed out that this system could channel into government computers information on all workers. A provision for token sanctions against employers hiring illegal aliens intimidated all Latin Americans or their descendants legally in the country and was strongly opposed by their organizations. Herman Baca of the Committee for Chicano Rights said that such legislation would "only lead to an increase in violence and to the creation of an apartheid-type system for Chicanos."[9] Existing employer sanctions have rarely been enforced, and when they were it was to show a "good face" to organized labor (for example, the early 1982 arrests of Los Angeles homeowners implicated in the holding of Mexican and Indonesian slaves). Sanctions offer employers a pretext for committing unfair labor practices, such as refusing to hire a nonwhite or arbitrarily firing a union organizer. They can also be used as an excuse for lower wages, on the ground that an employer's costs have risen because of the time spent checking documents. Under the pressure for screening new employees, labor unions might have to police members instead of expanding membership.

Consistent with the immigration proposals of Presidents Carter and Reagan, Simpson-Mazzoli included an amnesty for those alien workers who could show five or more years continuous residency. Few Mexican migrant workers would qualify, since they rarely stay continuously for more than a few months. Amnesty is a process by which criminals or political prisoners are pardoned by the state; it is inapplicable to workers—since when under capitalism is it a crime to sell one's labor power cheaply to an employer? Human beings can do illegal things but can a human being *be* illegal?

Bills like Simpson-Mazzoli, together with the stepped-up pace of illegal entry by political refugees from the Caribbean and Central America, created the conditions for an unprecedented crackdown on aliens in the 1980s. Indeed, in 1981 the Reagan administration proposed legislation to give the president "broad new emergency powers to deal with a mass migration of illegal aliens," including the authority to seal any harbor, port, airport, or road to prevent unwanted aliens from getting into the country; to restrict travel by U.S. citizens both domestically and to any country named in an emergency declaration; to put apprehended aliens into detention camps from which they could be released only at the discretion of the attorney general, who also could transfer them from one facility to another at will; and to exempt the government from virtually all environmental laws in setting up detention camps. The Simpson-Mazzoli bill required an increased budget for the U.S. Border Patrol, the country's only national police force; Reagan had already increased the patrol's budget and for fiscal 1982 requested $35 million for the development of permanent detention centers. If the detention areas holding Haitian political refugees in Florida in 1981 were any indication, such centers would amount to concentration camps.

The main target of these draconian proposals is the Spanish-speaking community, whose largest component—nearly 20 million—is Mexican or Chicano; the intended effect is to deflect attention from the economic crisis and divide the multinational U.S. working class by scapegoating Mexicans. Ex-CIA director William Colby stated in 1978 that Mexican immigration would represent in future years a greater threat to the United States than would the Soviet Union. Under President Jimmy Carter, the Border Patrol started to receive training in counterinsurgency techniques, and work was begun on construction of a "tortilla curtain" of spiked steel-wire fencing many feet high along the U.S.-Mexican border. President Carter's secretary of labor, Ray Marshall, proposed closing the border on the "liberal" premise that to avoid the exploitation of undocumented workers their entry must be prevented or they must be deported. Conservative U.S. politicians like Senator Simpson have claimed that Mexican immigration threatens U.S. territorial and cultural integration with "Quebec-ization." This anti-Mexican hysteria serves to prepare public opinion for new legislation like the Simpson-Mazzoli bill and to rationalize past and future repression of political organizing among the Spanish-speaking, who may now number more than the black population. The 1980 census tabulated 6.4 percent Spanish-speaking and 11.7 percent black, with the former growing four times faster than the latter during the previous decade—but the Spanish-speaking were undercounted. Many Latin American workers legally in the country were fearful of divulging any information for fear of harassment or illegal deportation, and the Catholic Church's Ad Hoc Committee for Hispanic Affairs chose not to cooperate with the U.S. Census Bureau in taking the census on the grounds that the confidentiality of the information could not be guaranteed. Concern about racism and whether one can "prove" one's "legal" status keeps many Latinos "invisible."

Thus, what happens to Mexican immigrants is directly related to the struggle of Chicanos and other Latinos to improve their situation. While petty bourgeois and some better-paid Chicano proletarians no longer have as much in common with the migrants as they once did, they nonetheless are subject to stop-and-search raids by agents of the Immigration and Naturalization Service (INS) at their work places, in their cars, on buses, or on city sidewalks. Between the two poles "Chicano" and "Mexican migrant," there is a continuum built of kinship ties, relative length of immigrant residency in the Chicano community, similarities of work and life situations, and so forth. While in early 1982 Mexican Ambassador to the United States Hugo B. Margáin, a supporter of a guest-worker program who has close ties to the reactionary Monterrey Group, publicly ridiculed Chicanos as "not Mexicans,"[10] the fact is that Chicanos are aware and proud of their Mexican roots and have long been in the forefront of the defense of the human rights of Mexican immigrants. Where divisions most strongly occur is along *class* lines—for example, some petty-bourgeois bureaucrats or certain employers or labor foremen versus Mexican *and* Chicano workers.

So with the rise of a new militancy among citizens of Mexican descent in the 1960s and afterward (the so-called Chicano movement), greater efforts were made to separate and divide them from other oppressed minorities—including immigrant workers. But these efforts did not always succeed. Younger militants defined themselves as Chicanos, launched a Chicano political party and caucuses in the established parties, founded a youth militia ("Brown Berets"), advocated the rights of Chicana women, and undertook a consciousness-raising campaign to locate their roots in "la raza," or the race of Mexicans who have resisted subjugation since early times. But "la raza" also refers to the human race struggling to be free,[11] and expressions of solidarity became common between this movement's farm workers, welfare mothers, Vietnam war veterans, and youth in the United States, and rebellious peasants, slum dwellers, workers, and students in Mexico. Consequently, the Chicano movement was savagely repressed. Nonviolent mass demonstrations were broken up by gunfire, resulting in the killing and wounding of scores, especially in Los Angeles and Denver. At least one confessed police agent confirmed plots to assassinate Cesar Chavez, leader of the United Farm Workers of America (UFWA). FBI agents and police *provocateurs* streamed into the ranks of UFWA and most other progressive movements. The grand-jury system was used to incarcerate or harass many leaders and activists of all U.S. progressive movements, including that of Chicanos, some of whom were accused of having links with so-called terrorists struggling for Puerto Rican independence. With the advent of the Carter-Reagan social-welfare cutbacks, however, the Chicano movement momentarily lost momentum.[12] Meanwhile, many of the symbols of the new militancy were picked up by corporate advertisers, repackaged, and sold to the Hispanic public as part of the general effort to defuse radical movements and return to the "silent fifties" in a saccharine haze of nostalgia (even the first commercial Chicano movie, *Zoot Suit,* a 1981 musical depicting the anti-Mexican riots of 1943 led by U.S. sailors given furloughs by their racist officers, contributed to this nostalgia). But the "Vietnam syndrome" would not fade away, and in the new wave of protest marches against the draft and U.S. intervention in El Salvador the most notable development was the emergence of Latinos as leaders and large numbers of Chicano participants who had radicalized in their churches, schools, or *barrios.*

It is not surprising, therefore, that U.S. policy on policing immigrants is an open expression of racism and class oppression. According to unpublished census data submitted by INS to the U.S. Select Commission on Immigration some 95 percent of those detained, arrested, and deported by the Border Patrol is of Mexican origin even though the Mexican component of the undocumented population is by 1980 figures only 45 percent. As Attorney Peter Schey of the National Center for Immigrants' Rights has confirmed, almost all those deported are psychologically or physically forced to sign "voluntary" departure forms—and 35 percent of the deportees are not even legally deportable in the first place! The potential deportee is given only three hours to react to the "proceedings," as INS routinely circumvents laws protecting even minimal rights granted U.S. residents.[13] In daily practice that is how Latin American neighborhoods, housing significant numbers of recent immigrants, are terrorized. The practice of "voluntary" deportation is used to crush labor-organizing activities and to discipline labor. Factory roundups, sudden deportations of workers fighting for enforcement of Occupational Safety and Health Administration (OSHA) safety standards or better wages, and the replacement of deported workers with other new arrivals weaken labor's hand. According to Attorney Schey, if even 10 percent of those threatened with deportation were to refuse to sign voluntary departure forms, the resultant bottleneck in processing detainees would slow down the pace of factory roundups and seriously reduce capital's advantages from such practices.

Paramilitary units of the Ku Klux Klan periodically roam the border, and the INS (or in the Latin American vocabulary, *la migra*) in early 1981 and again in 1982 stepped up the pace of factory roundups of alleged illegals for deportation. In a landmark decision in January 1982, U.S. District Judge Prentice H. Marshall of Chicago ruled that the INS can no longer surround or enter factories and residences and harass, detain, or forcibly interrogate all persons of "Hispanic appearance" in the area. But this finding was ignored in May 1982 when INS's "Operation Jobs" arrested 5,635 workers at their workplaces, 87 percent of whom were Mexican, on the pretext that illegals were taking jobs from Americans. Yet of the few who applied for their jobs, most were rejected, and within days most of the detained were released and back at work. Joaquin Avila, president of the prestigious Mexican American Legal Defense and Educational Fund (MALDEF, the Chicano equivalent of the NAACP), told the press, "We're appalled at the raids. This will seriously affect the rights of Hispanics when they seek employment." By September 1982, deportations of Mexicans were numbering about 1,000 a day and generating tensions in Chicano neighborhoods, whose older residents were comparing the deportation drive to 1954's "Operation Wetback." This historical comparison is significant, for then as now, mass deportations accompanied mass importations of Mexican workers—and capital cannot prosper without both.[14]

Besides fortifying the legal fiction of the border, the immigration policies of both Carter and Reagan were directed at nipping in the bud growing organizing activity among the undocumented workers themselves. Starting in 1974, in such urban areas as Los Angeles-San Diego and such rural ones as Maricopa County, Arizona, undocumented workers formed unions or participated in strikes in such companies as the following: Farah clothing (El Paso, Texas); Cyclone Automotive Products (Los Angeles, UAW Local 645); Reflectolite Products, Inc. (Los Angeles, International Brotherhood of General Workers); Nissin, Electrosound, Kraco, and Tigart Industries (Los Angeles, United Electrical Radio and Machine Workers of America—UE); and National Steel and Shipbuilding Company (San Diego). Unions of carpenters, upholsterers, furniture workers, shoemakers, metalworkers, and restaurant employees also engaged in brisk organizing among Mexicans. About a third of the Teamsters' Los Angeles membership is said to be undocumented Mexicans. Faced with declining memberships, the garment workers' ILGWU, the UAW, the International Longshoremen's and Warehousemen's Union, the United Steelworkers of America, the International Association of Machinists, and the Retail Clerks International Union in greater Los Angeles have increased organizing the undocumented. Also, undocumented farmworkers in Oregon, Ohio, New Jersey, Florida, Texas, Arizona, and other states have mounted significant organizing drives.[15]

Cesar Chavez's UFWA has a membership of 30,000, down from a peak of 50,000, and faces a resurgent movement to destroy it launched by large-scale growers and the Reagan administration. UFWA and most of U.S. organized labor could benefit from the energy emerging among the so-called undocumented workers. It would not be the first time—UFWA itself received most of its early impetus and membership from the undocumented and the 1905–1921 period of U.S. labor history witnessed a radicalization and organization of European immigrants that built many of today's established unions (e.g., ILGWU). That earlier period also produced a capitalist-sponsored hysteria against foreigners, culminating in the "Palmer Raids" (named after Attorney General A. Mitchell Palmer), which violently deported thousands of aliens and communists. The 1921–1924 immigration restrictions were similarly, though not exclusively, related to a new militancy and organization among previously unorganized "tractable" workers. It was then that U.S. employers began preferring Mexican immigrants, since importing and deporting them involved a shorter distance and lower costs.[16]

In response to the Reagan immigration proposals, many organizations of immigrant workers decided to unite into the National Coordinating Council of Mexican Workers in the United States. A strong force behind this move was the independent International Coordinating Committee (ICC), which claims a membership of 25,000 unionized undocumented workers. In 1980, ICC convened in Mexico City the First International Conference for the Full Rights of Undocumented Workers, which passed a Bill of Rights for the Undocumented Worker, endorsed by Mexico's Labor Congress (CT). CT has created a protection agency and a "resistance fund" for the undocumented. Important elements in both CT and AFL-CIO subsequently began to explore with ICC the possible formation of a common strategy that would turn back capital's attacks on the undocumented. (In early 1982, ICC's main affiliates—the International Brotherhood of General Workers, the Arizona Farm Workers Union, the Texas Farm Workers Union, and the Florida Farm Workers Union—merged into a single organization called the American Federation of Workers, AFW.) CT, AFL-CIO, and AFW attempts at forming a common strategy to defend the rights of the least organized are in the interest of all labor, provided that the AFW independents do not give in to the miserable tradition of sweetheart contracts and corrupt and violent trade-union bossism (*charrismo*) that have so often blemished organized labor's history.

Similar moves toward unity were evidenced at a three-day regional meeting convened by labor and religious groups in Los Angeles in the fall of 1981, which brought together delegates from more than 500 trade union, church, academic, political, and community organizations to deal with "economic dislocation" (runaway shops, layoffs, etc.). Mexico's telephone workers' and electrical workers' unions (both in CT) sent delegates, as did the Solidev electronic workers' union from Tijuana; in the late 1970s, it had organized an independent union among women workers and won a contract with Solitron Devices Corp., the first such victory by independents, among non-U.S. workers all over the world to overcome superexploitation by giant U.S. firms exporting abroad labor-intensive parts of the production process. And in early 1982 Los Angeles was the scene of the largest demonstration concerning migration issues ever held. It brought together representatives of the organizations that had attended the 1981 economic-dislocation conference and thousands of Mexican and Chicano residents to protest renewed factory roundups and deportations. The immediate spark igniting the demonstration was the U.S. government's decision to begin deportation proceedings against an estimated 100,000 Mexicans who held temporary visas (known as "Silva letters") that allowed them to remain pending regularization of their status.[17] Some 20,000 U.S.-born (and therefore U.S.-citizen) children of Silva-letter parents were suddenly threatened with immediate deportation—clearly an illegal act. The parents' refusal to report to the INS and the unified response of Chicano organizations, together with international support expressed from Mexico, suggested a new level of militancy emerging among workers of both countries.

A New Level of Labor Militancy

CT's support for Mexican workers in the United States was not fortuitous. It represented one of various attempts at bringing Mexico's new labor militancy under some kind of control. Traditionally, migrant workers had returned to Mexico with a greater awareness of the forces affecting their lives, and although some had become hopelessly materialistic and selfish others had assumed a more active role in local, regional, or even national struggles to change the conditions that forced them to migrate in the first place. Such was the case, for example, with Ramón Danzós Palomino, who returned from the United States to lead an independent peasant movement in the 1960s and soon rose to a top leadership position in the Mexican Communist Party (PCM). A key tactic of the ICC group of unionized undocumented workers from the outset has been to organize migrants inside Mexico *before* their departure. Consequently, the 1973–1977 phase of labor insurgency in Mexico, which already had taken the first steps toward emphasizing national solidarity among all workers and oppressed groups, entered a second phase in 1978–1982 that built up this solidarity and then sought to extend it internationally. In this and other regards, CT leaders marshaled a major effort to outflank rank-and-file militants by adopting their rhetoric and claiming to share their main goals.

Thus, for example, in 1978 CTM convoked a national assembly of CT (the first since the Labor Congress's creation twelve years earlier) that promptly endorsed some of the DT *electricistas'* demands, including nationalization of key TNCs, banks, insurance companies, and other financial institutions; a forty-hour work week; nationalization of food, textile, and construction enterprises; and defense of the rights of the undocumented—all steps rhetorically backed by the PRI. Although rank-and-file democrats saw this new tack of CT as a case of "waving the red flag to fight the red flag," the DT wing of the new labor militancy welcomed it, since it actively participated in the assembly and to this day retains CT affiliation. CT's attempts at accommodation with labor militants partially succeeded at first, since the savage acts of repression of 1976–1977 and the state's imposition of *topes* (wage ceilings) had caused all of labor to focus the fight on defending economic rights. In contrast with the preceding period, growing numbers of strikes now came from within the ranks of CT and CTM. The new labor insurgency continued to gain recruits, but the *charros,* old and new, used the economists protests to reassert influence over DT. For one thing, they were able to win certain concessions from capital or the state, which undercut DT's strength. On the other hand, a second rank of democratizers, who had held back in the earlier period, came to the fore in many CT unions. As a result, starting in 1978 thousands more workers gained experience in mounting pickets, disputing issues in strike committees, and organizing against capital and class-collaborationist union elements.

By 1980, people were fed up with the *topes,* and a fresh wave of strikes swept through various sectors of the economy, including automotive, rubber, mining, steel, metallurgy, electric, textiles, food, plastics, the telephone and postal services, airlines, buses, and so forth. Doctors, nurses, students, teachers, and even baseball players went out on strike. There were 130 strikes and 4,000 "labor conflicts"—and the pace continued through 1981 and 1982. Once again troops were used to break the more militant of these strikes, such as that at a DINA-Renault auto plant. The state also strengthened antistrike legislation. For example, Article 923 of the 1980 Federal Labor Law permits the president of the Conciliation and Arbitration Board, itself an administrative unit of the Ministry of Labor, to deny registration to a labor union and to deny the existence of a strike (all unions and the members of their executive committees have to register with the government). A special law prohibits a single national university union of professors, students, and workers advocated by the university union, SUNTU (where the PCM is strongest, though challenged by a "left opposition"). Recently approved legislation severely restricts worker rights and academic freedom in the university, and many sectors of the labor force have been submitted to Chapter B of Article 123 of the Constitution, which outlaws strikes by state employees. (Chapter A includes a clause prohibiting strikes among "special workers" whose labor may be deemed to have special social value—e.g., baseball players.) A *requisa* law, Mexico's equivalent of the U.S. Taft-Hartley Act, allows the state to take over strike-plagued industries considered vital to the national interest. This law was used against the

Coordinadora Democrática Nacional de Telefonistas seeking to represent more than 10,000 (mostly woman) telephone company workers (in addition, 500 militants were fired and automation was introduced). In the state of Nuevo León, seat of the Monterrey Group, any strike is automatically declared by the state government "an act of treason."

In spite of such obstacles, striking workers persisted in their struggle until the state relaxed the *topes* or granted them wage hikes—the first major breakthrough being achieved by 3,200 workers at General Motors who sustained a 106-day strike in 1980 that drew the support of many other unions. By early 1981, for the first time in many years, workers gained wage hikes that approximated the official 30 percent annual rate of inflation. Nevertheless, the purchasing power of the 5 million Mexicans earning the minimum wage had dropped 25 percent in 1980, and any partial recovery was soon wiped out by the 1982 peso devaluations and massive layoffs.

Mexico's annual May Day demonstration is usually a staid affair, full of pomp and circumstance, but by 1981 this was no longer the case. CT rejected the requests of SUNTU and the leftist coalition, Authentic Work Front (FAT), to march with its delegation past President López Portillo's reviewing stand. Many of those who did shouted anti-*charro* and anti-imperialist slogans. Meanwhile, some 10,000 SUNTU and FAT militants held a separate demonstration, and an estimated 300,000 workers showed up for still another demonstration called by the independents' UOI. In other words, the new labor militancy did not simply collapse under the double blows of repression and cooptation.

Strikes involving transport, automotive, oil, steel, electric, textile, food-processing, agricultural, and many other workers swept the nation in 1981 and 1982. Labor militants began once again to combine the earlier political and economic aspects of their demands, seeking not only jobs and decent wages but also the replacement of *charro* leaders. Less naive than in 1976, they directed fewer appeals to *señor presidente:* many had become not only anti-*charro* but also antistate (bus drivers in Mexico City struck *against* CTM). Some set about keeping their own "democratic" leaders in line, suspecting that the state had infiltrated their movement in order to sell it out— a case in point being the 1981 strike by some 10,000 Volkswagen workers in Puebla whose main aim was to replace the Ortega Arenas "independent" leadership with genuine independents. They claimed that UOI leader Juan Ortega Arenas, a lawyer, was in cahoots with the government, which sought to use his "Marxist" leadership of the independents to outflank the rest of the new labor insurgency; once they got rid of his appointees, they returned to work. There soon followed a nationwide movement to purge followers of Arenas from UOI sparked by workers from Volkswagen and the aviation and rubber industries. Meanwhile, the state broke its contract with Metropolitan University employees, whose independent union SITUAM lost the strike but won university-wide elections a year later. Similar crackdowns on the most leftist and militant university unions in other states were escalated—yet the new militancy persisted.

One of the most significant aspects of the strikes in this period was the growing emphasis on solidarity with other strikers. This was exemplified by the teachers' movement, which began in 1980 with a series of state-level strikes by schoolteachers demanding wage hikes and the democratization of their union locals and soon became national in scope. The teachers' main demands were honest elections of the leadership of their union (membership over half a million) and an end to the repression of their and other popular movements. In two states, Chiapas and Oaxaca, democratically elected union representatives were briefly allowed to assume leadership, but by early 1982 at least four of the teachers' leaders had been assassinated, others had "disappeared," and scores more had been arrested. Various national marches on Mexico City numbered well over 100,000 people and included peasant and worker delegations with whom the teachers formed solidarity alliances. The insistence that their battle against *charrismo* be linked to the rank-and-file worker-peasant movement against the same evil exemplifies how people from the intermediate classes who are being driven economically toward proletarian living conditions can become an explosive force in Mexico's future—especially when the fight begins as one against their *own* oppression.[18]

Inspired in part by the militant example of the teachers, many segments of the peasant and labor rank-and-file movement have established committees of solidarity in various centers of labor agitation. As part of this trend, some have emphasized rehiring those workers laid off for political reasons or as part of the government's austerity program. In addition, growing numbers of the democratic labor movement have showed up for demonstrations called by the National Front Against Repression (FNCR) and the National Defense Committee for Political Prisoners, Persecuted, Disappeared, and Exiled, leftist-dominated coalitions that champion their cause (and its victims). As the labor insurgency continues, so too does the pace of state repression—whether rural or urban. In July 1981, for instance, thirty imprisoned members of the independent peasant organization CNPA went on a hunger strike to demand punishment for the "intellectual authors" of 100 peasant assassinations and 12 disappeared comrades, plus satisfaction of 315 registered land claims—*all* during the previous twelve months. A Veracruz peasant meeting in solidarity with the hunger strikers was violently attacked, leaving 11 more dead. The hunger strike ended with a presidential agreement to meet some of the demands.

The growing seriousness, complexity, and interweaving of issues in the new labor insurgency became especially clear with the over-lapping of interests—including ethnic ones—involved in two major actions of 1980–1981 relating to oil and nuclear energy. In January 1981, some 10,000 peasants (mostly Indians) blockaded roads to the Cactus petrochemical plant, which supplies about two-thirds of the natural gas used inside Mexico, and the Cactus and Reforma oilfields in the southeastern state of Chiapas. Troops arrived, the blockade was lifted, and the state agreed to negotiate peasant claims of damage to crops and livestock caused by pollution from the plant.

Similarly, in the winter of 1980–1981, Purepecha Indian peas-ants (particularly women) of the Santa Fé community along the shores of Michoacán's tourist haven Lake Pátzcuaro (famous for its butterfly fishing nets) resisted the state's efforts to build an experi-mental nuclear energy center on their land. Purepecha women made contact with U.S. Indians more familiar with the devastation caused by uranium tailings and the nuclear industry's assault on their land and lives; they learned that the U.S. nuclear industry was holding back on further construction at home, preferring to "transfer" the risk to Indian lands in Mexico, Canada, and other countries. They were then able to persuade the men that the new job opportunities would lead only to sickness and death for their people, while the traditional fishing industry might well be de-stroyed. They were less successful in convincing the otherwise pro-gressive nuclear workers' union—SUTIN—which perceived the issue as one of jobs for its members and part of Mexico's "anti-imperialist" *(sic)* effort to achieve energy "independence." But they did win the support of the local tourist magnates, whose own vested self-interest was clearly not nuclear. Eventually, they united all the Indian communities along Lake Pátzcuaro's shores and forced the government to declare publicly that no nuclear center would ever be built in the state of Michoacán.

This incident shows another aspect of the peasant struggle—the growing awareness among educated Mexican Indians and peasant women of their common plight with Indians and oppressed peo-ples elsewhere. Eight hundred Indian delegates from as far north as Alaska and as far south as Patagonia attended the Second Meeting of Independent Indian Organizations of Mexico, Central America, and the Caribbean, held in Michoacán in March 1981. There was the usual language problem, overcome by the use of Spanish, plus photographs, slides, paintings, and a strong spirit of communality and sharing. The main organizing themes of the workshops were class analysis, international proletarian struggle, genocide, and the importance of recognizing a common Indian heritage. Among the anti-imperialist resolutions passed were ones of solidarity with the people of El Salvador and a ringing denunciation of the U.S.-based Summer Linguistics Institute, accused of having links to the CIA and of destroying indigenous cultures through its programs of "sterilization of women" and "Bible translation."[19] Such growing Indian militancy has evoked ferocious state repression, which in turn has only served to spread class and race consciousness among the Indian population. In 1981, the 6-million-strong Supreme Council of Indian Peoples (founded in 1979) successfully led a popular campaign that frustrated the state's traditional practice of imposing pro-government candidates in elections for the official National Indigenous People's Council, which incorporates eighty-five regional councils and represents 9 million Indians. The Supreme Council's democratic slate of candidates triumphed in all but a few areas.

Both the Indians' Supreme Council and the peasants' CNPA condemned the 1980 Law of Agrarian Development (LDA) and Mexican Alimentation System (SAM) that presumably would make the country self-sufficient in food production by 1982, calling them "bureaucratic and authoritarian control measures over rural producers accelerating the development of *latifundia* under a new legal cover." Financed in part by the World Bank, the new programs channeled tied credits, technical inputs, and commercial, warehousing, and transport facilities to subsistence farmers who were expected to "produce more" and share risks with the state in the development of agro-industries. LDA's Article 32 called for the "voluntary association of *ejidos* or communities with each other, with *colonos*, and with small proprietors—the phrase "small proprietors" is a code word for *neolatifundistas,* private property in the sense of big capital. The small proprietor would provide capital and the means of production, while the *ejidatorio* or smallholder would provide the land and labor. Nothing was said about the rights of the "voluntarily associated" peasants and workers to organize into labor unions in order to confront the bosses, the small proprietors. The new law also permitted the expropriation of "idle" *ejido* or Indian land while allowing "certificates of inviolability" for any "intensively used" cattle land. Combined with the earlier legalization of *ejido* rental, LDA and SAM produced an intensified assault on smallholder and subsistence farming by big capital and the state. The peasants' continued proletarianization was disguised through their association with the state or small proprietors.

Anticipating this, the Agrarian Reform Ministry's Co-op Development director, Marcos Dávila Ledesma, resigned in 1980, claiming that the peasants' basic problem—their lack of equipment and collective organization to market their own products—would only be aggravated. Absence of adequate transport and a peasant-controlled market, Dávila told the press, had led to the transfer of about 500 billion pesos ($22 billion) from 1940 to 1980 to "middlemen" and others who conducted and profited from the marketing of agrarian production. "It's a curious coincidence," he added, "that at the current value of the peso this sum is equivalent to the fixed assets of industry and commerce." But the official peasant organization CNC backed SAM, 60 percent of whose resources went to irrigated districts—the heartland of *neolatifundismo* and agribusiness. CNC understood well that by tying discontented and desperate subsistence producers to the state, SAM would help undermine the independents' CNPA and the Indians' Supreme Council. CNC also claimed much of the credit for the creation of 2,000 clinics serving 10 million rural inhabitants—part of the state's program to stem the decline in the health conditions of the agricultural work force.

By the end of 1982 the Mexican government was claiming that the drive to make the nation once more self-sufficient in food production was a success. But by its own definition of self-sufficiency (as *dietary* self-sufficiency) this was not true. Moreover, according to Banco de México figures, food imports continued apace. For example, while corn imports dropped from 4.2 million tons in 1980 to 2.8 million in 1981, bean imports declined only slightly, soybean imports doubled, and other food imports increased. Imports of basic grains were projected to reach more than 10 million tons a year by 1983.

As impressive as was the rise in unifying independent peasant and Indian organizing activity during the post-1978 phase of the new labor insurgency was the linking of rural struggles to those of the urban poor, who also moved to unify on the national level. In 1979, the National Network of Popular Colonies brought together fourteen organizations of slum dwellers, including Mexico City's Union of Popular Colonies, Monterrey's Land and Liberty Popular Front (50 neighborhoods), Durango's Popular Front (20 communities), and the Popular Defense Committee of Chihuahua

(300,000 slum dwellers, whose leader was assassinated in 1981). These slum militants began to join forces with DT, independent unionists, the student movement, and the "land for the tiller" peasant movement led by the CNPA. In the northeast the Coalition of Independent Organizations for the Defense of Popular Economy (founded in 1978) incorporated slum dwellers, workers, peasants, students, and housewives. Illustrative of the alliance building was the work of Acapulco's Colonia Anfiteatro, which mobilized tens of thousands of the urban poor to march on the state capital, linking "no eviction" demands against an urban "beautification" scheme sponsored by the tourist industry to a call by students and faculty to "unfreeze" funds at the state university. Despite increased repression, organizers in the proletarian slum areas have stepped up their activities, while in many cities spontaneous marches and street barricades have stopped bus fare increases and won other gains. A noteworthy example is the city's takeover of public transport in the Federal District in the fall of 1981, a long-standing demand of leftist and popular forces. While by no means the only cause, the immediate provocation was an attack on buses in the Netza slum area by thousands of residents who were protesting recent fare increases.

By mid-1981, two national meetings of networks of organizations of the urban poor had been held, resulting in their consolidation into the National Council of Popular Urban Movements (CONAMUP). CONAMUP's principal demand was that every poor family has the right to a piece of land for a dwelling. It denounced the state's urban development plans for their refusal to deal with more than the *colonias proletarias* and their failure to touch the interests of the bourgeoisie; such plans were called "speculative and corporate," directed by private banking and real-estate interests largely responsible for the urban poor's housing problems in the first place. As an alternative to this "privatization of the economy," CONAMUP called for greater state intervention to assist the entire working class. It pledged to continue the struggle of the immiserated to manage their own lives and to build multiclass coalitions to resist state repression and bring about genuine social change.

There still exist formidable obstacles to Mexican labor's winning its basic democratic rights, not the least of which are the deepening economic crisis and the state's increasingly repressive role. Many workers fall easy prey to CTM's enforcement of wage ceilings, calls for reduced work weeks (the norm is forty-eight hours), and approval of temporary plant shutdowns or automation as "lesser evils" to more mass layoffs. CTM has also imitated the AFL-CIO's policy of "givebacks" to help resolve the economic crisis. In June

1982, for instance, CTM asked workers to donate 1 percent of their salaries to the government, and even the communist-dominated Unified Socialist Party of Mexico (PSUM) agreed that workers should donate some of their wages to "the national cause." In the fall of 1982, Ford, GM, and other big companies closed down their production plants for limited periods—with CTM approval.

Illustrative of the state's stepped-up repressive role are the strikes at the Pascual Soft Drinks plant in Mexico City and the ACERMEX steel complex in 1982. On May 31, a company goon squad attacked the Pascual strikers, killing two workers and wounding fifteen others; the following day the *granaderos* and city police forcibly ejected the workers from the plant. CTM agreed to support the workers only if they disassociated themselves from the legal advisors of the left-wing PMT. Once they agreed, CTM got the company to grant them their economic demands—but then the company declared bankruptcy and dismissed all 2,046 of its employees. CTM defended the company, while the employees demanded the rehiring of all workers and state expropriation of the firm. Similarly, 1,300 workers led by anti-*charro* elements at ACER-MEX, a steel company owned by the ALFA fraction of the Monterrey Group since 1980, had their 157-day strike broken on June 17, 1982, by an alliance of the state labor conciliation boards, the *charros*, the *granaderos* and the police, and the ALFA group. Some 350 workers were fired, and then ALFA sold ACERMEX to the Hermes group, which was led in part by the PRI's Federal District mayor Carlos Hank González. During the ACERMEX struggle, which had really begun five years earlier, hundreds of leaders were dismissed, arrested, or kidnapped; two were assassinated.

But Mexico's *charros* are running scared. With the ground shaking beneath them, they do not take kindly to cartoons like the one showing one worker asking another, "Trade-union democracy? Where?"—to which the other, clad in prisoner's garb, replies, "Well, in Mexico, in Poland. . . ." And so, in late March 1982, CTM was forced by private employers' resistance to state-decreed wage increments and pressure from rank-and-file workers to threaten a general strike. CTM boss Velázquez publicly pleaded with private enterprise to come to its senses, asking it "not to play with fire." As quoted in the daily *Uno Más Uno* of March 25, 1982, Velázquez lay bare the true character and class-collaborationist role of CTM: "If we change tactics or abandon the workers to their luck, employers won't have time to realize what will happen: imagine a mob let loose on the streets, out of control."

A notable feature of the new labor militancy has been its popular, rather than political party, base. The various left-wing parties have sought to expand and organize the worker and peasant movements, but their role has been minor. Despite a fairly general receptivity to socialist programs, there is a widespread resistance to political parties or groups. Mexico's masses have taken the first steps toward organization on their own. Even those workers within the reformist DT tendency have responded more from felt needs than to democratic leadership initiatives.

Within the independent wing of the movement there has emerged a small but important group that seeks to coordinate strike actions and all those militants who take as their point of departure that there must be class independence from both the state and the *charros, caciques,* and self-proclaimed individual leaders. In 1982, the Coordinadora Sindical Nacional (COSINA) was founded, with the aim of coordinating the defense of democratic demands made by rank-and-file labor militants and of seeking to unify the various social movements and labor strikes. Thirty labor unions, twenty rank-and-file "currents," and a wide range of popular democratic organizations attended the founding congress. Among the popular organizations were the antirepression FNCR, the peasants' CNPA, the urban poor's CONAMUP, and the schoolteachers' CNTE (National Network of Education Workers). The executive committee included worker representatives from the telephone, subway, university, steel, textile, nuclear, and bottling unions. Four central demands were approved: an end to the austerity program, the unlimited right to strike, union democracy, and an end to all repression.

Political Parties and Elections

From the outset, the new labor insurgency confronted state power. This tended to propel it toward a natural alliance with leftist political parties, prohibited by the political reform from participating in the mass organizations. For the Left to achieve any meaningful political power it had to relate to the unions, for only in mass organizations could a political base be established. The Left in fact attempted to do this but confronted two additional obstacles: an anticommunist hysteria sponsored by the *charros,* and a feisty antiparty, independent mood among rank-and-file union militants. With the state attempting to prevent democratic union tendencies from getting out of hand and the Left seeking to advance them, the nation's political struggle came to gravitate around the labor movement, urban and rural. The effects and directions of labor's struggle became disputed within state circles, within each class, within each political party, and ultimately between parts of the state and key fractions of each major social class (including the bourgeoisie).

The PRI soon began speaking of the political reform program's going too far. At the end of 1978, PRI president Carlos Sansores Pérez stated: "Our people are not sufficiently prepared for democracy."[20] The Left, of course, views the reforms as not having gone far enough. Without establishing a stronger base among the masses, the Left is vulnerable to a new wave of repression, which might eliminate the limited space opened to it by the reforms. This is a fundamental cause of most of the Left's continuing its activities in Congress, on public television, and in the press. Yet the first Chamber of Deputies session with participation by leftist political parties passed amendments to the Federal Labor Law further restricting workers' rights while allowing the Left's legislative proposals to die in committee or voting them down on the floor (not one executive proposal was rejected by the Chamber).

Nonetheless, much of the Left views the political-reform program as one to be preserved and expanded in the fight against fascistic elements that have become more organized and active during the post-1968 intensification of the class war. Though unwinnable, national elections provide space for the Left to air its views. This space is a limited bourgeois-democratic concession managed by the state; in practice it is more bourgeois than democratic since individual and collective rights continue to be violated at the levels of freedom of expression, association, juridical protection, and the rights to unionize and strike. By shifting so much energy into electoral and propaganda battles, the Left runs the risk of becoming cut off from the struggles of workers and peasants at their workplaces at a historic moment when these fights have taken on central importance. Indeed, one of the aims of the state's political-reform program is precisely that.

There are a number of political parties in Mexico's Left, but two stand out: the Mexican Communist Party (PCM) and the Mexican Workers Party (PMT), symbols of the "old left" and the "new left" respectively. In the 1979 congressional elections, the PCM became the nation's third largest electoral force, garnering 5.4 percent of the vote. Struggling to shed its image of being against "God, Home, and Country," the PCM has admitted priests into its ranks, publicized the family life of Communists, and condemned the Soviet intervention in Afghanistan. It denies that it is Eurocommunist, but its 1981 convention replaced the goal of "dictatorship of the proletariat" with "workers' democratic power" and rebaptized its Marxist-Leninist ideology as "scientific socialism." It even began admitting Trotskyists into its ranks, causing old Stalinists to roll their eyes. Though its flag is still the hammer and sickle, it has shaved its Lenin beard and covered its oriental eyes with the dark glasses of the Latin American intellectual; its strength lies in the universities and among publicists, scholars, and youth. Its weakness is lack of a base in the trade unions, and its strategy is to bore from within the government-controlled unions rather than to woo the workers toward new organizations. Its all-consuming mission is to unify the many leftist and progressive parties and movements into a single cohesive political force.

It took a big step in this direction in late 1981 when, together with the much larger PMT, it announced the founding of PSUM, which merged the two largest leftist parties with three smaller pro-communist formations, the Mexican People's Party (PPM), the Revolutionary Socialist Party (PSR), and the Socialist Movement for Action and Unity (MAUS). Thus, Latin America's oldest Communist Party dissolved itself. The new unity on the Left lasted less than two months, during which time many Mexicans rallied to the opportunity for unifying popular movements that the PSUM's creation seem to augur. But the PMT's top leadership soon broke with PSUM, leaving the PMT weakened and the PSUM largely in the hands of the old PCM. Later, a small Left-reformist group called the Movement of Popular Action (MAP, founded in 1981) dissolved itself to join the PSUM, whose 1982 presidential candidate was the former PCM secretary-general, Arnaldo Martínez Verdugo. MAP brought into the PSUM Left-nationalist intellectuals and democratic trade unionists like those among the electrical and nuclear workers; two MAP founders, the prominent political scientist Arnaldo Córdova and economist Rolando Cordera, now represent PSUM in Congress.

The PMT, a loose organization of populist-oriented Marxist-Leninists, claims to have put down roots among workers, peasants, unemployed, and students, with municipal committees and base groups in a dozen states. Organized in the wake of the student insurgency of 1968, it avoids mention of a revolutionary transition to socialism and instead calls for enforcing the 1917 Constitution, which has plenty of potentially socialist clauses. Since all Mexicans are taught to revere the Constitution, a progressive blueprint for its time betrayed by every government since 1940, the PMT gains a sympathetic ear. Instead of a Lenin beard it wears a Mexican mustache, and rather than singing the rousing strains of the "Internationale," which frightens Mexicans, it tries to march them to the bouncing bars of "La Cucaracha," the light sinister music that once led Villa's ragtag armies to their heroic victories. On its flag, the

PMT has replaced hammer and sickle with monkey wrench and machete (one reason it left the PSUM was the new group's retaining the old PCM symbol). The PMT has frequently sneered at electioneering, but in the 1979 congressional elections its well-known leader, civil engineer Heberto Castillo, had himself photographed pulling the lever for the Communist Party. Like the PCM, the PMT thinks a violent revolution from below the only way out but postpones it to a remote future. But unlike the PCM it shows the weaknesses of a populist party: up-today-and-down-tomorrow activists, lack of inner discipline, and a vague ideology. It has lost some key regional cadre to the PSUM but remains a vital force whose leader is widely respected in the general populace. It sought but did not obtain registration for the 1982 elections, which it therefore boycotted.

On the other hand, the state allowed four smaller leftist parties to register and run presidential candidates in 1982: the Trotskyists' Revolutionary Workers Party (PRT); the Popular Socialist Party (PPS); the Socialist Workers Party (PST); and the Social Democratic Party (PSD). A section of the Fourth International run by European intellectuals like economist Ernest Mandel, the PRT rests on a column of students and teachers who advocate a worker-peasant alliance to bring down the regime in the style of proletarian Petrograd and the Ukrainian Soviet. For the 1982 elections it launched a presidential candidate on a "Left unity" platform that attracted a handful of smaller leftist groups—Rosario Ibarra de la Piedra, the mother of one of Mexico's "disappeared ones," who had gained great respect for appearing at every demonstration for popular causes in spite of repeated death threats against herself and her family (one of whom was driven to suicide in 1981). Influential in linking up proletarian and peasant women's struggles with those of feminist activists, Rosario Ibarra is the unofficial leader of the anti-repression front FNCR; throughout the land she is referred to affectionately as "*la señora.*"

Since its founding in the 1940s by dissident intellectuals from the official party and labor leaders like the late Vicente Lombardo Toledano, the PPS has experienced many splits and gained a reputation for being a PRI front within the Marxist-Leninist Left. Like the PST, it views the PRI as an independent political formation with a national revolutionary tradition grown cold. The PPS and PST argue that the task of the Left is to revive that tradition by building a fire under the ruling party. Founded by disciples of ex-president Luis Echeverría, the PST seeks ties with the Socialist International of Willy Brandt and similar Western social democrats, but the International prefers working with real power—the

PRI, one of its affiliates, though not an official member. Also court-ing the International is the PSD, founded in early 1981 by PRI dissidents, state technocrats, and small and medium-scale busi-nesspeople disenchanted with the PRI's ability to deliver the goods.

Until the elections of 1979 and 1982, Mexicans rarely had any chance to vote for Left-opposition candidates and so grew accus-tomed to casting "protest votes" for the candidates of the always present conservative PAN, the nation's second largest electoral force with 13 percent of the votes cast in the 1979 congressional elections. Founded in 1939 by Catholic conservatives to fight the populist reforms of Cárdenas, PAN for years filled its coffers with donations from capitalists favoring laissez-faire economics. Never getting very far as the party of the urban entrepreneurs and great landowners, it began developing in the 1960s a more populist poli-tics attacking corruption in government. Today PAN draws little support from the directors of the most powerful industrial-financial groups, who have accepted Keynesian thinking and pre-fer to work with the ruling PRI-government or to penetrate its ranks (they recognize that the chances of dislodging the PRI through elections are nil). So now PAN draws its electoral strength from the intermediate classes in the big cities and provincial towns; it also whips up support among religious-oriented peasants and a few workers with its new populist rhetoric. In the 1970s a new neopopulist party, the Mexican Democratic Party (PDM), was founded to serve part of PAN's old constituency: the conservative Catholics frightened by the anticlerical tradition of Mexican *políticos*. The ultra-rightist Sinarquistas affiliate with the PDM.[21]

Both the Left and the Right repeatedly object to Mexico's by now traditional electoral fraud. In 1981, after much violence, the PCM-COCEI coalition in Oaxaca succeeded in having a rerun of munici-pal elections in Juchitán—and won. But this was viewed by most Mexicans as an exception to the rule that when defeated, the PRI wins by official count. In late 1981 and early 1982, a number of city halls were occupied by irate citizens protesting electoral fraud and corruption. The states of México, Coahuila, Oaxaca, and Yucatán were particularly affected by such occupations, many of which were sparked by PAN militants who claimed they had won earlier elections.

Thus, in both the political and economic arenas Mexico's populace was far more agitated than usual in the months preceding a presidential election that normally elicits little public interest be-yond the question of who the PRI's candidate will be. No one bothers to wonder who the potential nominees might be or which way the three sectors of the PRI might swing in their use of intraparty power, since the arena in which the candidate is selected is not the three sectors but the inner circles of the state bureaucracy and the bourgeoisie. Needless to say, the PRI candidate automatically wins the election, since the PRI controls the vote-counting procedure. Indeed, in 1976 not one opposition party bothered to run a presidential candidate, although communist Valentín Campa, former rail strike leader of 1958, mounted an extra-official campaign that reportedly drew over a million "annulled" [invalid] votes. It was initially believed that the 1982 elections might reverse this trend, since a number of opposition parties had decided to test the waters of the political-reform program by fielding candidates, but few of those that sought registration as legal parties were approved by the PRI-dominated electoral commission.

The PRI announced its candidate almost a year in advance of the 1982 elections, by far and away the earliest announcement of the official party's presidential choice in history. This in itself suggested the depths of the political and economic crisis shaking Mexico. The *destapado* (from cock-fight jargon, referring to the unhitching of the band on the cock's feet as he enters the fray), Miguel de la Madrid Hurtado, was, like López Portillo, not a veteran of PRI internal politics. Author of López Portillo's Global Development Plan, he was a product of the private sector, a Harvard-educated technocrat who soon gathered around him a pre-inauguration "kitchen cabinet" of twenty-four fellow technocrats, sixteen of whom had done their postgraduate studies abroad. Only four politicians were included in this closed group. The selection of de la Madrid represented a blow to the state and PRI bureaucracies, whose ability to control the private sector was thereby called into question. Almost immediately Minister of Labor and PRI president Javier García Paniagua, a reformer, resigned—an indication that a vocal figure for revitalizing the PRI was unwilling to back the party's own presidential candidate.

Using state funds, the PRI proceeded to spend a fortune on its U.S.-style campaign, particularly through the purchase of television time (and votes). Given the skyrocketing foreign debt, this use of national revenues was viewed by most Mexicans as a disgraceful waste. De la Madrid campaigned on a platform of "moral rebirth" of the nation, echoing the anticorruption theme of his predecessor, whose administration turned out to be the most venal since Alémán's; as an indication of his own honesty, de la Madrid acknowledged that Mexico did indeed have a number of "disappeared" citizens. Apparently unpersuaded, more than half the nation's potential voters did not vote for him on election day (July

4), and over a million votes were annulled. The state's count showed the PRI with 74 percent, PAN 14 percent, the PSUM 5 percent, and other opposition parties the remainder. (The largest leftist party, the PMT, boycotted the election.) Since a PRI vote is virtually obligatory on the part of the swollen state bureaucracy and the 70 percent or so of the urban and rural work force it controls, these official results surprised no one—indeed, the next day's headlines did not bother to announce the winner. They focused on the turnout, proclaiming "Apathy Defeated!" Opposition poll watchers came up with a different tabulation, however. Based on reports from every state, they found that PAN got 20 to 30 percent of the vote, PSUM 10 to 15 percent, PRT 4 to 8 percent, and PRI only 40 to 50 percent.

Thus, state propaganda to the contrary, voter apathy and anti-PRI sentiment remained a problem that was only partially alleviated by the previous six years of political reform. The opposition's 100 seats in Congress were divided up after the elections as follows: PAN, 50; PSUM 17; PDM, 12; PST, 11; and PPS, 10. Many protested that they were short-changed, especially the PRT, which received no congressional seats even though its presidential candidate—"*la señora*"—drew far more votes (even by official count) than anyone had expected. She was denied a seat in the newly elected Congress on the absurd grounds that PRT did not garner enough congressional votes in the election to merit a representative. Most Mexicans felt the government was denying her a seat because it did not want national television carrying her electrifying speeches. With the fading of the electoral hoopla and of the international wire services' habitual humming of the electorate's endorsement of Mexico's "stable guided democracy," the state now got back to the more serious business of coping with rising popular discontent and its own insolvency.

Revolution and World Financial Panic Postponed: Expropriating the Banks

In his final state-of-the-nation address, on September 1, 1982, President López Portillo, a verbose, philosophical, and somewhat visionary man, spent several hours listing the accomplishments of his administration. High GNP growth rates, $27 billion invested in the petroleum industry, a recent reduction in food imports, more jobs created than ever before—the list seemed dreamlike. To stay awake, members of Congress periodically clapped their hands. After three hours of this annual ritual, television and radio listeners began turning off their sets.

They made a serious mistake, for the president went on to address the big questions, those on everyone's mind: Where did all the oil revenues go? Why were the state and even some private Mexican capitalists facing insolvency? What was happening to the peso? What would be done with the estimated $12 billion in foreign currency recently frozen in Mexican bank accounts (so-called Mexdollars)? How would Mexico ever pay either the interest or the principal on its foreign debt—the highest in the world? In view of the economy's petrolization, dollarization, and relative decapitalization, and the body politic's shakiness, how could social upheaval be avoided, or at least postponed? Finally, who would foot the bill—and accept the blame—for the country's economic doldrums: top state bureaucrats or private bankers and industrialists, all of whom had grown fat off oil revenues during the boom years?

López Portillo answered most of these questions in the final part of his address. He placed much of the blame for the economic crisis squarely on the shoulders of the great powers, whose high interest rates and unfair treatment of the less industrialized countries had contributed to the rapid rise in their foreign debt. The rest he blamed on Mexico's private bankers, who, he said, had looted the nation far more than had any colonialist power. Those watching the television screen could see the faces of the leaders of CCE and ABM fall. The president accused the bankers of sacking the country of $50 billion and stashing it in U.S. banks and real estate. Then, his voice quivering and his eyes filling with tears, he woke up every member of Congress with the announcement that he was expropriating the nation's private banks, with compensation for their owners. In one memorable moment, expected by no one, the state had saved itself and much of Mexican private capital by scapegoating the bankers and scooping up bank deposits, the banks' investments in over one hundred industries, and outstanding bank debts (estimated at $6 billion). After a moment of shocked silence, all but the CCE and ABM representatives stood up and applauded.

López Portillo's bank decree was a desperate attempt to patch up the state's economic hemorrhage, steal the thunder of the Left, divert the new labor insurgency, and reassert state autonomy. More thoroughgoing Cárdenas-style reforms, whether in the areas of oil, technology, or heavy industry, or against the TNCs altogether, would have forced Mexico into an anti-imperialist posture in practice as well as rhetoric—and where would that have left

Mexico's ruling class, without imperialism's support? That is why López Portillo moved against unproductive capital—the private banks—and not against imperialism or industry. The move itself was political, giving the state more "nationalist" breathing room with which to manipulate the class struggle. Even its economic motives met the approval of imperialism, which feared a Mexican default on the foreign debt (representing 10 percent of the combined debt of the less industrialized countries and Eastern Europe) that might ignite a chain reaction of defaults among the less industrialized nations and a world financial panic. About two-thirds of the total Third World debt was owed to private banks, and 22 percent of that amount was on the books of just nine U.S. firms (far in excess of the banks' total equity capital). Mexico's debt represented 17.1 percent of U.S. bank loans to Third World countries and the Eastern bloc. The three largest U.S. banks—Citibank, Chase Manhattan, and Bank of America—reportedly had an estimated 40 percent of their capital tied up in Mexico. Their executives hailed López Portillo's decree, saying it was needed to save the private banks from insolvency. Nevertheless, there remained the nagging fear that if Mexico moved "further to the Left," or if Brazil and Argentina followed "the Mexican way," an international financial collapse might indeed occur.

In spite of frequent differences of opinion and emphasis, the Mexican state maintains a harmonious relationship with imperialism, which only aggravates its crisis. Why? Because the state, like foreign capital, has to struggle to show *its* national legitimacy, to prove to a skeptical public its Mexican and independent character rather than its IMF-dictated and dependent character. This is one more reason that the Mexican government emphasizes its independent foreign policy—whether in its claim to 200 miles of offshore fishing rights (a bone in the throat of U.S. tuna fishermen), its hypocritical advocacy of the human rights of Mexican migrant workers, or its critiques of U.S. intervention in Central America.

The newly expanded alliance between the state and ABM was by no means broken by López Portillo's action, but it was refashioned. A respected advocate of state-directed economic reform was appointed to head the expanded national bank, but almost all executive and managerial appointments to the bank and its related institutions came from the private sector or its allies in the state bureaucracy—the very people who had fashioned López Portillo's alliance for production and Mexico's economic crisis in the first place. Even the bankers, although they feigned crocodile tears, accepted the expropriation after the nation's leading justices publicly endorsed the president's action. The new state bank head announced that shares in the banks and its nonfinancial holdings would be sold to the public—a sign that the ex-owners could yet recoup their losses. (Nonetheless, to test their strength, some prominent CCE members talked of an employers' lockout to protest the government's insensitivity to the rights of private property, and threatened a court suit; neither was forthcoming.) The expropriation brought into state hands half of Mexico's bank assets; the state already had the other half and, as we noted earlier, had set them to working for private monopoly capital. Since no new value is produced by banks, which carry out a service function in the economy, how could López Portillo's bold action portend any real economic change in Mexico's future?

In his address, López Portillo had assured organized labor that its Workers' Bank would be unaffected by the decree. Moreover, he announced that the 200,000 or so bank employees who for years had sought the right to unionize would now have a union. The Left called this "preventive unionization." The new bank union was placed under Chapter B of Article 123 of the Constitution, thereby depriving bank employees of the right to strike, and CTM started moving its *charros* into the union's leadership.

On September 3, nearly a million people overflowed Mexico City's Zócalo square to back the president at a state-sponsored rally. The PRI whipped up a euphoria of nationalism, comparing López Portillo's action to Cárdenas' 1938 oil nationalization and to the "moment of glory" of Zapata and Villa. The comparison was spurious: there was no mass movement involved in the bank takeover, even though the Left and the new labor militancy had long advocated such a step—in fact, a few hours after the official rally some 100,000 rain-drenched militants from independent labor and left-wing organizations flowed into the Zócalo to express their critical support of the bank expropriation.

While the state had clearly bought precious time politically by expropriating the banks and fanning the flames of nationalism, thereby postponing antistate activity, a number of questions remained unresolved. There was no move to raise wages or put a million laid-off workers back to work: the key themes were sacrifice and defense of "the nation's honor." And while the president blamed the bankers and announced easier, lower interest credit lines for small and medium-size businesses, what of the *políticos* who had pocketed much of the oil revenue? The private banks possessed information on this question. Had the state occupied them in part in order to avoid a scandal of bureaucratic robbery? The leftist weekly *Proceso* once more rose above normal standards of self-censorship and published articles, with photographs, about multimillion-dollar homes acquired or being built by Federal District boss Carlos Hank González and police chief General Arturo Durazo Moreno, as well as by López Portillo himself.

All of Mexico's opposition parties, except for PAN and PDM, critically supported the takeover of the banks. Among much of Left, including MAP, PPS, PST, and many Communists in PSUM (minus national labor figure Valentín Campa, however), a view emerged that the entire "political class" is not subservient to the bourgeoisie and imperialism, and that at least some of the techno-bureaucracy is an "intermediate class" (sometimes called a "governing class") that can be pushed to the left by popular mobilization. These elements, particularly MAP, advocated a form of nationalism that might fuel, and benefit from, the recent splits within the PRI and the techno-bureaucracy. Meanwhile, the popular fight for basic economic and political rights from below continued—led by the growing networks of independent workers, peasants, and slum dwellers. Responding to a generalized demand for more unity and to a specific call by independent-left groups (mainly labor's COSINA and the monthly magazine *Punto Crítico*), all the left-wing parties and popular mass organizations (PMT, PSUM, PRT, PST, CNPA, CONAMUP, etc.) founded in September the National Front for Wage Defense and Against Austerity and Scarcity. Yet in October a parallel organization, called the National Committee of Defense of the Popular Economy, was founded by PSUM, PMT, PSD, and other groups seeking to push the government into expropriating other private firms besides the banks. The PRT and *Punto Crítico* condemned the creation of this organization as "a divisive and reformist maneuver."

In late 1982, three currents of nationalism were fighting to define the future course of Mexico. The first was the demagogic version of the PRI, illustrated by outgoing President López Portillo's earlier alliance for production and incoming President de la Madrid's lifting of price controls, 53 percent devaluation of the peso, and acceptance of the IMF's austerity conditions in exchange for a $3.9 billion IMF credit and a further $5 billion advanced by private foreign creditors. Second was the only partially unified leftist version, including a socialist-oriented minority of the PRI. This current called for more nationalizations, particularly of the foreign-dominated pharmaceutical and food-processing industries—and, in some cases, complete independence of popular mass organizations from the state. Third was the right-wing version offered by the Monterrey Group, ex-bankers, and some other big capitalists, who sought to win over the discontented intermediate classes and claimed that only privatization of the economy could "save the nation." Some of these were presumably behind the rumors of a military coup d'état that prevailed during the final months of López Portillo's *sexenio*. While some Mexicans discounted the rumors as the "normal nonsense that happens every six years," the fact remains that it was not normal but was a recent phenomenon dating from 1976. And it was not nonsense, which helps explain why Defense Minister Galván, who heads the army, went out of his way to deny the rumors.

One thing is certain: the past fifteen years of repression in Mexico that has led to its censure by Amnesty International for failing to resolve the question of 500 disappeared people and countless political assassinations will not abruptly end. Any independent leftist or progressive mass mobilizations, such as those in 1980–1982 among Latin America's largest teachers' union, the peasants' CNPA, or the urban poor's CONAMUP, will be tolerated even less by the government since they will now be portrayed as antipatriotic during these difficult times "for all Mexicans." On the other hand, worsening economic conditions for the majority of Mexicans, many of whom are heading for the United States in quest of short-term work, may swell the number of people engaging in protest activities and polarize the class struggle more intensely—both nationally and internationally. As the crisis in capital accumulation continues, and as monopoly capital tightens its grip over people's lives in both Mexico and the United States, working and progressive people will increasingly have to forge international networks of unity and struggle if a better future is to dawn.

Conclusion

Today the global factory means the fate of a Mexican worker will in
large part also determine what happens to a worker in Detroit.
—Harley Shaiken
New York Times, March 21, 1982

What of Mexico's future prospects for economic development
and political democracy on behalf of the majority of its citizens?
Even in years of high GNP growth, two-thirds of industry operates
at a level below capacity and half the work force cannot find a
regular job. Yet the infrastructural and industrial bases for economic development exist in Mexico at a level beyond those of most
other Latin American countries. Similarly, although most of Mexico is arid or semi-arid land divided by jagged mountains and vol-
canoes, there exist abundant natural resources, including the
human resources of the Mexican people, whose creative energies
and productive capacities, in spite of widespread malnutrition and
disease, should not be underestimated.

Nevertheless, Mexico finds itself in a vicious circle of debt, maldistribution of income, and petrolization and dollarization of the
economy, which serve to maintain capital accumulation on behalf
of a few. The crisis is rooted in the integration of the state with
domestic monopoly capital and transnational corporations, which
has resulted in a subordinated industrialization and relative decapitalization. This in turn has transformed the class structure and
body politic, with peasant and labor protests occurring in the 1970s
and early 1980s largely in those areas most influenced by monopoly
capital and with popular demands for democratization being repressed more—and coopted less—by a technocratic-authoritarian
state whose room for maneuver has been much reduced.

Mexico's experience suggests that the development of productive capacity in Department I (production of the means of production), if it is dependent on the "good will" of the transnational
corporations, will only accelerate the accumulation of capital at the
centers of world capitalism and further tie the subordinate country
to imperialism and its lending institutions. A more appropriate
strategy for Mexico would be to put far more emphasis on developing education—from literacy campaigns to research-and-

313

development institutes—in order to generate the long-term capacity for indigenous technological growth. Moreover, to have any chance to end the vicious circle of uneven development, dependence on foreign capital, and monopolization of wealth by a few, it would have to break through the integrated blocs of power established in the triumvirate of state/private capital/foreign capital, nationalize the commanding heights of the economy, and, through national planning, begin to bring into convergence the nation's own resource uses, community needs, economic demands, and production. It is evident that Mexico's occasional anti-imperialist proclamations will continue to be an exercise in futility unless accompanied by anti-imperialist practice and a class (social) revolution. The neopopulist nationalism of recent bourgeois governments has masked the increased amount of proletarian and peasant labor power that is being provided at a low cost to foreign capital (and its associated partners within the Mexican bourgeoisie and the state bureaucratic sector).

The resulting intensification of class struggle, demands for democratization, and criticisms of economic dependence have provided a new opportunity for forging a socialist, anti-imperialist alternative—the main reason behind the state's frenetic effort to carry through a token political reform to deflect or absorb popular opposition. Many Mexicans have begun to organize themselves on a class or class-fraction basis (the peasants' CNPA, the urban poor's CONAMUP, independent labor's UOI, etc.), as well as to become involved in the first experiments at creating a nationwide defense of these organizations (Committees of Solidarity, COSINA, the National Front for Wage Defense and Against Austerity and Scarcity, etc.). At the same time, moves to unify the Left and to lay out specific programs of democratic and socialist demands have gained momentum.

With the growth of these democratic demands, it is possible that many of the elements informally linked through the diverse repressive apparatuses of the state—including paramilitary and police forces, prison officials (widely accused of torture), some of the military's officer corps, and so forth—will consider uniting with those of the current right-wing offensive led by the Monterrey group's *mano dura* fraction, the *neolatifundistas* least integrated with monopoly capital, the minority upper echelons of the divided intermediate classes, and parts of the Church hierarchy in order to "stabilize" the situation and "restore the fatherland to order and progress." Any strategy for Mexico's democratization, therefore, must carefully plan responses to the combination of military repression and increased foreign economic aid that has always occurred during times of crisis or escalated social mobilization. Dependent bourgeoisies across Latin America have often welcomed a military dictatorship as their last defense against a popular movement. Some Church, military, bourgeois, and intermediate-class elements may uphold the alternative of civilian "constitutional" rule, but the ultimate check on such repression is an increase in the strength of the nascent mass democratic movements.

In the 1970s and early 1980s, workers not only in Mexico but also in the United States engaged in struggle to democratize their unions and resist the work-place speed-ups, declines in real wages, layoffs, and other hardships imposed because of the economic crisis facing capital. Despite much harassment and bureaucratic despotism, rank-and-file candidates for the presidencies of such important unions as the 1.2 million-member United Steelworkers of America and the 170,000-member Oil, Chemical and Atomic Workers' Union came within a hair's breadth of being elected—while in Mexico, as we have seen, the struggle was even more intense. The discontent shaking labor in both countries, together with growing signs of support for undocumented migrant workers appearing among major unions, has caused many capitalists and the governments of both nations to be concerned about what the future may hold. Genuine union democracy and incipient international workers' unity constitute threats that capitalists seek to avoid at all costs.

As our discussion of migration and Mexico's labor insurgency has shown, there are many signs of the incipient internationalization of labor's struggle. Expressions of mutual support for strikers in textiles, electronics, agriculture, and mining have begun to flow back and forth across the border as workers increasingly come to recognize that they have a "common enemy." For example, in 1978–1979 a militant strike at the huge Nacozari copper mine in Sonora (near Cananea) was opposed by CTM. Ex-miners, young miners, and the region's unemployed led the strike movement. They sought, and received, support from the United Mine Workers in the United States. (Nevertheless, their movement was ruthlessly put down by army troops, police, and CTM's armed goons.) The chances for workers' struggles to succeed would improve considerably if, in incremental steps, expressions of solidarity—backed up by concrete support—were to spread through the ranks of Mexican and U.S. workers in mining, agriculture, and the steel, oil, electronics, nuclear, petrochemical, aviation, and automotive industries—to name just a few of the interrelated pivots of today's international economy. Bridging the information gap that keeps

workers uninformed of one another's struggles would be an important first step (and has been a major accomplishment of international conferences like the one on economic dislocation held in Los
Angeles in 1981).

Younger Mexican and U.S. industrial workers have much in
common: whether in Puebla or Pittsburgh, they voice disdain for
intellectuals and self-proclaimed labor leaders, aspire to material
goals, snap their fingers to the same music, and feel an intense class
hatred that seeks an outlet. Some of the young and more highly
skilled Mexican autoworkers have even begun to speak seriously
about internationalizing the class struggle, and the U.S. automobile
industry's decentralization and restructuring has the potential of
revitalizing the class struggle on both sides of the border. Many
U.S. labor leaders now endorse the sentiment expressed by Harley
Shaiken, a labor and technology specialist, as reported in the *New
York Times* of March 21, 1982: "Today the global factory means the
fate of a Mexican worker will in large part also determine what
happens to a worker in Detroit. It's not just a moral concern any
longer. The global factory mandates that unions have closer contact and communications." When Mexican workers win a strike,
achieve more say-so in the production process, or extend their
network of Committees of Solidarity, or when Latin Americans
overthrow dictatorships that outlaw democratic trade unionism,
U.S. runaway plants are dealt a serious blow.

As the example of the development of Mexico's north as a new
low-wage, less unionized pivot for the automobile industry
confirms, industrial workers in both countries have suffered the
effects of runaway plants and capital's increased mobility. The
short-term response of U.S. labor unions has been to try to stop
plant closings through worker "givebacks" (since imitated by Mexico's CT)—but as this fails to solve the problem, workers are beginning to doubt its effectiveness. Other recommended solutions have
been fines for capitalists who close their plants or the sealing of the
U.S.-Mexican border to keep out "scabs" who undermine the effort
to unionize workers in the competitive (nonmonopoly) sectors.
These are equally ineffective since capital-flight restrictions are impossible to enforce given monopoly capital's power relative to that
of the workers and since sealing the border can be accomplished
only through a fascist-like militarization that undermines the interests of all workers.

The analysis presented in this book suggests that industrial workers cannot maintain their previous gains in the class struggle with
the old strategies of confronting monopoly capital in a national
context and paying little attention to the struggles of the

nonunionized. Monopoly capital's increased mobility nationally and internationally has put *all* workers (including farmworkers and slum sweatshop employees) at a distinct disadvantage. Securing economic gains for workers in both the monopoly and competitive sectors of capital, then, has come to depend more than ever before on building an international alliance that seeks to guarantee the interests of all workers against their common enemy: monopoly capital. As we have seen, some of the most dynamic segments of Mexico's recent labor insurgency have been the rural proletariat/peasantry, the urban poor, and the undocumented emigrant workers—whose energies can vitalize other parts of the labor movement (without whose support the older unions might evanesce).

There are many obstacles to constructing such an alliance, including the racist hysteria being orchestrated by reactionary elements in the United States, the class-collaborationist history of the official labor confederations having the most political clout (AFL-CIO and CT), and the antilabor role of the two nations' governments. But as both capital and labor internationalize, sheer necessity is pushing labor to take on the international economy and to adopt, however gradually and unevenly, a strategy of international workers' solidarity and action—an important step toward the eventual establishment of a worker-controlled political and economic system: socialism.

Notes

These notes draw attention to matters of theoretical clarification, points of controversy, and supplementary information, as well as to sources of quotations or particularly useful documentation. Further documentation may be gleaned from the Selected Bibliography. The abbreviations FCE, INAH, SEP, and UNAM respectively stand for: Fondo de Cultura Económica, Instituto Nacional de Antropología e Historia, Secretaría de Educación Pública, and Universidad Nacional Autónoma de México.

Introduction

1. Each part includes, where appropriate, explanations of concepts or terms being introduced; normally, however, definitional and theoretical problems or controversies are dealt with in the notes. (A glossary of frequently used abbreviations and Spanish terms is included at the end of the book.) Concerning the statistics and research offered here, historical and contemporary statistics must be treated with a certain caution. The tables and figures presented cannot pretend to some ideal level of exactitude; there are too many controversies to permit that. They do, however, reflect a consensus among scholars or, in case of doubt, the more modest of the estimates available. The main purpose is to show proportions, not to give exact figures. In the case of the factual record of events, personalities, and the historical course of social change, the situation is similar. Only in cases of new research or of sufficient doubt or controversy are points amplified in the notes. There exists an abundant literature on Mexico (more than that on any other Latin American country), and many examples are included in the Selected Bibliography.

Chapter 1: Conquest and Colonization

1. Karl Marx, *Capital* (New York: International Publishers, 1967), 1:751. Chapters 26 and 31–33 of Part 1 of *Capital* explain the role of "original accumulation" in the birth of the capitalist era. Its role in earlier noncapitalist class systems is explored by Alexander V. Chayanov, "Sobre la teoría de los sistemas económicos no capitalistas," *Cuadernos Políticos* 5 (June–September 1975): 15–31; John Clammer, ed., *The New Economic Anthropology* (London: Macmillan, 1978); Maurice Godelier, *Perspectives in Marxist Anthropology* (New York: Cambridge University Press, 1977); Claude Meillassoux, *Mujeres, graneros y capitales* (Mexico City: Siglo XXI, 1977); and Claudia Von Werlhof, "Frauenarbeit: der

318

Blinde fleck in der Kritik der Politischen Okonomie," *Beiträge zur feministischen Theorie und Praxis* 1 (1978): 18–32.

2. *Cf.* Alex D. Krieger, "Early Man in the New World," in *Prehistoric Man in the New World,* ed. Jesse D. Jennings and Edward Norbeck (Chicago: University of Chicago Press, 1964).

3. *Cf.* Robert S. MacNeish, "The Origins of American Agriculture," *Antiquity* 154 (June 1965); and "The Origins of New World Civilization," *Scientific American* (November 1964); Richard E. Blanton, *Monte Alban: Settlement Patterns at the Ancient Zapotec Capital* (New York: Academic Press, 1978), and, with Steve Kowalewski, Gary Feinman, and Eva Fisch, "Regional Evolution in the Valley of Oaxaca, Mexico," *Journal of Field Archaeology* 6 (1979): 369-90; Friedrich Katz, *The Ancient American Civilizations* (New York: Praeger, 1972), chaps. 3–5; Georges C. Vaillant, *Aztecs of Mexico* (Garden City, N.Y.: Doubleday, 1962), chap. 2; Kent Flannery, *Early Mesoamerica Village* (New York: Academic Press, 1978); and William Sanders and Barbara Price, *Mesoamerica* (New York: Random House, 1968).

4. The Olmecs' society flourished in both the highlands and lowlands of Mexico from about 800 to 400 B.C. Olmec artisans sculpted giant human heads—some weighing up to twenty tons—as well as diverse objects in clay and jade, including the characteristic half-human figures with grinning jaguar teeth and claws. They and their successors used signs and mathematical symbols, suggesting that the writing and calendar developed later by the Maya were already known. Many scholars attribute the first full-fledged appearance of the state in Mexico to the Olmec period.

5. Monte Albán civilization (ca., 250 B.C.-A.D. 900), centered in the Valley of Oaxaca southeast of Mexico City, was characterized by intensive agriculture based on irrigation and terraces, high population density, long-distance trade (in obsidian, for example), and production of both cotton and cochineal (later to become important Mexican exports to Spain and Europe).

6. Gordon Willey, "The Structure of Ancient Maya Society, Evidence from the Southern Lowlands," and Egon Z. Vogt, "Some Implications of Zinancantan Social Structure for the Study of the Ancient Maya," in *Ancient Mesoamerican Selected Readings,* ed. John A. Grahame (Palo Alto: Stanford University Press, 1966).

7. I have discussed the relevant historiographical problems at length in "Prescott and His Sources: A Critical Appraisal," *Hispanic American Historical Review* 48, no. 1 (February 1968): 59–74. Two mythologies have emerged from the filtering of information through European eyes: the Indian as "lazy primitive," and the Indian as "noble savage." The first underlies the image so widespread in U.S. schoolbooks and newspapers: a dozing Mexican, his face hidden by a wide-rimmed sombrero, his body draped in a sarape, his back up against a cactus plant. The second has been revived by the 1960s series of books about a Yaqui wise man named "Don Juan" (Euro-Spanish, not Yaqui, nomenclature) who defines the route to happiness as individual and mysterious rather than social or obvious. This myth of supernatural wisdom—the "noble savage" in modern dress—was made socially acceptable by its drug-related profitability and by institutional forces aimed at deflecting social-protest activities into politically safe channels.

8. A *chinampa* does not float. It consists of a platform layered with mud and aquatic plants built out into a lake or body of fresh water and usually attached to the shore by the roots of an *ahuehuete* tree. Quite productive, allowing up to three harvests a year, the *chinampa* system of production under Nahua Indian direction is still in use and provides an important part of Mexico City's vegetables today.

9. The Aztecs' tributary mode of production included features of the "Asiatic" mode of production, described by Marx as one directed by a centralized state that oversees giant irrigation works, sends the army to quell revolt or conquer new areas, grants land-usufruct rights to villagers, and generally utilizes the economy for the pleasure of the ruler and his lackies rather than for the expansion of economic surplus and the human advancement of peoples. Yet the Aztec system was more dynamic than that of other societies dominated by the Asiatic mode of production and included other forms of production as well, all of which were dominated by the tributary system, without which the Aztecs could not survive. The complexity of the problem is explained in Roger Bartra, *El modo de producción asiático: problemas de la historia de los países coloniales* (Mexico City: Era, 1969); and Alberto J. Pla, *Modo de producción asiático y las formaciones económico-sociales Inca y Azteca* (Mexico City: El Caballito, 1979). A lucid elementary introduction to Marx's thoughts on modes of production is Ross Gandy, *Marx and History: From Primitive Society to the Communist Future* (Austin: University of Texas Press, 1979).

10. Though closely related to the state, the priesthood was independent economically, living off the labor of the populace, tributes, and the required provision of goods for religious festivities and rites. The clergy ran the schools in most *calpulli* and educated the ruling class and much of the bureaucracy. The priesthood sought to bring other religions into its domain, smashing idols or, more commonly, incorporating other deities—much as the Spaniards were to do. See Georges Baudot, *Utopie et histoire au Mexique: Les premiers chroniqueurs de la civilisation mexicaine, 1520–1569* (Toulouse: Ed. Edouard Privat, 1976); and Robert Ricard, *The Spiritual Conquest of Mexico* (Berkeley: University of California Press, 1966).

11. See Pedro Carrasco and Johanna Broda, eds., *Economía política e ideología en el México prehispánico* (Mexico City: Nueva Imagen, 1978); and Pedro Carrasco et. al., *Estratificación social en la Mesoamérica prehispánica* (Mexico City: INAH, 1976).

12. See Hernando Cortés, *Cartas de relación de la conquista de la Nueva España escritas al Emperador Carlos V, y otros documentos relativos a la conquista, años de 1519–1527,* ed. Charles Gibson, Josef Stummvoll, and Frans Unterkircher (Graz, 1960); and Bernal Díaz del Castillo, *Discovery and Conquest of Mexico, 1517–1521* (New York: Farrar, Strauss, and Cudahy, 1956).

13. The *mayeques* were those who did not belong to *calpullis*. While not having to pay tribute, they did have to till the nobility's lands and were transferred to the owners' heirs, thus constituting a hereditary closed group, subject to state laws. They derived from early Aztec times, and their ranks did not increase with later Aztec conquests. The *tlacotin*, or what the Europeans called slaves, had various rights—including the right to take their owners to court for mistreating them. Except in the case of traitors' descendants, one was neither born into slavery nor destined to remain a slave; slaves could own other slaves. Many *tlacotin* were porters for the merchants. Toward the end of the fifteenth century, slave-buying for the purposes of human sacrifice came into prominence, usually in distant regions such as the Yucatán, where the Maya specialized in selling slaves.

14. With the exception of the impressive irrigation works, some notable poetry, and exquisite metal work, especially in gold, the Aztecs did not achieve the scientific and artistic heights of some of Mexico's earlier civilizations. Their public education system, religion, and statecraft, on the other hand, were considerably developed.

15. Henry F. Dobyns, "Estimating Aboriginal American Population," *Current Anthropology,* 7 (1966): 395–449. Statistics fluctuate widely in this difficult area, but experts agree that Tenochtitlán contained about 300,000 people, making it larger than Madrid or Rome.

16. The ripping out of the victims' hearts with an obsidian knife, the ritual meal of parts of the deceased in order to commune with the gods, and other repulsive features of the Aztecs' sacrificial rites have earned them a bad name among Judeo-Christian peoples. But no religion has been immune from the savagery of bloody warfare and human slaughter, always based, as religion is, on the material realities of struggle for power. Many descendants of Mexico's original peoples became appalled at the barbarism of Catholic practices (Crusades, Inquisition, burning of heretics, etc.)—that is, in the peculiar forms in which they suffered them, beginning with the Spanish Conquest. The number of Indians who perished at the hands of the Spaniards far exceeded the number killed in Aztec sacrifices.

17. Many Aztec deities represented the forces of nature, so critical in the agricultural production and trade, which—with the booty of conquest—formed the material basis of Aztec life. In today's Mexico City, at the site of what once was a temple to Coatlicue (earth goddess and mother of the gods), stands the church of the Madonna of Guadalupe, built by the Spaniards (with Indian labor). Every year, Indians from outlying regions flock to this now Catholic temple to pay homage to the (virgin) mother of Jesus Christ—or the ancient mother of the gods. Some Aztec prayers continue to be expressed in Catholic ceremonies for today's Indians.

18. A highly durable and self-reproductive grain that grows in a variety of climates and does not require irrigation, maize was a crucial factor in the transition to sedentary agriculture, village and community development, and class societies. To this day, it accounts for nearly 75 percent of the daily energy intake of most of Mesoamerica's peoples.

19. Cited in Andre Gunder Frank, *Latin America: Underdevelopment or Revolution?* (New York: Monthly Review Press, 1969), pp. 233–34. Indians (and African slaves) were brought *to* the northern silver mines—so the bishop presumably had in mind Indian labor power.

20. Possibly the Indians' only biological revenge was to provide the *conquistadores* with syphilis, which the conquerors returned to Europe where it flourished (although some Latin American nationalists deny this and scholars dispute the question with obscure erudition).

21. Other demographic estimates compound the horror, showing far larger figures for 1520 and subsequent years but a higher rate of population decline among Indians. See Woodrow Borah, *The Aboriginal Population of Central Mexico on the Eve of the Spanish Conquest* (Berkeley: University of California Press, 1963); Dobyns, "Estimating Aboriginal American Population"; and Enrique Florescano, *Estructuras y problemas agrarios de México (1500–1821)* (Mexico City: Sepsetentas, 1971) and idem, *Precios del maíz y crisis agrícolas en México (1708–1810)* (Mexico City: Colegio de México, 1969).

22. Eric R. Wolf, *Sons of the Shaking Earth* (Chicago: University of Chicago Press, 1959), p. 200.

23. J. I. Israel, *Race, Class and Politics in Colonial Mexico* (London: Oxford University Press, 1975), p. 39. Indians sometimes fared better on haciendas, to which some retreated. See François Chevalier, *Land and Society in Colonial Mexico* (Berkeley: University of California Press, 1963), chap. 8.

24. The word *cacique* comes from the Arawak "kassiquan" ("to have or maintain a house"). The Spaniards imported this term from the Caribbean to apply to coopted Indian authorities.

25. On the institutional role and actual practices of the Inquisition, the ecclesiastical tribunals, and state juridical organs, consult Michel Foucault, *Vigilar y castigar*, 4th ed. (Mexico City: Siglo XXI, 1980). Father Zumárraga was the first Inquisitor and aimed his persecutions at both unruly colonists and at Indians

following non-Christian ways or otherwise resisting the clergy's demands, especially in the instances of land-grabbing, tribute-exacting former Indian nobles. Punishment of this latter "sin" was one of the causes of the Mixton Rebellion of 1541.

26. Segundo Montes, *El compadrazgo* (San Salvador: Uca Editores, 1979). For regional case studies confirming continuity of pre-Columbian social practices, consult Ida Altman and James Lockhart, eds., *Provinces of Early Mexico: Varieties of Spanish-American Regional Evolution* (Los Angeles: UCLA Latin American Center Publications, 1976). The Spaniards, for economic and cultural reasons based on their own history (of which the Conquest itself was a supreme manifestation), were sufficiently *macho* not to need these Indian antecedents of *machismo*—which the colonists and clergy transformed and deepened through all their practices of class, race, and sex exploitation. Through subsequent centuries of fighting against class domination and foreign intervention, Mexico's masses came to internalize *part* of *machismo* as a positive virtue of courageous resistance to injustice.

27. To an extent this was true also for Africans who became tied to the slave trade—the slaves' labor, as well as Africa's gold, ivory, and spices, went to the enrichment of European colonists, traders, planters, merchants, manufacturers, bankers, and royal heads of state.

28. Most non-Mexican (and some Mexican) historians ever since have emphasized these "moral" concerns of the Crown and yet dismissed as hopelessly "biased" the research of Bishop Bartolomé de Las Casas, known as the "Protector General of the Indians." See, for example, Lewis Hanke, *The Spanish Struggle for Justice in the Conquest of America* (Boston: Little, Brown and Company, 1965). Las Casas, an angry churchman who sought to protect the human rights of Mexico's original inhabitants at a time when they faced possible extinction from slaughter and disease, interpreted the Conquest as a product of bloody power and pillage in his *Historia de las Indias*, (2 vols. Madrid, 1957) and *Very Short Account of the Destruction of the Indies* (1552). Other priests backed Las Casas to such an extent that a papal bull of Pope Paul III in 1537 declared the Indians "free."

29. On the prevalent forms of labor recruitment in colonial Mexico, consult Charles Gibson, *The Aztecs under Spanish Rule* (Stanford: Stanford University Press, 1964); and Juan A. Villamarin and Judith E. Villamarin, *Indian Labor in Mainland Colonial Spanish America* (Newark: University of Delaware Latin American Studies Program, 1975).

30. Other variations included the persistence of agricultural *repartimiento* in parts of Oaxaca and Guadalajara until the eighteenth century. In most of Oaxaca, on the other hand, Indians retained much of their own land in plots twice the size (per family) of the plots they hold today. In Yucatán, private *encomiendas* were not abolished until 1786, and Indians were also subjected to labor drafts by Crown officials. In New Spain's northeast, a frontier area of mixed agriculture (cattle and food), free labor was supplemented by a system called *congrega*, in which landowners captured nomadic Indians who attacked them and brought them back to work their farms as prisoners of war. In central New Spain, where the majority of the population lived, agrarian estates were almost all worked by free labor.

31. Marx, *Capital*, I:753–54. Thus, even if in a certain sense, as Randall argues, "the acquisition of Mexico was not economically profitable for Spain," it was certainly so for other Europeans. The costs of empire always reduce and increasingly tend to undermine the gains—yet one can only speculate how Spain might have fared *without* Mexican silver. See Laura Randall, *A Comparative History of Latin America, 1500–1914* (Ann Arbor, Mich., 1977), volume on Mexico, p. 113.

32. Adam Smith, *An Inquiry into the Nature and Causes of the Wealth of Nations* (New York: Random House, 1937), pp. 204–7, cited in James D. Cockcroft, Andre Gunder Frank, and Dale L. Johnson, *Dependence and Underdevelopment: Latin America's Political Economy* (New York: Anchor, 1972), p. 21.

33. Cited in John Lynch, *Spain under the Hapsburgs* (London: Oxford Basil Blackwell, 1964), vol. 1, p. 141.

34. Cited in Frank, *Latin America*, pp. 235–36. H. G. Ward (*Mexico in 1827*, 2 vols. [London: Henry Colburn, 1828]), a British diplomat and a contemporary of von Humboldt, described agriculture as based on "circles of consumption" surrounding the mines and cities.

35. Lucas Alamán, *Historia de México desde los primeros movimientos que prepararon su independencia en el año 1808 hasta la época presente* (Mexico City: J. M. Lara, 1849–52), vol. 1, p. 101.

36. José María Quiroz, "Memoria de estatuto. Idea de la riqueza que daba la masa circulante de Nueva España a sus naturales producciones," in *Colección de documentos para la historia del comercio exterior de México* (Mexico City, 1959); Eric Van Young, "Urban Market and Hinterland: Guadalajara and Its Region in the Eighteenth Century," *Hispanic American Historical Review* 59, no. 4 (1979): 593–635; and Ramón María Serrera, *Guadalajara ganadera: Estudio regional novohispano, 1760–1805* (Seville: Esc. de Estudios Hispano-Americanos, 1977).

37. Doris M. Ladd, *The Mexican Nobility at Independence 1780-1826* (Austin: University of Texas Press, 1976), pp. 50–51.

38. Enrique Semo, *Historia mexicana: economía y lucha de clases* (Mexico City: Era, 1978), pp. 83–87, 163–69; Friedrich Katz, "Labor Conditions in XIX Century Mexican Haciendas." *Hispanic American Historical Review*, 54, no. 1 (February 1974): 1–47; and John H. Coatsworth, "Obstacles to Economic Growth in Nineteenth-Century Mexico," *The American Historical Review* 83, no. 1 (February 1978): 87–88.

39. To cite but one example: "They had known grinding poverty under the old regime, and were finding it perpetuated and sometimes increased under the new one; but it seemed less painful now because the Franciscans, after their gentle founder, made of poverty a virtue" (R. C. Padden, *The Hummingbird and the Hawk: Conquest and Sovereignty in the Valley of Mexico, 1503–1541* [Columbus: Ohio State University Press, 1967], p. 241). Description of lower class revolts in the following pages is intended to offset the main literature on colonial Mexico in its overemphasis on Indian, African, and *casta* adaptation to class domination, acculturation, etc.—not because such did not occur, but because in dwelling on these elements the literature underemphasizes or glosses over the basic *class* contradiction (and corresponding repression) engendering such adaptation. Moreover, adaptation was a two-way process, with most colonists and their descendants adopting aspects of Indian culture, such as *huaraches* (sandals), foods like *frijoles* (beans) and maize, technology like the *mano* (pestle) and *metate* (mortar) used to beat maize into dough for tortillas (the national "bread" of Indian and mestizo Mexico), *pulque* (a fermented drink from the century plant, rich in minerals and vitamins B and C), etc. Indeed, *pulque* production and commercialization, even though participated in by Indians, particularly women, developed into a booming business with the bulk of the profits appropriated by the elites or their Indian allies, while for the Indian masses *pulque* served as a reciprocity bond—its consumption to celebrate successful harvests or religious occasions helped them retain a social identity they could respect throughout the colonial period (indeed, until the present). See William B. Taylor, *Drinking, Homicide and Rebellion in Colonial Mexican Villages* (Stanford: Stanford University Press, 1979).

40. James D. Cockcroft, *Intellectual Precursors of the Mexican Revolution, 1900–1913* (Austin: University of Texas Press, 1968; Mexico City: Siglo XXI, 1971), pp. 53, 156.

41. Though differing in emphasis, works on the colonial and postcolonial period document this general picture and provide more examples of revolt besides those highlighted here. On the Great Chichimeca War, see Philip Wayne Powell, *Soldiers, Indians and Silver: The Northward Advance of New Spain, 1550–1600* (Berkeley: University of California Press, 1969); and idem, *Mexico's Miguel Caldera: The Taming of America's First Frontier* (Tucson: University of Arizona Press, 1977). For other Indian revolts, consult María Teresa Huerta and Patricia Palacios, eds., *Rebeliones Indígenas de la época colonial* (Mexico City: SEP/INAH, 1976); and Leticia Reina, *Las rebeliones campesinas en México (1819–1906)* (Mexico City: Siglo XXI, 1980).

42. See Peter Gerhard, "A Black Conquistador in Mexico," *Hispanic American Historical Review* 58, no. 3 (1978): 451–59.

43. Cited in Stanley J. Stein and Barbara H. Stein, *The Colonial Heritage of Latin America* (New York: Oxford University Press, 1970), p. 57.

44. Archivo General de Indias (Seville), section i, Patronato real 224. Later *visitadores* (e.g., Pedro de Quiroga and Juan de Palafox y Mendoza) verified widespread class conflict and hatred "in all classes of society" for Spanish colonialism.

45. For a focus on the class character of these *tumultos*, consult Chester Guthrie, "Riots in Seventeenth-Century Mexico City: A Study in Social History with Special Emphasis on the Lower Classes" (Ph.D. diss., University of California-Berkeley, 1937); and N. J. Stowe, "The Tumulto of 1624: Turmoil at Mexico City" (Ph.D. diss., University of Southern California, 1970).

46. For more on the army, see Christon I. Archer, *The Army in Bourbon Mexico, 1760–1810* (Albuquerque: University of New Mexico Press, 1977).

47. P. J. Bakewell, *Silver Mining and Society in Colonial Mexico: Zacatecas, 1546–1700* (Cambridge: Cambridge University Press, 1971), pp. 223–35; Richard Boyer, "Mexico in the Seventeenth Century: Transition of a Colonial Society," *Hispanic American Historical Review* 57, no. 3 (1977): 455–78; D. A. Brading, *Miners and Merchants in Bourbon Mexico, 1763–1810* (Cambridge: Cambridge University Press, 1971), pp. 8–12; Israel, *Race, Class, and Politics*, pp. 30–33; and Lynch, *Spain under the Hapsburgs*, vol. 2, pp. 199–200. This recent scholarship revises the Borah argument that epidemics led to the mid-seventeenth century mining decline and the Chaunu thesis of Mexico's failure as a market—see Woodrow Borah, *New Spain's Century of Depression* (Berkeley: University of California Press, 1951), pp. 5–44; and Pierre Chaunu and Huguette Chaunu, *Seville et l'Atlantique, 1504–1650* (Paris, 1955–59), vol. VIII.

48. Brading, *Miners and Merchants;* Walter Howe, *The Mining Guild of New Spain and Its Tribunal General, 1770–1821* (New York: Greenwood Press, 1968); and Robert W. Randall, *Real del Monte: A British Mining Venture in Mexico* (Austin: University of Texas Press, 1972).

49. Ladd, *Mexican Nobility*, pp. 34–36. See also Richard Lindley, "Kinship and Credit in the Structure of Guadalajara's Oligarchy, 1800–1830" (Ph.D. diss., University of Texas, 1976); and Louisa Schell Hoberman, "Merchants in Seventeenth-Century Mexico City," *Hispanic American Historical Review* 57, no. 3 (1977): 479–503.

50. Some of the humbler guilds, like candlemakers and cobblers, allowed Africans, mulattoes, and mestizos to rise to the upper ranks. A mestizo's status varied from being relegated to the bottom with Africans and mulattoes in the prestigious trades (metalsmiths, armourers, needlemakers) to becoming master craftsmen in select guilds (milliners, glove-makers, porcelain-makers).

51. See note 47 above.
52. Peter Singelmann, "Peripheral Capitalist Development and the Persistence of Peasant Production: the Contradictions of an Incomplete Transition" (paper presented at Fifth World Congress of Rural Sociology, Mexico City, August 7–12, 1980; mimeo.).
53. Gibson, *Aztecs under Spanish Rule*.
54. Jeffrey Bortz, "Wage Determination in Mexico," Ms. (1981); and idem, "Industrial Wages in Mexico City, 1939–1975" (Ph.D. diss., UCLA, 1982).

Chapter 2: Independence and Civil War, 1770–1880

1. Various economic historians have begun to adopt this 1770–1800 periodization of Mexican history. See, for example, Gilberto Argüello, *En torno al poder y a la ideología dominantes en México* (Puebla: Universidad Autónoma de Puebla, 1977). While this chapter's analysis of Mexico's nineteenth-century political economy is my own, I wish to thank historians Argüello and Barbara A. Tenenbaum for their helpful suggestions and informed insights.
2. For a good summary of the ideological program of the Bourbon reforms, consult Josefina Cintrón Tiryakian, "Campillo's Pragmatic New System: A Mercantile and Utilitarian Approach to Indian Reform in Spanish Colonies of the Eighteenth Century," *History of Political Economy* 10, no. 2 (1978): 233–57. As early as 1743, Philip V's Minister of State, and of the Navy, War, and the Indies, José del Campillo y Cossío, had outlined a series of reforms anticipating those of Charles III. Other political economists and *proyectistas* followed in Campillo's footsteps (e.g., Ustariz, Ulloa, and Ward). However, the more radical reform ideas, such as Charles III's 1786 ordinance "that all the natives shall enjoy an adequate endowment of landed property" and engage in production "for their own profit," were never implemented. For differences in emphasis on political concessions to criollos, contrast the "revolution in government" argument in D. A. Brading, *Miners and Merchants in Bourbon Mexico, 1763–1810* (New York: Cambridge University Press, 1971), with Peggy K. Liss, "Mexico en el Siglo XVIII," *Historia Mexicana* 27 (1977–78): 273–315. Criollos did obtain more positions in the bureaucracy, mining, commerce, and the militia, but real power remained with the Spaniards.
3. Enrique Florescano, *Precios del maíz y crisis agrícolas en México (1708–1810)* (Mexico City: Colegio de México, 1969), pp. xvi–xvii, *passim*.
4. Cited in R. W. Van Alstyne, *The Rising American Empire* (New York: Oxford University Press, 1960), p. 81.
5. Cited in Enrique Semo, *Historia mexicana: economía y lucha de clases* (Mexico City: Era, 1978), p. 204.
6. Doris M. Ladd, *The Mexican Nobility at Independence, 1780–1826* (Austin: University of Texas Press, 1976), pp. 29, 52.
7. Cited in R. A. Humphreys and John Lynch, *The Origins of the Latin American Revolutions, 1808–1826* (New York: Alfred A. Knopf, 1966), p. 27. On tensions between criollos and *peninsulares*, consult Hugh M. Hammill, Jr., *The Hidalgo Revolt: Prelude to Mexican Independence* (Gainesville: University of Florida Press, 1966); Salvador de Madariaga, *The Fall of the Spanish American Empire* (New York: Collier, 1963); and H. G. Ward, *Mexico in 1827* (London: Henry Colburn, 1828), vol. 1.
8. Cited in Florescano, *Precios del maíz*, p. 191.
9. On the role of the Spanish army in Mexico, see Christon I. Archer, *The Army in Bourbon Mexico, 1760–1810* (Albuquerque: University of New Mexico Press,

1977); and Lyle McAllister, *The "Fuero Militar" in New Spain, 1764–1800* (Gainesville: University of Florida Press, 1957). The *fueros militares* were minor privileges not to be confused with a "praetorian tradition," which had only an incipient basis in colonial Mexico.

10. Alexander von Humboldt, *Ensayo político sobre el Reino de la Nueva España* (Mexico City: Ed. Porrúa, 1966), p. 452.
11. Karl Marx, *Grundrisse* (New York: Vintage, 1973), p. 60.
12. Cf. Karl Marx, *Capital* (New York: International Publishers, 1967), vol. 3, p. 123.
13. There are various versions of Hidalgo's exact words, but this is the one used most frequently.
14. Cited in Humphreys and Lynch, *Origins of the Latin American Revolutions*, p. 263.
15. Carlos María de Bustamante, *Cuadro histórico*, vol. 2, pp. 610–11, and José María Luis Mora, *México y sus revoluciones*, vol. 3, pp. 33, 362, all cited in Ladd, *Mexican Nobility*, p. 114.
16. A minority of criollos fought General Calleja in unsuccessful revolts led by such independence advocates as López Rayón, Bravo, Verduzco, Mier y Terán, and Guerrero.
17. Ladd, *Mexican Nobility*, and Argüello, personal conversations, respectively.
18. See John H. Coatsworth, "Obstacles to Economic Growth in Nineteenth-Century Mexico," *The American Historical Review* 83, no. 1 (February 1978): 80–100, and idem, *Growth against Development: The Economic Impact of Railroads in Porfirian Mexico* (DeKalb: Northern Illinois University Press, 1981).
19. Cited in James D. Cockcroft, Andre Gunder Frank, and Dale L. Johnson, *Dependence and Underdevelopment: Latin America's Political Economy* (New York: Anchor, 1972), p. 30.
20. Mariano Otero, *Obras* (Mexico City: Ed. Porrúa, 1967), vol. 1, p. 178.
21. Barbara A. Tenenbaum, "Merchants, Money, and Mischief: The British in Mexico, 1821–1862," *The Americas* (January 1979): 335.
22. Cited in Lewis Hanke, ed., *History of Latin American Civilization: Sources and Interpretations* (Boston: Little, Brown, 1967), p. 25. In 1981 Mexican Freemasonry claimed 1.7 million members, 26 of 31 state governors, and 8 holders of Cabinet posts.
23. Cited in James M. Callahan, *American Foreign Policy in Mexican Relations* (New York: Macmillan, 1932), p. 34.
24. The full text of this letter, dated February 19, 1848, is reproduced in Moisés Gonzáles Navarro, *Raza y tierra: la guerra de castas y el henequén* (Mexico City: Colegio de Mexico, 1970), pp. 309–10.
25. Cited in Alonso Aguilar, *Dialéctica de la economía mexicana* (Mexico City: Nuestro Tiempo, 1968), p. 188.
26. Ponciano Arriaga, *Voto particular del C. Ponciano Arriaga sobre el derecho de propiedad* (San Luis Potosí: Impresa "Al Libro de Caja," 1959). Actually, the breaking up of communal lands had begun in earnest after Mexico gained independence—it reached its apex with the Liberal Reform. See Roger Bartra, *Estructuras agrarias y clases sociales* (Mexico City: Era, 1976).
27. Otero, *Obras*, p. 162.
28. Arriaga, *Voto particular*.
29. Even though a capitalist state reflects a class hegemony over dominated classes, there are many forms such a state may assume. Various mediation agencies exist in the political arena headed by the state and socially within different fractions of the hegemonic class. The state is never the sum of its various apparatuses or forms; nor is it the sum of interests of the dominant class. Class struggle defines the concrete forms assumed by any state.

30. John M. Hart, *Anarchism and the Mexican Working Class, 1860–1931* (Austin: University of Texas Press, 1978), p. 41.

Chapter 3: Dictatorship and Revolution, 1880–1920

1. Social Darwinism as a rationale for free-enterprise capitalism, rugged individualism, and racially biased "natural" superiorities enjoyed its heyday throughout the world in the latter part of the nineteenth century. See James D. Cockcroft, *Intellectual Precursors of the Mexican Revolution, 1900–1913* (Austin: University of Texas Press, 1968; paperback edition, 1976).

2. Cited in Charles C. Cumberland, *Mexico: The Struggle for Modernity* (New York: Oxford University Press, 1968), p. 196.

3. Cited in Josefina Vázquez de Knauth, *Nacionalismo y educación en México* (Mexico City: Colegio de México, 1970), p. 55.

4. See Marta Loyo Camacho and Javier Rodríquez Piña, *Historia de la migración mexicana a los Estados Unidos* (Mexico City: Universidad Autónoma Metropolitana Azcapotzalco: *Reporte de Investigación 82*, 1982).

5. See John Womack, Jr., *Zapata and the Mexican Revolution* (New York: Alfred A. Knopf, 1969), pp. 39–50; and Arturo Warman, *. . . y venimos a contradecir* (Mexico City: Ediciones de la Casa Chata, 1976), pp. 73–74.

6. See Frans J. Schryer, "A Ranchero Economy in Northwestern Hidalgo, 1880–1920," *Hispanic American Historical Review* 59, no. 3 (1979); and "The Role of the Rancheros of Central Mexico in the Mexican Revolution," *Canadian Journal of Latin American Studies* 4, no. 7 (1979).

7. Cited in Andre Gunder Frank, *Latin America: Underdevelopment or Revolution* (New York: Monthly Review Press, 1969), p. 238.

8. Jorge Basurto, *El proletariado industrial en México, 1850–1930* (Mexico City: UNAM, 1975), pp. 25–27. Throughout the nineteenth century, Mexico's main productive processes were taken over by capital, leading to a formal subsumption of laborers to capital's despotism and an "original accumulation" of capital. By 1900, many laborers were experiencing real subsumption to capital—that is, they were acting as free wage labor unfettered by intermediate or noncapitalist forms of labor discipline such as slavery, serfdom, debt-peonage, piecework, sharecropping, etc. This marked an important step in the transition to capital accumulation on an extended scale, a transition never completed. See Domenico E. Sindico, "Modernization in XIX Century Sugar Haciendas: The Case of Morelos (From Formal to Real Subjection of Labor to Capital)," *Latin American Perspectives* 7, no. 4 (Fall 1980): 83–99.

9. While in the name of "objectivity" an occasional U.S. scholar has attempted to play down the significance of Mexico's emergent industrial proletariat and its major pre-1911 party (PLM), or the influence of the 1906–1908 strikes in undermining the Díaz regime, Mexican scholars have generally agreed on their pivotal importance. See, for example, the unanimity on this point among the different interpretations of the Revolution offered in *Interpretaciones de la revolución mexicana*, ed. Héctor Aguilar Camín (Mexico City: Nueva Imagen, 1979). The single bloodiest massacre during the Porfiriato occurred on January 8, 1907, when troops opened fire on striking textile workers in the Río Blanco area of Veracruz. Estimates of the number of dead go as high as 1,000. The best researched account is Salvador Hernández, "Tiempos libertarios. El magonismo en México: Cananea, Río Blanco y Baja California," in *La clase obrera en la historia de México: De la dictadura porfirista a los tiempos libertarios*, ed.

Ciro R. S. Cardoso et al. (Mexico City: Siglo XXI, 1980), pp. 101–248. The standard monograph on the PLM is Cockcroft, *Intellectual Precursors.*

10. Cockcroft, *Intellectual Precursors,* p. 27.
11. Kenneth J. Grieb, "Standard Oil and the Financing of the Mexican Revolution," *California Historical Quarterly* 19, no. 1 (March 1971).
12. Cockcroft, *Intellectual Precursors,* p. 159.
13. Ibid., p. 175.
14. Cited in Antonio Díaz Soto y Gama, *La revolución agraria del sur y Emiliano Zapata, su caudillo* (1960), p. 133. I am grateful to Michoacán *ejidatarios,* some of whom lived on haciendas until 1935, for explaining from their own life histories the lack of participation by *acasillados* and what actually happened.
15. U.S. Department of State, *Papers Relating to the Foreign Relations* (Washington, D.C.: Government Printing Office, 1914), p. 444.
16. Jesús Silva Herzog, *Breve historia de la Revolución Mexicana* (Mexico City: FCE, 1947), vol. 1, pp. 34–35.
17. Alvaro Obregón, *Discursos* (Mexico City: Biblioteca de la Dirección General de Educación Militar, 1932), vol. 1, p. 279.
18. Salvador Alvarado, *La reconstrucción de México: Un mensaje a los pueblos de América* (Mexico City: J. Ballesca y Cia., 1919), vol. 3, pp. 91–94.
19. Actually, the arms and munitions were U.S.-made, purchased in the United States by Huerta agents, and shipped via Europe to decoy U.S. federal authorities. The fact that they finally ended on a German steamer of the American-Hamburg line was coincidental and not originally planned. No matter—Wilson needed a pretext for asserting U.S. power in determining the course of events inside Mexico. See Michael G. Meyer, "The Arms of the Ypiranga," *Hispanic American Historical Review* 50, no. 3 (August 1970): 543–56. Carranza's forces objected strongly to the U.S. occupation of Veracruz, in part because *they* sought (and received) German arms. Later, Germany would raise the Mexico question as part of its global ambitions. On January 16, 1917, German Foreign Secretary Arthur Zimmermann telegrammed the German Ambassador to the United States: "Top secret. We contemplate starting unrestricted submarine warfare the first of February. In spite of that, we will try to keep the U.S. neutral. In case we don't, we make a proposal to Mexico for an alliance on the following basis: make war together, make peace together, generous financial assistance and our agreement that Mexico must recover its lost territory in Texas, New Mexico and Arizona." But the United States did not stay neutral, and Germany's imaginative ambitions with regard to Mexico came to naught.
20. U.S. Department of State, *Papers Relating to the Foreign Relations,* p. 510.
21. Edith O'Shaughnessy, *A Diplomat's Wife in Mexico* (New York: Harper, 1916), p. 290.
22. Robert E Quirk, *The Mexican Revolution, 1914–1951: The Convention of Aguascalientes* (New York: The Citadel Press, 1963), pp. 109–11.
23. Ibid., pp. 135–38.
24. Rosendo Salazar, *La Casa del Obrero Mundial* (Mexico City: Costa-Amic, 1963), as well as other works by Salazar, especially, with Jose G. Escobedo, *Las pugnas de la gleba, 1907–1922* (Mexico City, 1922), 2 vols. (see vol. 1, pp. 157–60).
25. Arnaldo Córdova, "México: Revolución burguesa y política de masas," in *Interpretaciones,* ed. Camín, pp. 55–89.
26. Cited in Robert F. Smith, *The United States and Revolutionary Nationalism in Mexico, 1916–1932* (Chicago: University of Chicago Press, 1972), p. 576.
27. Ibid., pp. 580–81.
28. Cited in Ferdinand Lundberg and Lyle Stuart, *The Rich and the Super-rich* (New York: Bantam, 1969), p. 890; and Scott Nearing and Joseph Freeman, *Dollar Diplomacy* (New York: Monthly Review Press, 1969), p. 273.

29. Womack, *Zapata,* pp. 300–17, 346–51.
30. See Marx's writings, *The 18th Brumaire* and *Class Struggles in France.*
31. See Herzog, *Beve historia.*
32. See Adolfo Gilly, *La revolución interrumpida* (Mexico City: El Caballito, 1971) and the interpretations offered in *Interpretaciones,* ed. Camín.
33. Gilly, *La revolución interrumpida.*

Chapter 4: Roots of the Modern State, 1920–1940

1. See Roderic A. Camp, *Mexico's Leaders: Their Education and Recruitment* (Tucson: University of Arizona Press, 1980); Arnaldo Córdova, "México: Revolución burguesa y política de masas," in *Interpretaciones de la revolución mexicana,* ed. Héctor Aguilar Camín (Mexico City: Nueva Imagen, 1979), pp. 76–77; Merilee Grindle, "Patrons and Clients in the Bureaucracy: Career Networks in Mexico," *Latin American Research Review* 12 (1977): 37–66; Nora Hamilton, *The Limits of State Autonomy: Post-Revolutionary Mexico* (Princeton, N.J.: Princeton University Press, 1982); Juan Felipe Leal, *La burguesía y el estado mexicano* (Mexico City: El Caballito, 1972); Peter H. Smith, *Labyrinths of Power: Political Recruitment in Twentieth Century Mexico* (Princeton, N.J.: Princeton University Press, 1979); Mark Wasserman, "Persistent Oligarchs: Vestiges of the Porfirian Elite in Revolutionary Chihuahua, Mexico 1920–1935" (paper presented at the Sixth Conference of Mexican and U.S. Historians, Chicago, September 1981). On the class character of corruption and its historical roots in this period, consult Rosario Castellanos et al., *La Corrupcion* (Mexico City: Nuestro Tiempo, 1969).
2. Hamilton, *Limits of State Autonomy.*
3. Antonio Gramsci, *Selections from the Prison Notebooks* (New York: International Publishers, 1971); idem, *La política del estado moderno* (Barcelona: Ed. Peninsula, 1971); and idem, *Obras completas* (Mexico City: Juan Pablos Editor, S.A., 1975).
4. While the state in any society performs a variety of functions and can take many different forms, it is always the organizer of society in the interests of the class structure taken as a whole. The state is rooted in the economic infrastructure from which it springs and which it in turn affects. It retains a certain autonomy from the infrastructure; develops in the general interests of the ruling class (or combination of dominant classes or class fractions); and serves to reproduce and reinforce the prevalent economic conditions of life. Like the infrastructure, the state develops on the basis of contending classes and, as examples given later in this work reveal, itself plays an active role in class formation (and even class creation), as well as in capital accumulation. When emergent, vital bourgeois fractions are pushing the economic process forward and seeking both economic and political hegemony, they often confront the resistance of older ruling-class fractions, including indolent large landowners, some of the merchant bourgeoisie, certain bankers tied to outside interests (cf. the opposition to Limantour, 1907–1911), etc. Simultaneously, all these dominant economic interests may be threatened in common by aroused underclasses, especially those being proletarianized by capitalism's relentless advance: e.g., peasants and workers as during the 1910–1920 Revolution. Short of revolutionary transformation of both the economy and the polity, the next best solution in such situations, from the point of view of those benefiting from the overall exploitative structure, is to delegate (or accept) sufficient power on the state's part (autonomy) to, in Engels's words, meet "the economic necessities of the national situation" (Engels, letter to Danielson, June 18, 1892, cited in Hal Draper, *Karl Marx's Theory of Revolution: State and Bureaucracy* [New York: Monthly Review

Press, 1977], p. 585). In the case of Mexico, an old state apparatus had to be dismantled (1910–1917) and a new one constructed (1917–1938); but the state itself remained a class (capitalist) state.

5. John Child, *Unequal Alliance: The Inter-American Military System, 1938–1978* (Boulder: Westview Press, 1980), p. 13 (based on U.S. War Department, War Plans Division, "General Mexican War Plan," Entry 282, RG 165 and Entry 365, RG 407, U.S. National Archives).

6. Cited in Lorenzo Meyer, *México y Estados Unidos en el conflicto petrolero (1917–1942)* (Mexico City: Colegio de México, 1968), p. 87.

7. Ambassador Morrow's shrewd appeals to Mexican dignity stood in stark contrast to how Mexican migrant workers were being treated in the United States. There, Mexicans were treated as scapegoats for whatever economic problems arose for the U.S. working class. Samuel Gompers, president of the American Federation of Labor (AFL), emphasized the Mexicans' alleged inferior productive capacity, while Theodore Lothrop Stoddard spoke of the cultural inferiority of Mexicans. In 1920 Stoddard affirmed in his book *The Rising Tide of Labor against White World-Supremacy* (New York: C. Scribners' Sons, pp. 107–08) that the Mexican migrant was undesirable because he was "born communist." C. M. Goethe tried to demonstrate scientifically that Mexicans are racially inferior in his article "Immigration from Mexico," published in *The Alien in Our Midst; or, "Selling Our Birthright for a Mess of Pottage"* by two other champions of white supremacy, Madison Grant and Charles Davidson (New York: The Galton Publishing Co., Inc., 1930). The economic crises of 1907, 1921, 1929–34, 1947, 1954, 1974, and 1980–82 all witnessed the scapegoating of Mexican migrant workers for problems created by the capitalist system itself—and massive deportations and harassment of Mexican immigrants. The attacks on Mexicans became so severe during the Depression that in 1932 the head of the U.S. Department of Agriculture had to rush to the aid of U.S. employers in agriculture, mining, and industry desperate for cheap Mexican migrant labor by publicly declaring, "We have depended upon these people; they are not a social burden but honest men and workers who have helped so much to develop this country" (Archivo de la Secretaría de Relaciones Exteriores 41-26-139, IV/241 (73) (03)/1, Jan. 27, 1932). See also Mercedes Carreras de Velasco, *Los mexicanos que devolvió la crisis, 1929–1932* (Mexico City: Secretaría de Relaciones Exteriores, 1974); Jorge Bustamante and James Cockcroft, "One More Time: The 'Undocumented,'" *Radical America* 15, no. 6 (November–December 1981): 7–16; and James Cockcroft, "Mexican Migration Crisis and the Internationalization of Labor Struggle," *Contemporary Marxism* 5 (July 1982): 48–61.

8. Cited in Robert F. Smith, "The Morrow Mission and the International Commission of Bankers on Mexico: The Interaction of Finance Diplomacy and the New Mexican Elite," *Journal of Latin American Studies* 1, no. 2 (November 1969): 150.

9. A diligent examination of this entrenchment of foreign economic interests is Leopoldo Solís's *La realidad económica mexicana: retrovisión y perspectivas* (Mexico City: Siglo XXI, 1971).

10. Cited in Smith, "The Morrow Mission," p. 162.

11. Cited in James W. Wilkie, *The Mexican Revolution: Federal Expenditure and Social Change since 1910* (Berkeley: University of California Press, 1967), p. 62.

12. The Cristero Revolt was a complex affair, mixing agrarian protest with anticommunism, antigovernment rebellion, and the redemptive qualities of the Virgin of Guadalupe. The Catholic Church, divided between progressives and conservatives as David C. Bailey has shown (*Viva Cristo Rey! The Cristero Rebellion and the Church-State Conflict in Mexico* [Austin: University of Texas Press, 1974]), backed it. Contrasting interpretations are offered in Jean Meyer, *La cristiada. La*

guerra de los cristeros, 3 vols. (Mexico City: Siglo XXI, 1974); and Robert E. Quirk, *The Mexican Revolution and the Catholic Church, 1910–1929* (Bloomington: Indiana University Press, 1960). See also James W. Wilkie, "The Meaning of the Cristero Religious War against the Mexican Revolution," *A Journal of Church and State,* no. 2 (Spring 1966): 214–33, and José Díaz Román Rodríguez, *El movimiento cristero* (Mexico City: Nueva Imagen, 1979).

13. Cited in Arnaldo Córdova, *La ideología de la revolución mexicana* (Mexico City: Era, 1973), p. 328.

14. *Futuro,* May 1934, pp. 54–61. See also Arnaldo Córdova, *La clase obrera en la historia de México: En una época de crisis (1928–1934)* (Mexico City: Siglo XXI, 1980), p. 164.

15. See footnote 7, above.

16. See Ramona Falcón, "El surgimiento del agrarismo cardenista—Una revisión de las tesis populistas," *Historia Mexicana* 28, no. 3 (January–March 1978): 333–86.

17. Cited in Wayne A. Cornelius, Jr., "Nation-Building, Participation, and Distribution: The Politics of Social Reform under Cárdenas," in *Development Episodes in Comparative Politics: Crisis, Choice, and Change,* ed. Gabriel A. Almond and Scott C. Flanagan (Boston: Little, Brown and Company, 1973), p. 84.

18. Cited in Cordova, *La ideología,* p. 235. A key figure in this intellectual heritage of socialist education was Spanish pedagogue Francisco Ferrer Guardia, who founded the Escuela Moderna in Barcelona, 1901, and co-founded with a group of anarchists the International League for Rational Education of Children, 1907. Ferrer Guardia was executed in 1909 by the Spanish government as an alleged chief of the antimonarchist revolutionary movement. European anarchists made his case a *cause célèbre,* as did Mexican anarchists who headed the Precursor Movement against Díaz. After Díaz's overthrow, organized labor's Casa del Obrero Mundial set up workers' schools modeled on Ferrer Guardia's principles (James D. Cockcroft, *Intellectual Precursors of the Mexican Revolution, 1900–1913* [Austin: University of Texas Press, 1968, paperback ed., 1976], pp. 175, 223).

19. See Gramsci, *Prison Notebooks.* Such a hegemonic project normally takes form in times of crisis, often during a transition from one stage of economic development to another; also, during a period of political transition (itself related to economic change). In the course of a given crisis, a particular class or class fraction (often the ascendant one) attempts to carry through the transition and the class goals it seeks through ideological combat, alliance-building, and other forms of political struggle. The aim of the project is to gain dominance over the state and its ideological apparatuses, to transform the state in corresponding ways, to subordinate or defeat rival projects and the class interests behind them—in sum, to alter the balance of power in society as a whole. A hegemonic project is not necessarily clear or well articulated, confused as it is by the contestants' formations of new alliances of class and social forces—new "power blocs" (cf. Morones's alliance with Obregón and, briefly, Calles, both of whom in turn were busy expanding their capitalist interests in chickpeas and construction, respectively). Moreover, hegemonic projects are risky since they imply a change in basic social relations and the dominant ideology, with corresponding instability (cf. the Cárdenas period). There is no guarantee that the contest will not lead to the common ruin of the contesting forces, or that the doors will not be opened to a more revolutionary (or counterrevolutionary) transformation of society. Yet the circumstances of crisis and class antagonism usually do lead to one or another form of hegemonic project built on new alliances. History is full of such experiences.

20. Wilkie, *The Mexican Revolution,* p. 265.

332   *Mexico*

21. Cited in Joe C. Ashby, *Organized Labor and the Mexican Revolution under Lázaro Cárdenas* (Chapel Hill: University of North Carolina Press, 1967), p. 27.
22. Ibid., p. 273.
23. The full text of this historic speech may be found in Lázaro Cárdenas, *Palabras y documentos públicos de Lázaro Cárdenas, 1928–1940*, vol. 2 (Mexico City: Siglo XXI, 1978).
24. Cited in Ashby, *Organized Labor*, p. 37.
25. David L. Raby, "Los maestros rurales y los conflictos sociales en México, 1931–1940," *Historia Mexicana* 18, no. 2 (October–December 1968).
26. Lyle C. Brown, "General Lázaro Cárdenas and Mexican Presidential Politics, 1933–1940: A Study in the Acquisition and Manipulation of Political Power" (Ph.D. diss., University of Texas, 1964), p. 211.
27. Jesús Silva Herzog, *El petróleo mexicano* (Mexico City, 1941), p. 5; personal interview, 1964.
28. Cited in Albert L. Michaels, "The Crisis of Cardenismo," *Journal of Latin American Studies* 2 (May 1970): 51.
29. Nora L. Hamilton, "The State and Class Conflict: Mexico during the Cárdenas Period," in *Classes, Class Conflict, and the State*, ed. Maurice Zeitlin (Cambridge: Winthrop Publishers, Inc., 1980), p. 358.
30. Cited in Michaels, "Crisis of Cardenismo," p. 57.
31. Various authors have employed the concept "corporativism" to Mexico's political system. For a summary, see Arnaldo Córdova, "El desafío de la izquierda mexicana," *Nexos* 18 (June 1979): 3–15.
32. E.g., David Apter, *The Politics of Modernization* (Chicago: University of Chicago Press, 1965); Gino Germani, *Política y sociedad en una época de transición* (Buenos Aires, 1965), and idem, with Torcuato S. di Tella and Octavio Ianni, *Populismo y contradicciones de clase en Latinoamérica* (Mexico City: Era, 1973); Octavio Ianni, *La formacíon del estado populista en América Latina* (Mexico City: Siglo XXI, 1975); G. Ionescu and E. Gellner, *Populism* (London, 1970); and Aníbal Quijano Obregón and Francisco Weffort, *Populismo, marginalidad y dependencia* (San José, Costa Rica, 1973). For an incisive summary of the problem, consult Ernesto Laclau, *Politics and Ideology in Marxist Theory* (London: New Left Books, 1977).
33. Laclau, *Politics and Ideology in Marxist Theory*, p. 184.

Chapter 5: The Transformation of Agriculture and Industry

1. See Alonso Aguilar and Jorge Carrión, *La burguesía, la oligarquía y el estado* (Mexico City: Nuesto Tiempo, 1972), pp. 185–86.
2. The emphasis on retaining and honoring parts of leaders' anatomies has its precedents in the second quarter of the nineteenth century. In 1838, when a conservative government was in power, the bones of Iturbide (the leader who declared Mexico independent in 1821 and was executed after the revolt of Santa Anna and Guadalupe Victoria in 1824) were removed to Mexico City's cathedral. The blown-off leg of Santa Anna became an object of homage for his followers, even as, later, one of Santa Anna's artificial limbs was to command similar adoration. It is generally believed that the wily Santa Anna encouraged this cult as a weapon in his struggle for state power with rival caudillos.
3. Marcela Lagarde, "El indigenismo, un proceso ideológico" (Tesis de Licenciatura, Escuela Nacional de Antropologia e Historia, 1974), p. 79; Ricardo Pozas and Isabel H. de Pozas, *Los indios en las clases sociales de México* (Mexico City: Siglo XXI, 1971), pp. 99–100. While little has actually been done for the survivors of the Conquest or their descendants except when they themselves have fought for

their rights, it remains significant that in the ideological superstructure of Mexico the Indian is granted—however cynically—at least some recognition of legitimacy. This contrasts with the situation in the United States, where phrases like "the only good Indian is a dead Indian" and media portrayals of figures like the mythical Lone Ranger and his aide Tonto (Spanish for "dumb") perpetuate a profoundly racist culture with roots going back to the genocidal wars conducted by U.S. colonists and their descendants against Amerindians. This is of little solace to Mexico's Indians, however, as they suffer continued exploitation and reduction made more difficult to combat by the mask of *indigenismo*.

4. Such is the criterion of the Mexican Census Bureau. However, there are many rural towns with slightly more than 2,500 residents that resemble "urban" areas in no way whatsoever.

5. Roger Bartra, "Peasants and Political Power in Mexico: A Theoretical Model," *Latin American Perspectives* 2, no. 2 (Summer 1975).

6. Rodolfo Stavenhagen et al., *Neolatifundismo y explotación de Emiliano Zapata a Anderson Clayton & Co.* (Mexcio City: Nuestro Tiempo, 1968), pp. 19, 30–31, 75–78, 86–87; see also John W. Barchfield, "La política agraria de México contemporáneo," *Revista de México Agrario* 10, no. 3 (1977).

7. In his Ph.D. dissertation "Industrial Wages in Mexico City, 1939–1975" (History Department, UCLA, 1982), Jeffrey Bortz has done the most complete research to be found on Mexican wage scales and labor's contribution to industrial growth. Consult also his "Problemas de la medición de la afiliación sindical," *A* 1, no. 1 (September–December 1980): 29–66; "El salario obrero en el Distrito Federal 1939–1975," *Investigación Económica* 36, no. 4 (October–December 1977): 129–70; and (with Ricardo Pascoe P.) "Salario y clase obrera en la acumulación de capital en Mexico," *Coyoacán* 1, no. 2 (January–March 1978): 79–93.

8. See Fred Hirsch, *An Analysis of Our AFL-CIO Role in Latin America or Under the Covers with the CIA* (San Jose, Calif., 1974): and Jack Scott, *Yankee Unions, Go Home! How the AFL Helped the U.S. Build an Empire in Latin America* (Vancouver, B.C.: New Star Books, 1978).

9. Ibid.

10. For illustrative examples, see María Guadalupe Acevedo López and Gilberto Silva Ruiz, "Análisis de las situaciones de clase de los trabajadores mexicanos" (Tesis de Licenciatura en Sociologia, UNAM, 1973).

11. Since unions exaggerate their membership numbers, it is impossible to establish an accurate accounting of CTM's share of unionized workers.

12. Bortz, "Industrial Wages in Mexico City." Two standard works documenting these phenomena are Pablo Gonzáles Casanova, *La democracia en México* (Mexico City: Siglo XXI, 1965); and Ifigenia M. de Navarrete, "Income Distribution in Mexico," in *Mexico's Recent Economic Growth*, ed. Enrique Pérez López et al. (Austin: University of Texas Press, 1967), pp. 133–72.

13. *Latin American Weekly Report*, November 16, 1979, and *International Herald Tribune*, April 20, 1980.

14. José Luis Ceceña, *México en la órbita imperial* (Mexico City: El Caballito, 1970); Salvador Cordero H., "Concentración industrial y poder económico en México," *Cauadernos del CES* 18 (1977); and González Casanova, *La democracia en México*.

15. TNCs are corporations that have their base in one country but draw much of their income, raw materials, and operating capital from several other countries, through ownership of foreign subsidiaries, joint ventures with foreign governments or investors, and a host of other means. The compelling force behind the rise of TNCs is the need for corporations to grow and maintain their profitability, as well as to gain control over as much of the world's resources and

capital as possible. The TNC, a logical outgrowth of monopoly capital that has outgrown nations, constitutes the economic heart of modern imperialism. The term "transnational" is preferable to "multinational" because it is a less ideological and more accurate concept, combining the control aspects implicit in "national" with the global aspects of "trans." For elaboration, see James D. Cockcroft, "Impact of Transnational Corporations on Chile's Social Structure," *Summation* 5, nos. 1 and 2 (Summer 1975): 7–32; revised in *Cauadernos Políticos* 10 (October–December 1976): 64–82. On imperialism, consult V. I. Lenin, *Imperialism, the Highest Stage of Capitalism* (New York: International Publishers, 1972); Samir Amin, *Accumulation on a World Scale: A Critique of the Theory of Underdevelopment*, 2 vols. (New York: Monthly Review Press, 1974); and Paul Sweezy, "Some Problems in the Theory of Capital Accumulation," *Monthly Review*, (May 1974); pp. 38–55.

16. Ceceña, *México en la órbita imperial;* and Fernando Fajnzylber and Trinidad Martínez Tarrago, *Las empresas transnacionales: expansión a nivel mundial y proyección en la industria mexicana* (Mexico City: FCE, 1976).
17. Peter Baird and Ed McCaughan, *Beyond the Border: Mexico and U.S. Today* (New York: NACLA, 1979), p. 190.
18. Fajnzylber and Martínez Tarrago, *Las empresas transnacionales.*
19. Cited in NACLA, *Mexico 1968* (New York: NACLA, 1968), p. 37. Cf. D. W. Barraesen, *The Border Industrialization Program of Mexico* (Lexington, Mass.: D. C. Heath, 1971); Alma Chapoy Bonifaz, *Empresas multinacionales* (Mexico City: El Caballito, 1975); Peter G. Van der Spek, "Mexico's Booming Border Zone: A Magnet for Labor-Intensive American Plants," *Journal of Interamerican Economic Affairs* 29 (Spring/Summer 1976); and Liborio Villalobos Calderón, "La industria maquiladora extranjera en México: mal necesario de una sociedad subdesarrollado," *Relaciones Internacionales* (UNAM) (April–June 1973).
20. Miguel Wionzcek, *Inversión y technología extranjera en América Latina* (Mexico City: Cuadernos de Joaquín Mortiz, 1971) and Banco de México figures for the 1965–1970 period. Since 1970, changes in the Banco de México's statistical categories and TNCs' increased reluctance to provide all data have made it more difficult to assess accurately the depth of foreign capital's penetration of the economy and methods employed. But the trends described here are universally recognized.
21. *The Financial Times,* February 3, 1969.
22. Y. U. A. Sergeyev and N. Yu Strugatshya, "Scientific and Technical Development, the Monopolies and the Patent System," reprinted from Russian research journal *SSHA: Ekonomik, Politika, Ideologiya* in *Idea* 15, no. 2 (Summer 1971); and UNCTAD, *Transfer of Technology* (New York: UN Conference on Trade and Development Secretariat [UNCTAD], Junta del Acuerdo de Cartegena, TD/107, Dec. 29, 1971).
23. Fajnzylber and Martínez Tarrago, *Las empresas transnacionales.*
24. Business International Corporation, "Nationalism in Latin America" (September 1970), pp. 21, 29. The more industrialized countries' sales of technology to the less-industrialized developing countries (LDCs) derive from the historic tendency of capital to expand more rapidly in Department I than in Department II of production (articles of consumption). Earlier in the history of the more industrialized countries, Department I's high organic composition of capital (ratio of constant capital, or instruments and raw materials of production, to variable capital, or labor power—the only source of surplus value and profit) had been balanced by a lower organic composition in Department II, allowing for an acceptable generalized rate of profit. (Growth in the organic composition of capital generates the tendency of the rate of profit to fall.) As more and more workers became unionized in countries like the United States,

the organic composition of capital rose in Department II, putting more pressure on capitalists to find other areas to reestablish the accustomed balance of rates of profit. They found those areas in LDCs undertaking industrialization, at first in those countries' Department II of production and eventually in their Department I as well. A 1972 AID report made its central point this more recent need for "steadily increasing foreign sales of U.S. capital goods and technologically intensive products" ("Technical Cooperation with Iran," *Report to the Agency for International Development,* April 11, 1972, p. 9).

25. Quoted in Richard S. Newfarmer and W. F. Mueller, *Multinational Corporations in Brazil and Mexico: Structural Sources of Economic and Noneconomic Power* (Washington, D.C.: Report to the Subcommittee on Multinational Corporations of the Committee on Foreign Relations, U.S. Senate, August 1975), p. 17.
26. See Gary Gereffi, "Drug Firms and Dependency in Mexico: the Case of the Steroid Hormone Industry" (Yale University & Harvard University Center for International Affairs, mimeo, 1977).
27. Fajnzylber and Martínez Tarrago, *Las empresas transnacionales;* and Bernardo Sepúlveda and Antonio Chumacero, *La inversión extranjera en México* (Mexico City: FCE, 1973).
28. The "package" is priced cheaper as a whole than it would be if its component parts were sold separately. See UNCTAD, *Transfer of Technology,* pp. 2–3.
29. Cook Industries, however, is in decline and Japanese firms play a larger role now.
30. The World Bank helped finance the irrigation projects in Mexico's northwest and then in the late 1960s began pouring monies into Mexico's livestock-export sector. By 1971, AID accounted for one-third of the budget of Mexico's International Center for the Improvement of Corn and Wheat.
31. Cynthia Hewitt de Alcántara, *La modernización de la agricultura mexicana, 1940–1970* (Mexico City: Siglo XXI, 1978), p. 297.
32. James D. Cockcroft, unpublished field notes, 1963.
33. François Chevalier, "The Ejido and Political Stability in México," in *The Politics of Conformity in Latin America,* Claudio Veliz, ed. (London: Oxford University Press, 1967), p. 182.
34. John W. Barchfield, "The Structure of Power and the Deformation of Agrarian Reform in Mexico," *Revista del México Agrario* 14 (1981).
35. See "Agriculture," years 1970 and 1975, Table 9, this chapter.
36. Ernest Feder, *Imperialismo fresa* (Mexico City: Ed. Campesina, 1978).
37. Hewitt de Alcántara, *Modernización,* pp. 300–01.
38. Alonso Aguilar and Fernando Carmona, *México: riqueza y miseria* (Mexico City: Nuestro Tiempo, 1967), p. 65.
39. Alonso Aguilar, "La burgesía no sólo manda, gobierna," *Estrategia* 28 (July–August 1979): 2–32.
40. Good summaries of this process are: *The Economic Intelligence Unit* (London), 1970; and René Villarreal, "Del proyecto de crecimiento y sustitución de importaciones al desarrollo y sustitución de exportaciones," *Comercio Exterior* 25, no. 3 (March 1975): 315–23. Clark W. Reynolds, an advocate of U.S. investments in Mexican development, confirms the picture given here in his well-researched *The Mexican Economy: Twentieth-Century Structure and Growth* (New Haven: Yale University Press, 1970).
41. Banco de México, annual reports; and Carlos Perzabal, *Acumulación capitalista dependiente y subordinada: el caso de México (1940–1978)* (Mexico City: Siglo XXI, 1979), p. 128.
42. See note 19, above.
43. Leo Fenster, "Mexican Auto Swindle," *The Nation,* June 2, 1969, pp. 693–97.
44. *Business Trends,* 1972, 1977. Of Mexican-owned manufacturing firms, 6 percent

accounted for 94 percent of their fixed capital, 90 percent of their value of production, and 70 percent of their employed personnel; of nonforeign commercial firms, 1.8 percent absorbed 73 percent of their capital and 63.9 percent of their income; similar monopolization occurred in services. See Aguilar and Carmona, *México,* pp. 27–28; and Gregorio Vidal, "Estado mexicano, capital monopolista y oligarquía financiera," *Iztapalapa* 2, no. 3 (July–December 1980): 48–73.

45. See Jaime Osorio Urbina, "Superexplotación y clase obrera: el caso mexicano," *Cuadernos Políticos* 6 (October–December 1975): 5–23.
46. David Barkin, "Mexico's Albatross: The U.S. Economy," and Stephen R. Niblo, "Progress and the Standard of Living in Contemporary Mexico," *Latin American Perspectives* 2, no. 2 (Summer 1975); and Alonso Aguilar and Fernando Carmona, "Sobre el estado en México," *Estrategia* 38 (March–April 1981): 1–44.
47. Aguilar, "La burguesía no sólo manda, gobierna."
48. For more on Nafinsa, consult Nafinsa's annual reports; Frank R. Brandenburg, *The Making of Modern Mexico* (Englewood Cliffs, N.J.: Prentice-Hall, 1964); *Estrategia* 28 and 38 (July–August 1979, March–April 1981); and J. T. Dock Houk, *Financing and Problems of Development Banking* (New York, 1967).
49. Aguilar and Carmona, "Sobre el estado en México."

Chapter 6: Classes and the State

1. Alonso Aguilar and Fernando Carmona, *México: riqueza y miseria* (Mexico City: Nuestro Tiempo, 1967), p. 35.
2. Moisés González Navarro, "Mexico: The Lopsided Revolution," in *Obstacles to Change in Latin America,* ed. Claudio Veliz (London: Oxford University Press, 1965), pp. 206–29.
3. México, Michoacán, Hidalgo, Guanajuato, Chihuahua, Sinaloa, Tlaxcala, Jalisco, Oaxaca, and Chiapas. Most of the rest of out-migration flows from Durango, Veracruz, and Zacatecas.
4. Armando Bartra, "Colectivización o proletarización: el caso del Plan Chontalpa," *Cuadernos Agrarios* 1, no. 4 (1978): 56–110.
5. *Excelsior,* July 15, 1975, as summarized by Philip Russell, *Mexico in Transition* (Austin, Tex.: Colorado River Press, 1977), p. 112.
6. Arturo Warman, . . . *y venimos a contradecir: los campesinos de Morelos y el estado nacional* (Mexico City: Ediciones de la Casa Chata, 1976), p. 15.
7. See Luisa Paré, *El proletariado agrícola en México* (Mexico City: Siglo XXI, 1977).
8. Claude Meillassoux, *Mujeres, graneros y capitales* (Mexico City: Siglo XXI, 1977).
9. Paré, *El proletariado.*
10. James D. Cockcroft (with UAM-Azcapotzalco Migration Research Team), *Trabajadores de Michoacán: historia de un pueblo migrante* (imisac Ediciones "Contraste," 1982).
11. Cited in Cheryl Payer, "The World Bank and the Small Farmer," *Monthly Review* 32, no. 6 (November 1980): 35.
12. Ibid.
13. AID, U.S. Delegation, World Conference on Agrarian Reform and Rural Development, Rome, July 12–21, 1979, "Integration of Women in Development" (mimeo., May 24, 1979).
14. Hannes Lorenzen, "Investment in the Poor: A World Bank Project in Mexico" (Rome Declaration Group, Gartenhofstrasse 27, Zurich, 1980, mimeo.); and

John W. Barchfield, "The Structure of Power and the Deformation of Agrarian Reform in Mexico," *Revista del México Agrario* 14 (1981).

15. Veronika Bennholdt-Thomsen, "Investition in die Armen. Zur Entwicklungsstrategie der Weltbank," *Lateinamerika, Analysen und Berichte*, no. 4 (1980).

16. James D. Cockcroft, unpublished field notes, 1973.

17. Roger Bartra et al., *Caciquismo y poder político en el México rural* (Mexico City: Siglo XXI, 1975).

18. Paré, *El proletariado.*

19. Armando Bartra, "Sobre las clases sociales en el campo mexicano," *Cuadernos Agrarios*, no. 1 (1976).

20. See Aguilar and Carmona, *México;* Alonso Aguilar and Jorge Carrión, *La burguesía, la oligarquía y el estado* (Mexico City: Nuestro Tiempo, 1972); Frank R. Brandenburg, *The Making of Modern Mexico* (Englewood Cliffs, N.J.: Prentice-Hall, 1964); Salvador Cordero H., "Concentración industrial y poder económico en México," *Cuadernos del CES* 18 (1977); idem, with Rafael Santín, "Los grupos industriales, una nueva organización en México," *Cuadernos del CES* 23 (1977); Juan Manuel Fragoso, Elvira Concheiro, and Antonio Gutiérrez, *El poder de la gran burguesía* (Mexico City: Ediciones de Cultura Popular, 1979); Robert Jones Shafer, *Mexican Business Organizations* (Syracuse, N.Y.: Syracuse University Press, 1973); and various authors in *Capitalismo monopolista de estado*, 2 vols. (Mexico City: Edicones de Cultura Popular, 1972).

21. Clark W. Reynolds, *The Mexican Economy: Twentieth-Century Structure and Growth* (New Haven: Yale University Press, 1970).

22. For case studies of Monterrey, see Jesús Puente Leyva, *Distribución del ingreso en un área urbana: el caso de Monterrey* (Mexico City: Siglo XXI, 1969); Menno Vellinga, *Industrialización, burguesía y clase obrera en México: el caso de Monterrey* (Mexico City: Siglo XXI, 1979); and Diana R. Villarreal G. and Rosa Albina Garavito Elías, *Proceso de marginalización y desarrollo capitalista* (Mexico City: Universidad Autónoma de Nuevo León, 1975). For historical background, consult Alex M. Saragoza, "The Formation of a Mexican Elite: The Industrialization of Monterrey, Nuevo León, 1880–1920" (Ph.D. diss., University of California-San Diego, 1979).

23. Harry Braverman, *Labor and Monopoly Capital* (New York: Monthly Review Press, 1974), p. 415.

24. *Uno Más Uno*, November 14, 1979.

25. Salvador Hernández, "The PRI and the Mexican Student Movement of 1968: A Case Study of Repression" (M.A. Thesis, Sociology, University of British Columbia, 1970), p. 42.

26. Carlos Alberto Torres, oral commentary at the Thirteenth Congress of Latin American Sociologists, Panama, November 22, 1979.

27. *Uno Más Uno*, December 3, 1980. On capital's structural obstacles to women's equality, consult Heleieth I. B. Saffioti, "Women, Mode of Production, and Social Formations," *Latin American Perspectives* 4, nos. 1 and 2 (Winter and Spring 1977): 36. I wish to thank professors Veronika Bennholdt-Thomsen and Claudia von Werlhof of the Sociology Department of the Universität Bielefeld for their many hours of theoretical struggle with me on the issues involved in the woman question, which assisted me in its discussion throughout this work. While not in complete agreement with their pioneering views in the area of sex and class, I have benefited from such works of theirs as the following: Bennholdt-Thomsen, "Subsistence Reproduction and Extended Reproduction: A Contribution to the Discussion about Modes of Production," working paper of the Fakultät fur Soziologie, Universität Bielefeld, West Germany (1979), and von Werlhof, "Notes on the Relation Between Sexuality and Economy," *Review*

4, no. 1 (Summer 1980): 33–42; and "Frauenarbeit: der Blinde fleck in der Kritik der Politischen Ökonomie," *Beiträge zur feministischen Theorie und Praxis* 1 (1978): 18–32.

28. For elaboration, see James D. Cockcroft, "Subordinated Technological Development: The Case of Mexico," in *Research in Social Movements, Conflicts and Change*, ed. Louis Kriesberg, (Greenwich, Conn.: JAI Press, Inc., 1982), vol. 4, pp. 183–207; and idem, "Impact of Transnational Corporations on Chile's Social Structure," *Summation* 5, nos. 1 and 2 (Summer 1975): 7–32 (revised in *Cuadernos Politicos* 10 [October-December 1976]: 64–82).

29. Drawing on Marx's thesis that in 1847 both the aristocracy and the bourgeoisie were too weak to rule Germany, Engels wrote: "The present situation in Germany is nothing but a compromise between the nobility and the petty bourgeoisie; it results in putting the administration in the hands of a third class: the bureaucracy" ("The Status Quo in Germany," in Friedrich Engels, *Werke* [Berlin: Dietz Zerlag, 1964–1968]), vol. 4, p. 44. This instance of the bureaucracy as a "class," however, cannot be compared with Mexico's situation where the Mexican and foreign bourgeoisies can scarcely be described as "too weak to rule" and the petty bourgeoisie is impotent compared with that of 1847 Germany: consequently the Mexican bureaucracy has not emerged as a distinct cohesive class. There exists a vast literature on the Mexican state, but it is lacking in case studies integrated with a thoroughgoing analysis of the bureaucracy. The best overview in English on the issues involved is William Loeffler, "Class, State, Hegemony: Theoretical Issues and Mexico" (Ph.D. diss., Sociology, Rutgers University, 1982).

30. For a more dynamic class analysis of bureaucratic groups in the future, one would have to look at the degree to which the jobs of bureaucrats have become proletarianized. For the United States, Braverman *(Labor and Monopoly Capital)* has shown that many bureaucrats, clerks, office workers, service and retail-trade employees, etc., have become a "wage-working proletariat in a new form"; often their work is more manual than intellectual and produces profits or commodities for capitalists at wages lower than those of industrial workers (capital as a social relation). Similar trends have begun to emerge in relatively industrialized Latin American countries dependent on foreign technology.

31. There is a paucity of literature on Mexico's intermediate classes. Three monographs are: Gabriel Careaga, *Mitos y fantasía de la clase media en México* (Mexico City: Joaquín Mortiz, 1974); Francisco López Cámara, *El desafío de la clase media* (Mexico City: Joaquín Mortiz, 1971); and José Calixto Rangel Contla, *La pequeña burguesía en la sociedad mexicana, 1895 a 1960* (Mexico City: UNAM, 1972).

32. Fernando Fajnzylber and Trinidad Martínez Tarrago, *Las empresas transnacionales: expansión a nivel mundial y proyección en la industria mexicana* (Mexico City: FCE, 1976), p. 354; and Víctor Bernal Sahagún, *The Impact of Multinational Corporations on Employment and Income: The Case of Mexico* (Geneva: International Labor Office, 1976), p. 146.

33. Karl Marx, *Capital* (New York: International Publishers, 1967), I: 599.

34. See Bortz's works referred to in note 7, chap. 5.

35. See Javier Aguilar García, "Historia sindical de General Motors y la huelga de 1980," *A* 1, no. 1 (September–December 1980): 91–105; and idem, "El sindicalismo del sector automotriz 1960–1976," *Cuadernos Políticos* 16 (April–June 1978): 44–64; Peter Baird and Ed McCaughan, *Beyond the Border: Mexico and the U.S. Today* (New York: NACLA, 1979); Monica-Claire Gambrill et al., *Maquiladoras* (Mexico City: Centro de Estudios Económicos y Sociales del Tercer Mundo, 1981); José Othón Quiroz Trejo, "Proceso de trabajo en la industrial automotriz terminal: formas de dominación capitalista y respuestas proletarias," *CELA Cuaderno* 40 (1980); idem, "Proceso de trabajo en la industria

automotriz," *Cuadernos Políticos* 26 (October–December 1980): 64–76; and José Luis Reyna and Raúl Trejo Delarbre, *La clase obrera en la historia de México: de Adolfo Ruiz Cortines a Adolfo López Mateos (1952–1964)* (Mexico City: Siglo XXI, 1982).

36. Susan Eckstein, *The Poverty of Revolution: the State and the Urban Poor in Mexico* (Princeton, N.J.: Princeton University Press, 1977). Cf. Wayne Cornelius, *Politics and the Migrant Poor in Mexico City* (Stanford: Stanford University Press, 1975); María Patricia Fernández, "'Chavalas de Maquiladora'—A Study of the Female Labor Force in Ciudad Juárez' Offshore Production Plants" (Ph.D. diss., Rutgers University, 1980); and Gambrill et al., *Maquiladoras*.

37. Notwithstanding, the recent literature on marginalization *is* useful in its description of racism, sexism, oppression, and so-called internal colonialism asserted by stronger groups—for an annotated bibliography, see Antonia Murga Franssinetti, "La marginalidad en América Latina: una bibliografía commentada," *Revista Mexicana de Sociología* 40, no. 1 (1978): 221–331. Critiques of the marginalization approach include Veronika Bennholdt-Thomsen, "Marginalidad en América Latina: una crítica de la teoría" (MS., Universität Bielefeld, Soziologie, 1981); James D. Cockcroft, "Immiseration, Not Marginalization," *Latin American Perspectives* (in press); and "Pauperización, no marginalización," *Coyoacán* 15 (May 1983): 34–52; Pedro Moctezuma and Bernardo Navarro, "Clase obrera, ejército industrial de reserva y movimientos sociales urbanos de las clases dominados en México: 1970–1976," *Teoría y Política* 1, no. 2 (October–December 1980): 53–72; Jorge Montaño, *Los problemas de la ciudad en los asentamientos espontáneos* (Mexico City: Siglo XXI, 1976); Janice Perlman, *O Mito da marginalidade* (Rio de Janeiro, 1977); and Aníbal Quijano Obregón, *Imperialismo y "marginalidad" en América Latina* (Lima, 1977).

38. Marx, *Capital*, I: 633. This is the seed for Marx's polemic against Malthus, treated for the Mexican case by Luis A. Serrón, *Scarcity, Exploitation, and Poverty: Malthus and Marx in Mexico* (Norman: University of Oklahoma Press, 1980). Two pioneering works on contemporary urbanization relating to this are Manuel Castells, *La cuestión urbana* (Mexico City: Siglo XXI, 1975); and Jean Lojkine, *El marxismo, el estado y la cuestión urbana* (Mexico City: Siglo XXI, 1979).

39. Marx, *Capital*, I: 644–45. It is not true that Marx called the various forms of surplus population the "dangerous classes," a colloquial term he applied only to vagabonds, criminals, and prostitutes—and then in quotation marks. Nor did he ever suggest that the most downtrodden, the so-called lumpenproletariat, could serve only reactionary causes. He recognized in the suffering of the surplus population the same degradation of work that increasingly alienates all the proletariat as capitalism develops.

40. Marx, *Capital*, I: 645.

41. Moctezuma and Navarro, "Clase obrera." On Netza, consult Maximiliano Iglesias, *Netzahualcóyotl: testimonios históricos*, 3 vols. (Mexico City: Taller de Impresiones Populares, 1978–1982); and Martín de la Rosa, *Promoción popular y lucha de clases: análisis de un caso, Netzahualcóyotl* (Mexico City: Taller de Impresiones Populares, 1979).

42. Jorge Alonso et al., *Lucha urbana y acumulación de capital* (Mexico City: Editorial de la de Casa Chata, 1980); José Antonio Alonso, *Las costureras domésticas de Netzahualcóyotl* (Puebla: Universidad Autónoma de Puebla, 1981); and idem, *Sexo, trabajo y marginalidad urbana* (Mexico City: Editorial Edicol, 1981); and Cristina Padilla, "Maquiladoras de Santa Cecilia: marginadas o asalariadas?" (Tesis de Licenciatura, Universidad Ibero-Americana, 1978). See also note 27.

43. Alonso et al., *Lucha urbana*, p. 245. For elaboration, see Paul Singer, *Economía política de la urbanización* (Mexico City: Siglo XXI, 1975).

44. Ibid.

45. See Eckstein, *Poverty or Revolution.*
46. See note 24, chap. 5.
47. Sol Tax, *Penny Capitalism* (Chicago: University of Chicago Press, 1963).
48. Comments John G. Taylor: "In one period, sections of the semi-proletariat can be attracted to socialist-based movements emerging from the urban and rural proletariat; in another period they could equally well rally behind a populist movement based on indigenous industrial capital and rural smallholders; in other periods, they can even aspire to the political ideologies of the urban petite-bourgeoisie. The contradictoriness and ambivalence of political movement among this large and powerful section of the proletariat must, therefore, be situated primarily within the place it necessarily occupies 'on the periphery' of production" (*From Modernization to Modes of Production: A Critique of the Sociologies of Development and Underdevelopment* [Atlantic Highlands, N.J.: Humanities Press, 1979], p. 240).
49. De la Rosa, *Promoción popular,* p. 139. *See also* Armando Bartra, "Sobre las clases sociales," (1978) and Eckstein, *Poverty of Revolution.*
50. Eckstein, *Poverty of Revolution,* pp. 101, 107.
51. There are other reasons for noting the political potential of the immiserated. Those authors who have emphasized the role of dependence in leading to the development of metropolitan centers of capitalism at the expense of ex-colonial countries have generally blurred or ignored the internal class dynamics of nations dominated by imperialism, reducing their "analysis" of the poor to a unilinear view of "hopeless marginalization." In the case of Mexico, the class dynamics are far more complex, more deeply rooted in the growth of domestic monopoly capital and a strong state, and more pregnant with hope and change than any vulgar theory of dependence or marginalization would suggest. Misguided theory, like erroneous theoretical premises in general, leads not only to faulty political strategy but also, in this case, to one form of "hopeless" conclusion or another—in a word, *defeatism.*

Chapter 7: The Crisis, 1968–1977

1. A folk saying encapsulates the point better than any sociological treatise: "Pobre México, tan lejos de Dioz y tan cerca de los Estados Unidos" ("Poor Mexico, so far from God and so near to the United States").
2. In 1966 Bo Anderson and I first developed an analysis of Mexican cooptation techniques in the article "Control and Cooptation in Mexican Politics." I expanded and refined the analysis the following year in "Coercion and Ideology in Mexican Politics." Both articles appear in James D. Cockcroft, Andre Gunder Frank, and Dale L. Johnson, *Dependence and Underdevelopment: Latin America's Political Economy* (New York: Anchor Books, 1972), pp. 219–68.
3. NACLA, *Mexico 1968* (New York: NACLA, 1968).
4. *NACLA Report on the Americas,* January/February 1978. Cf. the following issues of the same journal: July/August 1976; January 1977; March 1977; July/August 1977; September/October 1977; January/February 1978; March/April 1978; May/June 1978; and September/October 1978. The author gratefully acknowledges the assistance of Professor Sheldon Liss of the University of Akron's History Department for compilation of much of this material. The *New York Times* reported on November 22, 1977, that the FBI "conducted extensive operations in Mexico to undermine Communist groups there that it said might

filter across the border." More than a hundred pages of material released under the Freedom of Information Act are available for consultation at the FBI headquarters in Washington.

5. Such was the case, for example, with the worker-peasant-student Coalition of Oaxaca (COCEO) and Coalition of the Isthmus (COCEI). Among quarreling leftist parties, some have accused the Socialist Workers Party (PST) of subordinating peasants it has organized in Veracruz to the state-administered coffee and tobacco corporations TABAMEX and INMECAFE.

6. For an excellent elaboration on the crisis in capital accumulation, consult Manuel Castells, *The Economic Crisis and American Society* (Princeton, N.J.: Princeton University Press, 1980); and idem, *La teoría marxista de las crisis económicas y las transformaciones del capitalismo* (Mexico City: Siglo XXI, 1978), along with various issues of *Monthly Review*. On the character of the production process, see Harry Braverman, *Labor and Monopoly Capital* (New York: Monthly Review Press, 1974); and María Patricia Fernández, "'Chavalas de Maquiladora'—A Study of the Female Labor Force in Ciudad Juárez' Offshore Production Plants" (Ph.D. diss. Rutgers University, 1980).

7. Juan Castaingts Teillery, "Los precios de producción en el modelo de acumulación mexicano," *Iztapalpa* 2, no. 3 (July–December 1980): 5–38. Jeffrey Bortz offers a similar analysis of Mexico's weak accumulation process in his works cited in note 7 of Chapter 5 and links it to Mexico's comparatively low productivity with excellent tables of statistics in "Wage Determination in Mexico" (unpublished MS, 1981). On the relation between Mexico's subcapitalization and generation of employment discussed in the next paragraph, consult Mario Margulis, "Petróleo, indocumentados y maquiladoras: teoría de la renta y transferencia de valor," *Arte, Sociedad, Ideología* 6 (1979): 103–19.

8. Nafinsa-Unida, "A Strategy to Develop Capital Goods in Mexico" (Mexico City: Nacional Financiera, 1977).

9. Banco de México, annual reports.

10. For a sampling of issues involved in recent debates about unequal exchange, see Charles Bettelheim's critique of Emmanuel, in Arghiri Emmanuel, *Unequal Exchange: A Study of Imperialism of Trade* (New York: Monthly Review Press, 1972); and Harry Magdoff's illuminating historical discussion in his *Imperialism: From the Colonial Age to the Present* (New York: Monthly Review Press, 1978).

11. Alonso Aguilar, "La burguesía no sólo manda, gobierna," *Estrategia* 28 (July–August 1979): 2–32.

12. *Uno Más Uno*, January 15, 1978.

13. Cited in *NACLA Report on the Americas*, "Dateline." July–August 1977.

14. James D. Cockcroft, unpublished field notes, 1981.

15. Basic primers on the world petroleum industry are Anthony Sampson, *The Seven Sisters* (New York: Bantam Books, 1975); Michael Tanzer, *The Political Economy of International Oil and the Underdeveloped Countries* (Boston: Beacon Press, 1969); idem, *The Energy Crisis: World Struggle for Power and Wealth* (New York: Monthly Review Press, 1974). Five U.S. oil giants reportedly earned $30 billion between 1962 and 1968 while paying federal taxes of only $1.4 billion (4.7 percent)—such low taxes amount to a subsidy by other U.S. taxpayers, one vastly augmented in 1981 by the Reagan administration's tax giveaway to big oil.

16. James D. Cockcroft, unpublished field notes, 1964.

17. The phrasing is that of Professor John J. Johnson of Stanford University, as quoted by *Newsweek*, August 23, 1965—and the message is carried through the panoply of U.S. military training institutions from Panama to Puerto Rico that have provided instruction for most Latin American dictators and presidents in recent decades.

18. Cited in *The News* (Mexico City), July 21, 1981.
19. ABM, *Informe del congreso directivo a la convención anual* (1973).
20. *Uno Más Uno*, March 11, 1978.
21. *El Día*, May 17, 1975.

Chapter 8: The Crisis Prolonged, 1978–1982

1. *Proceso*, September 22, 1980.
2. *Cencos*, February 1980, p. 5.
3. *Proceso*, November 14, 1977.
4. Ibid., April 6, 1981. For an excellent analysis of the different, conflicting tendencies with the Mexican Church, consult Martín de la Rosa, "La iglesia católica mexicana y el conflicto social, 1965–1979" (Ph.D. diss., Ecole des Hautes Etudes, Sciences Sociales, 1981).
5. Because the migrants come and go with such frequency and are difficult to count, their exact numbers are unknown; all empirical studies concur that the size of the Mexican undocumented population in the United States at various moments during the years 1975, 1976, and 1977 was at least 235,000 and no more than 2.9 million. I have elaborated on Mexican migration in the following works: "Mexican Migration, Crisis, and the Internationalization of Labor Struggle," *Contemporary Marxism* 5 (July 1982): 48–61; (with Jorge Bustamante), "Unequal Exchange in the Binational Relationship: The Case of Immigration Labor," in *Mexican-U.S. Relations: Conflict or Convergence?* ed. Carlos Vásquez and Manuel García y Griego (Los Angeles: UCLA Chicano Studies Research Center, 1982); "One More Time: The 'Undocumented,'" *Radical America* 15, no. 6 (November–December 1981): 6–15; "Mexico-E.U.: la frontera invisible," *Nexos* 42 (June 1981); and (with Universidad Autónoma Metropolitana-Azcapotzalco Migration Research Team), *Trabajadores de Michoacán: historia de un pueblo migrante* (Morelia: IMISAC, 1982) and *Migración y problemas fronterizos* (forthcoming). I want to thank the many members of the UAM-Azcapotzalco Migration Research Team for their suggestions and ongoing work in this area for broadening the understanding of this complex subject.
6. *Latin American Weekly Report*, February 8, 1980.
7. Manuel Castells, *La teoría marxista de las crisis económicas y las transformaciones del capitalismo* (Mexico City: Siglo XXI, 1978), p. 15.
8. Prevailing immigration law (U.S. Congress, 7 U.S.C., Section 1324) permits an employer to hire undocumented workers, and the employer can decide unilaterally if the migrant will be treated as a worker or as a "criminal." Sanctioned by what in fact is a labor law disguised as an immigration law, the position of the undocumented worker is an almost totally defenseless one. The structural characteristics of inequality historically produced in the relations between the two countries here takes on an intensified micro-dimensional form: boss/slave.
9. Herman Baca, various press conferences, and interview reprinted in Committee on Chicano Rights, *A Chicano Perspective on the President's Immigration Proposals* (1981, available from CCR, 1837 Highland Ave., National City, CA 92050).
10. Various press clippings, including reports on press conferences held by Herman Baca, Jorge Bustamante, and James Cockcroft in San Ysidro, California, January 27, 1982 (*San Diego Union* and the *Tribune* of San Diego, January 28, 1982).
11. Since their incorporation into the United States after the 1848 U.S. conquest of almost half of Mexico's territory, Mexicans in the Southwest have experienced

an extreme racism second only to that suffered by Indians in the region. Swindled out of their properties, robbed, attacked, lynched, and abused without fair judicial recourse, they and their descendants supposedly protected under the Treaty of Guadalupe Hidalgo have put up a stiff but usually futile resistance. See the pioneering work of Rodolfo Acuña, *Occupied America: A History of Chicanos* (New York: Harper & Row, 1981). In New Mexico, the movement to reclaim lands stolen from Mexicans after the Treaty of Guadalupe Hidalgo took on a new militance in the 1960s under the initial leadership of Reies Lopez Tijerina. There developed increased contact between this rural movement and other civil rights and progressive groups in the United States. Thus a wider public came to know of the land and cultural claims of these Mexican descendants and also of the repression they have suffered, the endless legal charges and harassments, and the vigilante arson and assaults that still take place with official complacency or complicity.

12. A few used the movement to climb the social ladder (Chicanos have their "Uncle Toms," known as *tíos tacos* for their aping of "anglo" ways); others grew disillusioned with the lack of progress and wandered into mystical cults; some became so busy struggling to survive economically that they had "little time for politics"—but a significant number kept up the political struggle and remain active today.

13. Interview with Peter Schey, December 23, 1981.

14. There is an unmistakable historical pattern of capital's using increased deportations at those moments when it seeks more, not less, immigrant labor—the deportations serve to make the migrants more tractable, as well as to drain off any surplus that accumulates in the labor pool—see Ernesto Galarza, *Merchants of Labor: The Mexican Bracero Story* (Santa Barbara: McNally & Loftin, 1964).

15. I gratefully acknowledge the assistance of the following persons for their information on this new labor militancy among so-called undocumented workers: Pete Beltran of UAW, Humberto Camacho of UE, Juan Gutiérrez of the American Federation of Workers, and José Luis Pérez Conchola of the Centro de Información e Estudios Migratorios—the first three in Los Angeles and the last-named in Tijuana—and Raúl Hinojosa of *Sin Fronteras* magazine (Chicago).

16. See Kitty Calavita, "The Dialectics of U.S. Immigration Policy, 1820–1924, with Implications for the Contemporary Debate," *Contemporary Crisis* (Fall 1981).

17. The granting of the letters stemmed from a 1977 class-action lawsuit filed and won in the U.S. Supreme Court by Refugio Silva, charging that quotas for people in the Western Hemisphere who wished to immigrate were applied in a discriminatory fashion (e.g., Mexican quotas were used to let in Cuban refugees).

18. I want to thank members of the teachers' strike movement, particularly Juana María Gandy, for their generous help in providing information on their struggle.

19. James D. Cockcroft, unpublished field notes, 1981.

20. Cited in *Latin America Political Report,* December 15, 1978.

21. I want to thank Ross Gandy for his assistance in sorting out the many opposition parties and their positions in Mexico. The only significant one not discussed in the text lost its registration by its poor showing in the 1982 elections and is unlikely to make a comeback. It is the PARM (Authentic Party of the Mexican Revolution), a neopopulist party whose ideology is indistinguishable from PRI's. Many of its leaders for decades have been aging male generals or veterans of the 1910–1920 Revolution. PARM claims that what the PRI does it can do better. Most Mexicans are all too familiar with what the PRI does, and the promise of doing it better hardly excites them.

Glossary

ABM: Asociación de Banqueros Mexicanos, or Mexican Bankers' Association, private organizational heart of Mexican financial capital.

Agiotistas: Moneylenders.

Agrarista: Militant peasant demanding land reform since the late 1920s.

AID: Agency for International Development (U.S. government).

ALFA group: Part of Monterrey's big finance capital based partly on the steel industry and petrochemicals.

Aparcero: Partner in small farm plot, private or ejidal.

Arrendatario capitalista: A renter of land who pays the *hacendado* or *latifundista* rent and retains the profits from production.

Avecinado: Squatter accepted by the community.

Bajío: Greater Guanajuato area in central Mexico, rich in mining, agriculture, and manufacture; traditional "food basket."

Baldío laws: "Vacant land" decrees of 1863, 1883, and 1894 used to dispossess Indians of their landholdings and to concentrate land in the hands of the *latifundistas.*

BARAPEM: Batallón de Radio-Patrullas del Estado de México, or Radio-Patrol Battalion of the State of Mexico, an elite paramilitary unit used to attack "land invaders" in Mexico City and to harrass the poor.

Bracero: Term used to describe a Mexican migrant worker in the United States after the 1942–1964 Emergency Farm Labor Program agreed to between the U.S. and Mexican governments.

Cacique: Local boss.

Caciquismo: System or practice of *caciques.*

Calpulli: An Aztec community endowed with commonly held, inalienable land; evolved into religious, military, or administrative unit.

CAM: Congreso Agrario Mexicano, or Mexican Agrarian Council, an independent peasant organization later coopted by the government.

CANACINTRA: Cámara Nacional de Industrias de Transformación, or National Chamber of Transformation Industries, a state-affiliated organization of small and medium manufacturers, now including monopoly firms; part of CCE.

Capitulación: A contract awarded the leader of an overseas expedition by the Spanish Crown, granting him restricted rights and holding him to various obligations.

Casa de Contratación: Spain's Board of Trade.

Casta: Race mixture.

Caudillo: Strong regional leader, sometimes achieving national power; military strongman.

CCE: Consejo Coordinador Empreserial, or Management Coordinating Council, incorporating heads of all major private and state-affiliated capitalist organizations; the voice of Mexican monopoly capital.

CCI: Confederación Campesina Independiente, or Independent Peasant Confederation, a radical peasant organization founded in the 1960s and later coopted by the government.

344

Central: An organization of leaders and/or militants in any movement, linking up different regions or elements.

CGOCM: Confederación General de Obreros y Campesinos de México, or General Confederation of Workers and Peasants of Mexico, established in 1933; an early foundation of organized labor's CTM (created in 1936).

Charrismo: Corruption, violence, and anti-democratic behavior associated with *charros* (union bosses).

Charro: Derogatory but common term for trade-union leader involved in corruption, violence, or anti-democratic behavior.

Chinampa: So-called floating gardens used by Aztecs; some remain near Mexico City.

Científicos: Porfirio Díaz' braintrust of Positivists and Social Darwinists who grew wealthy while providing a proforeigner capitalist ideology for the oligarchic-capitalist state.

CNC: Confederación Nacional Campesina, or National Peasant Confederation, the official confederation of peasants.

CNH: Consejo Nacional de Huelga, or National Strike Council (of student organizations, 1968).

CNOP: Confederación Nacional de Organizaciones Populares, or National Confederation of Popular Organizations, the so-called middle class sector of the PRI; incorporates diverse elements, including the urban poor.

CNT: Central Nacional de Trabajadores, or National Central of Workers, a labor confederation; part of CT.

COCEI/COCEO: Worker-peasant-student Coalition of the Isthmus and Coalition of Oaxaca, independent progressive mass movements.

Colonia proletaria: An urban slum.

Colonos: Private possessors of state lands in agrarian colonies.

Compadrazco: Godparenthood; a patriarchical form of strengthening class hierarchy and patron-client relations.

Comunero: Member of a village community or *ejido.*

CONAMUP: Coordinadora Nacional de Movimientos Urbanos Populares, or National Council of Popular Urban Movements, a network of organizations of the urban poor seeking radical reforms, founded in 1981.

CONASUPO: Compañía Nacional de Subsistencias Populares, or National Company of Popular Goods, state agency meant to provide low-cost food for the masses.

CONCAMIN: Confederación de Cámaras de Industria, or Confederation of Chambers of Industries, a state-affiliated organization of industrial firms, including CANACINTRA and joint Mexican-foreign enterprises; some ties to state fraction of bourgeoisie; part of CCE.

CONCANACO: Confederación de Cámaras Naciónales de Comercio, or Confederation of National Chambers of Commerce, a state-affiliated organization of big commercial capital; some ties to state fraction of bourgeoisie; part of CCE.

Consulado: Merchant guild.

COPARMEX: Confederación Patronal de la República de México, or Employers' Confederation, of the Mexican Republic, a private organization of capitalists, mainly from Monterrey Group; part of CCE.

Corregidor: Local Spanish official in charge of districts, tribute collection, and all local residents.

COSINA: Coordinadora Sindical Nacional, or National Trade Union Council, a network of popular organizations of rank-and-file workers founded in 1982 to coordinate the defense of democratic demands.

Criollos: Spanish-descended whites born in colonial Mexico.

CROM: Confederación Regional Obrera Mexicana or Regional Mexican Worker Confederation, a state-backed national labor organization influential in the 1918–1929 period.

CT: Congresso de Trabajo, or Congress of Labor, the official labor umbrella organization incorporating leaders from CTM, CNT, and other labor confederations or unions.

CTM: Confederación de Trabajadores Mexicanos, or Confederation of Mexican Workers, the official national labor confederation, with an estimated 2 million members.

Cúspide: Summit.

CYDSA: Celulosa y Perisados, S.A., a chemical group within the Monterrey Group.

Democratic Tendency (DT): Anti-*charro,* reform-minded trade unionists within CTM and MSR.

Diezmo: One-tenth of produce delivered to the Catholic Church hierarchy by peasants, artisans, and other small producers (mostly phased out).

Ejidal: Of or relating to *ejidos.*

Ejidatario: Owner of a parcel of an *ejido.*

Ejido: Traditional Indian village land, often communal; now 90 percent noncollective units composed of individual holdings.

Empresario del estado: High-salaried manager or director of a state enterprise, usually part of bureaucratic fraction of the bourgeoisie.

Encomendero: Holder of an *encomienda* and its Indian labor and product.

Encomienda: Crown decree allowing a conquistador to have access to Indians and their labor, but not their land.

FAT: Frente Auténtico del Trabajo, or Authentic Labor Front, an independent trade-unionist front outside CTM.

FNCR: Frente Nacional Contra la Represión, or National Front Against Repression, a leftist coalition influential in national politics.

Fotonovelas: Cheap, mass-circulation paperback novels with simple vocabulary and drawings or photographs.

Frijoles: Beans, the main source of protein in the Mexican diet.

Fuero: A special right, privilege, or jurisdiction.

Gachupín: Derogatory term for Spaniard or *peninsular.*

GDP: Gross Domestic Product.

GNP: Gross National Product.

Golpe militar: Military *coup d'état.*

Granaderos: Elite riot-squad corps.

Hacendado: Owner of an hacienda; large landholder.

Hacienda: Large landholding, often with industrial installations within its boundaries.

IMF: International Monetary Fund.

Indigenismo: Ideology of respect for the Indian heritage and the Indian peoples; used by all forces seeking political power as well as by the government to destroy Indian culture and integrate Indians into the national economy.

Ingenio: (Sugar)mill.

INI: Instituto Nacional Indigenista, or National Indian Institute, a state agency helping to integrate Indians into the national economy.

Jefe: Boss.

Jornalero: Day laborer.

Ladino: Spanish-speaking Indian who assimilates into white or mestizo culture.

Latifundio, latifundium: Large landholding.

Latifundista: Large landholder.

Letrados: University-trained lawyers who often became part of Spanish bureaucracy.

Maize: Corn.

MAP: Movimiento de Acción Popular, or Movement of Popular Action, dissolved into PSUM.

Maquiladora: Assembly plant.

MAUS: Movimiento de Acción y Unidad Socialista, or Socialist Movement for Action and Unity, dissolved into PSUM.

Mayeques: Bondsmen tilling Aztec nobility's lands.

Mayordomo: Foreman or administrator of a farm or hacienda.

Mestizo: Person of mixed Indian/white descent.

Milpa: Small parcel of land, often producing corn.

Minifundio, minifundium: Small land parcel; subsistence plot.

Minifundista: Holder of a *minifundium;* subsistence farmer.

Misceláneas: One-room stores selling tobacco, soft drinks, cookies, oils, etc.

Monterrey group: A conservative and reactionary cluster of big and medium capitalists, dominated by the ALFA and VISA groups.

Mordida: "Little bite," or bribe.

MSR: Movimiento Sindical Revolucionario, or Revolutionary Trade Union Movement, incorporating dissident electrical workers and other "Democratic Tendency" unionists.

Mulatto: Afro-white person.

Municipio: Administrative unit of cluster of towns or communities.

Nacionalero: Occupier of state land whose status has not been regularized.

Nafinsa: Nacional Financiera, an industrial development bank of state and private capital, with the state holding the majority of shares.

Neolatifundismo: System of accumulating a grid of landholdings, often under different names or ruses, under a single landowner.

Obraje: Textile workshop.

PAN: Partido de Acción Nacional, or National Action Party (right wing).

Patrón: Employer or "boss."

Patronazgo: Godfather system.

PCM: Partido Comunista Mexicano, or Mexican Communist Party, dissolved into PSUM.

PDM: Partido Democrático Mexicano, or Mexican Democratic Party (right wing).

PEMEX: Petróleos Mexicanos, the state-owned oil complex.

Peninsulares: Spaniards born in Spain.

Personalismo: A kind of "spoils system" based on personal contacts and favors.

PMT: Partido Mexicano de Trabajadores, or Mexican Workers' Party (left-wing anti-government party).

PNR: Partido Nacional Revolucionario, or National Revolutionary Party, founded in 1929 and early forerunner of the governing PRI.

Político: Politician.

Porros: Armed thugs operating as goon squads against the Left and against popular movements seeking reform.

PPM: Partido del Pueblo Mexicano, or Mexican People's Party, a Left split from the PPS; dissolved into PSUM.

PPS: Partido Popular Socialista, or Popular Socialist Party (reformist).

Predio: A farm of any size.

Prestanombres: Mexicans lending their names to foreign capitalists to help them get around nationalist laws regulating foreign investment.

PRI: Partido Revolucionario Institucional, or Institutional Revolutionary Party, official political party running government.

PRM: Partido de la Revolución Mexicana, or Party of the Mexican Revolution, established in 1938 to replace the PNR; direct forerunner of today's governing PRI.

PRT: Partido Revolucionario de Trabajadores, or Revolutionary Workers' Party (Trotskyist).

PSD: Partido Social Democrático, or Social Democratic Party (reformist).

PSR: Partido Socialista Revolucionario, or Revolutionary Socialist Party, a left split from the PST; dissolved into the PSUM.

348 *Mexico*

PST: Partido Socialista de Trabajadores, or Socialist Workers' Party (reformist).

PSUM: Partido Socialista Unificado de México, or Unified Socialist Party of Mexico, founded in 1981 as a left-unity party incorporating the PCM, PPM, PSR, MAUS, and MAP.

Ranchero: Small landholder or farmer, owning or renting a *rancho.*

Rancho: Small estate or homestead farm owned or rented.

Reforma política: A political reform package, cosmetic in character, introduced by President José López Portillo (1976–1982).

Repartimiento: Labor share-out system based on royal permissions and payments in wages.

SAM: Sistema de Alimentación Mexicana, or Mexican Alimentation System, introduced by government in 1980 to try to make Mexico self-sufficient in food production.

Sepafin: Secretaría de Patrimonio y Fomento Industrial, or Ministry of National Properties and Industrial Promotion.

Sexenio: Six-year administration of a president, the single term in office prescribed by the 1917 Constitution.

Sinarquistas: Extreme-right, neo-fascist organization, strong in 1930s and still active today.

SUTERM: Largest electrical workers' union.

Técnico: Technocrat.

Tienda de raya: Company store.

Tlacotin: So-called slaves, about 5 percent of population under the Aztecs.

TNC: Transnational corporation.

Topes: Wage ceilings.

Tumultos: Underdog riot-revolts in colonial Mexico's cities.

UNAM: Universidad Nacional Autónoma de México, or National University of Mexico.

UOI: Unidad Obrera Independiente, or Independent Worker Unity, the organization of independent trade unionists outside CTM; strong in the automotive and aviation industries.

Vidrio group: Part of Monterrey's big finance capital, based in part on the glass and bottling industry.

VISA group: Part of Monterrey's big finance capital, based in part on the brewery industry.

Visitador: Inspector appointed by the Crown.

Zambo: Afro-Indian person.

Selected Bibliography

This selected bibliography does not pretend to be comprehensive, although it is representative of the general literature on Mexico. It aims to accomplish two purposes. First, the lay reader can find here basic introductory texts, readable overviews, interesting case studies, and some standard bibliographical works. Second, the scholar can find recent works published in Mexico or Europe that supplement or advance well-known earlier works in both Spanish and English. The abbreviations FCE, INAH, SEP, and UNAM respectively stand for: Fondo de Cultura Económica, Instituto Nacional de Antropología e Historia, Secretaría de Educación Pública, and Universidad Nacional Autónoma de México. A more complete version of the bibliography can be obtained from the author at Friends Lake, Chestertown, N.Y. 12817.

Acuña, Rodolfo. *Occupied America: A History of Chicanos.* New York: Harper & Row, 1981.
Aguilar, Alonso and Carrión, Jorge. *La burguesía, la oligarquía y el estado.* Mexico City: Nuestro Tiempo, 1972.
Aguilar Camín, Hector, ed. *Interpretaciones de la revolución mexicana.* Mexico City: Nueva Imagen, 1979.
Aguilar García, Javier. *La política sindical en México: industria del automovil.* Mexico City: Era, 1982.
Aguilar Mora, Manuel. *El bonapartismo mexicano.* 2 vols. Mexico City: Juan Pablos Editor, 1982.
Aguilera, Manuel. *La desnacionalización de la economía mexicana.* Mexico City: FCE, 1975.
Aguirre Beltrán, Gonzalo. *La población negra de México, 1519–1810.* Mexico City, 1946.
Alonso, Antonio. *El movimiento ferrocarrilero en México, 1958–1959.* Mexico City: Era, 1972.
Alonso, Jorge, ed. *Lucha urbana y acumulación de capital.* Mexico City: Ediciones de la Casa Chata, 1980.
Alperovich, M. S. *Historia de la independencia en México.* Mexico City: Grijalbo, 1967.
Alvarez, Alejandro. "El movimiento obrero ante la crisis económica." *Cuadernos Políticos* 16 (April–June 1978).
Anderson, Rodney D. *Outcasts in Their Own Land: Mexican Industrial Workers, 1906–1911.* DeKalb: Northern Illinois University Press, 1976.
Angeles, Luis. *Crisis y coyuntura de la economía mexicana.* Mexico City: El Caballito, 1978.

350 *Mexico*

Anguiano, Arturo. *El estado y política obrera del cardenismo.* Mexico City: Era, 1978.

Archer, Christon I. *The Army in Bourbon Mexico, 1760–1810.* Albuquerque: University of New Mexico Press, 1977.

Arizpe, Lourdes. *Migración, etnicismo y cambio económico: un estudio sobre migrantes campesinos a la ciudad de México.* Mexico City: Colegio de México, 1978.

Ashby, Joe C. *Organized Labor and the Mexican Revolution under Lázaro Cárdenas.* Chapel Hill: University of North Carolina Press, 1967.

Baird, Peter and McCaughan, ed. *Beyond the Border: Mexico and the U.S. Today.* New York: NACLA, 1979.

Bakewell, P. J. *Silver Mining and Society in Colonial Mexico: Zacatecas, 1546–1700.* Cambridge: Cambridge University Press, 1971.

Barchfield, John W. *Peasants, Politics, and Development in Mexico.* New Brunswick, N.J.: Transaction Books, 1982.

Barkin, David. *Desarrollo regional y reorganización campesina.* Mexico City: Nueva Imagen, 1978.

————et al. *Las relaciones México/Estados Unidos,* Mexico City: Nueva Imagen, 1980.

————and Esteva, Gustavo. *Inflación y democracia: el caso de México.* Mexico City: Siglo XXI, 1979.

Bartra, Armando. "Sobre las clases sociales en el campo mexicano." *Cuadernos Agrarios* 1 (1976).

Bartra, Roger. "Capitalism and the Peasantry in Mexico." *Latin American Perspectives* 9 (Winter 1982).

————. *Estructrura agraria y clases sociales en México.* Mexico City: Era, 1974.

————. *El poder despótico burgués.* Mexico City: Era, 1978.

————et al. *Caciquismo y poder político en el México rural.* Mexico City: Siglo XXI, 1975.

Basáñez, Miguel. *La lucha por la hegemonía en México: 1968–1980.* Mexico City: Siglo XXI, 1981.

Basurto, Jorge. *El conflicto internacional en torno al petróleo de México.* Mexico City: Siglo XXI, 1976.

————. *El proletariado industrial en México, 1850–1930.* Mexico City: UNAM, 1975.

Bazant, Jan. *Alienation of Church Wealth in Mexico.* Cambridge: Cambridge University Press, 1971.

————. *A Concise History of Mexico from Hidalgo to Cárdenas, 1805–1940.* New York: Cambridge University Press, 1977.

Bazin, Maurice and Anderson, Sam. *Ciencia e Independencia.* 2 vols. Lisbon: Livros Horizonte, 1977.

Benítez, Fernando. *Las indios de México,* 4 vols. Mexico City: Era, 1972.

Bennett, Douglas and Sharpe, Kenneth. "Controlling the Multinationals: The Illogic of Mexicanization." In Lawrence V. Gould and Harry Targ, eds., *Global Dominance and Dependence.* Brunswick, Ohio: King's Court Communications, 1981.

Bennholdt-Thomsen, Veronika. "Investment in the Poor: Analysis of World Bank Policy." *Social Scientist* 91–92 (1980).

————. "Toward a Class Analysis of Agrarian Sectors: Mexico." *Latin American Perspectives* 7 (Fall 1980).

Bermúdez, Antonio J. *The Mexican Petroleum Industry: A Case Study in Nationalization.* Stanford: Stanford University Institute of Latin American Studies, 1963.

Bernal Sahagún, Víctor. *Anatomía de la publicidad en México, monopolios, enajenación y desperdicio.* Mexico City: Nuestro Tiempo, 1974.

————. *Impact of Multinational Corporations on Employment and Income: The Case of Mexico.* Geneva: ILO, 1976.

Bernstein, Marvin D. *The Mexican Mining Industry, 1890–1950*. Albany: State University of New York, 1965.

Blair, Calvin P. *The Political Economy of Mexican Development*. Austin: University of Texas Press, 1981.

Blaisdell, Lowell L. *The Desert Revolution: Baja California, 1911*. Madison: University of Wisconsin Press, 1962.

Boils, Guillermo. *Los militares en México, 1915–1974*. Mexico City: El Caballito, 1975.

Bonfil Batalla, Guillermo, ed. *Utopia y revolución*. Mexico City: Nueva Imagen, 1981.

Bortz, Jeffrey. "Industrial Wages in Mexico City, 1939–1975." Ph.D. diss., UCLA, 1982.

Brachet, Viviane. *La población de los estados mexicanos, 1824–1895*. Mexico City: INAH, 1976.

Brading, D. A. *Haciendas and Ranchos in the Mexican Bajío: León, 1700–1860*. Cambridge: Cambridge University Press, 1979.

—————. *Miners and Merchants in Bourbon Mexico, 1763–1810*. Cambridge: Cambridge University Press, 1971.

Brandenburg, Frank R. *The Making of Modern Mexico*. Englewood Cliffs, N.J.: Prentice-Hall, 1964.

Burbach, Roger and Flynn, Patricia. *Agribusiness in the Americas*. New York: Monthly Review Press, 1980.

Bustamante, Jorge and Cockcroft, James D. "Unequal Exchange in the Binational Relationship: The Case of Immigration Labor." In Carlos Vásquez and Manuel García y Griego, eds., *Mexico-U.S. Relations: Conflict or Convergence?* Los Angeles: UCLA Chicano Studies Research Center, 1982.

Calvert, Peter. *The Mexican Revolution 1910–1914: The Diplomacy of Anglo-American Conflict*. New York: Cambridge University Press, 1968.

Camarillo, Albert. *Chicanos in a Changing Society*. Cambridge, Mass.: Harvard University Press, 1979.

Camp, Roderic A. *Mexican Political Biographies, 1935–1975*. Tucson: University of Arizona Press, 1976.

Campa, Valentín. *Mi testimonio*. Mexico City: Ediciones de Cultura Popular, 1978.

Cárdenas, Lázaro. *Ideario político*. Mexico City: Era, 1972.

Cardenas, Gilbert. "Immigrant Women in the Labor Force." Unpublished ms. Austin: University of Texas, 1981.

Cardoso, Ciro F. S. *México en el siglo XIX*. Mexico City: Nueva Imagen, 1980.

—————, ed. *Formación y desarrollo de la burguesía en México, siglo XIX*. Mexico City: Siglo XXI, 1978.

Cardoso, Lawrence A. *Mexican Emigration to the United States, 1897–1931*. Tucson: University of Arizona Press, 1980.

Carr, Barry. *El movimiento obrero y la política en México, 1910–1929*. 2 vols. Mexico City: SepSetentas, 1976.

Castellanos Guerrero, Alicia. *Ciudad Juárez: La vida fronteriza*. Mexico City: Nuestro Tiempo, 1981.

Castillo, Heberto and Paoli, Francisco J. *El poder robado*. Mexico City: Edamex, 1980.

Castrejón Diez, Jaime and Pérez Lizaur, Marisol. *Historia de las universidades estatales*. 2 vols. Mexico City: SEP, 1976.

Ceceña, José Luis. *México en la orbita imperial*. Mexico City: El Caballito, 1970.

Centro de Estudios Históricos del Movimiento Obrero Mexicano. *Cuadernos Obreros*, various vols.

Centro de Estudios Internacionales. *Indocumentados: mitos y realidades*. Mexico City: Colegio de México, 1979.

—————. *Las perspectivas del petróleo mexicano*. Mexico City: Colegio de México, 1979.

Centro de Investigación y Docencia Económicas (CIDE). *Economía mexicana*. Mexico City: CIDE, 1980.

Chance, John K. *Race and Class in Colonial Oaxaca.* Stanford: Stanford University Press, 1978.

Chávez Orozco, Luis. *La agonía del artesanado mexicano.* Mexico City: Aloma, 1958.

Chávez, Elias. *Los priistas.* Mexico City: Ed. Proceso, 1980.

Chevalier, François. *Land and Society in Colonial Mexico.* Berkeley: University of California Press, 1963.

Coatsworth, John H. *Growth Against Development: The Economic Impact of Railroads in Porfirian Mexico.* DeKalb: Northern Illinois University Press, 1981.

Cockcroft, James D. "Immiseration, Not Marginalization." *Latin American Perspectives* (in press, 1983).

—————. "Mexican Migration, Crisis, and the Internationalization of Labor Struggle." *Contemporary Marxism* 5 (July 1982).

—————. *Intellectual Precursors of the Mexican Revolution, 1900–1913.* Austin: University of Texas Press, 1968.

—————and Gandy, Ross. "The Mexican Volcano." *Monthly Review* 33 (May 1981).

—————and UAM-Azcapotzalco Migration Research Team, eds. "Migración, problemas fronterizos, y crisis." *Revista "A"* 7 (December 1982).

—————. *Testimonios de la migración.* Mexico City: Ed. Trillas, 1983.

—————. *Trabajadores de Michoacán: historia de un pueblo migrante.* Mexico City: imisac Ediciones "Contraste," 1982.

Colón Reyes, Linda Ivette. "La manufactura textil mexicana, antes de la fundación del banco de avío [1830]." *Revista Mexicana de Ciencias Políticas y Sociales* 83 (January–March 1976).

Congreso Latinoamericano de Petroquímica. *Petroquímica en México.* Mexico City, 1978.

Consejo Nacional de Ciencia y Desarrollo. *El petróleo en México y en el mundo.* Mexico City: 1979.

Contreras, Ariel José. *México 1940: Industrialización y crisis política.* Mexico City: Siglo XXI, 1977.

Cordera, Rolando and Tello, Carlos. *México la disputa por la nación.* Mexico City: Siglo XXI, 1981.

Córdova, Arnaldo. *La ideología de la revolución mexicana.* Mexico City: Era, 1973.

—————. *La política de masas del cardenismo.* Mexico City: Era, 1974.

—————. *La política de masas y el futuro de la izquierda en México.* Mexico City: Era, 1979.

Cornelius, Wayne. *Politics and the Migrant Poor in Mexico City.* Stanford, Ca.: Stanford University Press, 1975.

Cosío Villegas, Daniel, ed. *Historia moderna de México.* 10 vols. Mexico City: Hermes, 1955–63.

Costeloe, Michael. *Church Wealth in Mexico: A Study of the "Juzgado de Capellanías" in the Archbishopric of Mexico, 1800–1856.* Cambridge: Cambridge University Press, 1967.

Cross, Harry E. and Sandos, James A. *Rural Development in Mexico and Recent Migration to the United States.* Berkeley: Institute of Governmental Studies, University of California, 1982.

Cué Cánovas, Agustín. *La industria en México, 1521–1845.* Mexico City: Centenario, 1959.

Cumberland, Charles C. *The Mexican Revolution: The Constitutionalist Years.* Austin: University of Texas Press, 1972.

De la Luz Arriaga, María. "El magisterio en lucha." *Cuadernos Políticos* 27 (January–March 1981).

De la Peña, Sergio. *La formación del capitalismo en México.* Mexico City: Siglo XXI, 1975.

De la Rosa M., Martin. "La Iglesia católica en México: del Vaticano II a la CELAM (1965–1979)." *Cuadernos Políticos* 19 (January–March 1979).

De Oliveira, Orlandina. "Industrialization, Migration and Entry Labor Force Changes in Mexico City." Ph.D. diss., University of Texas, 1975.

División General de Estadística. *X Censo General de Población, 1980.* Mexico City: 1982.

Dixon, Marlene; Martínez, Elizabeth; and McCaughan, Ed. "Chicanas and Mexicanas Within a Transnational Working Class." *Our Socialism* 1, no. 1 (March 1983).

Dunbar Ortiz, Roxanne. *Roots of Resistance: Land Tenure in New Mexico, 1680–1980.* Los Angeles: UCLA Chicano Studies Research Center, 1980.

Eckstein, Susan. *The Poverty of Revolution: The State and the Urban Poor in Mexico.* Princeton: Princeton University Press, 1977.

Elliott, John H. *Imperial Spain, 1469–1716.* New York: St. Martin's Press, 1962.

Elu de Lenero, María del Carmen. *El trabajo de la mujer en México.* Mexico City: Instituto Mexicano de Estudios Sociales, 1975.

Esteva, Gustavo. *La batalla en el México rural.* Mexico City: Siglo XXI, 1980.

————. *El estado y la comunicación.* Mexico City: Nueva Política, 1979.

Everett, Michael D. "The Role of the Mexican Trade Unions, 1950–1963." Ph.D. diss., Washington University (St. Louis), 1967.

Fabela, Isidro and Fabela, Josefina E., eds. *Documentos históricos de la Revolución Mexicana.* 27 vols. Mexico City: FCE, 1964–73.

Fajnzylber, Fernando and Martínez Tarrago, Trinidad. *Las empresas transnacionales: expansión a nivel mundial y proyección en la industria mexicana.* Mexico City: FCE, 1976.

Falcón, Romana. "El surgimiento del agrarismo cardenista: una revisión de las tesis populistas." *Historia Mexicana* 27 (1977–78).

Farriss, N. M. *Crown and Clergy in Colonial Mexico, 1750–1821: The Crisis of Ecclesiastical Privilege.* London: London University Press, 1968.

Favre, Henri. *Cambio y continuidad entre los mayas de México.* Mexico City: Siglo XXI, 1973.

Feder, Ernest. *Imperialismo fresa.* Mexico City: Ed. Campesina, 1978.

————. *Lean Cows—Fat Ranchers: The International Ramifications of Mexico's Beef Cattle Industry.* Berlin: Research Institute of the Berghof Stiftung, 1979.

Fernández Hurtado, Ernesto. *Cincuenta años de banca central.* Mexico City: FCE, 1976.

Fernández, María Patricia. "'Chavalas de Maquiladora': A Study of the Female Labor Force in Ciudad Juárez' Offshore Production Plants." Ph.D. diss., Rutgers University, 1980.

Fernández, Raúl A. *The United States-Mexico Border.* Notre Dame, Ind.: University of Notre Dame Press, 1977.

Fitzgerald, E. V. K. "The State and Capital Accumulation in Mexico." *Journal of Latin American Studies* 10 (November 1978).

Flores, Esteban T. "La circulación internacional del trabajo y la lucha de clases." *Historia y Sociedad* 20 (1978).

Florescano, Enrique. *Origen y desarrollo de los problemas agrarios de México, 1500–1821.* Mexico City: Era, 1976.

Fowler Salamini, Heather. *Agrarian Radicalism in Veracruz, 1920–1938.* Lincoln: University of Nebraska Press, 1971.

Fragoso, Juan Manuel, Gutiérrez, Elvira Concheiro, and Gutiérrez, Antonio. *El poder de la gran burguesía.* Mexico City: Ediciones de Cultura Popular, 1979.

Frank, Andre Gunder. *Mexican Agriculture, 1521–1630.* Cambridge: Cambridge University Press, 1979.

Frost, Elsa Cecilia, Meyer, Michael C., and Vázquez, Josefina Z., eds. *Labor and Laborers Through Mexican History.* Tucson: University of Arizona Press, 1979.

Fuentes Molinar, Olac. *Educación y política en México.* Mexico City: Nueva Imagen, 1981.

Galarza, Ernesto. *Merchants of Labor: The Mexican Bracero Story.* Santa Barbara: McNally & Loftin, 1964.

Gambrill, Mónica-Claire et al. *Maquiladoras.* Mexico City: Centro de Estudios Económicos y Sociales del Tercer Mundo, 1981.

Gamio, Manuel. *Mexican Immigration to the United States.* New York: Dover, 1971.

Gandy, Ross and Hodges, Donald. *Mexico 1910–1976: Reform or Revolution?* London: Zed Press, 1979.

García Cantú, Gastón. *Las invasiones norteamericanas en México.* Mexico City: Era, 1971.

García Rivera, Emilio. *Historia documental del cine mexicano.* 10 vols. Mexico City: Era, 1969–82.

Garcia, J. Chris. *La Causa Política: The Chicano Political Experience.* Notre Dame, Ind.: University of Notre Dame Press, 1974.

Garcia, Mario T. *Desert Immigrants: The Mexicans of El Paso, 1880–1920.* New Haven: Yale University Press, 1981.

Garza, Gustavo and Schteingart, Martha. *La acción habitacional del estado en México.* Mexico City: Colegio de México, 1978.

Gibson, Charles. *The Aztecs under Spanish Rule.* Stanford, Ca.: Stanford University Press, 1964.

Gilly, Adolfo. *La revolución interrumpida.* Mexico City: El Caballito, 1971.

Gómez, Marte R. *Las comisiones agrarias del sur.* Mexico City: Porrúa, 1961.

———. *La reforma agraria en las filas villistas, años 1913 a 1915 y 1920.* Mexico City: Instituto Nacional de Estudios Históricos de la Revolución Mexicana, 1966.

Gómez-Quiñones, Juan. *Sembradores, Ricardo Flores Magón and the Partido Liberal Mexicano: A Eulogy and Critique.* Los Angeles: UCLA Chicano Studies Research Center, 1973.

——— and Leobardo Arroyo, Luis. *Orígenes del movimiento obrero chicano.* Mexico City: Era, 1978.

González, Luis. *Historia de la Revolución Mexicana, 1934–1940: Los días del presidente Cárdenas.* Mexico City: Colegio de México, 1981.

González Casanova, Pablo. *El estado y los partidos políticos en México.* Mexico City: Era, 1981.

———, ed. *La clase obrera en la historia de México.* 22 vols. Mexico City: Siglo XXI, 1980–83.

———and Florescano Enrique, eds. *México hoy.* Mexico City: Siglo XXI, 1979.

González Salazar, Gloria. "Participation of Women in the Mexican Labor Force." In June Nash and Helen I. Safa, eds., *Sex and Class in Latin America.* New York: Praeger, 1976.

Grayson, George W. *The Politics of Mexican Oil,* Pittsburgh: University of Pittsburgh Press, 1981.

Green, Rosario. *Estado y banca transnacional en México.* Mexico City: Nueva Imagen, 1981.

Grindle, Merille S. *Bureaucrats, Politicians, and Peasants in Mexico.* Berkeley: University of California Press, 1977.

Hale, Charles A. *Mexican Liberalism in the Age of Mora.* New Haven: Yale University Press, 1968.

Hall, Linda B. *Alvaro Obregón: Power and Revolution in Mexico 1911–1920.* College Station: Texas A&M University Press, 1981.

Halsell, Grace. *The Illegals.* New York: Stein and Day, 1978.

Hamill, Hugh M. Jr. *The Hidalgo Revolt: Prelude to Mexican Independence.* Gainesville: University of Florida Press, 1966.

Hamilton, Earl P. *American Treasure and the Price Revolution in Spain, 1501–1650.* Cambridge, Mass.: Harvard University Press, 1934.

Hamilton, Nora L. *Mexico: The Limits of State Autonomy.* Princeton: Princeton University Press, 1982.

Hamnett, Brian R. "Mexico's Royalist Coalition: The Response to Revolution, 1808–1821." *Journal of Latin American Studies* 12 (1981).

————. *Politics and Trade in Southern Mexico, 1750–1821.* Cambridge: Cambridge University Press, 1971.

Hart, John M. *Anarchism and the Mexican Working Class, 1860–1931.* Austin: University of Texas Press, 1978.

Hellman, Judith. *Mexico in Crisis.* New York: Holmes & Meier, 1978.

Hernández, Salvador. *Magonismo y movimiento obrero en México: Cananea y Río Blanco.* Mexico City: UNAM, 1977.

Hewitt de Alcántara, Cynthia. *La modernización de la agricultura mexicana, 1940–1970.* Mexico City: Siglo XXI, 1978.

Huacuja R., Mario and Woldenberg, José. *Estado y lucha política en el México actual.* Mexico City: El Caballito, 1979.

Huerta, María Teresa and Palacios, Patricia, eds. *Rebeliones indígenas de la época colonial.* Mexico City: SEP/INAH, 1976.

Ianni, Octavio. *El estado capitalista en la época de Cárdenas.* Mexico City: Era, 1977.

Instituto de Investigaciones Sociales (UNAM). *El perfil de México en 1980.* 3 vols. Mexico City: Siglo XXI, 1970–71.

Instituto Michoacano de Investigaciones Sociales, A.C. *Qué es el SAM?* Morelia: IMISAC, 1981.

Israel, J. I. *Race, Class, and Politics in Colonial Mexico.* London: Oxford University Press, 1975.

Jauregui, Jesús et al. *Tábamex: un caso de integración vertical de la agricultura.* Mexico City: Nueva Imagen, 1980.

Juárez, Antonio. *Las corporaciones transnacionales y los trabajadores mexicanos.* Mexico City: Siglo XXI, 1979.

Katz, Friedrich. *The Secret War in Mexico: Europe, the United States, and the Mexican Revolution.* Chicago: University of Chicago Press, 1981.

————, ed. *La servidumbre agraria en México en la época porfiriana.* Mexico City: Era, 1980.

Keremitsis, Dawn. *La industria textil mexicana en el siglo XIX.* Mexico City: SepSetentas, 1973.

Knowlton, Robert J. *Church Property and the Mexican Reform, 1856–1910.* DeKalb: Northern Illinois University Press, 1976.

Labastida, Horacio, ed. *Documentos para el estudio de la industrialización en México, 1837–1845.* Mexico City: Secretaría de Hacienda y Crédito Público, 1977.

Ladd, Doris M. *The Mexican Nobility at Independence 1780–1826.* Austin: University of Texas Press, 1976.

Leal, Juan Felipe. *México: Estado, burocracia y sindicatos.* Mexico City: El Caballito, 1975.

León-Portilla, Miguel. *Visión de los vencidos, relaciones indígenas de la conquista.* Mexico City: UNAM, 1972.

Lewis, Oscar. *Five Families: Mexican Case Studies in the Culture of Poverty.* New York: Random House, 1959.

Lewis, Sasha. *Slave Trade Today: American Exploitation of Illegal Aliens.* Boston: Beacon Press, 1979.

Lieuwen, Edwin. *Mexican Militarism: The Political Rise and Fall of the Revolutionary Army, 1910–1940.* Albuquerque: University of New Mexico Press, 1968.

Liss, Peggy Korn. *Mexico under Spain, 1521–1556: Society and the Origins of Nationality.* Chicago: University of Chicago Press, 1975.

Lomnitz, Larissa. *Networks and Marginality: Life in a Mexican Shantytown.* New York: Academic Press, 1977.

López Acuña, Daniel. *La salud desigual en México.* Mexico City: Siglo XXI, 1980.

López y Rivas, Gilberto. *La guerra del 47 y la resistencia popular a la ocupación.* Mexico City: Nuestro Tiempo, 1976.

Loyo, Aurora. *El movimiento magisterial de 1958.* Mexico City: Era, 1979.

Loyo Camacho, Marta and Rodríguez Piña, Javier. *Historia de la migración mexicana a los Estados Unidos.* Mexico City: UAM-Azcapotzalco, *Reporte de Investigación* 82 (1982).

Loyola Díaz, Rafael. *La crisis Obregón-Calles.* Mexico City: Siglo XXI, 1980.

Lozoya, Jorge A. *El ejército mexicano: 1910–1965.* Mexico City: Colegio de México, 1970.

Lynch, John. *Spain under the Hapsburgs.* Oxford: Basil Blackwell, 1964.

Maciel, David R., ed. *La otra cara de México: el pueblo chicano.* Mexico City: El Caballito, 1977.

Margulis, Mario. *Contradicciones en la estructura agraria y transferencias de valor.* Mexico City: Colegio de México, 1979.

Márquez Fuentes, Manuel and Rodríguez Araujo, Octavio. *El Partido Comunista Mexicano.* Mexico City: El Caballito, 1973.

Mejía Fernández, Miguel. *Política agraria en México en el siglo XIX.* Mexico City: Siglo XXI, 1979.

Méndez González, Rosalinda. "Capital Accumulation and Mexican Immigration to the United States." Ph.D. diss., University of California–Irvine, 1981.

Meyer, Jean. *El sinarquismo: ¿un fascismo mexicano? 1937–1947.* Mexico City: J. Mortiz, 1979.

Meyer, Lorenzo. *México y los Estados Unidos en el conflicto petrolero, 1917–1942.* Mexico City: Colegio de México, 1972.

Meyer, Michael C. *Huerta: A Political Portrait.* Lincoln: University of Nebraska Press, 1972.

———. *Mexican Rebel: Pascual Orozco and the Mexican Revolution, 1910–1915.* Lincoln: University of Nebraska Press, 1967.

——— and Sherman, William L. *The Course of Mexican History.* New York: Oxford University Press, 1979.

Michaels, Albert L. "The Crisis of Cardenismo." *Journal of Latin American Studies* 2 (May 1970).

Mirandé, Alfredo and Enríquez, Evangelina. *La Chicana: The Mexican-American Woman.* Chicago: University of Chicago Press, 1979.

Monsivais, Carlos. "Notas sobre cultura popular en México." *Latin American Perspectives* 5 (Winter 1978).

Montáñez, Carlos and Aburto, Horacio. *Maíz: Política institucional y crisis agrícola.* Mexico City: Nueva Imagen, 1979.

Moore Lappé, Frances and Collins, Joseph. *Food First: Beyond the Myth of Scarcity.* Boston: Houghton Mifflin, 1977.

Mora, Magdalena and del Castillo, Adelaida R., eds. *Mexican Women in the United States: Struggles Past and Present.* Los Angeles: UCLA Chicano Studies Research Center, 1980.

Morales, Patricia. *Indocumentados mexicanos.* Mexico City: Grijalbo, 1982.

NACLA Report on the Americas. "Power Struggle: Labor and Imperialism in Mexico's Electrical Industry." September–October 1977.

NACLA. *Mexico 1968.* New York: NACLA, 1968.

Newfarmer, Richard S. and Mueller, W. F. *Multinational Corporations in Brazil and*

Mexico. U.S. Senate, Report to the Subcommittee on Multinational Corporations of the Committee on Foreign Relations, August 1975.

Niemeyer, E. Victor. *Revolution at Querétero: The Mexican Constitutional Convention of 1916–1917.* Austin: University of Texas Press, 1974.

North, Lisa and Raby, David. "The Dynamic of Revolution and Counter-Revolution: Mexico under Cárdenas, 1934–1940." *LARU Studies* (Toronto) 2, no. 1 (1977).

Novelo, Victoria and Urteaga, Augusto. *La industria en los magueyuales: Trabajo y sindicatos en ciudad Sahagún.* Mexico City: Nueva Imagen, 1979.

Oliva de Coll, Josefina. *La resistencia indígena ante la Conquista.* Mexico City: Siglo XXI, 1974.

Orozco, Jose Clemente. *Autobiografía.* Mexico City: Era, 1970.

Orozco, Lourdes. "Explotación y fuerza de trabajo en México: los trabajadores transitorios." *Cuadernos Políticos* 16 (April–June 1978).

Ortiz de la Tabla Ducasse, Javier. *Comercio exterior de Veracruz, 1778–1821: Crisis de dependencia.* Seville: Escuela de Estudios Hispano-Americanos de Sevilla, 1978.

Othón Quiroz Trejo, José. "Proceso de trabajo en la industria automotriz terminal: formas de dominación capitalista y respuestas proletarias." *CELA Cuaderno* (UNAM) 40 (1980).

Paoli, Francisco J. and Montalvo, Enrique. *El socialismo olvidado de Yucatán.* Mexico City: Siglo XXI, 1977.

Paré, Luisa. *El proletariado agrícola en México.* Mexico City: Siglo XXI, 1977.

———, ed. *Ensayos sobre el problema cañero.* Mexico City: UNAM, 1979.

———. *Polémica sobre las clases sociales en el campo mexicano.* Mexico City: Macehual, 1979.

Payer, Cheryl. *The Debt Trap: The IMF and the Third World.* New York: Monthly Review Press, 1974.

———. *The World Bank: A Critical Analysis.* New York: Monthly Review Press, 1982.

Paz, Octavio. *The Labyrinth of Solitude.* New York: Grove Press, 1966.

Pellicer de Brody, Olga and Mancilla, Esteban L. *El entendimiento con los Estados Unidos y la gestión del desarrollo establizador.* Mexico City: Colegio de México, 1978.

Pérez Rayón, Nora. "Marco teórico para el análisis de la fuerza de trabajo femenina." *Reporte de Investigación* Mexico City: UAM-Azcapotzalco, 1981.

Perry, Laurens Ballard. *Juárez and Díaz: Machine Politics in Mexico.* Dekalb: Northern Illinois University Press, 1978.

Perzabal, Carlos. *Acumulación capitalista dependiente y subordinación: el caso de México, 1940–1978.* Mexico City: Siglo XXI, 1979.

Poniotowska, Elena. *Fuerte es el silencio.* Mexico City: Era, 1980.

Portes, Alejandro, and Walton, John. *Labor, Class and the International System.* New York: Academic Press, 1981.

Potash, Robert A. *El Banco de Avío de México.* Mexico City: FCE, 1959.

Problemas del Desarrollo (Mexico City). "Petróleo y energéticos." Vol. 37 (1979).

Quijano, José Manuel. *México: Estado y Banca Privada.* Mexico City: Editorial CIDE, 1981.

Quirk, Robert E. *The Mexican Revolution 1914–1915: The Convention of Aguascalientes.* Bloomington: University of Indiana Press, 1960.

Raat, W. Dirk. *Revoltosos: Mexico's Rebels in the United States, 1903–1923.* College Station: Texas A&M University Press, 1981.

Raby, David. *Educación y revolución social en México.* Mexico City: SepSetentas, 1974.

Rama, Ruth and Rello, Fernando. *Agroindustrias transnacionales y política alimentaria en México.* Mexico City: Terra Nova, 1982.

Ramírez Rincano, Mario. "Perfiles de la política obrera-empresarial." *Revista Mexicana de Sociología* 36 (July–September, 1974).
Reavis, Dick. *Without Documents*. Austin: Condor Publishing Co., 1978.
Reed, Nelson. *The Caste War of Yucatán*. Stanford: Stanford University Press, 1964.
Reina, Leticia. *Rebeliones campesinas en México, 1819–1906*. Mexico City: Siglo XXI, 1980.
Reisler, Mark. *By the Sweat of Their Brow: Mexican Immigrant Labor in the United States, 1900–1940*. Westport, Conn.: Greenwood Press, 1976.
Revista Punto Crítico (Mexico City). "Lucha de clases 1972–1982." 1982.
Reyna, José Luis and Weinert, Richard S., eds. *Authoritarianism in Mexico*. Philadelphia: Institute for the Study of Human Issues, 1977.
Ríos-Bustamante, Antonio, ed. *Mexican Immigrant Workers in the U.S.* Los Angeles: UCLA Chicano Studies Research Center, 1981.
Rippy, Merrill. *Oil and the Mexican Revolution*. Luden, Netherlands: E. J. Brill, 1972.
Robles, Martha. *Educación y sociedad en la historia de México*. Mexico City: Siglo XXI, 1977.
Rodríguez Araujo, Octavio. *La reforma política y los partidos en México*. Mexico City: Siglo XXI, 1979.
Romero, Fred E. *Chicano Workers: Their Utilization and Development*. Los Angeles: UCLA Chicano Studies Research Center, 1979.
Ruiz, Ramón Eduardo. *The Great Rebellion*. New York: W. W. Norton, 1981.
Russell, Philip. *Mexico in Transition*. Austin, Tx.: Colorado River Press, 1977.
Samora, Julian. *Los Mojados: The Wetback Story*. Notre Dame, Ind.: University of Notre Dame Press, 1971.
Saxe-Fernández, John. *Petróleo y estrategia: México y Estados Unidos en el contexto de la política global*. Mexico City: Siglo XXI, 1980.
Schryer, Frans J. *The Rancheros of Pisaflores: The History of a Peasant Bourgeoisie in Twentieth-Century Mexico*. Toronto: University of Toronto Press, 1980.
Science for the People (Cambridge, Mass.). "Science and Technology in Latin America." June 1973.
Semo, Enrique. *Historia mexicana: economía y lucha de clases*. Mexico City: Era, 1978.
————, ed. *México: un pueblo en la historia*. 5 vols. Puebla: Universidad Autónoma de Puebla, 1981–83.
Sepúlveda, Bernardo et al. *Las empresas transnacionales en México*. Mexico City: Colegio de México, 1974.
Shulgovski, Anatoli. *México en la encrucijada de su historia*. Mexico City: Ediciones de Cultura Popular, 1968.
Singelmann, Peter. "Rural Collectivization and Dependent Capitalism: The Mexican Collective Ejido." *Latin American Perspectives* 18 (Summer 1978).
Singlemann, Peter, Quesada, Sergio, and Tapia, Jesús. "Land Without Liberty: The Continuities of Peripheral Capitalist Development and Peasant Exploitation among the Cane Growers in Morelos, Mexico." *Latin American Perspectives* 34 (Summer 1982).
Siqueiros, David Alfaro. *Me llamaban el Coronelazo*. Mexico City: Grijalbo, 1977.
Smith, Peter H. *Labyrinths of Power: Political Recruitment in Twentieth-Century Mexico*. Princeton: Princeton University Press, 1979.
Smith, Robert F. *The United States and Revolutionary Nationalism in Mexico 1916–1932*. Chicago: University of Chicago Press, 1972.
Somavia, Juan et al. *Movimiento sindical y empresas transnacionales*. Mexico City: Nueva Imagen, 1979.
Sommers, Joseph. *After the Storm*. Albuquerque: University of New Mexico Press, 1968.
Sosnick, Stephen H. *Hired Hands: Seasonal Farm Workers in the United States*. Santa Barbara: McNally & Loftin, 1978.

Spalding, Hobart A. Jr. *Organized Labor in Latin America.* New York: Harper and Row, 1977.

Stavenhagen, Rodolfo. "Capitalism and the Peasantry in Mexico." *Latin American Perspectives* 18 (Summer 1978).

Super, John C. "Querétero Obrajes: Industry and Society in Provincial Mexico, 1600–1810." *Hispanic-American Historical Review* 56 (May 1976).

Tello, Carlos. *La política económica en México, 1970–1976.* Mexico City: Siglo XXI, 1979.

Tenenbaum, Barbara A. "The Age of Agiotistas, 1821–1856." Unpublished ms., University of South Carolina, 1980.

————. "The Politics of Penury: Mexican Fiscal Policies and Political Program, 1848–1856." Ph.D. diss., Harvard University, 1973.

————. "Straightening Out Some of the Lumpen in the Development." *Latin American Perspectives* 2 (Summer 1975).

Trejo Delarbre, Raúl. "The Mexican Labor Movement: 1917–1975." *Latin American Perspectives* 3 (Winter 1976).

U.S. Senate, Committee on Foreign Relations and Joint Economic Committee. *Mexico's Oil and Gas Policy: An Analysis.* Washington, D.C., December 1978.

Unión de Comuneros "Emiliano Zapata." *Primer encuentro regional de la UCEZ.* Mexico City: Taller de Impresiones Populares, 1981.

Vallejo, Demetrio. *Las luchas ferrocarrileras que conmovieron a México: orígenes, hechos y verdades historicas.* Mexico City: Hombre Nuevo, 1975.

Vallens, Vivian M. *Working Women in Mexico During the Porfiriato, 1880–1910.* San Francisco: R&E Research Associates, 1978.

Vanderwood, Paul J. *Disorder and Progress: Bandits, Police, and Mexican Development.* Lincoln: University of Nebraska Press, 1981.

Various authors. "Estado y clase obrera en México." *Revista "A"* 1 (September–December 1980).

Various authors. "Hacienda mexicana en el cambio: siglos XIX y XX." *Revista Mexicana de Ciencias Políticas y Sociales* 24 (January –March 1978).

Various authors. *El petróleo.* Mexico City: Colegio de México, 1978.

Various authors "Mexico in the Eighties." *Latin American Perspectives* 32 (Winter 1982).

Various political parties. *Encuestas y debates: la reforma política y la izquierda.* Mexico City: Nuestro Tiempo, 1979.

Vasconcelos, José. *Obras completas.* 4 vols. Mexico City: Libreros Mexicanos Unidos, 1961.

Vaughan, Mary Kay. *The State, Education, and Social Class in Mexico, 1880–1928.* Dekalb: Northern Illinois University Press, 1981.

Vicens Vives, J., ed. *Historia Social y económica de España y América.* 5 vols. Barcelona: Ed. Vicens Viva, 1954.

Vilar, Pierre. *Crecimiento y desarrollo, economía e historia: reflexiones sobre el caso español.* Barcelona: Ed. Ariel, 1964.

Villamarin, Juan A. and Villamarin, Judith E. *Indian Labor in Mainland Colonial Spanish America.* Newark, Del.: University of Delaware Latin American Studies Program, 1975.

Villarreal, René. *El disequilibrio externo en la industrialización de México, 1929–1975.* Mexico City: FCE, 1976.

Warman, Arturo. *Ensayos sobre el campesinado en México.* Mexico City: Nueva Imagen, 1980.

————. *. . . . y venimos a contradecir: los campesinos de Morelos y el estado nacional.* Mexico City: Ediciones de la Casa Chata, 1976.

Weaver, Thomas and Downing, Theodore E., eds. *Mexican Migration.* Tucson: University of Arizona Press, 1976.

Weyl, Nathaniel and Weyl, Sylvia. *The Reconquest of Mexico: The Years of Lázaro Cárdenas.* New York: Oxford University Press, 1939.

Wolf, Eric R. *Peasant Wars of the Twentieth Century.* New York: Harper and Row, 1969.

————. *Sons of the Shaking Earth.* Chicago: University of Chicago Press, 1974.

Womack, John Jr. *Zapata and the Mexican Revolution.* New York: Alfred A. Knopf, 1969.

Zermeño, Sergio. *México: una democracia utópica, el movimiento estudiantil del 68.* Mexico City: Siglo XXI, 1978.

Index

Index
371